# HESIOD

# I

LCL 57

# HESIOD

## THEOGONY
## WORKS AND DAYS
## TESTIMONIA

EDITED AND TRANSLATED BY

## GLENN W. MOST

HARVARD UNIVERSITY PRESS

CAMBRIDGE, MASSACHUSETTS

LONDON, ENGLAND

2006

S/o Blkwl. ¹²/₀₆ 21.60

Library of Congress Catalog Card Number 2006041322
CIP data available from the Library of Congress

ISBN-13: 978-0-674-99622-9
ISBN-10: 0-674-99622-4

*Composed in ZephGreek and ZephText by*
*Technologies 'N Typography, Merrimac, Massachusetts.*
*Printed and bound by Edwards Brothers,*
*Ann Arbor, Michigan, on acid-free paper.*

# CONTENTS

# ACKNOWLEDGMENTS

The very first Loeb I ever bought was *Hesiod, The Homeric Hymns and Homerica.* After more than a third of a century of intense use, my battered copy needed to be replaced—and not only my copy: even when it was first published in 1914, Evelyn-White's edition was, though useful, rather idiosyncratic, and the extraordinary progress that scholarship on Hesiod has made since then has finally made it altogether outdated. The Homeric parts of that edition have now been replaced by two volumes edited by Martin West, *Homeric Hymns. Homeric Apocrypha. Lives of Homer* and *Greek Epic Fragments from the Seventh to the Fifth Centuries BC;* the present volumes are intended to make the rest of the material contained in Evelyn-White's edition, Hesiod and the poetry attributed to him, accessible to a new generation of readers.

Over the past decade I have taught a number of seminars and lecture courses on Hesiod to helpfully thoughtful and critical students at Heidelberg University, the Scuola Normale Superiore di Pisa, and the University of Chicago: my thanks to all of them for sharpening my understanding of this fascinating poet.

Various friends and colleagues read the introduction, text, and translation of this edition and contributed numerous corrections and improvements of all sorts to them.

# ACKNOWLEDGMENTS

I am especially grateful to Alan Griffiths, Filippomaria Pontani, Mario Telò, and Martin West.

Finally, Dirk Obbink has put me and all readers of these volumes in his debt by making available to me a preliminary version of his forthcoming edition of Book 2 of Philodemus' *On Piety*, an important witness to the fragmentary poetry ascribed to Hesiod.

Glenn W. Most
Firenze, January 2006

# ABBREVIATIONS AND SYMBOLS

| | |
|---|---|
| *BE* | *Bulletin épigraphique* |
| DK | Hermann Diels, Walther Kranz, *Die Fragmente der Vorsokratiker,* fifth edition (Berlin, 1934–1937) |
| *FGrHist* | Felix Jacoby, *Die Fragmente der griechischen Historiker* (Berlin and Leiden, 1923–1958) |
| *FHG* | Carolus et Theodorus Müller, *Fragmenta Historicorum Graecorum* (Paris, 1841–1873) |
| GP² | Bruno Gentili, Carlo Prato, *Poetae Elegiaci,* second edition (Leipzig-Munich and Leipzig, 1988–2002) |
| *JöByzG* | *Jahrbuch der österreichischen Byzantinischen Gesellschaft* |
| K. A. | Rudolf Kassel, Colin Austin, *Poetae Comici Graeci* (Berlin-New York, 1983–2001) |
| *OCT*³ | Friedrich Solmsen, Reinhold Merkelbach, M. L. West, *Hesiodi Theogonia, Opera et Dies, Scutum, Fragmenta selecta,* third edition (Oxford, 1990) |
| *SEG* | *Supplementum Epigraphicum Graecum* |
| *SH* | Hugh Lloyd-Jones and Peter Parsons, *Supplementum Hellenisticum* (Berlin, 1983) |

# ABBREVIATIONS

# INTRODUCTION

"Hesiod" is the name of a person; "Hesiodic" is a designation for a kind of poetry, including but not limited to the poems of which the authorship may reasonably be assigned to Hesiod himself. The first section of this Introduction considers what is known and what can be surmised about Hesiod; the second provides a brief presentation of the various forms of Hesiodic poetry; the third surveys certain fundamental aspects of the reception and influence of Hesiodic poetry; the fourth indicates the principal medieval manuscripts upon which our knowledge of the *Theogony* (*Th*), *Works and Days* (*WD*), and *Shield* is based; and the fifth describes the principles of this edition. There follows a brief and highly selective bibliography.

## HESIOD'S LIFE AND TIMES

The *Theogony* and the *Works and Days* contain the following first-person statements with past or present indicative verbs:[1]

---

[1] This list includes passages in which the first person is indicated not by the verb but by pronouns, and excludes passages in which the first person verb is in a different grammatical form and expresses a preference or a judgment rather than a fact (e.g., *WD* 174–75, 270–73, 475–76, 682–84).

1. *Th* 22–34: One day the Muses taught Hesiod song while he was pasturing his lambs under Mount Helicon: they addressed him scornfully, gave him a staff of laurel, breathed into him a divine voice with which to celebrate things future and past, and commanded him to sing of the gods, but of themselves first and last.

2. *WD* 27–41: Hesiod and Perses divided their allotment, but Perses seized more than was his due, placing his trust in law-courts and corruptible kings rather than in his own hard work.

3. *WD* 633–40: The father of Hesiod and Perses sailed on ships because he lacked a fine means of life; he left Aeolian Cyme because of poverty and settled in this place, Ascra, a wretched village near Helicon.

4. *WD* 646–62: Hesiod never sailed on the open sea, but only crossed over once from Aulis to Chalcis in Euboea, where he participated in the funeral games of Amphidamas; he won the victory there and dedicated the trophy, a tripod, to the Muses of Helicon where they first initiated him into poetry and thereby made it possible for him to speak knowledgeably even about seafaring.

Out of these passages a skeletal biography of Hesiod can be constructed along the following lines. The son of a poor emigrant from Asia Minor, born in Ascra, a small village of Boeotia, Hesiod was raised as a shepherd, but one day, without having had any training by human teachers, he suddenly found himself able to produce poetry. He attributed the discovery of this unexpected capability to a mystical experience in which the Muses themselves initiated him into the craft of poetry. He went on to achieve success in poetic competitions at least once, in Chalcis; unlike his father, he did not have to make his living on the high seas. He quarreled with his brother Perses about their inheritance, accusing him of laziness and injustice.

We may add to these bare data two further hypothetical suggestions. First, Hesiod's account of his poetic initiation does not differ noticeably from his other first-person statements: though we moderns may be inclined to disbelieve or rationalize the former—indeed, even in antiquity Hesiod's experience was often interpreted as a dream, or dismissed as the result of intoxication from eating laurel leaves, or allegorized in one way or another—Hesiod himself seems to regard all these episodes as being of the same order of reality, and there is no more reason to disbelieve him in the one case than in the others. Apparently, Hesiod believed that he had undergone an extraordinary experience, as a result of which he could suddenly produce poetry.[2] Somewhat like Phemius, who tells Odysseus, "I am self-taught, and a god has planted in my mind all kinds of poetic paths" (*Odyssey* 22.347–48), Hesiod can claim to have been taught directly by a divine instance and not by any merely human instructor. Hesiod's initiation is often described as having been a visual hallucination, but in fact it seems to have had three separate phases: first an exclusively auditory experience of divine voices (Hesiod's

[2] Other poets, prophets, and lawgivers from a variety of ancient cultures—Moses, Archilochus, and many others—report that they underwent transcendental experiences in which they communed with the divine on mountains or in the wilderness and then returned to their human audiences with some form of physical evidence proving and legitimating their new calling. Within Greek and Roman literary culture, Hesiod's poetic initiation went on to attain paradigmatic status.

Muses, figures of what hitherto had been a purely oral poetic tradition, are "shrouded in thick invisibility" [*Th* 9] and are just as much a completely acoustic, unseen and unseeable phenomenon as are the Sirens in the *Odyssey*); then the visual epiphany of a staff of laurel lying before him at his feet (Hesiod describes this discovery as though it were miraculous, though literal-minded readers will perhaps suppose that he simply stumbled upon a carved staff someone else had made earlier and discarded there, or even upon a branch of a peculiar natural shape); and finally the awareness within himself of a new ability to compose poetry about matters past and future (hence, presumably, about matters transcending the knowledge of the human here and now, in the direction of the gods who live forever), which he interprets as a result of the Muses having breathed into him a divine voice.

And second, initiations always denote a change of life, and changes of life are often marked by a change of name: what about Hesiod's name? There is no evidence that Hesiod actually altered his name as a result of his experience; but perhaps we can surmise that he could have come to understand the name he had already received in a way different from the way he understood it before his initiation. Etymologically, his name seems to derive from two roots meaning "to enjoy" (*hēdomai* > *hēsi-*) and "road" (*hodos*)[3]—"he who takes pleasure in the journey," a perfectly appropriate name for the son of a mercantile seaman who had to travel for his living and expected that his son would follow him in this profession or in a closely related

[3] The ancient explanations for Hesiod's name (see Testimonia T27–29) are untenable.

one. But within the context of the proem to the *Theogony* in which Hesiod names himself, his name seems to have a specific and very different resonance. For Hesiod applies to the Muses the epithet *ossan hieisai,* "sending forth their voice," four times within less than sixty lines (10, 43, 65, 67), always in a prominent position at the end of the hexameter, and both of the words in this phrase seem etymologically relevant to Hesiod's name. For *hieisai,* "sending forth," is derived from a root meaning "to send" which could no less easily supply the first part of his name (*hiēmi* > *hēsi-*) than the root meaning "to enjoy" could; and *ossan,* "voice," is a synonym for *audē,* "voice," a term that Hesiod uses to indicate what the Muses gave him (31, cf. 39, 97, and elsewhere) and which is closely related etymologically and semantically to *aoidē,* the standard term for "poetry" (also applied by Hesiod to what the Muses gave him in 22, cf. also 44, 48, 60, 83, 104, and elsewhere). In this context it is difficult to resist the temptation to hear an implicit etymology of "*Hēsi-odos*" as "he who sends forth song."[4] Perhaps, then, when the Muses initiated Hesiod into a new life, he resemanticized his own name, discovering that the appellation that his father had given him to point him towards a life of commerce had always in fact, unbeknownst to him until now, been instead directing him towards a life

---

4 To be sure, these terms for "voice" and "poetry" have a long vowel or diphthong in their penultimate syllable, whereas the corresponding vowel of Hesiod's name is short. But the other etymologies that Hesiod provides elsewhere in his poems suggest that such vocalic differences did not trouble him very much (nor, for that matter, do they seem to have bothered most other ancient Greek etymologists).

of poetry. If so, Hesiod will not have been the only person whom his parents intended for a career in business but who decided instead that he was really meant to be a poet.

This is as much as—indeed it is perhaps rather more than—we can ever hope to know about the concrete circumstances of Hesiod's life on the basis of his own testimony. But ancient and medieval readers thought that they knew far more than this about Hesiod: biographies of Hesiod, full of a wealth of circumstantial detail concerning his family, birth, poetic career, character, death, and other matters, circulated in antiquity and the Middle Ages, and seem to have been widely believed.[5] In terms of modern conceptions of scholarly research, these ancient biographical accounts of Hesiod can easily be dismissed as legends possessing little or no historical value: like most of the reports concerning the details of the lives and personalities of other archaic Greek poets which are transmitted by ancient writers, they probably do not testify to an independent tradition of biographical evidence stretching with unbroken continuity over dozens of generations from the reporter's century back to the poet's own lifetime. Rather, such accounts reflect a well attested practice of extrapolation from the extant poetic texts to the kind of character of an author likely to produce them. But if such ancient reports probably tell us very little about the real person Hesiod who did (or did not) compose at least some of the poems transmitted under his name, they do provide us with precious indications concerning the reception of those poems, by concretely suggesting the nature of the

[5] See Testimonia T1–35 for a selection of some of the most important examples.

image of the poet which fascinated antiquity and which has been passed on to modern times. We will therefore return to them in the third section of this Introduction.

If many ancient readers thought they knew far more about Hesiod's life than they should have, some modern scholars have thought that they knew even less about it than they could have. What warrant have we, after all, for taking Hesiod's first-person statements at face value as reliable autobiographical evidence? Notoriously, poets lie: why should we trust Hesiod? Moreover, rummaging through poetic texts in search of evidence about their authors' lives might well be considered a violation of the aesthetic autonomy of the literary work of art and an invitation to groundless and arbitrary biographical speculation. And finally, comparative ethnographic studies of the functions and nature of oral poetry in primitive cultures, as well as the evidence of other archaic Greek poets like Archilochus, have suggested to some scholars that "Hesiod" might be not so much the name of a real person who ever existed independently of his poems but rather nothing more than a designation for a literary function intrinsically inseparable from them. Indeed, the image that Hesiod provides us of himself seems to cohere so perfectly with the ideology of his poems that it might seem unnecessary to go outside these to understand it, while, as we shall see in in the second section of this Introduction, attempts to develop a coherent and detailed narrative regarding the exact legal situation of Hesiod and his brother Perses as this is presented in different portions of the *Works and Days* have often been thought to founder on self-contradictions. Can we be sure that Hesiod ever really did have a brother named Perses with whom he had a legal quarrel, and that Perses is not instead merely a useful fiction, a convenient addressee to whom to direct his poem? And if we cannot be entirely sure about Perses, can we really be sure about Hesiod himself?

The reader should be warned that definitive answers to these questions may never be found. My own view is that these forms of skepticism are most valuable not because they provide proof that it is mistaken to understand Hesiod's first-person statements as being in some sense autobiographical (for in my opinion they cannot provide such proof) but rather because they encourage us to try to understand in a more complex and sophisticated way the kinds of autobiographical functions these statements serve in Hesiod's poetry. That is, we should not presuppose as self-evident that Hesiod might have wished to provide us this information, but ask instead why he might have thought it a good idea to include it.

There was after all in Hesiod's time no tradition of public autobiography in Greece which has left any discernable traces. Indeed, Hesiod is the first poet of the Western cultural tradition to supply us even with his name, let alone with any other information about his life. The difference between the Hesiodic and the Homeric poems in this regard is striking: Homer never names himself, and the ancient world could scarcely have quarreled for centuries over the insoluble question of his birthplace if the *Iliad* or *Odyssey* had contained anything like the autobiographical material in the *Theogony* and *Works and Days*. Homer is the most important Greek context for understanding Hesiod, and careful comparison with Homer can illumine not only Hesiod's works but even his life. In antiquity the question of the relation between Homer and Hesiod was usually understood in purely chronological terms, involving the relative priority of the one over the other (both positions were frequently maintained); additionally, the widely felt sense of a certain rivalry between the two founding traditions of Greek poetry was often projected onto legends of a competition between the two poets at a public contest, a kind of archaic shoot-out at the oral poetry corral.[6] In modern times, Hesiod has (with a few important exceptions) usually been considered later than Homer: for example, the difference between Homeric anonymity and Hesiodic self-disclosure has often been interpreted as being chronological in nature, as though self-identification in autobiographical discourse represented a later stage in the development of subjectivity than self-concealment. But such a view is based upon problematic presuppositions about both subjectivity and discourse, and it cannot count upon any historical evidence in its support. Thus, it seems safer to see such differences between Homeric and Hesiodic poetry in terms of concrete circumstances of whose reality we can be sure: namely, the constraints of production and reception in a context of poetic production and consumption which is undergoing a transition from full orality to partial literacy. This does not mean, of course, that we can be certain that the Hesiodic poems were *not* composed after the Homeric ones, but only that we cannot use *this* difference in the amount of apparently autobiographical material in their poems as evidence to decide the issue.

Both Homer's poetry and Hesiod's seem to presuppose a tradition of fully oral poetic composition, performance,

[6] See Testimonia T1–24.

reception, and transmission, such as is idealized in the *Odyssey*'s Demodocus and Phemius, but at the same time to make use of the recent advent of alphabetic writing, in different and ingenious ways. Most performances of traditional oral epic in early Greece must have presented only relatively brief episodes, manageable and locally interesting excerpts from the vast repertory of heroic and divine legend. Homer and Hesiod, by contrast, seem to have recognized that the new technology of writing afforded them an opportunity to create works which brought together within a single compass far more material than could ever have been presented continuously in a purely oral format (this applies especially to Homer) and to make it of interest to more than a merely local audience (this applies to both poets). Homer still focuses upon relatively brief episodes excerpted out of the full range of the epic repertoire (Achilles' wrath, Odysseus' return home), but he expands his poems' horizons by inserting material which belonged more properly to other parts of the epic tradition (for example, the catalogue of ships in *Iliad* 2 and the view from the wall in *Iliad* 3) and by making frequent, more or less veiled allusions to earlier and later legendary events and to other epic cycles. As we shall see in more detail in the following section, Hesiod gathered together within the single, richly complicated genealogical system of his *Theogony* a very large number of the local divinities worshipped or otherwise acknowledged in various places throughout the Greek world, and then went on in his *Works and Days* to consider the general conditions of human existence, including a generous selection from popular moral, religious, and agricultural wisdom. In Homer's sheer monumental bulk, in Hesiod's cosmic range, and in the pan-Hellenic aspirations of both poets, their works move decisively beyond the very same oral traditions from which they inherited their material.

Indeed, not only does Hesiod use writing: he also goes to the trouble of establishing a significant relation between his poems that only writing could make possible. In various passages, the *Works and Days* corrects and otherwise modifies the *Theogony*: the most striking example is *WD* 11, "So there was not just one birth of Strifes after all," which explicitly rectifies the genealogy of Strife that Hesiod had provided for it in *Th* 225. Thus, in his *Works and Days* Hesiod not only presupposes his audience's familiarity with his *Theogony*, he also presumes that it might matter to them to know how the doctrines of the one poem differ from those of the other. This is likely not to seem as astonishing to us as it should, and yet the very possibility of Hesiod's announcement depends upon the dissemination of the technology of writing. For in a context of thoroughgoing oral production and reception of poetry, a version with which an author and his audience no longer agree can be dealt with quite easily, by simply replacing it: it just vanishes together with the unique circumstances of its presentation. What is retained unchanged, from performance to performance, is the inalterable core of tradition which author and audience together continue to recognize as the truth. In an oral situation, differences of detail between one version and another are defined by the considerations of propriety of the individual performance and do not revise or correct one another: they coexist peacefully in the realm of compatibly plausible virtualities. By contrast, Hesiod's revision of the genealogy of Eris takes advantage of the newer means of communication afforded by writing.

For his emphatic repudiation of an earlier version presupposes the persistence of that version in an unchanged formulation beyond the circumstances in which it seemed correct into a new situation in which it no longer does; and this persistence is only made possible by writing.

But if the novel technology of writing provided the condition of possibility for Hesiod's announcement, it can scarcely have motivated it. Why did he not simply pass over his change of view in silence? Why did he bother to inform the public instead? An answer may be suggested by the fact that in the immediately preceding line, Hesiod has declared that he will proclaim truths (*etētyma: WD* 10) to Perses. Of these announced truths, this one must be the very first. Hesiod's decision publicly to revise his earlier opinion is clearly designed to increase his audience's sense of his reliability and veracity—paradoxically, the evidence for his present trustworthiness resides precisely in the fact that earlier he was mistaken: Hesiod proves that he will now tell truths by admitting that once he did not.

Hesiod's reference to himself as an *author* serves to *authorize* him: it validates the truthfulness of his poetic discourse by anchoring it in a specific, named human individual whom we are invited to trust because we know him. Elsewhere as well in Hesiod's poetry, the poet's self-representation is always in the service of his self-legitimation. In the *Theogony,* Hesiod's account of his poetic initiation explains how it is that a merely mortal singer can have access to a superhuman wisdom involving characters, times, and places impossibly remote from any human experience: the same Muses who could transform a shepherd into a bard order him to transmit their knowledge to human listeners (*Th* 33–34) and, moreover, vouch for its truthfulness (*Th*

28).[7] In the *Works and Days,* Hesiod's account of his father's emigration and of his quarrel with his brother creates the impression that he is located in a real, recognizable, and specific socio-economic context: he seems to know what he is talking about when he discusses the importance of work and of justice, for he has known poverty and injustice and can therefore draw from his experiences the conclusions that will help us to avoid undergoing them ourselves. And in the same poem, Hesiod's acknowledgement of his lack of sailing experience serves not only to remind his audience that he is not reflecting only as a mere mortal upon mortal matters but is still the very same divinely inspired poet who composed the *Theogony,* but also to indicate implicitly that, by contrast, on every other matter that he discusses in this poem his views are based upon extensive personal experience.

In contrast with Hesiod, Homer's anonymity seems best

[7] The Muses, to be sure, declare that they themselves are capable of telling falsehoods as well as truths (*Th* 27–28). But if the Muses order Hesiod "to sing of the race of the blessed ones who always are, but always to sing of themselves first and last" (*Th* 33–34), they are presumably not commanding him to tell falsehoods, but to celebrate the gods truthfully. The point of their assertion that they can tell falsehoods is not that Hesiod's poetry will contain falsehoods, but that ordinary human minds, in contrast to the gods', are so ignorant that they cannot tell the difference, so similar are the Muses' falsehoods to their truths (*etymoisin homoia: Th* 27). Their words are a striking but conventional celebration of their own power: Greek gods typically have the capacity to do either one thing or else the exact opposite, as they wish, without humans being able to determine the outcome (cf. e.g. *Th* 442–43, 447; *WD* 3–7).

understood simply as the default option, as his continuation of one of the typical features of oral composition: for the audience of an orally composed and delivered text, there can be no doubt who its author is, for he is singing or declaiming before their very eyes, and hence there is no necessity for him to name himself. Homer's poetry is adequately justified, evidently, by the kinds of relationships it bears to the archive of heroic legends latent within the memories of its audience: it needs no further legitimation by his own person. In the case of Hesiod, however, matters are quite different: his self-references justify his claim to be telling "true things" (*alēthea: Th* 28) and "truths" (*etētyma: WD* 10) about the matters he presents in the *Theogony* and *Works and Days*, and the most reasonable assumption is that this poetic choice is linked to those specific matters (to which we will turn in the second section of this Introduction) at least as much as to Hesiod's personal proclivities. To derive from the obvious fact that these self-references are well suited to the purpose of self-justification the conclusion that they bear no relation to any non-poetic reality is an obvious *non sequitur*: the fact that they have a textual function is not in the least incompatible with their also having a referential one, and the burden of proof is upon those who would circumscribe their import to the purely textual domain.

As for Hesiod's approximate date and his chronological relation to Homer, certainty is impossible on the evidence of their texts. Passages of the one poet that seem to refer to the poems or to specific passages of the other poet are best understood not as allusions to specific texts that happen to have survived, but rather as references to long-lived oral poetic traditions which pre-dated those texts and eventually issued in them. Homeric and Hesiodic poetic traditions must have co-existed and influenced one another for many generations before culminating in the written poems we possess, and such apparent cross-references clearly cannot provide any help in establishing the priority of the one poet over the other. A more promising avenue would start from the assumption that each of the two poets probably belonged to the first generation of his specific local culture to have experienced the impact of writing, when old oral traditions had not yet been transformed by the new technology but the new possibilities it opened up were already becoming clear, at least to creative minds. A rough guess along these lines would situate both poets somewhere towards the end of the 8th century or the very beginning of the 7th century BC. But it is probably impossible to be more precise.[8] Did writing come first to Ionia and only somewhat later to Boeotia? If so, then Homer might have been somewhat older than Hesiod. Or might writing have been imported rather early from Asia Minor to the Greek mainland—for example, might Hesiod's father even have brought writing with him in his boat from Cyme to Ascra? In that case Hesiod could have been approximately coeval with Homer or even slightly older. In any case, the question, given the information at our disposal, is probably undecidable.

[8] Hesiod's association with Amphidamas (*WD* 654–55) has sometimes been used to provide a more exact date for the poet, since Amphidamas seems to have been involved in the Lelantine War, which is usually dated to around 700 BC. But the date, duration, and even historical reality of this war are too uncertain to provide very solid evidence for dating Hesiod with any degree of precision.

## HESIODIC POETRY

### Hesiod's Theogony

Hesiod's *Theogony* provides a comprehensive account of the origin and organization of the divinities responsible for the religious, moral, and physical structure of the world, starting from the very beginning of things and culminating in the present regime, in which Zeus has supreme power and administers justice.

For the purposes of analysis Hesiod's poem may be divided into the following sections:

1. *Proem* (1–115): a hymn to the Muses, telling of their birth and power, recounting their initiation of Hesiod into poetry, and indicating the contents of the following poem.

2. *The origin of the world* (116–22): the coming into being of the three primordial entities, Chasm, Earth, and Eros.

3. *The descendants of Chasm 1* (123–25): Erebos and Night come to be from Chasm, and Aether and Day from Night.

4. *The descendants of Earth 1* (126–210): Earth bears Sky, and together they give birth to the twelve Titans, the three Cyclopes, and the three Hundred-Handers; the last of the Titans, Cronus, castrates his father Sky, thereby producing among others Aphrodite.

5. *The descendants of Chasm 2* (211–32): Night's numerous and baneful progeny.

6. *The descendants of Earth 2* (233–69): Earth's son Pontus begets Nereus, who in turn begets the Nereids.

7. *The descendants of Earth 3* (270–336): Pontus' son

Phorcys and daughter Ceto produce, directly and indirectly, a series of monsters.

8. *The descendants of Earth 4* (337–452): children of the Titans, especially the rivers, including Styx (all of them children of Tethys and Ocean), and Hecate (daughter of Phoebe and Coeus).

9. *The descendants of Earth 5* (453–506): further children of the Titans: Olympian gods, born to Rhea from Cronus, who swallows them all at birth until Rhea saves Zeus, who frees the Cyclopes and is destined to dethrone Cronus.

10. *The descendants of Earth 6* (507–616): further children of the Titans: Iapetus' four sons, Atlas, Menoetius, Epimetheus, and Prometheus (including the stories of the origin of the division of sacrificial meat, of fire, and of the race of women).

11. *The conflict between the Titans and the Olympians* (617–720): after ten years of inconclusive warfare between the Titans and the Olympians, Zeus frees the Hundred-Handers, who help the Olympians achieve final victory and send the defeated Titans down into Tartarus.

12. *Tartarus* (721–819): the geography of Tartarus and its population, including the Titans, the Hundred-Handers, Night and Day, Sleep and Death, Hades, and Styx.

13. *The descendants of Earth 7* (820–80): Earth's last child, Typhoeus, is defeated by Zeus and sent down to Tartarus.

14. *The descendants of Earth 8* (881–962): a list of the descendants of the Olympian gods, including Athena, the

Muses, Apollo and Artemis, Hephaestus, Hermes, Diony-
sus, and Heracles.[9]

15. *The descendants of Earth* 9 (963–1022): after a con-
cluding farewell to the Olympian gods and the islands,
continents, and sea, there is a transition to a list of the chil-
dren born of goddesses, followed by a farewell to these and
a transition to a catalogue of women (this last is not in-
cluded in the text of the poem).

Already this brief synopsis should suffice to make it ob-
vious that the traditional title *Theogony* gives only a very
inadequate idea of the contents of this poem—as is often
the case with early Greek literature, the transmitted title is
most likely not attributable to the poet himself, and corre-
sponds at best only to certain parts of the poem. "Theo-
gony" means "birth of the god(s)," and of course hun-
dreds of gods are born in the course of the poem; and yet
Hesiod's poem contains much more than this. On the one
hand, Hesiod recounts the origin and family relations of at
least four separate kinds of entities which are all certainly
divine in some sense but can easily be distinguished by us
and were generally distinguished by the Greeks: (1) the fa-
miliar deities of the Greek cults venerated not only in
Boeotia but throughout Greece, above all the Olympian
gods and other divinities associated with them in Greek re-
ligion, like Zeus, Athena, and Apollo; (2) other Greek gods,

---

[9] Many scholars believe that Hesiod's authentic *Theogony*
ends somewhere in this section or perhaps near the beginning of
the next one (precisely where is controversial), and that the end of
the poem as we have it represents a later continuation designed to
lead into the *Catalogue of Women*. This question is discussed fur-
ther below.

primarily the Titans and the monsters, most of whom play some role, major or minor, in Greek mythology, but were almost never, at least as far as we can tell, the object of any kind of cult worship; (3) the various parts of the physical cosmos conceived as a spatially articulated whole (which were certainly regarded as being divine in some sense but were not always personified as objects of cult veneration), including the heavens, the surface of the earth, the many rivers and waters, a mysterious underlying region, and all the many things, nymphs, and other divinities contained within them; and (4) a large number of more or less personified embodiments of various kinds of good and bad moral qualities and human actions and experiences, some certainly the objects of cult veneration, others surely not, ranging from Combats and Battles and Murders and Slaughters (228) to Eunomia (Lawfulness) and Dike (Justice) and Eirene (Peace) (902). And on the other hand, the synchronic, systematic classification of this heterogeneous collection of Greek divinities is combined with a sustained diachronic narrative which recounts the eventual establishment of Zeus' reign of justice and includes not only a series of dynastic upheavals (Sky is overthrown by Cronus, and then Cronus by Zeus) but also an extended epic account of celestial warfare (the battle of the Olympians against the Titans and then of Zeus against Typhoeus).

To understand Hesiod's poem, it is better to start not from its title and work forwards but instead from the state of affairs at which it eventually arrives and work backwards. At the conclusion of his poem, Hesiod's world is all there: it is full to bursting with places, things, values, experiences, gods, heroes, and ordinary human beings, yet these all seem to be linked with one another in systematic relationships and to obey certain systematic tendencies; chaotic disorder can easily be imagined as a terrifying possibility and indeed may have even once been predominant, but now seems for the most part a rather remote menace. For Hesiod, to understand the nature of this highly complex but fully meaningful totality means to find out where it came from—in ancient Greece, where the patronymic was part of every man's name, to construct a genealogy was a fundamental way to establish an identity.

Hesiod recognizes behind the elements of human experience the workings of powers that always are, that may give or withhold unpredictably, that function independently of men, and that therefore may properly be considered divine. Everywhere he looks, Hesiod discovers the effects of these powers—as Thales will say about a century later, "all things are full of gods."[10] Many have been passed on to him through the Greek religion he has inherited, but by no means all of them; he may have arrived at certain ones by personal reflection upon experience, and he is willing to reinterpret even some of the traditional gods in a way which seems original, indeed rather eccentric (this is especially true of Hecate[11]). The values that these gods

[10] Aristotle *De anima* A 5.411a7 = Thales 11 A 22 D-K, Fr. 91 Kirk-Raven-Schofield.

[11] Hesiod's unparalleled attribution of universal scope to Hecate (*Th* 412–17) derives probably not from an established cult or personal experience but from consideration of her name, which could be (mis-)understood as etymologically related to *hekēti*, "by the will of" (scil. a divinity, as with Zeus at *WD* 4), so that Hecate could seem by her very name to function as an intermediary between men and any god at all from whom they sought favor.

embody are not independent of one another, but form patterns of objective meaningfulness: hence the gods themselves must form part of a system, which, given their anthropomorphism, cannot but take a genealogical form.

The whole divine population of the world consists of two large families, the descendants of Chasm and those of Earth, and there is no intermarrying or other form of contact between them. Chasm (not, as it is usually, misleadingly translated, "Chaos") is a gap upon which no footing is possible: its descendants are for the most part what we would call moral abstractions and are valorized extremely negatively, for they bring destruction and suffering to human beings; but they are an ineradicable and invincible part of our world and hence, in some way, divine. The progeny of Chasm pass through several generations but have no real history. History, in the strong sense of the concrete interactions of anthropomorphic characters attempting to fulfill competing goals over the course of time, is the privilege of the progeny of Earth, that substantial foundation upon which alone one can stand, "the ever immovable seat of all the immortals" (117–18).

Hesiod conceives this history as a drastically hyperbolic version of the kinds of conflicts and resolutions familiar from human domestic and political history.

We may distinguish two dynastic episodes from two military ones. Both dynastic episodes involve the overthrow of a tyrannical father by his youngest son. First Earth, resenting the fact that Sky has concealed within her their children, the Cyclopes and Hundred-Handers, and feeling constricted by them, engages Cronus to castrate his father the next time he comes to make love with her; then Cronus himself, who has been swallowing his children by

Rhea one after another lest one of them dethrone him, is overthrown by Zeus, whom Rhea had concealed at his birth, giving Cronus a stone to swallow in his stead (Zeus manages to be not only Cronus' youngest son but also his oldest one, because Cronus goes on to vomit out Zeus' older siblings in reverse sequence). The two stories are linked forwards by Sky's curse upon his children and his prophecy that vengeance would one day befall them (207–10) and backwards by Rhea's seeking advice from Earth and Sky on how to take revenge upon Cronus for what he has done both to his children and to his father (469–73). There is of course an unmistakable irony, and a fitting justice, in the fact that Cronus ends up suffering at the hands of his son a fate not wholly different from the one he inflicted upon his own father, though cosmic civility has been making some progress in the meantime and his own punishment is apparently not as primitive and brutal as his father's was. Zeus too, it turns out, was menaced by the threat that a son of his own would one day dethrone him, but he avoids this danger and seems to secure his supremacy once and for all by swallowing in his turn not his offspring but their mother, Metis (886–900).

The two military episodes involve scenes of full-scale warfare. First the Olympians battle inconclusively against the Titans for ten full years until the arrival of new allies, the Hundred-Handers, brings them victory. This episode is linked with the first dynastic story by the fact that Zeus liberates first the three Cyclopes, then the three Hundred-Handers (whose imprisonment in Earth had provoked her to arrange Sky's castration): the first group of three provides him his characteristic weapons, thunder, thunderbolts, and lightning, while the second group assures his victory. In broad terms the Hesiodic Titanomachy is obviously modeled upon the Trojan War familiar from the Homeric tradition: ten years of martial deadlock are finally broken by the arrival of a few powerful new allies (like Neoptolemus and Philoctetes) who alone can bring a decisive victory. At the end of this war the divine structure of the world seems complete: the Olympians have won; the Titans (and also, somewhat embarrassingly, the Hundred-Handers) have been consigned to Tartarus; its geography and inhabitants can be detailed at length. The *Theogony* could have ended here, with Zeus in his heaven and all right with the world. Instead, Hesiod has Earth bear one last child, Typhoeus, who engages in a second military episode, a final winner-take-all duel with Zeus. Why? One reason may be to close off the series of Earth's descendants, which had begun long ago with Sky (126–27), by assigning to the first mother of us all one last monstrous offspring (821–22): after Typhoeus, no more monsters will ever again be born from the Earth. But another explanation may also be imagined, a theologically more interesting one. The birth of Typhoeus gives Zeus an opportunity to demonstrate his individual prowess by defeating in single-handed combat a terrifying adversary and thereby to prove himself worthy of supremacy and rule. After all, the Titanomachy had been fought by all the gods together, and had been decided by the intervention of the Hundred-Handers: in this conflict Zeus had been an important warrior (687–710, 820) but evidently not the decisive one. Like the *Iliad*, Hesiod's martial epic must not only include crowd scenes with large-scale havoc but also culminate in a single individual duel which proves incontestably the hero's superiority. It is only after his victory in this single combat that Zeus, bowing to popular acclaim, can officially assume the kingship and assign to the other gods their honors (883–85), and then wed Themis (Justice) and father Eunomia (Lawfulness), Dike (Justice), and Eirene (Peace, 902). Zeus' rule may well have been founded upon a series of violent and criminal deeds in a succession of divine generations, but as matters now stand his reign both expresses and guarantees cosmic justice and order, and it is certainly a welcome improvement upon earlier conditions.

Theogonic and cosmogonic poetry was limited neither to Hesiod nor to Greece. Within Greek culture, Hesiod's poem certainly goes back to a variety of local oral traditions which he has selected, compiled, systematized, and transformed into a widely disseminated written document; some of these local traditions Hesiod no doubt thereby supplanted (or they survived only by coming to an accommodation with his poem), but others continued to remain viable for centuries, as we can tell from sources like Plutarch and Pausanias. At the same time, Hesiod's *Theogony* is the earliest fully surviving example of a Greek tradition of written theogonies and cosmogonies in verse, and later in prose, ascribed to mythic poets like Musaeus and Orpheus and to later historical figures like Pherecydes of Syros and Acusilaus of Argos in the 5th century BC (and even the Presocratic philosophers Parmenides and Empedocles stand in this same tradition, though they interpret it in a radically original way); in the few cases in which the fragmentary evidence permits us to form a judgment, it is clear that such authors reflect traditions or personal conceptions different from Hesiod's yet at the same time have written under the strong influence of Hesiod's *Theogony*.

Moreover, Greece itself was only one of numerous an-
cient cultures to develop such traditions of theogonic and
cosmogonic verse. In particular, the *Enûma Eliš*, a Babylo-
nian creation epic, and various Hittite mythical texts con-
cerning the exploits of the god Kumarbi present striking
parallels with certain features and episodes of Hesiod's
*Theogony:* the former tells of the origin of the gods and
then of war amongst them, the victory and kingship of
Marduk, and his creation of the world; the latter recount a
myth of succession in heaven, including the castration of a
sky-god, the apparent eating of a stone, and the final tri-
umph of a weather-god corresponding to Zeus. There can
be no doubt that Hesiod's *Theogony* represents a local
Greek inflection upon a cultural *koine* evidently wide-
spread throughout the ancient Mediterranean and Near
East. But despite intensive research, especially over the
past decades, it remains unclear precisely what the histori-
cal relations of transmission and influence were between
these various cultural traditions—at what time or times
these mythic paradigms were disseminated to Greece and
by what channels—and exactly how Hesiod's *Theogony* is
to be evaluated against this background. In any case, it
seems certain that this Greek poem is not only a local ver-
sion but a characteristically idiomatic one. For one thing,
there is no evidence that Greek cosmogonic poetry in or
before Hesiod was ever linked to any kind of cult practice
in the way that, for example, the *Enûma Eliš* was officially
recited as part of the New Year festival of the city of Baby-
lon. And for another, even when the accounts of Hesiod
and the Near Eastern versions seem closest, the differ-
ences between them remain striking—for example, the
castration of the sky-god, which in other traditions serves

to separate heaven and earth from one another, in Hesiod seems to have not this function but rather that of preventing Sky from creating any more offspring and constricting Earth even further. Thus the Near Eastern parallels illumine Hesiod's poem, but they enrich its meaning rather than exhausting it.

### Hesiod's Works and Days

Hesiod's *Works and Days* provides an exhortation, addressed to his brother Perses, to revere justice and to work hard, and indicates how success in agriculture, sailing, and other forms of economic, social and religious behavior can be achieved by observing certain rules, including the right and wrong days for various activities.

For the purposes of analysis Hesiod's poem may be divided into the following sections:

1. *Proem* (1–10): a hymn to Zeus, extolling his power and announcing Hesiod's project of proclaiming truths to Perses.[12]

2. *The two Strifes* (11–41): older than the bad Strife that fosters war and conflict there is also her sister, the good Strife that rouses men to work, and Perses should shift his allegiance from the former to the latter.

3. *The myth of Prometheus and Pandora* (42–105): men suffer illness and must work for a living because Zeus punished them with Pandora for Prometheus' theft of fire.

4. *The races of men* (106–201): the current race of men, unlike previous ones, has a way of life which is neither idyl-

---

[12] Various ancient sources report that some copies of the poem lacked this proem, cf. Testimonia T42, 49, 50.

lic nor incapable of justice, but it will be destroyed as those earlier ones were unless it practices justice.

5. *Justice and injustice* (202–285): justice has been given not to animals but to men, and Zeus rewards justice but punishes injustice.

6. *Work* (286–334): work is a better way to increase one's wealth than is violence or immorality.

7. *How to deal with men and gods* (335–80): general precepts regarding religion and both neighborly and domestic economics.

8. *Advice on farming* (381–617): precepts to be followed by the farmer throughout the course of the whole year.

9. *Advice on sailing* (618–93): precepts on when and how best to risk seafaring.

10. *Advice on social relations* (694–723): specific precepts regarding the importance of right measure in dealings with other people.

11. *Advice on relations with the gods* (724–64): specific precepts on correct behavior with regard to the gods.

12. *Good and bad days* (765–821): days of good and bad auspices for various activities as these occur during the course of every month.

13. Conclusion (822–28).

As in the *Theogony,* so too here: the title of the *Works and Days* gives only a very inadequate idea of its contents, emphasizing as it does the advice on farming (and perhaps also on sailing, cf. "works" *WD* 641) and the list of good and bad days, at the expense of the matters discussed in the rest of the poem. But if it is evident that the *Works and Days* is not only about works and days, it is less clear just what it *is* about, and how the works and days it does discuss are to be understood within the context of its other concerns.

Above all, what is the relation between the two main themes of the poem, work and justice? Rather than being linked explicitly to one another, they seem to come into and go out of focus complementarily. Hesiod begins by asking Zeus to "straighten the verdicts with justice yourself" (9–10), but in the lines that immediately follow it is for her inciting men to work that he praises the good Strife (20–24). The myth of Prometheus and Pandora is presented as an explanation for why men must work for a living (42–46), and the list of evils scattered by Pandora into the world, though it emphasizes diseases, does include toil (91). But in the story of the races of men that follows, it is only the first race whose relation to work is given prominence—the golden race need not work for a living (113, 116–19)—but in the accounts of all the subsequent races it is justice and injustice that figure far more conspicuously (134–37, 145–46, 158, 182–201) than work does (only 151, 177). The fable about the hawk and nightingale, which immediately follows, introduces a long section on the benefits of justice and the drawbacks of injustice (202–85), from which the theme of work is almost completely absent (only 231–32). And yet the very next section (286–334) inverts the focus, extolling the life of work and criticizing sloth, and subordinating to this theme the question of justice and injustice (320–34). And in the last 500 lines of the poem, filled with detailed instructions on the proper organization of agricultural and maritime work and other matters, the theme of justice disappears almost entirely (only 711–13).

To be sure, the themes of justice and work are linked closely in the specific case of the legal dispute between

Hesiod and Perses, whom the poet accuses of trying to achieve prosperity by means of injustice and not of hard work. But even if we could believe in the full and simple reality of this dispute (we shall see shortly that difficulties stand in the way of our doing so), it would provide at best a superficial and casual link between these themes, scarcely justifying Hesiod's wide-ranging mythological and anthropological meditation. Again, there is indeed a certain tendency for Hesiod to direct the sections on justice towards the kings as addressees (202, 248, 263) and those on work towards Perses (27, 286, 299, 397, 611, 633, 641), as is only natural, given that it is the kings who administer justice and that Hesiod could scarcely have hoped to persuade them to go out and labor in the fields. And yet this tendency is not a strict rule—there are also passages addressed to Perses in which Hesiod encourages him to pursue justice (213, 274)—and to invoke it here would merely redescribe the two kinds of themes in terms of two sets of addressees without explaining their systematic interconnection.

In fact, for Hesiod a defining mark of our human condition seems to be that, for us, justice and work are inextricably intertwined. The justice of the gods has imposed upon human beings the necessity that they work for a living, but at the same time this very same justice has also made it possible for them to do so. To accept the obligation to work is to recognize one's humanity and thereby to acknowledge one's place in the scheme of things to which divine justice has assigned one, and this will inevitably be rewarded by the gods; to attempt to avoid work is to rebel in vain against the divine apportionment that has imposed work upon human beings, and this will inevitably be punished. Human beings, to be understood as human, must be seen in contrast with the other two categories of living beings in Hesiod's world, with gods and with animals; and indeed each of the three stories with which Hesiod begins his poem illuminates man's place in that world in contrast with these other categories.

The story of Prometheus and Pandora defines human work as a consequence of divine justice: Prometheus' theft of fire is punished by the gift of Pandora to men. Whereas in the *Theogony*'s account of Prometheus the emphasis had been upon the punishment of Prometheus himself in the context of the other rebellious sons of Iapetus, and Pandora (not yet named there) had been responsible only for the race of women, in the *Works and Days* the emphasis is laid upon the punishment of human beings, with Pandora responsible for ills that affect all human beings as such. The necessity that we work for a living is part of Zeus' dispensation of justice; we will recall from the *Theogony* that Prometheus had been involved in the definitive separation between the spheres of gods and of men (*Th* 535–36), and now we understand better what that means. We ourselves might think it unfair that human beings must suffer for Prometheus' offence. But that is not for us to decide.

Hesiod's "story" (106) of the races of men helps us to locate our present human situation in comparison and contrast with other imaginable, different ones. The golden and silver races express in their essential difference from us the two fundamental themes of the *Works and Days,* on the one hand the terrible necessity of working and taking thought for the future (something that the golden race, unlike us, did not need to do, for they did not toil for their living and did not grow old), on the other hand the obligation and the possibility to conduct our life in accordance with justice (something that the silver race, unlike us, was constitutionally incapable of doing). Our race, the iron one, alone remains open-ended in its destiny, capable either of following justice and hence flourishing or practicing injustice and hence being destroyed; our choice between these two paths should be informed by the models of good and bad behavior furnished by the traditional stories about the members of the race of bronze and of the heroes, the great moral paradigms of Greek legend.

Finally, Hesiod establishes justice as an anthropological universal in his "fable" (202) of the hawk and nightingale, by contrasting the condition of men with that of animals. For animals have no justice (274–80), and nothing prevents them from simply devouring one another. But human beings have received justice from Zeus; and if Zeus' justice means they must toil in the fields for their living, at least they thereby manage to nourish themselves in some way other than by eating their fellow-men. The point of Hesiod's fable is precisely to highlight the difference between the situations of human beings and of animals: if the kings to whom it is addressed do indeed "have understanding" (202), then this is how they will understand it, and they will not (literally or figurally) devour (literal or figural) songsters.

In summary, the world of the *Works and Days* knows of three kinds of living beings and defines them systematically in terms of the categories of work and justice: the gods always possess justice and never need to work; human beings are capable of practicing justice and are obliged to work for a living; and animals know nothing of either justice or work. For a human being to accept his just obligation to work is to accept his place in this world.

Thus the first part of the *Works and Days* provides a conceptual foundation for the necessity to work in terms of human nature and the organization of the world. The rest of the poem goes on to demonstrate in detail upon this basis just how, given that Zeus has assigned work to men, the very same god has made it possible (but certainly not inevitable) for them to do this work well. The world of non-human nature is one grand coherent semiotic system, full of divinely engineered signs and indications which human beings need to read aright if they are to perform successfully the endless toil which the gods have imposed upon them. The stars that rise and set, the animals that call out or behave in some striking way, are all conveyors of specific messages, characters in the book of nature; Hesiod's mission is to teach us to read them. If we manage to learn this lesson, then unremitting labor will still remain our lot, and we will never be free from various kinds of suffering; but at least, within the limits assigned to mankind, we will flourish. The farmer's and sailor's calendars semioticize the year in its cyclical course as a series of signals and responses; then the list of auspicious and inauspicious days with which the poem ends carves a different section out of the flow of time, this time in terms of the single month rather than of the whole year, demonstrating that there is a meaningful and potentially beneficial logic in this narrower temporal dimension as well.[13] And the same human

[13] Some scholars, mistakenly in my view, have assigned lines 765–828, the so-called "*Days*," to some other, later author than Hesiod, because of what they take to be the superstitious charac-

willingness to acknowledge divine justice that expresses itself in the domain of labor by adaptation to the rules of non-human nature manifests itself in the rest of this second half of the *Works and Days* in two further domains: in that of religion, by avoiding various kinds of improper behavior which are punished by the gods; and in that of social intercourse, by following the rules that govern the morally acceptable modes of competition and collaboration with other men. Thus a profound conceptual unity links all parts of the poem from beginning to end, from the hymn to Zeus and the praise of the good Strife through the most detailed, quotidian, and, for some readers at least, superstitious precepts.

At the same time, the *Works and Days* is a fitting sequel to the *Theogony*. If Hesiod's earlier poem explains how Zeus came to establish his rule of justice within the world, his later one indicates the consequences of that rule for human beings. Human beings were certainly not completely absent from the *Theogony*, but by the same token they obviously did not figure as its central characters either. But in the *Works and Days* they take center stage. With this shift of focus from gods (in their relation to other gods and to men) to men (in their relation to other men and to gods) comes an obvious change in both the tone and the rhetorical stance of the later poem, which can be seen most immediately in the difference between the virtual absence of imperatives and related grammatical forms in Hesiod's first poem and their extraordinary frequency in

---

ter of this passage and because it presupposes a lunar calendar not used elsewhere by Hesiod.

his second one. Both poems deal with values, and espe-
cially with the most fundamental value of all, justice. But
the *Theogony* views these values from the perspective of
the gods who embody them always and unconditionally,
while the *Works and Days* considers them from the view-
point of human beings who may fail to enact them properly
and therefore must be encouraged to do so for their own
good. That is why the *Theogony* is a cosmogony, but the
*Works and Days* is a protreptic.

Hesiod's protreptic is directed ultimately to us, but it is
addressed in the first instance to someone whom he calls
his brother Perses and whose degree of reality or unreality
has been the object of considerable scholarly controversy.
Two observations about Perses seem incontestable. The
first is that he plays a far more prominent role in the first
half of the poem than in its second half: in the general part
that comprises its first 334 lines his name appears six times,
in the sections containing specific precepts that comprise
its last 494 lines it appears only four times (and three of
these passages occur within the space of only 30 lines, be-
tween 611 and 641). The second is that the various refer-
ences to Perses seem to presuppose a variety of specific sit-
uations involving Hesiod's relation with him that cannot
easily be reconciled with one another within the terms of a
single comprehensible dramatic moment: Perses prefers
to waste his time watching quarrels and listening to the
assembly rather than working for his living, but he will not
be able to do this a second time, for Hesiod suggests that
the two of them settle with straight judgments here and
now their quarrel, which arose after they had divided their
allotment when Perses stole many things and went off,
confiding in the corruptible kings (27–41); Perses should

revere Justice rather than Outrageousness (213); Perses should listen to what Hesiod tells him, obey Justice and forget violence (274–76); Hesiod will tell Perses, "you great fool" (286), what he thinks, namely that misery is easy to achieve but excellence requires hard work (286–92); Perses, "you of divine stock" (299), should continue working in order to have abundant means of life (299–301); "foolish Perses" (397) has come to ask Hesiod for help but will receive nothing extra from him, and should work so that he and his own family will have sufficient means of life (396–403); Perses should harvest the grapes in mid-September (609–11); the father of Hesiod and Perses, "you great fool" (633), used to sail in boats to make a living; Perses should bear in mind all kinds of work in due season, but especially sailing (641–42). Who won the law suit, and indeed whatever became of it? Has Perses remained a fool or become an obedient worker? Some scholars have concluded from these discrepancies that Perses is a purely fictional character with no reality outside of Hesiod's poem; others have tried to break down the *Works and Days* into a series of smaller poems, each of which would be tied to a specific moment in Hesiod's relation with his brother. It may be preferable, instead, to understand the adverb *authi* ("right here," 35) in Hesiod's invitation to his brother to "decide our quarrel right here with straight judgments" (35–36) as referring not to some real legal tribunal existing independently from the *Works and Days* but rather to the sphere of effectiveness of this very poem. There is no reason not to believe that Perses existed in reality just as much as Hesiod himself did; but Hesiod could certainly have been convinced enough of the power of his poetry to be able to ascribe to its protreptic such persuasive force that even the recalcitrant Perses would be swayed by it, so that the man who had begun as his bitter opponent would end up becoming so completely identified with the anonymous addressees of his didactic injunctions as to be almost fully assimilated to them. That is, the *Works and Days* does not represent a single moment of time or a single dramatic situation: instead, the dynamic development of the poem measures out a changing situation to which the conspicuous changes in the characterization of Perses precisely correspond. Whether or not additionally there is an actual legal dispute between Hesiod and Perses being fought out in the courts (and we cannot exclude this possibility altogether), the most pertinent arena for reconciling their differences, the one in which their quarrel will be decided by "straight judgments, which come from Zeus, the best ones" (36), is this very poem.

Like his *Theogony*, Hesiod's *Works and Days* is a characteristically original version of a genre of wisdom literature which existed in Greece and was also widespread throughout the ancient world. While fewer other Greek poems like the *Works and Days* seem to have been composed than ones like the *Theogony*, there can be no doubt that Hesiod's poem goes back to earlier oral traditions in Greece. Indeed, some poems were extant in antiquity that were considered similar enough to Hesiod's that they were ascribed to him (they are discussed in the second section of this Introduction), and after Hesiod other gnomic poets, especially Phocylides and Theognis, followed his lead in this genre. From other ancient cultures, comparable works providing various kinds of religious, social, and agricultural instruction have survived in Sumerian (examples include the very ancient *Instructions of Šuruppak*, collections of proverbs and admonitions, an agricultural handbook ascribed to Ninurta, and a dialogue between a father and his misguided son), Akkadian (above all the *Counsels of Wisdom,* full of advice on proper dealings with gods and men, and other works addressed to sons, kings, and princes), Egyptian (where one of the most important literary genres was called "instruction"), Aramaic (the language of the earliest known version of the widely disseminated story of Ahiqar), Hebrew (the book of Proverbs), and other ancient languages. There are many striking parallels both in detail and in general orientation between Hesiod's poem and its non-Greek counterparts, and it seems evident that we can best understand Hesiod if we see him as working, consciously or unconsciously, within this larger cultural context. But, at least until now, no other work has ever been discovered which rivals his own in depth, breadth, and unity of conception.

### The Hesiodic Catalogue of Women or Ehoiai, and the Shield

Besides the *Theogony* and the *Works and Days,* one additional poem is transmitted in medieval manuscripts of Hesiod, the *Shield* (i.e. of Heracles). But this text must be understood, at least in part, as an outgrowth of the *Catalogue of Women* or *Ehoiai,* which survives only in fragments; hence it will be necessary to discuss the two together.

The *Theogony* reaches a splendid climax in Zeus' defeat of Typhoeus (868), followed, perhaps not unexpectedly, by a list of the offspring of that monster (869–80). Now Zeus' investiture as king of the Olympians and his distribution of honors to the other gods can finally occur and be recounted, albeit with surprising brevity (881–85). There follows a catalogue of seven marriages of Zeus and of the offspring they produce—now that he has resolved his career difficulties he can set about starting a family. Each entry is of decreasing length; the list begins with Zeus thwarting a potential threat to his rule by swallowing Metis (886–900), includes his expectable and climactic fathering of Eunomia (Lawfulness), Dike (Justice), Eirene (Peace, 902), and the Muses (915–17), and culminates in his marriage to Hera, his legitimate spouse (886–923); this is followed, perhaps not unsuitably, by the births, achieved without a sexual partner, of Athena and Hephaestus (924–29). There follows a series of very short indications of other gods and mortals who united with one another and in some cases gave birth to other gods or mortals (930–62)—in only 33 lines, 10 couples (including Zeus three more times) and 10 children. This is followed by a farewell to the Olympian gods and the divinities who make up the natural surroundings of the Eastern Mediterranean, and then by a transition to a catalogue of the goddesses who slept with mortals and produced children (963–68); this catalogue, though it gives the impression of being somewhat less summary than the preceding one, still manages to compress 10 mothers and 19 children into only 50 verses (969–1018). This is then followed by a transition from the just concluded list of goddesses who slept with mortals to the announcement of a new list of mortal women (1019–22). Either with this announcement, or just before it, ends the *Theogony* as it is transmitted by the medieval manuscripts.

It is extremely difficult to resist the impression that towards its close our *Theogony* peters out quite anticlimactically, and it is just as difficult to imagine why Hesiod should have set out to make his poem create this effect. Moreover, the last two lines of the transmitted text, "And now sing of the tribe of women, sweet-voiced Olympian Muses, daughters of aegis-holding Zeus" (1021–22), are identical to the first two lines of another poem ascribed to Hesiod in antiquity, the *Catalogue of Women* or *Ehoiai* (Fr. 1.1–2). The most economical explanation of all this is that the ending of our *Theogony* has been adapted to lead into that other poem; and if, as most scholars believe, the *Catalogue* of which it is possible to reconstruct the outlines and many details postdates Hesiod significantly, then the modifications to the *Theogony* can only have been the work, not of Hesiod himself, but rather of a later editor. Where exactly Hesiod's own portion of the text ceases and the inauthentic portion begins remains controversial; most scholars locate the border somewhere between lines 929 and line 964, but there can be no certainty on this question.[14]

The *Catalogue of Women* is a systematic presentation in five books of a large number of Greek legendary heroes and episodes, beginning with the first human beings and continuing down to Helen and the time just before the be-

---

[14] Here as in other cases, the difficulty of resolving this question is increased by the fact that it has sometimes been formulated erroneously: for the scholarly hypothesis that everything (or almost everything) up to a given line must be entirely the work of Hesiod and everything thereafter entirely the work of a later poet or poets supposes, far too simplistically, that later accretions always take the form of supplementary additions to a fully unchanged text, and not, more realistically, that of more or less extensive modifications and adaptations of the inherited text as well.

ginning of the Trojan War. The organizational principle is genealogical, in terms of the heroes' mortal mothers who were united with divine fathers; the repeated, quasi-formulaic phrase with which many of these women are introduced, *ē hoiē* ("or like her"), gave rise to another name for the poem, the *Ehoiai*. The *Catalogue of Women* was one of Hesiod's best known poems in antiquity and seems to have enjoyed particular popularity in Greek Egypt. But because it did not form part of the selection of three poems that survived antiquity by continuous transmission, for many centuries it was lost except in the form of citations by other ancient authors who were so transmitted.

Two developments over the past century or so, however, have restored to us a good sense of its general structure as well as a considerable portion of its content. The first is the discovery and publication of a large number of Hesiod papyri from Egypt: for example, Edgar Lobel's publication in 1962 of Volume XXVIII of the Oxyrhynchus Papyri, containing exclusively Hesiodic fragments, singlehandedly provided almost as much new material from the poem as had hitherto been available altogether, and already in 1985 West estimated that the remains of more than 50 ancient copies of the *Catalogue* had been discovered.[15] One very rough measure of the growth in the sheer number of extant fragments of the poem over the past century is the difference between the 136 testimonia and fragments that Rzach was able to collect in his 1902 Teubner edition and the 245 in Merkelbach and West's *Fragmenta*

[15] M. L. West, *The Hesiodic Catalogue of Women* (Oxford 1985), pp. 35, 1.

*Hesiodea* of 1967.[16] Since then many more testimonia and fragments have been added, and new ones continue to be discovered each year.

This increase in the surviving material has gone hand in hand with a second development, the gradual recognition on the part of scholars that in the genealogical sections of his *Library,* a handbook of Greek mythology of the 1st or 2nd century AD, Pseudo-Apollodorus made extensive use of the *Catalogue of Women,* and that in consequence this extant work could be used, though with great caution, to reconstruct a considerable part of Hesiod's lost one, not only in outline but also in some detail. It must be acknowledged that there is still no direct, adequate, non-circular proof for the correctness of the large-scale organization which has been deduced for the *Catalogue* from Pseudo-Apollodorus, and it is not entirely impossible that today's scholarly reconstruction will be vitiated by tomorrow's papyrus. But as it happens, so far none of the papyri discovered since the work of Merkelbach and West has disproven their general view of the poem; in fact, each more recent discovery has confirmed their analysis, or at least been compatible with it. Moreover, as of yet no cogent alternative account has been proposed. It is for good reason, then, that almost all the scholarship on the *Catalogue* in the last decades has taken their work as a starting-point. Hence it

16 Of course these bare numbers are misleading for a number of reasons: there are empty numbers, cancelled numbers, and subdivided numbers; there are fragments that consist of a few letters and fragments that go on for a number of pages. These figures are intended only to give a general impression of the scale of the growth in our knowledge of the poem.

is their reconstruction that provides the basis for the presentation of the *Catalogue* in this Introduction and for the general organization of the fragments in the present edition, though I have disagreed with them in a number of questions of specific placement, and in the selection and evaluation of some of the fragments presented, and have provided a new numeration.[17]

As far as we can tell, the contents of the five books of the *Catalogue of Women* were arranged as follows:

Book 1: an introductory proem, then the descendants of Prometheus' son Deucalion (northern Greeks), beginning with his children, including Hellen; and then Hellen's descendants, including Aeolus and Aeolus' descendants.

Book 2: Aeolus' descendants, continued, beginning with Atalanta; then a new starting-point, the descendants of Inachus (Argives), including after a number of generations Belus, and Belus' descendants.

Books 3 and 4: Inachus' descendants, continued from the descendants of Belus' brother Agenor; then a new starting-point, the descendants of Pelasgus (Arcadians); then another new starting-point, the descendants of Atlas (with various geographical branches, including the

---

[17] The reader should be warned that numerous problems remain. Perhaps the most worrisome is the uncertainty whether the mother of Asclepius is Arsinoe or Coronis. In the present edition I assign the fragments identifying his mother as Arsinoe to Book 2 of the *Catalogue* (Fr. 53–60), another fragment concerning Coronis (without apparent reference to Asclepius) to unplaced fragments of the *Catalogue* (Fr. 164), and one or two fragments concerning Coronis' betrayal of Apollo to unplaced fragments of Hesiod's works (Fr. 239–40). Other scholars have distributed these fragments differently.

Pelopids); then yet another new starting-point, the descendants of Asopus (also geographically heterogeneous); one more starting-point, the descendants of Cecrops and of Erechtheus (Athenians), may well also have figured in Book 3 or 4.[18]

Book 5: the suitors of Helen and Zeus' plan for the destruction of the heroes.

As in the case of the *Theogony* and *Works and Days*, the *Catalogue of Women* has many analogues throughout the other cultures of the ancient world, and genealogy remained a primary form of historical explanation in Greece for centuries. Indeed, elements of catalogue poetry can also be found in Homer, especially in Odysseus' visit to the Underworld in *Odyssey* 11. But in this case too the (admittedly fragmentary) evidence seems to point to an idiosyncratic, original work of art of which the meaning is certainly enriched but cannot be entirely explained by these parallels. The Hesiodic *Catalogue* provides a human counterpart to Hesiod's *Theogony:* a general classification of all the major heroes and heroines of Greek mythology, organized genealogically from a definite beginning to a definite end and with all-encompassing pan-Hellenic ambitions. The whole rich panoply of Greek local legend is reduced to a very small number of starting-points, and from these are developed lines of descent that bind all the characters and events into a single history, an enormously complex but

---

[18] It is uncertain just where Book 3 ended and Book 4 began; the new starting-point of Pelasgus may have been set at the opening of Book 4 (so proposed in the present edition), or Pelasgus' descendants and at least the first descendants of Atlas may have formed part of Book 3 (so Merkelbach-West).

highly structured and, at least to a certain extent, unified story. As in the *Theogony*, the bare bones of genealogical descent often produce verse consisting of little more than proper names—in itself already a demonstration of a high degree of poetic skill, and doubtless a source of considerable pleasure to ancient audiences. And yet here too the severe structure is often enlivened by entertaining stories whose meaning goes well beyond what would be required for the purposes of strict genealogy. In comparison with Homer's tendency to humanize and sanitize Greek myth, the *Catalogue of Women* (like the *Theogony*) presents us with tantalizing glimpses of an astonishingly colorful, erotic, often bizarre, sometimes even grotesque world of legend: the monstrous Molionian twins (Fr. 13–15), Periclymenus with his deadly metamorphoses (Fr. 31–33), lovely swift Atalanta (Fr. 47–51), thievish Autolycus (Fr. 67–68), Mestra whom her father sells repeatedly in order to buy food for his blazing hunger (Fr. 69–71), Phineus and the Harpies (Fr. 97–105), Caenis whom her lover Poseidon transforms at her request into the man Caeneus (Fr. 165)—our view of Greek myth would certainly be far poorer without them. And finally, the *Catalogue of Women* seems to be driven diachronically by a single long-term narrative which corresponds on a different level to the complementary stories of the triumph of the justice of Zeus, which provides the backbone to the *Theogony*, and of the administration of that justice, which structures the *Works and Days*. In the *Catalogue* this narrative provides a vast preamble to the Trojan War, interpreting the heroic age as a long period of frequent and intimate intercourse (in all senses) between gods and men to which Zeus decides to put an end after Helen gives birth to Hermione

(Fr. 155.94ff.). Why exactly Zeus decides to kill off the heroes at this moment in world history is not clear, and the point of the extensive natural scene that follows in the text, with its lengthy account of weather conditions and a terrible snake (Fr. 155.129ff.), has not yet been satisfactorily explained. But it is clear that, for the author of this Hesiodic poem, the Trojan legends that inspired Homer were the most fitting possible *telos* at which to aim his own composition. After the *Catalogue* come the *Iliad* and *Odyssey* and other epic poems; and a long time after them comes the world of ordinary men and women.

The *Catalogue of Women* was almost always considered a genuine work of Hesiod's in antiquity, and this view has been followed by a few modern scholars as well. But most modern scholarship prefers to see the poem as a later, inauthentic addition to the corpus of Hesiod's poems. Various considerations, of unequal weight individually but fairly persuasive cumulatively, suggest that the *Catalogue* was probably composed sometime between the end of the 7th century and the middle of the 6th century BC (though of course the stories and names that fill it go back centuries earlier), well over a century after the lifetime of Hesiod. Given its character it is not in the least surprising that it was attributed at some point to Hesiod himself and was spliced into ancient editions of his poems, immediately following the *Theogony*.

The other poem transmitted in medieval manuscripts of Hesiod, the *Shield,* is at least partially an outgrowth of the *Catalogue of Women* and another striking example of the interaction between the Hesiodic and Homeric poetic traditions. The *Shield* begins with the phrase *Ē hoiē* ("Or like her"), familiar from the *Catalogue,* and indeed the first

56 lines were transmitted in antiquity as part of that poem
(cf. T52 and Fr. 139). They recount how Zeus slept with
Amphitryon's wife Alcmene the same night as Amphitryon
did, so that she gave birth to unequal twins, to Zeus' son
Heracles and Amphitryon's son Iphicles (1–56). To this
story is appended a much longer narrative telling how,
many years later, Heracles, aided by his nephew Iolaus,
slew Ares' son Cycnus and wounded Ares (57–480). Al-
most half of this narrative is filled by a lengthy and richly
detailed description of the shield that Heracles takes up in
preparation for his combat (139–321); in comparison, the
scenes preceding the duels are stiff and rather conven-
tional, and the fighting itself is dealt with in rather sum-
mary fashion.

Whereas in the *Iliad* and *Odyssey* Heracles is referred
to only about eighteen times, almost always in a marginal
role,[19] in the *Theogony* he has an important function as an
instrument of Zeus' justice, slaying monsters, liberating
Prometheus, and receiving as a reward for his labors a
place in Olympus and Hebe as his bride.[20] So too, he re-
curs repeatedly in a variety of different contexts in the *Cat-
alogue of Women,* as we would only expect of the greatest
hero of Greek legend—indeed he is already named in the
proem on a par with the other sexually productive male
Greek gods (Fr. 1.22).[21] So it is not surprising that a poet
who decided to provide a Hesiodic counterpart to the cele-
brated shield which Homer gives his hero Achilles in *Iliad*

[19] *Il.* 2.653, 658, 666, 679, 5.628, 638, 11.690, 14.266, 324,
15.25, 640, 18.117, 19.98, 20.145; *Od.* 8.224, 11.267, 601, 21.26.
[20] *Th* 289, 315, 317, 318, 332, 527, 530, 943, 951, 982.
[21] Then Fr. 22, 31–33, 117, 133, 138–41, 174–75.

18—that this is the point of the *Shield* is pretty obvious, and was already recognized by Aristophanes of Byzantium[22]—should have chosen Heracles to be the protagonist of his own poem. Yet it is remarkable how faithful this Hesiodic poet remains to his Homeric model at the same time as he elaborates upon it in an original and interesting way.

We may surely presume it as likely that in heroic times most real shields, if they were not constructed for purely defensive purposes but also bore any figural representations at all, were intended not to instruct enemies but to terrify them. Yet Homer assigns a practical shield of this sort not to Achilles but to Agamemnon, whose shield bears allegorical personifications of fear designed to strike fear into anyone who sees them (Gorgo, Deimos, Phobos: *Il.* 11.32–37). To the hero who matters to him most, Achilles, Homer grants a shield whose grand cosmological vision locates even the epic story of the *Iliad* as a whole within a wider and much more significant horizon of meaning, demonstrating its limits and thereby enlarging its import. Achilles' shield encloses within a heaven of the sun, moon, and stars (*Il.* 18.484–89) and the all-encompassing circle of Ocean (607–8) the earth as a world of human beings, divided first into two cities, one at peace (including a murder trial, 491–508) and one at war (509–40), and then into the basic agricultural activities, first fieldwork (plowing 541–49, reaping 550–60, wine harvest and festival 561–72) and then livestock (at war 573–86, at peace 587–89). Perhaps it was the cosmic scope or the juridical and agricultural content that struck some Hesiodic poet as belonging

[22] See Testimonium T52.

more rightly to his own tradition than to a Homeric one. In any case, when he chose to imitate the Homeric shield, he sought to surpass it by heightening it whenever possible. He begins with a terrifying shield, like Agamemnon's, which starts out with allegorical personifications (144–60) and then moves up the biological ladder from animals (snakes 161–67, boars and lions at war 168–77) through Lapiths and Centaurs (178–90) to the gods at war (191–200) and peace (201–7). He then supplements this by providing a variation on Achilles' cosmic shield: beginning with non-military strife (fishing 207–15, the mythic pursuit of Perseus by the Gorgons 216–37), he then gives his own two cities, one at war (237–69) and one at peace (270–85), followed by such peaceful activities as horsemen (285–86), agriculture (plowing 286–88, reaping 288–91, wine harvest 292–300) and non-military competition (athletic boxing and wrestling 301–2, hunting 302–4, athletic contests of horsemen and chariots 304–13), and he closes the whole composition with the ring of all-surrounding Ocean (314–17). Throughout the poem he demonstrates a consistent taste for hyperbolic and graphically violent, indeed often lurid detail which has earned him fewer admirers among modern readers than he deserves.

The *Shield* is generally dated to sometime between the end of the 7th and the first half of the 6th century BC. Its precise relation to the *Catalogue of Women* is controversial. Some have thought that the author of the *Shield* himself borrowed the first 56 lines of his poem from the *Catalogue* and therefore that the *Shield* postdates the *Catalogue*. But the two parts of the poem have in fact nothing whatsoever to do with one another except for the fact that they both have Heracles as protagonist, and it seems there-

fore much more likely that lines 1–56 of the *Shield* origi-
nally formed part of the *Catalogue* but that the rest of
the *Shield* arose independently of the *Catalogue* and was
later combined with the first part and included among
Hesiod's works by an ancient editor.

### Other Poems Ascribed to Hesiod

As in the case of the *Catalogue of Women* and *Shield,* the
fame of Hesiod's name attracted to it productions by other
poets which bore some affinity to his own, and thereby
helped ensure their survival in antiquity. But the other po-
ems which bore Hesiod's name circulated far less in antiq-
uity than the *Theogony* and the *Works and Days* did, and
they were excluded from at least some selected lists of his
works; so today they exist only in exiguous fragments if at
all, and often even their nature and structure remain quite
obscure.

One group of poems must have been comparable to the
*Catalogue of Women:*

1. The *Great Ehoiai* (Testimonia T42 and 66; Fr. 185–
201, and perhaps also 239, 241–43, 247–48). Given its title,
this poem clearly must have been broadly similar in con-
tent and form to the *Ehoiai;* and if the *Ehoiai* had five
books, then the *Great Ehoiai* must have consisted of even
more. Some of the stories the *Great Ehoiai* told coincide
with those in the *Catalogue,* others seem to have been dif-
ferent; in at least one case ancient scholars noted a discrep-
ancy between the versions of the same story they found in
the two works (Fr. 192). Very little is known about this
poem. It seems to have circulated scarcely at all in antiq-
uity outside the narrow confines of professional literary

scholarship: citations and reports from Pausanias and the scholia and commentaries to Pindar, Apollonius Rhodius, Aristotle and other authors make up all but one or two of the extant fragments, and only a single papyrus has so far been identified as coming from this poem (Fr. 189a).

2. *The Wedding of Ceyx* (T67–68; Fr. 202–5). The marriage of Aeolus' daughter Alcyone to Ceyx, the son of the Morning Star, was recounted in Book 1 of the *Catalogue of Women* (Fr. 10.83–98, 12; cf. Fr. 46); they seem to have loved one another so much that he called her Hera and she called him Zeus, and consequently Zeus punished them by transforming them into birds. Ceyx also plays a marginal role in the *Shield* (354, 472, 476) and is otherwise associated with Heracles (Fr. 189a); conversely, Heracles seems to have figured in *The Wedding of Ceyx* (Fr. 202–3, and cf. Fr. 291). What the content of this poem was—whether it was romantic and tragic, or epic, or something else—remains unknown; one fragment from it (Fr. 204) seems to evince a rather frosty wit.

3. The *Melampodia* (T42; Fr. 206–15, and perhaps also Fr. 253 and 295). Melampus was a celebrated seer in Greek legend who figured both in the *Catalogue of Women* (Fr. 35, 242) and in the *Great Ehoiai* (Fr. 199). The *Melampodia,* in at least three books (Fr. 213), must have recounted the exploits not only of Melampus himself but also of other famous seers like Teiresias (Fr. 211–12), Calchas and Mopsus (Fr. 214), and Amphilochus (Fr. 215). How these accounts were related to one another is not known.

4. *The Descent of Peirithous to Hades* (T42; Fr. 216, and perhaps also 243). A poem on this subject is attributed to Hesiod by Pausanias (T42). A papyrus fragment contain-

ing a dialogue in the Underworld between Meleager and Theseus in the presence of Peirithous (Fr. 216) is assigned by editors, plausibly but uncertainly, to this poem.

5. *Aegimius* (T37, 79; Fr. 230–38). A poem of this title, extant in antiquity, was attributed either to Hesiod or to Cercops of Miletus. Aegimius figures in the *Catalogue of Women* (Fr. 10) as a son of Dorus, the eponym of the Dorians; other sources report that Heracles helped him in battle, and that after Heracles' death he showed his gratitude by raising Heracles' son Hyllus together with his own sons. The fairly numerous fragments, mostly deriving from ancient literary scholars, indicate that the poem recounted myths, including those relating to Io (Fr. 230–32), the Graeae (Fr. 233), Theseus (Fr. 235), the golden fleece (Fr. 236), and Achilles (Fr. 237). But what the connection among such stories might have been and even what the poem was basically about are anyone's guess.

Another group of poems bears obvious affinities to the *Works and Days:*

1. The *Great Works* (T66; Fr. 221–22, and perhaps also 271–73). From its title it appears that this poem bore the same relation to the *Works and Days* as the *Great Ehoiai* bore to the *Catalogue of Women*. One of the surviving fragments is moralistic (Fr. 221), the other discusses the origin of silver (Fr. 222); both topics can be correlated with the *Works and Days*.

2. The *Astronomy* or *Astrology* (T72–78; Fr. 223–29, and perhaps also 118, 244–45, 261–62). A work bearing one or the other of these two titles was celebrated enough in the Hellenistic period for Aratus to have taken it as his model for his own *Phenomena,* according to Callimachus (T73); and it survived as late as the 12th century, when the

Byzantine scholar Tzetzes read and quoted it (T78; Fr. 227b). Most of the few remaining fragments that can be attributed to it with certainty regard the risings and settings of stars and constellations; the similarity of this topic to the astronomical advice in the *Works and Days* is obvious.

3. The *Precepts of Chiron* (T42, 69–71; Fr. 218–20, and perhaps also Fr. 240, 254, 271–73, 293). Until Aristarchus declared its inauthenticity (T69), a poem under this title was attributed in antiquity to Hesiod. Its content seems to have consisted of pieces of advice, some moral or religious (Fr. 218), some practical (Fr. 219–20); presumably they were put into the mouth of Chiron, the centaur who educated Achilles and Jason and appeared in the *Catalogue* (Fr. 36, 155, 162–63). No doubt it was the admonitions and precepts in Hesiods's *Works and Days* that suggested to some ancient readers that this poem too was his.

4. *Bird Omens* (T80; perhaps Fr. 295). In some copies of the *Works and Days* that poem was followed after its conclusion at line 828 by a poem called *Bird Omens;* the words in lines 826–28, "Happy and blessed is he who knows all these things and does his work without giving offense to the immortals, *distinguishing the birds* and avoiding trespasses," may either have been what suggested to some editor that such a poem could be added at this point or may even have been composed or modified by a poet-editor in order to justify adding such a poem. In either case, Apollonius Rhodius marked the poem as spurious (T80) and no secure fragment of it survives.

5. *On Preserved Foods* (T81). Athenaeus quotes some lines from a poem about preserved foods attributed to Hesiod by Euthydemus of Athens, a doctor who may have lived in the 2nd century BC; Athenaeus suggests that their

real author was Euthydemus himself, and there seems no reason to doubt him. Perhaps it was the general subject, advice regarding household matters, that suggested attributing the poem to the author of the *Works and Days*.

Finally, there were some poems assigned to Hesiod in antiquity of which the attribution is more difficult to explain:

1. *The Idaean Dactyls* (T1; Fr. 217). The two ancient reports about this poem show only that it told of the discovery of metals.

2. *Dirge for Batrachus* (T1). Nothing is known about this poem or about Batrachus except that the *Suda* identifies him as Hesiod's beloved. The fact that the personal name Batrachus is well attested only in Attica might suggest that the poem was attributed to Hesiod during a period of Athenian transmission or popularity of his poetry.

3. *The Potters* (T82; for the text, see Pseudo-Herodotus, *On Homer's Origins, Date, and Life* 32, pp. 390–95 West). A short hexametric poem found in an ancient biography of Homer and consisting first in a prayer to Athena to help potters if they will reward the poet, and then in imprecations against them if they should fail to do so, was also attributed by some ancient scholars to Hesiod, on the testimony of Pollux.

## HESIOD'S INFLUENCE
## AND RECEPTION

The ancient reception of Hesiod is a vast, complex, and very under-researched area. Here only a sketch of its very basic outlines and some indications of its fundamental tendencies can be provided.

While the Testimonia regarding Hesiod's life (T1–40) demonstrate that his biography was of interest in antiquity, there can be little doubt that it was of less interest than Homer's: Homer was by far the more culturally central poet of the two, and the absolute absence of information about his life could spur his many admirers' historical fantasy. Some details of Hesiod's biography were derived from his poems; he was supplied with a father, Dius (T1, 2, 95, 105), whose name arose out of a misunderstanding of *WD* 299; his mother's name, Pycimede (T1, 2, 105), which means "cautious-minded" or "shrewd," may have been invented on the basis of the character of his poetry. Various details seem to have been created out of a hostile reading of his poetry: thus Ephorus stated that Hesiod's father left Cyme not, as Hesiod claimed, because of poverty, but because he had murdered a kinsman (T25); and the various legends concerning the poet's death (T1, 2, 30–34) involve him as an innocent or sometimes even guilty party in a sordid tale of seduction, violation of hospitality, and murder, which seems fully to confirm his highly negative account of the race of iron men among whom he is destined to live. And yet his murderers are punished in a way that suggests the workings of divine justice (T2, 32–34); and as an infant, Hesiod is marked out by a miracle for future greatness as a poet (T26). Ancient scholarship attempted to determine the chronological relation between Homer and Hesiod (T3–24); the tendency to correlate the prestige of these two poets by inventing legends of competition between them led to the idea of their relative contemporaneity (T10–14), but the other options, that Homer was older than Hesiod (T5–9) and that Hesiod was older than Homer (T15–16), were both also well represented. The sequence Orpheus-Musaeus-Hesiod-Homer recurs a number of times in very different contexts (17, 18, 116a, 119bi and bii), but it is far from certain that it was always, or indeed ever, meant in a strictly chronological sense.

In the Archaic and Classical periods, Hesiod's *Theogony* and *Works and Days* both found a number of poets and prose writers who continued to work within the generic traditions he canonized, as indicated above in the sections discussing those poems. But it is the *Catalogue of Women* that seems to have had the greatest impact not only upon lyric poets like Stesichorus, Pindar (who at *Isthmian* 6.66–67 cites *WD* 412, attributing it to Hesiod by name), and Bacchylides (who mentions Hesiod by name and quotes from him a sentence not found in any of his extant works, Fr. 306) but also upon the tragic poets, who generally preferred to draw their material not from the *Iliad* and *Odyssey* but from the Epic Cycle and the Hesiodic *Catalogue*. It was in the Hellenistic period, however, that Hesiod reached the acme of his literary influence in ancient Greece: he provided a model of learned, civilizing poetry and a more modest alternative to pompous martial epic that made him especially prized by Callimachus himself (T73, 87) and by Callimachus' Greek (T73, 56) and Latin (T47, 90–92) followers. In particular, Hesiod was celebrated by ancient poets and in ancient poetics as a founder of literary genres (especially didactic poetry, but also the poem of instruction for princes); it was mostly through the mediation of Aratus, of Latin translations of this poet, and of Virgil that Hesiod was known in Late Antiquity and in the Latin Middle Ages. For Greek readers in Hellenistic and Imperial Egypt, the *Catalogue of Women* seems, at least to judge from the evidence of the papyri, to have been one of the most intensely studied archaic texts after Homer's epics; perhaps its systematic presentation of their own rich and sometimes bizarre mythology gave these readers a sense of orientation and consolation. To the same period may belong the essential conception of the extant version of the *Contest of Homer and Hesiod,* in which Homer pleases the crowd more than Hesiod does but the king nevertheless awards the prize for victory to Hesiod, because a poem about peace and agriculture should be deemed superior to one about war and bloodshed. Hesiod's poems continued to be set to music and performed privately, and perhaps also publicly, well into the Imperial period (T84–86), and as late as the 3rd or early 4th century AD his story of his poetic initiation was still capable of inspiring a technically gifted anonymous poet (T95) to compose a tour-de-force acrostic poem on this subject.

But the *Theogony* and *Works and Days* have had their greatest influence perhaps not so much as whole poetic constructs, but in terms of two of the myths they narrate. Hesiod's tale of Prometheus inspired the author of a tragedy attributed to Aeschylus (as well as Protagoras in Plato's dialogue of that title), and then went on from there to become one of the central myths of Western culture, usually with little regard for the details or even the general import of Hesiod's own treatment of the tale; the same applies to Hesiod's story of the races of men, which, isolated from its argumentative context and transformed (especially in Ovid's *Metamorphoses*) into an account not of the races but of the ages of men, bequeathed to later centuries the consoling image of a Golden Age, when life was easier and men were better and happier than they are now. So too, Hesiod's portrayal of his poetic initiation generated a whole tradition of such scenes, in Greek, Latin, and post-Classical literature.

Hesiod also plays a crucial role in the history of Greek religion and philosophy. He was the object of a cult at Thespiae (T104–5, 108), and was venerated not only at Orchomenus (T102–3), Helicon (T109), and Olympia (T110), but also as far away as Macedonia (T107) and Armenia (T106). Herodotus could quite rightly say that it was Hesiod's systematization of the various local traditions of Greek mythology, together with Homer's, which gave the Greeks their national religion (T98). And for that very reason, Hesiod was a preferred target of philosophers, starting with Xenophanes (T97) and culminating most famously in Plato (T99), who objected to the popular views of the nature of the gods as these were canonized in his poetry. Yet Hesiod's relation to Greek philosophy is in fact quite complicated. Already Aristotle seems uncertain as to whether he should count Hesiod as a true philosopher or not: in some passages he begins the history of philosophy with Thales, consigning Hesiod to the pre-philosophical theologians (so T117.c.i), while in others he considers Hesiod's accounts of such figures as Eros to be cosmological doctrines apparently worthy of serious attention (so T117.c.ii). Indeed, Hesiod's poetry has always seemed to occupy an ambiguous and unstable position somewhere between pure mythology, in which the gods are autonomous divine beings with their own personalities and destinies, and a rudimentary philosophy, in which the gods are merely allegorical designations for moral and rational categories of thought. Yet Hesiod's questions—what are the origin and structure of things? how can human beings achieve success and happiness in their lives?—are the very same ones that concerned all later Greek philosophers; and his answers, despite their often mythical form, continued to interest philosophers until the end of antiquity. Sometimes the philosophers expressed this interest in the form of outright attack (T97, 99, 100, 113, 118), rarely in that of unabashed praise (T114, 116ab), increasingly over the course of time in that of allegorical recuperation (T115, 116c, 117, 119–20). The difficulties of explaining the erudite, pagan, often rebarbative *Theogony* in particular to children in Imperial and, even more so, in Byzantine Christian schools led to a particularly rich set of allegorical scholia on this poem.

The Byzantine study of Hesiod was the culmination of the work of centuries of historians, rhetoricians, and literary scholars who devoted themselves to the edition, elucidation, and sometimes allegedly even plagiarism of his poems. Greek historiography, in such figures as Eumelus and Acusilaus, begins as the continuation of the *Theogony* and *Catalogue of Women* by other means (T121–22). The authors of Greek rhetorical manuals, developing and systematizing the work of earlier professionals like the rhapsodes (T83), sophists (T115), and rhetors (T123), applied their technical categories, with some success, to the rather recalcitrant set of his texts (T124–27). Greek literary scholarship starts, in the case of Hesiod as in so many other instances, with Aristotle, who wrote a treatise on *Hesiodic Problems* in one book (T128), and Hesiodic philology, though it always takes second place in the study of archaic epic to Homeric philology, continues to occupy the attention of more and less celebrated philologists until at least the end of antiquity (T129–50). One place of honor in the history of Hesiodic philology belongs to Plutarch, who wrote a biography of Hesiod (which does not survive) and a predominantly moralizing commentary on the *Works and Days* in at least four books, of which extensive excerpts are cited in the ancient scholia to that poem (T147); and another one should be assigned to the 5th century Neoplatonist Proclus, who wrote a mostly philosophical commentary on the same poem which often quotes Plutarch's commentary and of which many fragments are cited in the same scholia (T148).

## THE TRANSMISSION OF HESIOD'S POETRY

Hesiod's works are transmitted in very varying degrees of incompleteness by fragments from well over fifty ancient manuscripts, papyrus or parchment rolls or codices from Egypt dating from at least the 1st century BC to the 6th century AD; and numerous medieval and early modern manuscripts transmit his three extant poems—about 70 for the *Theogony*, over 260 for the *Works and Days*, about 60 for the *Shield*.[23] But the most important witnesses for constructing a critical edition are only about a dozen:

[23] The basic information about the transmission of Hesiod's poems is conveniently available in M.L. West, Commentary on *Th* 48–72, and Commentary on *WD*, 60–86; and in Solmsen-Merkelbach-West, *Hesiodi Theogonia* . . . , pp. ix-xxiii. For the symbols that indicate some further minor manuscripts cited only rarely in the apparatus to this edition, the reader is referred to West's commentaries.

S    Laurentianus 32,16, dated to 1280, containing *Th, WD,* and *Shield.*

B    Parisinus suppl. gr. 663, from the end of the 11th or the beginning of the 12th century, containing in part *Th* and *Shield.*

L    Laurentianus conv. soppr. 158, from the 14th century, containing the whole of *Th* and *Shield.*

R    Casanatensis 356, from the 13th or likelier 14th century, containing *Th* and most of *Shield.*

J    Ambrosianus C 222 inf., partly from the late 12th century, containing *WD* and *Shield.*

F    Parisinus gr. 2773, from the 14th century, containing *WD* and most of *Shield.*

Q    Vaticanus gr. 915, from a few years before 1311, containing *Th.*

K    Ravennas 120, from the 14th century, containing *Th.*

C    Parisinus gr. 2771, from the 10th or 11th century, containing most of *WD.*

D    Laurentianus 31,39, from the 12th century, containing *WD.*

E    Messanensis bibl. univ. F.V. 11, from the end of the 12th century, containing *WD.*

H    Vaticanus gr. 2383, dated to 1287, containing *WD.*

A    fol. 75 of Parisinus suppl. gr. 663 (indicated as B above) contains lines 87–138 of *Shield* written at the same time as B but by a different hand.

In addition, the following symbols designate groups of manuscripts:

*m*    Parisinus gr. 2763, Parisinus gr. 2833, Vratislaviensis Rehd. 35, and Mosquensis 469 (all 15th century).

| | |
|---|---|
| *b* | *m,* L, and R. |
| *n* | Marcianus IX. 6 (14th century) and Salmanticensis 243 (15th century). |
| *v* | Laurentianus conv. soppr. 15 (14th century), Panormitanus Qq-A-75 and Parisinus suppl. gr. 652 (both 15th century). |
| *a* | *n* and *v.* |
| *u* | Matritensis 4607, Ambrosianus D 529 inf., and Vaticanus gr. 2185 (all 15th century). |
| *k* | K and *u.* |
| *φ* | E and H. |

For the numbers which designate the papyri cited, the reader is referred to the editions of West[24] and of Solmsen-Merkelbach-West.[25]

## THIS EDITION

The aim of this edition is to make available to professional scholars, students, and interested general readers the texts of Hesiod's poetry and the Testimonia of his life and works as these are understood by current scholarship. This Loeb edition can make no claim to being a truly critical edition: I have not examined the papyri or the manuscripts and have relied instead upon the reports of editors I consider trustworthy. My general impression is that there is little to be gained at this point by a renewed *recensio* of the manu-

[24] West, Commentary on *Th*, pp. 64–65, and Commentary on *WD*, pp. 75–77.

[25] Solmsen-Merkelbach-West, *Hesiodi Theogonia* . . . , pp. xxvi-xxviii.

script evidence—in other words, recent editors seem to have done that job very well indeed.

There are three parts to this edition, and each requires a few words of explanation:

1. *Theogony, Works and Days, Shield.* The first two of these poems are found in vol. 1 of the present edition, the third one in vol. 2. For the texts of these three poems I have availed myself of what in my judgment is the best critical edition of each poem currently available: for the *Theogony* and *Works and Days,* West's commented editions to each poem;[26] for the *Shield,* Solmsen's edition in Solmsen-Merkelbach-West's Oxford Classical Text of Hesiod.[27] I have relied upon these editions for their reports of the manuscript evidence, but I have differed from their choice of readings whenever it seemed necessary to do so, often (but not always) in order to defend the transmitted reading against what I consider an unnecessary conjectural correction. As a general rule I have tried always to translate a Greek word wherever it occurs with the same English one; but of course that has not always been possible and I have not hesitated to sacrifice strict observance of that rule to the requirements of intelligibility. So too I have tried in general to give in the sequence of clauses and even words in the English translation a sense of the syntactical sequence of the Greek original, but that has not always been possible either.

2. *Fragments.* These are found in vol. 2 of the present

---

[26] West, Commentary on *Th,* pp. 111–49, and Commentary on *WD,* pp. 95–135.

[27] Solmsen-Merkelbach-West, *Hesiodi Theogonia . . . ,* pp. 88–107.

edition. Like virtually all contemporary scholars, I have been fundamentally guided in my understanding of the *Catalogue of Women* and the other fragments of Hesiodic poetry by the work of Merkelbach and West. But while I have gratefully followed their interpretation of the *Catalogue*'s general structure, I have chosen to differ from their detailed arrangement of the fragments when doing so yielded what seemed to me a more plausible result. I have also decided, after considerable hesitation, to provide a new numeration for the fragments; aware though I am of the inconveniences resulting from the multiplication of systems of numeration, I judged that the disadvantages in doing so at this point were considerably less than those entailed by continuing to follow the Merkelbach-West numbers, outdated, inconsistent, and confusing as these have become over the decades, in large part due to the very progress achieved by their own research. In any case the Merkelbach-West numbers are provided together with the Greek texts of the fragments, and a concordance of fragment numbers at the back of vol. 2 should make it possible without too much difficulty to shift back and forth between the two systems.[28] I have followed Merkelbach-West and other editors in grouping together under the general term of "fragments" both verbal citations or direct witnesses (fragments in the narrow sense) and reports about the contents of the poems (strictly speaking, Testimonia). But in arranging the fragments I have grouped to-

[28] To make this edition more convenient for the reader I have also included in these concordances the numbers of Hirschberger's recent, useful commentary on the *Catalogue of Women* and *Great Ehoiai*.

gether direct witnesses and verbal citations on the one hand and indirect Testimonia on the other in those cases in which both kinds of witnesses refer to exactly the same mythic datum, even at the occasional cost of briefly interrupting thereby the continuity of a direct witness to the *Catalogue;* I hope that this disadvantage (lessened by cross-references in the different parts of the same direct witness) will be found to be outweighed by the greater perspicuity in the resulting arrangement of the various kinds of witnesses. In the translations of fragments transmitted by papyri, I have attempted wherever possible to give a visual indication of what is actually transmitted on the papyrus and where, as well as to differentiate attested material from what is supplemented by editors (the latter is set off by square brackets []). So too I have tried to follow in the case of the fragments the rules noted above for the translation of the three fully extant poems; but here too I have preferred pragmatism and intelligibility to rigorously following rules without exceptions.

3. *Testimonia.* These are to be found in vol. 1 of the present edition. I have provided only a small sampling of what I consider to be the most interesting and important among the thousands of Testimonia provided by ancient Greek and Latin writers concerning the life and works of Hesiod. The Testimonia are divided into those concerning Hesiod's life, his works, and his influence and reception, with further subdivisions in each case. Readers should bear in mind that, while these classifications are useful, they are sometimes somewhat artificial; cross-references should help to direct readers to particularly important areas of overlap but can provide only a minimal orientation. A model and an indispensable help in the collection of

these Testimonia was provided by the corresponding sec-
tion in Felix Jacoby's edition of the *Theogony*;[29] the reader
who wishes to compare my collection with his will be aided
in doing so by the concordance of the two collections of
Testimonia at the back of this volume.

[29] Felix Jacoby, ed., *Hesiodi Carmina. Pars I: Theogonia*
(Berlin 1930), pp. 106–35.

# BIBLIOGRAPHY

### Critical editions

Friedrich Solmsen, R. Merkelbach, and M. L. West, eds. *Hesiodi Theogonia Opera et Dies Scutum: Fragmenta Selecta* (Oxford 1970, 1983², 1990³).
M. L. West, ed. *Hesiod. Theogony* (Oxford 1966).
——— *Hesiod: Works and Days* (Oxford 1978).
R. Merkelbach and M. L. West, eds. *Fragmenta Hesiodea* (Oxford 1967 = 1999).

### Other editions

Aloisius Rzach, ed. *Hesiodus Carmina*, editio maior (Leipzig 1902), editio minor (Leipzig 1902, 1908², 1913³ = Stuttgart 1958).
Hugh G. Evelyn-White, ed. *Hesiod: The Homeric Hymns and Homerica* (Cambridge, Mass., and London 1914).
Paul Mazon, ed. *Hésiode: Théogonie, Les Travaux et les Jours, le Bouclier* (Paris 1928, 1960⁵).
Felix Jacoby, ed. *Hesiodi Carmina. Pars I: Theogonia* (Berlin 1930).
Aristides Colonna, ed. *Hesiodi Opera et Dies* (Milano-Varese 1959).
Graziano Arrighetti, ed. *Esiodo: Opere* (Torino 1998).

# BIBLIOGRAPHY

## Scholia

Thomas Gaisford, ed. *Poetae minores Graeci,* vol. 3 (Oxford 1814, Leipzig 1823).

Hans Flach, ed. *Glossen und Scholien zur hesiodischen Theogonie* (Leipzig 1876).

Augustinus Pertusi, ed. *Scholia vetera in Hesiodi Opera et Dies* (Milano 1955).

Lambertus Di Gregorio, ed. *Scholia vetera in Hesiodi Theogoniam* (Milano 1975).

## Commentaries

### Theogony

Wolfgang Aly. *Hesiods Theogonie* (Heidelberg 1913).

M. L. West. *Hesiod. Theogony* (Oxford 1966).

Richard Hamilton. *Hesiod's Theogony* (Bryn Mawr 1990).

### Works and Days

Pierre Waltz, ed. *Hésiode, Les Travaux et les Jours* (Brussels 1909).

Paul Mazon, ed. *Hésiode. Les Travaux et les Jours* (Paris 1914).

Ulrich von Wilamowitz-Moellendorff, ed. *Hesiodos Erga* (Berlin 1928 = Dublin/Zürich 1962, 1970).

T. A. Sinclair, ed. *Hesiod: Works and Days* (London 1932).

M. L. West. *Hesiod: Works and Days* (Oxford 1978).

W. J. Verdenius. *A Commentary on Hesiod: Works and Days,* vv. 1–382 (Leiden 1985).

### Shield

Carlo Ferdinando Russo, ed. *Hesiodi Scutum* (Firenze 1950, 1965[2]).

BIBLIOGRAPHY

## Catalogue of Women

Martina Hirschberger. *Gynaikon Katalogos und Megalai Ehoiai: Ein Kommentar zu den Fragmenten zweier hesiodeischer Epen* (München 2004).

## Lexica

Johannes Paulson. *Index Hesiodeus* (Lund 1890 = Hildesheim 1962).

M. Hofinger. *Lexicon Hesiodeum cum indice inverso* (Leiden 1973–85).

William W. Minton. *Concordance to the Hesiodic Corpus* (Leiden 1976).

Joseph R. Tebben. *Hesiod-Konkordanz: A Computer Concordance to Hesiod* (Hildesheim and New York 1977).

## General collections of essays

Fondation Hardt. *Entretiens sur l'antiquité classique 7: Hésiode et son influence* (Genève 1962).

Ernst Heitsch, ed. *Hesiod = Wege der Forschung 44* (Darmstadt 1966).

Graziano Arrighetti, ed. *Esiodo: Letture critiche* (Milano 1975).

Apostolos N. Athanassakis, ed. *Essays on Hesiod I-II, Ramus 21:1–2* (1992).

Fabienne Blaise, Pierre Judet de la Combe, and Philippe Rousseau, eds. *Le métier du mythe. Lectures d'Hésiode* (Lille 1996).

# BIBLIOGRAPHY

## General studies

Friedrich Solmsen. *Hesiod and Aeschylus* (Ithaca 1949).

G. P. Edwards. *The Language of Hesiod in Its Traditional Context* (Oxford 1971).

Pietro Pucci. *Hesiod and the Language of Poetry* (Baltimore 1977).

Richard C. M. Janko. *Homer, Hesiod and the Hymns: Diachronic Development in Epic Diction* (Cambridge 1982).

William G. Thalmann. *Conventions of Form and Thought in Early Greek Epic Poetry* (Baltimore 1984).

Robert Lamberton. *Hesiod* (New Haven 1988).

Richard Hamilton. *The Architecture of Hesiodic Poetry* (Baltimore and London 1989).

Jenny Strauss Clay. *Hesiod's Cosmos* (Cambridge 2003).

## Theogony

Friedrich Schwenn. *Die Theogonie des Hesiodos* (Heidelberg 1934).

Hans Schwabl. *Hesiods Theogonie: Eine unitarische Analyse* (Wien 1966).

## Works and Days

Walter Nicolai. *Hesiods Erga: Beobachtungen zum Aufbau* (Heidelberg 1964).

Jean-Pierre Vernant. "Le mythe hésiodique des races: Essai d'analyse structurale," and "Le mythe hésiodique des races: Sur un essai de mise au point," in *Mythe et pensée chez les Grecs*, vol. 1 (Paris 1965), pp. 13–41 and 42–79.

Berkley Peabody. *The Winged Word: A Study of Ancient*

## BIBLIOGRAPHY

*Greek Oral Composition as Seen Principally Through Hesiod's Works and Days* (Albany 1975).

Jens-Uwe Schmidt. *Adressat und Paraineseform: Zur Intention von Hesiods 'Werken und Tagen'* (Göttingen 1986).

Stefanie Nelson. *God and the Land: The Metaphysics of Farming in Hesiod and Virgil* (New York and Oxford 1998).

Anthony T. Edwards. *Hesiod's Ascra* (Berkeley, Cal. 2004).

### Catalogue of Women

M. L. West. *The Hesiodic Catalogue of Women: Its Nature, Structure, and Origins* (Oxford 1985).

Paul Dräger. *Untersuchungen zu den Frauenkatalogen Hesiods* (Stuttgart 1997).

Richard Hunter, ed. *The Hesiodic* Catalogue of Women: *Constructions and Reconstructions* (Cambridge 2005).

### Shield

Andrew S. Becker. "Reading Poetry through a Distant Lens: Ecphrasis, Ancient Greek Rhetoricians, and the Pseudo-Hesiodic 'Shield of Herakles,'" *American Journal of Philology* 113 (1992) 5–24.

### Oriental sources and parallels

Peter Walcot. *Hesiod and the Near East* (Cardiff 1966).

James B. Pritchard, ed. *The Ancient Near East, vols. 1, 2* (Princeton 1958, 1975).

M. L. West. *The East Face of Helicon: West Asiatic Elements in Greek Poetry and Myth* (Oxford 1997).

Walter Burkert. *Babylon, Memphis, Persepolis: Eastern Contexts of Greek Culture* (Cambridge, Mass. 2004).

# BIBLIOGRAPHY

## Influence and reception

Carlo Buzio. *Esiodo nel mondo greco sino alla fine dell'età classica* (Milano 1938).

Athanasios Kambylis. *Die Dichterweihe und ihre Symbolik: Untersuchungen zu Hesiodos, Kallimachos, Properz und Ennius* (Heidelberg 1965).

Gerhard Vogel. *Der Mythos von Pandora; Die Rezeption eines griechischen Sinnbildes in der deutschen Literatur* (Hamburg 1972).

Hannelore Reinsch-Werner. *Callimachus hesiodicus: Die Rezeption der hesiodischen Dichtung durch Kallimachos von Kyrene* (Berlin 1976).

Alan Cameron. *Callimachus and His Critics* (Princeton 1995).

Christos Fakas. *Der Hellenistische Hesiod: Arats Phainomena und die Tradition der antiken Lehrepik* (Wiesbaden 2001).

Immanuel Musäus. *Der Pandoramythos bei Hesiod und seine Rezeption bis Erasmus von Rotterdam* (Göttingen 2004).

# HESIOD

# ΘΕΟΓΟΝΙΑ

Μουσάων Ἑλικωνιάδων ἀρχώμεθ᾽ ἀείδειν,
αἵ θ᾽ Ἑλικῶνος ἔχουσιν ὄρος μέγα τε ζάθεόν τε,
καί τε περὶ κρήνην ἰοειδέα πόσσ᾽ ἁπαλοῖσιν
ὀρχεῦνται καὶ βωμὸν ἐρισθενέος Κρονίωνος·
5 καί τε λοεσσάμεναι τέρενα χρόα Περμησσοῖο
ἢ Ἵππου κρήνης ἢ Ὀλμειοῦ ζαθέοιο
ἀκροτάτῳ Ἑλικῶνι χοροὺς ἐνεποιήσαντο,
καλοὺς ἱμερόεντας, ἐπερρώσαντο δὲ ποσσίν.
ἔνθεν ἀπορνύμεναι κεκαλυμμέναι ἠέρι πολλῷ
10 ἐννύχιαι στεῖχον περικαλλέα ὄσσαν ἱεῖσαι,
ὑμνεῦσαι Δία τ᾽ αἰγίοχον καὶ πότνιαν Ἥρην
Ἀργείην, χρυσέοισι πεδίλοις ἐμβεβαυῖαν,
κούρην τ᾽ αἰγιόχοιο Διὸς γλαυκῶπιν Ἀθήνην
Φοῖβόν τ᾽ Ἀπόλλωνα καὶ Ἄρτεμιν ἰοχέαιραν
15 ἠδὲ Ποσειδάωνα γαιήοχον ἐννοσίγαιον
καὶ Θέμιν αἰδοίην ἑλικοβλέφαρόν τ᾽ Ἀφροδίτην
Ἥβην τε χρυσοστέφανον καλήν τε Διώνην
Λητώ τ᾽ Ἰαπετόν τε ἰδὲ Κρόνον ἀγκυλομήτην

2

# THEOGONY

(1) Let us begin to sing from the Heliconian Muses, who possess the great and holy mountain of Helicon and dance on their soft feet around the violet-dark fountain and the altar of Cronus' mighty son.[1] And after they have washed their tender skin in Permessus or Hippocrene or holy Olmeius, they perform choral dances on highest Helicon, beautiful, lovely ones, and move nimbly with their feet. Starting out from there, shrouded in thick invisibility, by night they walk, sending forth their very beautiful voice, singing of aegis-holding Zeus, and queenly Hera of Argos, who walks in golden sandals, and the daughter of aegis-holding Zeus, bright-eyed Athena, and Phoebus Apollo, and arrow-shooting Artemis, and earth-holding, earth-shaking Poseidon, and venerated Themis (Justice) and quick-glancing Aphrodite, and golden-crowned Hebe (Youth) and beautiful Dione, and Leto and Iapetus and crooked-counseled Cronus, and Eos (Dawn) and great

[1] Zeus.

Ἠῶ τ᾽ Ἠέλιόν τε μέγαν λαμπράν τε Σελήνην
20 Γαῖάν τ᾽ Ὠκεανόν τε μέγαν καὶ Νύκτα μέλαιναν
ἄλλων τ᾽ ἀθανάτων ἱερὸν γένος αἰὲν ἐόντων.
  αἵ νύ ποθ᾽ Ἡσίοδον καλὴν ἐδίδαξαν ἀοιδήν,
ἄρνας ποιμαίνονθ᾽ Ἑλικῶνος ὕπο ζαθέοιο.
  τόνδε δέ με πρώτιστα θεαὶ πρὸς μῦθον ἔειπον,
25 Μοῦσαι Ὀλυμπιάδες, κοῦραι Διὸς αἰγιόχοιο·
"ποιμένες ἄγραυλοι, κάκ᾽ ἐλέγχεα, γαστέρες οἶον,
ἴδμεν ψεύδεα πολλὰ λέγειν ἐτύμοισιν ὁμοῖα,
ἴδμεν δ᾽ εὖτ᾽ ἐθέλωμεν ἀληθέα γηρύσασθαι."
  ὣς ἔφασαν κοῦραι μεγάλου Διὸς ἀρτιέπειαι,
30 καί μοι σκῆπτρον ἔδον δάφνης ἐριθηλέος ὄζον
δρέψασαι, θηητόν· ἐνέπνευσαν δέ μοι αὐδὴν
θέσπιν, ἵνα κλείοιμι τά τ᾽ ἐσσόμενα πρό τ᾽ ἐόντα,
καί μ᾽ ἐκέλονθ᾽ ὑμνεῖν μακάρων γένος αἰὲν ἐόντων,
σφᾶς δ᾽ αὐτὰς πρῶτόν τε καὶ ὕστατον αἰὲν ἀείδειν.
35   ἀλλὰ τίη μοι ταῦτα περὶ δρῦν ἢ περὶ πέτρην;
τύνη, Μουσάων ἀρχώμεθα, ταὶ Διὶ πατρὶ
ὑμνεῦσαι τέρπουσι μέγαν νόον ἐντὸς Ὀλύμπου,
εἴρουσαι τά τ᾽ ἐόντα τά τ᾽ ἐσσόμενα πρό τ᾽ ἐόντα,
φωνῇ ὁμηρεῦσαι, τῶν δ᾽ ἀκάματος ῥέει αὐδὴ
40 ἐκ στομάτων ἡδεῖα· γελᾷ δέ τε δώματα πατρὸς
Ζηνὸς ἐριγδούποιο θεᾶν ὀπὶ λειριοέσσῃ

19 ante 18 habent Π²S, ante 15 K, om. Π¹⁸L (exp. Hermann)
28 γηρύσασθαι Π¹ Π²n, γρ. L² ex Σ: μυθήσασθαι bvK
31 δρέψασαι Π¹(?)a: δρέψασθαι bKSΣΔ Aristides
32 θέσπιν Goettling: θείην codd.: θεσπεσίην Aristides
Lucianus    37 ἐντὸς Π¹Π²KV Etym.: αἰὲν a

4

Helius (Sun) and gleaming Selene (Moon), and Earth and great Ocean and black Night, and the holy race of the other immortals who always are.

(22) One time, they[2] taught Hesiod beautiful song while he was pasturing lambs under holy Helicon. And this speech the goddesses spoke first of all to me, the Olympian Muses, the daughters of aegis-holding Zeus: "Field-dwelling shepherds, ignoble disgraces, mere bellies: we know how to say many false things similar to genuine ones, but we know, when we wish, how to proclaim true things." So spoke great Zeus' ready-speaking daughters, and they plucked a staff, a branch of luxuriant laurel, a marvel, and gave it to me; and they breathed a divine voice into me, so that I might glorify what will be and what was before, and they commanded me to sing of the race of the blessed ones who always are, but always to sing of themselves first and last.

(35) But what is this to me, about an oak or a rock?[3] Come then, let us begin from the Muses, who by singing for their father Zeus give pleasure to his great mind within Olympus, telling of what is and what will be and what was before, harmonizing in their sound. Their tireless voice flows sweet from their mouths; and the house of their father, loud-thundering Zeus, rejoices at the goddesses'

[2] The Muses.

[3] A proverbial expression, possibly already so for Hesiod; its origin is obscure but its meaning here is evidently, "Why should I waste time speaking about irrelevant matters?"

σκιδναμένη, ἠχεῖ δὲ κάρη νιφόεντος Ὀλύμπου
δώματά τ᾽ ἀθανάτων· αἱ δ᾽ ἄμβροτον ὄσσαν ἱεῖσαι
θεῶν γένος αἰδοῖον πρῶτον κλείουσιν ἀοιδῇ
45 ἐξ ἀρχῆς, οὓς Γαῖα καὶ Οὐρανὸς εὐρὺς ἔτικτεν,
οἵ τ᾽ ἐκ τῶν ἐγένοντο, θεοὶ δωτῆρες ἐάων·
δεύτερον αὖτε Ζῆνα θεῶν πατέρ᾽ ἠδὲ καὶ ἀνδρῶν
ἀρχόμεναί θ᾽ ὑμνεῦσι θεαὶ λήγουσί τ᾽ ἀοιδῆς
ὅσσον φέρτατός ἐστι θεῶν κάρτει τε μέγιστος·
50 αὖτις δ᾽ ἀνθρώπων τε γένος κρατερῶν τε Γιγάντων
ὑμνεῦσαι τέρπουσι Διὸς νόον ἐντὸς Ὀλύμπου
Μοῦσαι Ὀλυμπιάδες, κοῦραι Διὸς αἰγιόχοιο.

τὰς ἐν Πιερίῃ Κρονίδῃ τέκε πατρὶ μιγεῖσα
Μνημοσύνη, γουνοῖσιν Ἐλευθῆρος μεδέουσα,
55 λησμοσύνην τε κακῶν ἄμπαυμά τε μερμηράων.
ἐννέα γάρ οἱ νύκτας ἐμίσγετο μητίετα Ζεὺς
νόσφιν ἀπ᾽ ἀθανάτων ἱερὸν λέχος εἰσαναβαίνων·
ἀλλ᾽ ὅτε δή ῥ᾽ ἐνιαυτὸς ἔην, περὶ δ᾽ ἔτραπον ὧραι
μηνῶν φθινόντων, περὶ δ᾽ ἤματα πόλλ᾽ ἐτελέσθη,
60 ἡ δ᾽ ἔτεκ᾽ ἐννέα κούρας, ὁμόφρονας, ᾗσιν ἀοιδὴ
μέμβλεται ἐν στήθεσσιν, ἀκηδέα θυμὸν ἐχούσαις,
τυτθὸν ἀπ᾽ ἀκροτάτης κορυφῆς νιφόεντος Ὀλύμπου·
ἔνθά σφιν λιπαροί τε χοροὶ καὶ δώματα καλά,
πὰρ δ᾽ αὐτῆς Χάριτές τε καὶ Ἵμερος οἰκί᾽ ἔχουσιν
65 ἐν θαλίῃς· ἐρατὴν δὲ διὰ στόμα ὄσσαν ἱεῖσαι

48 damn. Guyet λήγουσί Π¹S: λήγουσαί codd.

---

4 Line 48 is apparently unmetrical and is excised by some
scholars; I retain it, adopting (but without conviction) the banal-

lily-like voice as it spreads out, and snowy Olympus' peak resounds, and the mansions of the immortals. Sending forth their deathless voice, they glorify in their song first the venerated race of the gods from the beginning, those to whom Earth and broad Sky gave birth, and those who were born from these, the gods givers of good things; second, then, the goddesses, both beginning and ending their song, sing[4] of Zeus, the father of gods and of men, how much he is the best of the gods and the greatest in supremacy; and then, singing of the race of human beings and of the mighty Giants, they give pleasure to Zeus' mind within Olympus, the Olympian Muses, the daughters of aegis-holding Zeus.

(53) Mnemosyne (Memory) bore them on Pieria, mingling in love with the father, Cronus' son—Mnemosyne, the protectress of the hills of Eleuther—as forgetfulness of evils and relief from anxieties.[5] For the counsellor Zeus slept with her for nine nights, apart from the immortals, going up into the sacred bed; and when a year had passed, and the seasons had revolved as the months waned, and many days had been completed, she bore nine maidens—like-minded ones, who in their breasts care for song and have a spirit that knows no sorrow—not far from snowy Olympus' highest peak. That is where their bright choral dances and their beautiful mansions are, and beside them the Graces and Desire have their houses, in joyous festivities; and the voice they send forth from their mouths as

izing reading transmitted by one second-century papyrus and one thirteenth-century manuscript.        [5] Hesiod explains, paradoxically, that the Muses, born from Memory, serve the purpose of forgetfulness. Cf. also *Theogony* 98–103.

μέλπονται, πάντων τε νόμους καὶ ἤθεα κεδνὰ
ἀθανάτων κλείουσιν, ἐπήρατον ὄσσαν ἱεῖσαι.
   αἱ τότ' ἴσαν πρὸς Ὄλυμπον, ἀγαλλόμεναι ὀπὶ
   καλῇ,
ἀμβροσίῃ μολπῇ· περὶ δ' ἴαχε γαῖα μέλαινα
70  ὑμνεύσαις, ἐρατὸς δὲ ποδῶν ὕπο δοῦπος ὀρώρει
νισομένων πατέρ' εἰς ὅν· ὁ δ' οὐρανῷ ἐμβασιλεύει,
αὐτὸς ἔχων βροντὴν ἠδ' αἰθαλόεντα κεραυνόν,
κάρτει νικήσας πατέρα Κρόνον· εὖ δὲ ἕκαστα
ἀθανάτοις διέταξεν ὁμῶς καὶ ἐπέφραδε τιμάς.
75     ταῦτ' ἄρα Μοῦσαι ἄειδον Ὀλύμπια δώματ'
     ἔχουσαι,
ἐννέα θυγατέρες μεγάλου Διὸς ἐκγεγαυῖαι,
Κλειώ τ' Εὐτέρπη τε Θάλειά τε Μελπομένη τε
Τερψιχόρη τ' Ἐρατώ τε Πολύμνιά τ' Οὐρανίη τε
Καλλιόπη θ'· ἡ δὲ προφερεστάτη ἐστὶν ἁπασέων,
80  ἡ γὰρ καὶ βασιλεῦσιν ἅμ' αἰδοίοισιν ὀπηδεῖ.
ὅντινα τιμήσουσι Διὸς κοῦραι μεγάλοιο
γεινόμενόν τε ἴδωσι διοτρεφέων βασιλήων,
τῷ μὲν ἐπὶ γλώσσῃ γλυκερὴν χείουσιν ἐέρσην,
τοῦ δ' ἔπε' ἐκ στόματος ῥεῖ μείλιχα· οἱ δέ νυ λαοὶ
85  πάντες ἐς αὐτὸν ὁρῶσι διακρίνοντα θέμιστας
ἰθείῃσι δίκῃσιν· ὁ δ' ἀσφαλέως ἀγορεύων
αἶψά τι καὶ μέγα νεῖκος ἐπισταμένως κατέπαυσε·
τούνεκα γὰρ βασιλῆες ἐχέφρονες, οὕνεκα λαοῖς

74 διέταξε νόμους van Lennep (νόμοις Guyet)
83 ἐέρσην Π³ΒΚΣ Themistius: ἀοιδήν a Aristides Stobaeus

they sing is lovely, and they glorify the ordinances and the cherished usages of all the immortals, sending forth their lovely voice.

(68) They went towards Olympus at that time, exulting in their beautiful voice, with a deathless song; and around them the black earth resounded as they sang, and from under their feet a lovely din rose up as they traveled to their father. He is king in the sky, holding the thunder and the blazing thunderbolt himself, since he gained victory in supremacy over his father Cronus; and he distributed well all things alike to the immortals and devised their honors.

(75) These things, then, the Muses sang, who have their mansions on Olympus, the nine daughters born of great Zeus, Clio (Glorifying) and Euterpe (Well Delighting) and Thalia (Blooming) and Melpomene (Singing) and Terpsichore (Delighting in Dance) and Erato (Lovely) and Polymnia (Many Hymning) and Ourania (Heavenly), and Calliope (Beautiful Voiced)—she is the greatest of them all, for she attends upon venerated kings too. Whomever among Zeus-nourished kings the daughters of great Zeus honor and behold when he is born, they pour sweet dew upon his tongue, and his words flow soothingly from his mouth. All the populace look to him as he decides disputes with straight judgments; and speaking publicly without erring, he quickly ends even a great quarrel by his skill. For this is why kings are wise,[6] because when the populace is

---

[6] The phrase is ambiguous; alternative renderings would be "This is why there are wise kings" or "This is why wise men are (set up as) kings."

βλαπτομένοις ἀγορῆφι μετάτροπα ἔργα τελεῦσι
90 ῥηιδίως, μαλακοῖσι παραιφάμενοι ἐπέεσσιν·
ἐρχόμενον δ᾽ ἀν᾽ ἀγῶνα θεὸν ὡς ἱλάσκονται
αἰδοῖ μειλιχίῃ, μετὰ δὲ πρέπει ἀγρομένοισι.
τοίη Μουσάων ἱερὴ δόσις ἀνθρώποισιν.
ἐκ γάρ τοι Μουσέων καὶ ἑκηβόλου Ἀπόλλωνος
95 ἄνδρες ἀοιδοὶ ἔασιν ἐπὶ χθόνα καὶ κιθαρισταί,
ἐκ δὲ Διὸς βασιλῆες· ὁ δ᾽ ὄλβιος, ὅντινα Μοῦσαι
φίλωνται· γλυκερή οἱ ἀπὸ στόματος ῥέει αὐδή.
εἰ γάρ τις καὶ πένθος ἔχων νεοκηδέι θυμῷ
ἄζηται κραδίην ἀκαχήμενος, αὐτὰρ ἀοιδὸς
100 Μουσάων θεράπων κλεῖα προτέρων ἀνθρώπων
ὑμνήσει μάκαράς τε θεοὺς οἳ Ὄλυμπον ἔχουσιν,
αἶψ᾽ ὅ γε δυσφροσυνέων ἐπιλήθεται οὐδέ τι κηδέων
μέμνηται· ταχέως δὲ παρέτραπε δῶρα θεάων.
χαίρετε τέκνα Διός, δότε δ᾽ ἱμερόεσσαν ἀοιδήν·
105 κλείετε δ᾽ ἀθανάτων ἱερὸν γένος αἰὲν ἐόντων,
οἳ Γῆς ἐξεγένοντο καὶ Οὐρανοῦ ἀστερόεντος,
Νυκτός τε δνοφερῆς, οὕς θ᾽ ἁλμυρὸς ἔτρεφε Πόντος.
εἴπατε δ᾽ ὡς τὰ πρῶτα θεοὶ καὶ γαῖα γένοντο
καὶ ποταμοὶ καὶ πόντος ἀπείριτος οἴδματι θυίων
110 ἄστρά τε λαμπετόωντα καὶ οὐρανὸς εὐρὺς ὕπερθεν·
οἵ τ᾽ ἐκ τῶν ἐγένοντο, θεοὶ δωτῆρες ἐάων·
ὥς τ᾽ ἄφενος δάσσαντο καὶ ὡς τιμὰς διέλοντο,
ἠδὲ καὶ ὡς τὰ πρῶτα πολύπτυχον ἔσχον Ὄλυμπον.

91 ἀν᾽ ἀ[γ]ῶνα Π³L²ᵞᵖ. sch. BT Il. 24. 1: ἀνὰ ἄστυ codd.,
Stobaeus

being harmed in the assembly they easily manage to turn the deeds around, effecting persuasion with mild words; and as he goes up to the gathering they seek his favor like a god with soothing reverence, and he is conspicuous among the assembled people.

(93) Such is the holy gift of the Muses to human beings. For it is from the Muses and far-shooting Apollo that men are poets upon the earth and lyre-players, but it is from Zeus that they are kings; and that man is blessed, whomever the Muses love, for the speech flows sweet from his mouth. Even if someone who has unhappiness in his newly anguished spirit is parched in his heart with grieving, yet when a poet, servant of the Muses, sings of the glorious deeds of people of old and the blessed gods who possess Olympus, he forgets his sorrows at once and does not remember his anguish at all; for quickly the gifts of the goddesses have turned it aside.

(104) Hail, children of Zeus, and give me lovely song; glorify the sacred race of the immortals who always are, those who were born from Earth and starry Sky, and from dark Night, and those whom salty Pontus (Sea) nourished. Tell how in the first place gods and earth were born, and rivers and the boundless sea seething with its swell, and the shining stars and the broad sky above, and those who were born from them, the gods givers of good things; and how they divided their wealth and distributed their honors, and also how they first took possession of many-folded

---

105–15 exp. Goettling, neque ullus hic v. quem non sive expunxerint sive transposuerint viri docti

108–10 exp. Ellger Wilamowitz alii

111 (=46) om. Π³B Theophilus Hippolytus

# HESIOD

ταῦτά μοι ἔσπετε Μοῦσαι Ὀλύμπια δώματ' ἔχουσαι
115 ἐξ ἀρχῆς, καὶ εἴπαθ', ὅτι πρῶτον γένετ' αὐτῶν.

ἤτοι μὲν πρώτιστα Χάος γένετ'· αὐτὰρ ἔπειτα
Γαῖ' εὐρύστερνος, πάντων ἕδος ἀσφαλὲς αἰεὶ
ἀθανάτων οἳ ἔχουσι κάρη νιφόεντος Ὀλύμπου
Τάρταρά τ' ἠερόεντα μυχῷ χθονὸς εὐρυοδείης,
120 ἠδ' Ἔρος, ὃς κάλλιστος ἐν ἀθανάτοισι θεοῖσι,
λυσιμελής, πάντων τε θεῶν πάντων τ' ἀνθρώπων
δάμναται ἐν στήθεσσι νόον καὶ ἐπίφρονα βουλήν.

ἐκ Χάεος δ' Ἔρεβός τε μέλαινά τε Νὺξ ἐγένοντο·
Νυκτὸς δ' αὖτ' Αἰθήρ τε καὶ Ἡμέρη ἐξεγένοντο,
125 οὓς τέκε κυσαμένη Ἐρέβει φιλότητι μιγεῖσα.

Γαῖα δέ τοι πρῶτον μὲν ἐγείνατο ἶσον ἑωυτῇ
Οὐρανὸν ἀστερόενθ', ἵνα μιν περὶ πάντα καλύπτοι,
ὄφρ' εἴη μακάρεσσι θεοῖς ἕδος ἀσφαλὲς αἰεί,
γείνατο δ' οὔρεα μακρά, θεᾶν χαρίεντας ἐναύλους
130 Νυμφέων, αἳ ναίουσιν ἀν' οὔρεα βησσήεντα,
ἠδὲ καὶ ἀτρύγετον πέλαγος τέκεν οἴδματι θυῖον,
Πόντον, ἄτερ φιλότητος ἐφιμέρου· αὐτὰρ ἔπειτα
Οὐρανῷ εὐνηθεῖσα τέκ' Ὠκεανὸν βαθυδίνην

114 sq. damn. Seleucus, 115 Aristarchus    127 πάντα
καλύπτοι BV, K (sscr. ει), Cornutus v. l., Etym. Magnum: πάντα
καλύπτῃ a sch. in Pindarum Theophilus Cyrillus Stobaeus Etym.
Genuinum Meletius: alterutrum Π³: πᾶσαν ἐέργοι vel –ῃ sch. in
Homerum, Cornutus v. 1., Etym. Magnum

12

Olympus. These things tell me from the beginning, Muses who have your mansions on Olympus, and tell which one of them was born first.

(116) In truth, first of all Chasm[7] came to be, and then broad-breasted Earth, the ever immovable seat of all the immortals who possess snowy Olympus' peak and murky Tartarus in the depths of the broad-pathed earth, and Eros, who is the most beautiful among the immortal gods, the limb-melter—he overpowers the mind and the thoughtful counsel of all the gods and of all human beings in their breasts.

(123) From Chasm, Erebos and black Night came to be; and then Aether and Day came forth from Night, who conceived and bore them after mingling in love with Erebos.

(126) Earth first of all bore starry Sky, equal to herself, to cover her on every side, so that she would be the ever immovable seat for the blessed gods; and she bore the high mountains, the graceful haunts of the goddesses, Nymphs who dwell on the wooded mountains. And she also bore the barren sea seething with its swell, Pontus, without delightful love; and then, having bedded with Sky, she bore

---

[7] Usually translated as "Chaos"; but that suggests to us, misleadingly, a jumble of disordered matter, whereas Hesiod's term indicates instead a gap or opening.

Κοῖόν τε Κρεῖόν θ᾽ Ὑπερίονά τ᾽ Ἰαπετόν τε
135 Θείαν τε Ῥείαν τε Θέμιν τε Μνημοσύνην τε
Φοίβην τε χρυσοστέφανον Τηθύν τ᾽ ἐρατεινήν.
τοὺς δὲ μέθ᾽ ὁπλότατος γένετο Κρόνος
    ἀγκυλομήτης,
δεινότατος παίδων, θαλερὸν δ᾽ ἤχθηρε τοκῆα.
    γείνατο δ᾽ αὖ Κύκλωπας ὑπέρβιον ἦτορ ἔχοντας,
140 Βρόντην τε Στερόπην τε καὶ Ἄργην ὀβριμόθυμον,
οἳ Ζηνὶ βροντήν τ᾽ ἔδοσαν τεῦξάν τε κεραυνόν.
οἳ δ᾽ ἤτοι τὰ μὲν ἄλλα θεοῖς ἐναλίγκιοι ἦσαν,
μοῦνος δ᾽ ὀφθαλμὸς μέσσῳ ἐνέκειτο μετώπῳ·
Κύκλωπες δ᾽ ὄνομ᾽ ἦσαν ἐπώνυμον, οὕνεκ᾽ ἄρά
    σφεων
145 κυκλοτερὴς ὀφθαλμὸς ἔεις ἐνέκειτο μετώπῳ·
ἰσχὺς δ᾽ ἠδὲ βίη καὶ μηχαναὶ ἦσαν ἐπ᾽ ἔργοις.
    ἄλλοι δ᾽ αὖ Γαίης τε καὶ Οὐρανοῦ ἐξεγένοντο
τρεῖς παῖδες μεγάλοι <τε> καὶ ὄβριμοι, οὐκ
    ὀνομαστοί,
Κόττος τε Βριάρεώς τε Γύγης θ᾽, ὑπερήφανα τέκνα.
150 τῶν ἑκατὸν μὲν χεῖρες ἀπ᾽ ὤμων ἀίσσοντο,
ἄπλαστοι, κεφαλαὶ δὲ ἑκάστῳ πεντήκοντα
ἐξ ὤμων ἐπέφυκον ἐπὶ στιβαροῖσι μέλεσσιν·
ἰσχὺς δ᾽ ἄπλητος κρατερὴ μεγάλῳ ἐπὶ εἴδει.
    ὅσσοι γὰρ Γαίης τε καὶ Οὐρανοῦ ἐξεγένοντο
155 δεινότατοι παίδων, σφετέρῳ δ᾽ ἤχθοντο τοκῆι
ἐξ ἀρχῆς· καὶ τῶν μὲν ὅπως τις πρῶτα γένοιτο,

144–45 damn. Wolf

14

deep-eddying Ocean and Coeus and Crius and Hyperion and Iapetus and Theia and Rhea and Themis and Mnemosyne and golden-crowned Phoebe and lovely Tethys. After these, Cronus was born, the youngest of all, crooked-counseled, the most terrible of her children; and he hated his vigorous father.

(139) Then she bore the Cyclopes, who have very violent hearts, Brontes (Thunder) and Steropes (Lightning) and strong-spirited Arges (Bright), those who gave thunder to Zeus and fashioned the thunderbolt. These were like the gods in other regards, but only one eye was set in the middle of their foreheads; and they were called Cyclopes (Circle-eyed) by name, since a single circle-shaped eye was set in their foreheads. Strength and force and contrivances were in their works.

(147) Then from Earth and Sky came forth three more sons, great and strong, unspeakable, Cottus and Briareus and Gyges, presumptuous children. A hundred arms sprang forth from their shoulders, unapproachable, and upon their massive limbs grew fifty heads out of each one's shoulders; and the mighty strength in their great forms was dreadful.

(154) For all these, who came forth from Earth and Sky as the most terrible of their children,[8] were hated by their own father from the beginning. And as soon as any of them

---

[8] The exact reference is unclear, but apparently only the last two sets of three children each, the Cyclopes and the Hundred-Handers, are meant, and not additionally the first set of twelve Titans.

---

148 om., in mg. add. L¹, post 149 *m* (hic et II²¹)

15

πάντας ἀποκρύπτασκε καὶ ἐς φάος οὐκ ἀνίεσκε
Γαίης ἐν κευθμῶνι, κακῷ δ' ἐπετέρπετο ἔργῳ,
Οὐρανός· ἡ δ' ἐντὸς στοναχίζετο Γαῖα πελώρη
160 στεινομένη, δολίην δὲ κακὴν ἐπεφράσσατο τέχνην.
αἶψα δὲ ποιήσασα γένος πολιοῦ ἀδάμαντος
τεῦξε μέγα δρέπανον καὶ ἐπέφραδε παισὶ φίλοισιν·
εἶπε δὲ θαρσύνουσα, φίλον τετιημένη ἦτορ·
"παῖδες ἐμοὶ καὶ πατρὸς ἀτασθάλου, αἴ κ' ἐθέλητε
165 πείθεσθαι· πατρός κε κακὴν τεισαίμεθα λώβην
ὑμετέρου· πρότερος γὰρ ἀεικέα μήσατο ἔργα."
   ὣς φάτο· τοὺς δ' ἄρα πάντας ἕλεν δέος, οὐδέ τις
      αὐτῶν
φθέγξατο. θαρσήσας δὲ μέγας Κρόνος ἀγκυλομήτης
αἶψ' αὖτις μύθοισι προσηύδα μητέρα κεδνήν·
170 "μῆτερ, ἐγώ κεν τοῦτό γ' ὑποσχόμενος τελέσαιμι
ἔργον, ἐπεὶ πατρός γε δυσωνύμου οὐκ ἀλεγίζω
ἡμετέρου· πρότερος γὰρ ἀεικέα μήσατο ἔργα."
   ὣς φάτο· γήθησεν δὲ μέγα φρεσὶ Γαῖα πελώρη·
εἶσε δέ μιν κρύψασα λόχῳ, ἐνέθηκε δὲ χερσὶν
175 ἅρπην καρχαρόδοντα, δόλον δ' ὑπεθήκατο πάντα.
ἦλθε δὲ νύκτ' ἐπάγων μέγας Οὐρανός, ἀμφὶ δὲ Γαίῃ
ἱμείρων φιλότητος ἐπέσχετο, καί ῥ' ἐτανύσθη
πάντῃ· ὁ δ' ἐκ λοχέοιο πάις ὠρέξατο χειρὶ
σκαιῇ, δεξιτερῇ δὲ πελώριον ἔλλαβεν ἅρπην,
180 μακρὴν καρχαρόδοντα, φίλου δ' ἀπὸ μήδεα πατρὸς
ἐσσυμένως ἤμησε, πάλιν δ' ἔρριψε φέρεσθαι
ἐξοπίσω. τὰ μὲν οὔ τι ἐτώσια ἔκφυγε χειρός·

was born, Sky put them all away out of sight in a hiding-place in Earth and did not let them come up into the light, and he rejoiced in his evil deed. But huge Earth groaned within, for she was constricted, and she devised a tricky, evil stratagem. At once she created an offspring, of gray adamant, and she fashioned a big sickle and showed it to her dear sons.

(163) And she spoke, encouraging them while she grieved in her dear heart: "Sons of mine and of a wicked father, obey me, if you wish: we would avenge your father's evil outrage. For he was the first to devise unseemly deeds."

(167) So she spoke, but dread seized them all, and none of them uttered a sound. But great crooked-counseled Cronus took courage and at once addressed his cherished mother in turn with these words: "Mother, I would promise and perform this deed, since I do not care at all about our evil-named father. For he was the first to devise unseemly deeds."

(173) So he spoke, and huge Earth rejoiced greatly in her breast. She placed him in an ambush, concealing him from sight, and put into his hands the jagged-toothed sickle, and she explained the whole trick to him. And great Sky came, bringing night with him; and spreading himself out around Earth in his desire for love he lay outstretched in all directions. Then his son reached out from his ambush with his left hand, and with his right hand he grasped the monstrous sickle, long and jagged-toothed, and eagerly he reaped the genitals from his dear father and threw them behind him to be borne away. But not in vain did they fall

---

165 κε Goettling: κεν Sras: γε aK: τε Wac

# HESIOD

ὅσσαι γὰρ ῥαθάμιγγες ἀπέσσυθεν αἱματόεσσαι,
πάσας δέξατο Γαῖα· περιπλομένων δ᾿ ἐνιαυτῶν
185 γείνατ᾿ Ἐρινῦς τε κρατερὰς μεγάλους τε Γίγαντας,
τεύχεσι λαμπομένους, δολίχ᾿ ἔγχεα χερσὶν ἔχοντας,
Νύμφας θ᾿ ἃς Μελίας καλέουσ᾿ ἐπ᾿ ἀπείρονα γαῖαν.
μήδεα δ᾿ ὡς τὸ πρῶτον ἀποτμήξας ἀδάμαντι
κάββαλ᾿ ἀπ᾿ ἠπείροιο πολυκλύστῳ ἐνὶ πόντῳ,
190 ὣς φέρετ᾿ ἂμ πέλαγος πουλὺν χρόνον, ἀμφὶ δὲ
        λευκὸς
ἀφρὸς ἀπ᾿ ἀθανάτου χροὸς ὤρνυτο· τῷ δ᾿ ἔνι κούρη
ἐθρέφθη· πρῶτον δὲ Κυθήροισι ζαθέοισιν
ἔπλητ᾿, ἔνθεν ἔπειτα περίρρυτον ἵκετο Κύπρον.
ἐκ δ᾿ ἔβη αἰδοίη καλὴ θεός, ἀμφὶ δὲ ποίη
195 ποσσὶν ὕπο ῥαδινοῖσιν ἀέξετο· τὴν δ᾿ Ἀφροδίτην
ἀφρογενέα τε θεὰν καὶ ἐυστέφανον Κυθέρειαν
κικλήσκουσι θεοί τε καὶ ἀνέρες, οὕνεκ᾿ ἐν ἀφρῷ
θρέφθη· ἀτὰρ Κυθέρειαν, ὅτι προσέκυρσε Κυθήροις·
Κυπρογενέα δ᾿, ὅτι γέντο περικλύστῳ ἐνὶ Κύπρῳ·
200 ἠδὲ φιλομμειδέα, ὅτι μηδέων ἐξεφαάνθη.
τῇ δ᾿ Ἔρος ὡμάρτησε καὶ Ἵμερος ἕσπετο καλὸς
γεινομένῃ τὰ πρῶτα θεῶν τ᾿ ἐς φῦλον ἰούσῃ·
ταύτην δ᾿ ἐξ ἀρχῆς τιμὴν ἔχει ἠδὲ λέλογχε
μοῖραν ἐν ἀνθρώποισι καὶ ἀθανάτοισι θεοῖσι,

200 φιλομμειδέα Bergk: φιλο(μ)μηδέα vel –μήδεα (μει sscr. Mosqu. 469)

9 It is unclear what exactly the relation is between the Melian

18

from his hand: for Earth received all the bloody drops that shot forth, and when the years had revolved she bore the mighty Erinyes and the great Giants, shining in their armor, holding long spears in their hands, and the Nymphs whom they call the Melian ones on the boundless earth.[9] And when at first he had cut off the genitals with the adamant and thrown them from the land into the strongly surging sea, they were borne along the water for a long time, and a white foam rose up around them from the immortal flesh; and inside this grew a maiden. First she approached holy Cythera, and from there she went on to sea-girt Cyprus. She came forth, a reverend, beautiful goddess, and grass grew up around her beneath her slender feet. Gods and men call her (a) "Aphrodite," the foamborn goddess and (b) the well-garlanded "Cytherea," (a) since she grew in the foam, (b) and also "Cytherea," since she arrived at Cythera, (c) and "Cyprogenea," since she was born on sea-girt Cyprus, (d) and "genial," since she came forth from the genitals.[10] Eros accompanied her and beautiful Desire stayed with her as soon as she was born and when she went to the tribe of the gods; and since the beginning she possesses this honor and has received as her lot this portion among human beings and immortal gods—

nymphs, the ash trees with which they are closely associated, and human beings, who may have originated from one or the other of these: cf. *Theogony* 563, *Works and Days* 145.

[10] Hesiod interprets the first half of the name Ἀφροδίτη as though it were derived from ἀφρός ("foam"), and the second half of the traditional epithet φιλομμειδής ("smile-loving", here translated as "genial" for the sake of the pun) as though it were derived from μῆδος ("genitals").

205 παρθενίους τ᾽ ὀάρους μειδήματά τ᾽ ἐξαπάτας τε
τέρψίν τε γλυκερὴν φιλότητά τε μειλιχίην τε.
τοὺς δὲ πατὴρ Τιτῆνας ἐπίκλησιν καλέεσκε
παῖδας νεικείων μέγας Οὐρανός, οὓς τέκεν αὐτός·
φάσκε δὲ τιταίνοντας ἀτασθαλίῃ μέγα ῥέξαι
210 ἔργον, τοῖο δ᾽ ἔπειτα τίσιν μετόπισθεν ἔσεσθαι.

Νὺξ δ᾽ ἔτεκε στυγερόν τε Μόρον καὶ Κῆρα
    μέλαιναν
καὶ Θάνατον, τέκε δ᾽ Ὕπνον, ἔτικτε δὲ φῦλον
    Ὀνείρων.
214 δεύτερον αὖ Μῶμον καὶ Ὀιζὺν ἀλγινόεσσαν
213 οὔ τινι κοιμηθεῖσα θεῶν τέκε Νὺξ ἐρεβεννή,
215 Ἑσπερίδας θ᾽, αἷς μῆλα πέρην κλυτοῦ Ὠκεανοῖο
χρύσεα καλὰ μέλουσι φέροντά τε δένδρεα καρπόν·
καὶ Μοίρας καὶ Κῆρας ἐγείνατο νηλεοποίνους,
Κλωθώ τε Λάχεσίν τε καὶ Ἄτροπον, αἵ τε βροτοῖσι
γεινομένοισι διδοῦσιν ἔχειν ἀγαθόν τε κακόν τε,
220 αἵ τ᾽ ἀνδρῶν τε θεῶν τε παραιβασίας ἐφέπουσιν,
οὐδέ ποτε λήγουσι θεαὶ δεινοῖο χόλοιο,
πρίν γ᾽ ἀπὸ τῷ δώωσι κακὴν ὄπιν, ὅστις ἁμάρτῃ.
τίκτε δὲ καὶ Νέμεσιν πῆμα θνητοῖσι βροτοῖσι
Νὺξ ὀλοή· μετὰ τὴν δ᾽ Ἀπάτην τέκε καὶ Φιλότητα
225 Γῆράς τ᾽ οὐλόμενον, καὶ Ἔριν τέκε καρτερόθυμον.
αὐτὰρ Ἔρις στυγερὴ τέκε μὲν Πόνον ἀλγινόεντα
Λήθην τε Λιμόν τε καὶ Ἄλγεα δακρυόεντα
Ὑσμίνας τε Μάχας τε Φόνους τ᾽ Ἀνδροκτασίας τε

maidenly whispers and smiles and deceits and sweet delight and fondness and gentleness.

(207) But their father, great Sky, called them Titans (Strainers) as a nickname, rebuking his sons, whom he had begotten himself; for he said that they had strained to perform a mighty deed in their wickedness, and that at some later time there would be vengeance for this.

(211) Night bore loathsome Doom and black Fate and Death, and she bore Sleep, and she gave birth to the tribe of Dreams. Second, then, gloomy Night bore Blame and painful Distress, although she had slept with none of the gods, and the Hesperides, who care for the golden, beautiful apples beyond glorious Ocean and the trees bearing this fruit. And she bore (a) Destinies and (b) pitilessly punishing Fates, (a) Clotho (Spinner) and Lachesis (Portion) and Atropos (Inflexible), who give to mortals when they are born both good and evil to have, and (b) who hold fast to the transgressions of both men and gods; and the goddesses never cease from their terrible wrath until they give evil punishment to whoever commits a crime. Deadly Night gave birth to Nemesis (Indignation) too, a woe for mortal human beings; and after her she bore Deceit and Fondness and baneful Old Age, and she bore hard-hearted Strife.

(226) And loathsome Strife bore painful Toil and Forgetfulness and Hunger and tearful Pains, and Combats and Battles and Murders and Slaughters, and Strifes and

---

213–14 transp. Hermann

218–19 secl. Paley: om. Stobaeus 1. 3. 38 non respiciunt Σvet (habent Π⁴ codd. Stobaeus 1. 5. 5)

Νείκεά τε Ψεύδεά τε Λόγους τ᾽ Ἀμφιλλογίας τε
230 Δυσνομίην τ᾽ Ἄτην τε, συνήθεας ἀλλήλησιν,
Ὅρκόν θ᾽, ὃς δὴ πλεῖστον ἐπιχθονίους ἀνθρώπους
πημαίνει, ὅτε κέν τις ἑκὼν ἐπίορκον ὀμόσσῃ·

Νηρέα δ᾽ ἀψευδέα καὶ ἀληθέα γείνατο Πόντος
πρεσβύτατον παίδων· αὐτὰρ καλέουσι γέροντα,
235 οὕνεκα νημερτής τε καὶ ἤπιος, οὐδὲ θεμίστων
λήθεται, ἀλλὰ δίκαια καὶ ἤπια δήνεα οἶδεν·
αὖτις δ᾽ αὖ Θαύμαντα μέγαν καὶ ἀγήνορα Φόρκυν
Γαίῃ μισγόμενος καὶ Κητὼ καλλιπάρῃον
Εὐρυβίην τ᾽ ἀδάμαντος ἐνὶ φρεσὶ θυμὸν ἔχουσαν.
240 Νηρῆος δ᾽ ἐγένοντο μεγήριτα τέκνα θεάων
πόντῳ ἐν ἀτρυγέτῳ καὶ Δωρίδος ἠυκόμοιο,
κούρης Ὠκεανοῖο τελήεντος ποταμοῖο,
Πρωθώ τ᾽ Εὐκράντη τε Σαώ τ᾽ Ἀμφιτρίτη τε
Εὐδώρη τε Θέτις τε Γαλήνη τε Γλαύκη τε,
245 Κυμοθόη Σπειώ τε θοὴ Θαλίη τ᾽ ἐρόεσσα
Πασιθέη τ᾽ Ἐρατώ τε καὶ Εὐνίκη ῥοδόπηχυς
καὶ Μελίτη χαρίεσσα καὶ Εὐλιμένη καὶ Ἀγαυὴ
Δωτώ τε Πρωτώ τε Φέρουσά τε Δυναμένη τε
Νησαίη τε καὶ Ἀκταίη καὶ Πρωτομέδεια,
250 Δωρὶς καὶ Πανόπη καὶ εὐειδὴς Γαλάτεια
Ἱπποθόη τ᾽ ἐρόεσσα καὶ Ἱππονόη ῥοδόπηχυς
Κυμοδόκη θ᾽, ἣ κύματ᾽ ἐν ἠεροειδέι πόντῳ
πνοιάς τε ζαέων ἀνέμων σὺν Κυματολήγῃ
ῥεῖα πρηΰνει καὶ ἐυσφύρῳ Ἀμφιτρίτῃ,
255 Κυμώ τ᾽ Ἠιόνη τε ἐυστέφανός θ᾽ Ἁλιμήδη

Lies and Tales and Disputes, and Lawlessness and Reck-
lessness, much like one another, and Oath, who indeed
brings most woe upon human beings on the earth, when-
ever someone willfully swears a false oath.

(233) Pontus begot Nereus, unerring and truthful, the
oldest of his sons; they call him the Old Man, because he is
infallible and gentle, and does not forget established cus-
toms but contrives just and gentle plans.[11] Then, mingling
in love with Earth, he begot great Thaumas and manly
Phorcys, and beautiful-cheeked Ceto, and Eurybia, who
has a heart of adamant in her breast.

(240) And from Nereus and beautiful-haired Doris,
the daughter of Ocean the circling river, were born numer-
ous children of goddesses in the barren sea,[12] Protho and
Eucrante and Sao and Amphitrite, and Eudora and Thetis
and Galene and Glauce, Cymothoe and swift Speo and
lovely Thalia, and Pasithea and Erato and rosy-armed
Eunice, and graceful Melite and Eulimene and Agave, and
Doto and Proto and Pherusa and Dynamene, and Nesaea
and Actaea and Protomedea, Doris and Panope and fair-
formed Galatea, and lovely Hippothoe and rosy-armed
Hipponoe, and Cymodoce, who together with Cymatolege
and fair-ankled Amphitrite easily calms the waves in the
murky sea and the blasts of stormy winds, and Cymo and
Eone and well-garlanded Halimede, and smile-loving

[11] The point of this explanation is unclear.
[12] Many of the names of the Nereids reflect their role as sea
nymphs.

---

243 Πρωθώ Δ: Πρωτώ codd.

Γλαυκονόμη τε φιλομμειδὴς καὶ Ποντοπόρεια
Λειαγόρη τε καὶ Εὐαγόρη καὶ Λαομέδεια
Πουλυνόη τε καὶ Αὐτονόη καὶ Λυσιάνασσα
Εὐάρνη τε φυὴν ἐρατὴ καὶ εἶδος ἄμωμος
260 καὶ Ψαμάθη χαρίεσσα δέμας δίη τε Μενίππη
Νησώ τ' Εὐπόμπη τε Θεμιστώ τε Προνόη τε
Νημερτής θ', ἣ πατρὸς ἔχει νόον ἀθανάτοιο.
αὗται μὲν Νηρῆος ἀμύμονος ἐξεγένοντο
κοῦραι πεντήκοντα, ἀμύμονα ἔργ' εἰδυῖαι·
265 Θαύμας δ' Ὠκεανοῖο βαθυρρείταο θύγατρα
ἠγάγετ' Ἠλέκτρην· ἡ δ' ὠκεῖαν τέκεν Ἶριν
ἠυκόμους θ' Ἁρπυίας, Ἀελλώ τ' Ὠκυπέτην τε,
αἵ ῥ' ἀνέμων πνοιῇσι καὶ οἰωνοῖς ἅμ' ἕπονται
ὠκείῃς πτερύγεσσι· μεταχρόνιαι γὰρ ἴαλλον.

270 Φόρκυι δ' αὖ Κητὼ γραίας τέκε καλλιπαρήους
ἐκ γενετῆς πολιάς, τὰς δὴ Γραίας καλέουσιν
ἀθάνατοί τε θεοὶ χαμαὶ ἐρχόμενοί τ' ἄνθρωποι,
Πεμφρηδώ τ' εὔπεπλον Ἐννώ τε κροκόπεπλον,
Γοργούς θ', αἳ ναίουσι πέρην κλυτοῦ Ὠκεανοῖο
275 ἐσχατιῇ πρὸς νυκτός, ἵν' Ἑσπερίδες λιγύφωνοι,
Σθεννώ τ' Εὐρυάλη τε Μέδουσά τε λυγρὰ παθοῦσα·
ἡ μὲν ἔην θνητή, αἱ δ' ἀθάνατοι καὶ ἀγήρῳ,
αἱ δύο· τῇ δὲ μιῇ παρελέξατο Κυανοχαίτης
ἐν μαλακῷ λειμῶνι καὶ ἄνθεσιν εἰαρινοῖσι.
280 τῆς ὅτε δὴ Περσεὺς κεφαλὴν ἀπεδειροτόμησεν,
ἐξέθορε Χρυσάωρ τε μέγας καὶ Πήγασος ἵππος.

Glauconome and Pontoporea, Leagore and Euagore and
Laomedea, Polynoe and Autonoe and Lusianassa, and Eu-
arne, lovely in shape and blameless in form, and Psamathe,
graceful in body, and divine Menippe, and Neso and
Eupompe and Themisto and Pronoe, and Nemertes (In-
fallible), who has the disposition of her immortal father.
These came forth from excellent Nereus, fifty daughters
who know how to do excellent works.

(265) Thaumas married Electra, the daughter of deep-
flowing Ocean. She bore swift Iris and the beautiful-haired
Harpies, Aello and Ocypete, who with their swift wings
keep up with the blasts of the winds and with the birds; for
they fly high in the air.

(270) Then to Phorcys Ceto bore beautiful-cheeked
old women, gray-haired from their birth, whom both the
immortal gods and human beings who walk on the earth
call the Graeae, fair-robed Pemphredo and saffron-robed
Enyo, and the Gorgons who dwell beyond glorious Ocean
at the edge towards the night, where the clear-voiced
Hesperides are, Sthenno and Euryale, and Medusa who
suffered woes. She was mortal, but the others are immortal
and ageless, the two of them; with her alone the dark-
haired one[13] lay down in a soft meadow among spring
flowers. When Perseus cut her head off from her neck,
great Chrysaor and the horse Pegasus sprang forth; the lat-

---

[13] Poseidon.

---

258 Πουλυνόη Muetzell: -νόμη codd. (Σ^rec.)
270 γραίας: κούρας Koechly

τῷ μὲν ἐπώνυμον ἦν, ὅτ᾽ ἄρ᾽ Ὠκεανοῦ παρὰ πηγὰς
γένθ᾽, ὁ δ᾽ ἄορ χρύσειον ἔχων μετὰ χερσὶ φίλῃσι.
χὠ μὲν ἀποπτάμενος, προλιπὼν χθόνα μητέρα
μήλων,

285 ἵκετ᾽ ἐς ἀθανάτους· Ζηνὸς δ᾽ ἐν δώμασι ναίει
βροντήν τε στεροπήν τε φέρων Διὶ μητιόεντι·
Χρυσάωρ δ᾽ ἔτεκε τρικέφαλον Γηρυονῆα
μιχθεὶς Καλλιρόῃ κούρῃ κλυτοῦ Ὠκεανοῖο·
τὸν μὲν ἄρ᾽ ἐξενάριξε βίη Ἡρακληείη

290 βουσὶ πάρ᾽ εἰλιπόδεσσι περιρρύτῳ εἰν Ἐρυθείῃ
ἤματι τῷ, ὅτε περ βοῦς ἤλασεν εὐρυμετώπους
Τίρυνθ᾽ εἰς ἱερήν, διαβὰς πόρον Ὠκεανοῖο,
Ὄρθόν τε κτείνας καὶ βουκόλον Εὐρυτίωνα
σταθμῷ ἐν ἠερόεντι πέρην κλυτοῦ Ὠκεανοῖο.

295 ἡ δ᾽ ἔτεκ᾽ ἄλλο πέλωρον ἀμήχανον, οὐδὲν ἐοικὸς
θνητοῖς ἀνθρώποις οὐδ᾽ ἀθανάτοισι θεοῖσι,
σπῆι ἔνι γλαφυρῷ, θείην κρατερόφρον᾽ Ἔχιδναν,
ἥμισυ μὲν νύμφην ἑλικώπιδα καλλιπάρηον,
ἥμισυ δ᾽ αὖτε πέλωρον ὄφιν δεινόν τε μέγαν τε

300 αἰόλον ὠμηστήν, ζαθέης ὑπὸ κεύθεσι γαίης.
ἔνθα δέ οἱ σπέος ἐστὶ κάτω κοίλῃ ὑπὸ πέτρῃ
τηλοῦ ἀπ᾽ ἀθανάτων τε θεῶν θνητῶν τ᾽ ἀνθρώπων,
ἔνθ᾽ ἄρα οἱ δάσσαντο θεοὶ κλυτὰ δώματα ναίειν.
ἡ δ᾽ ἔρυτ᾽ εἰν Ἀρίμοισιν ὑπὸ χθόνα λυγρὴ Ἔχιδνα,

288 habent bQ, legit Tzetzes: om. Π16 Π22akS (add. in mg. S1)
295–336 versus expulerunt alios alii, aliasve distinxerunt
recensiones        300 αἰόλον Scheer (e Σrec): ποικίλον codd. Δ

26

ter received his name from being born beside the waters[14] of Ocean, the former from holding a golden sword[15] in his hands. Pegasus flew off, leaving behind the earth, the mother of sheep, and came to the immortals; he dwells in Zeus' house and brings the thunder and lightning to the counsellor Zeus. And Chrysaor, mingling in love with Callirhoe, glorious Ocean's daughter, begot three-headed Geryoneus, who was slain by Heracles' force beside his rolling-footed cattle in sea-girt Erythea on the day when he drove the broad-browed cattle to holy Tiryns, after he crossed over the strait of Ocean and killed Orthus and the cowherd Eurytion in the murky stable beyond glorious Ocean.

(295) She[16] bore in a hollow cave another monster, intractable, not at all similar to mortal human beings or to the immortal gods: divine, strong-hearted Echidna, half a quick-eyed beautiful-cheeked nymph, but half a monstrous snake, terrible and great, shimmering, eating raw flesh, under the hidden places of the holy earth. That is where she has a cave, deep down under a hollow boulder, far from the immortal gods and mortal human beings; for that is where the gods assigned her to dwell in glorious mansions. She keeps guard among the Arima[17] under the

---

[14] Hesiod derives Pegasus' name from πηγαί ("waters").

[15] Hesiod derives Chrysaor's name from χρύσειον ἄορ ("golden sword").

[16] Probably Ceto.

[17] Already in antiquity it was unknown whether this was a mountain range or a tribe of people, and where it was located, in Asia Minor or in Italy.

305 ἀθάνατος νύμφη καὶ ἀγήραος ἤματα πάντα.
　　τῇ δὲ Τυφάονά φασι μιγήμεναι ἐν φιλότητι
　　δεινόν θ' ὑβριστήν τ' ἄνομόν θ' ἑλικώπιδι κούρῃ·
　　ἡ δ ὑποκυσαμένη τέκετο κρατερόφρονα τέκνα.
　　Ὄρθον μὲν πρῶτον κύνα γείνατο Γηρυονῆι·
310 δεύτερον αὖτις ἔτικτεν ἀμήχανον, οὔ τι φατειόν,
　　Κέρβερον ὠμηστήν, Ἀίδεω κύνα χαλκεόφωνον,
　　πεντηκοντακέφαλον, ἀναιδέα τε κρατερόν τε·
　　τὸ τρίτον Ὕδρην αὖτις ἐγείνατο λύγρ' εἰδυῖαν
　　Λερναίην, ἣν θρέψε θεὰ λευκώλενος Ἥρη
315 ἄπλητον κοτέουσα βίῃ Ἡρακληείῃ.
　　καὶ τὴν μὲν Διὸς υἱὸς ἐνήρατο νηλέι χαλκῷ
　　Ἀμφιτρυωνιάδης σὺν ἀρηιφίλῳ Ἰολάῳ
　　Ἡρακλέης βουλῇσιν Ἀθηναίης ἀγελείης.
　　ἡ δὲ Χίμαιραν ἔτικτε πνέουσαν ἀμαιμάκετον πῦρ,
320 δεινήν τε μεγάλην τε ποδώκεά τε κρατερήν τε.
　　τῆς ἦν τρεῖς κεφαλαί· μία μὲν χαροποῖο λέοντος,
　　ἡ δὲ χιμαίρης, ἡ δ' ὄφιος κρατεροῖο δράκοντος.
　　[πρόσθε λέων, ὄπιθεν δὲ δράκων, μέσση δὲ χίμαιρα,
　　δεινὸν ἀποπνείουσα πυρὸς μένος αἰθομένοιο.]
325 τὴν μὲν Πήγασος εἷλε καὶ ἐσθλὸς Βελλεροφόντης·
　　ἡ δ' ἄρα Φῖκ' ὀλοὴν τέκε Καδμείοισιν ὄλεθρον,
　　Ὄρθῳ ὑποδμηθεῖσα, Νεμειαῖόν τε λέοντα,
　　τόν ῥ' Ἥρη θρέψασα Διὸς κυδρὴ παράκοιτις

　　307 κούρῃ αS: νύμφη k: utrumque b
　　321 τῆς ἦν West: τῆς δ' ἦν ab Herodianus et al. gramm.,
Herodianus rhetor: τῆς δ' αὖ kS　　323–24 (=Il. 6. 181–182)
damn. Wolf　　324 om. a

earth, baleful Echidna, an immortal nymph and ageless all her days.

(306) They say that Typhon, terrible, outrageous, lawless, mingled in love with her, a quick-eyed virgin; and she became pregnant and bore strong-hearted children. First she bore Orthus, the dog, for Geryoneus; second, she then gave birth to something intractable, unspeakable, Cerberus who eats raw flesh, the bronze-voiced dog of Hades, fifty-headed, ruthless and mighty; third, she then gave birth to the evil-minded Hydra of Lerna, which the goddess, white-armed Hera, raised, dreadfully wrathful against Heracles' force. But Zeus' son, the scion of Amphitryon, Heracles, slew it with the pitiless bronze, together with warlike Iolaus, by the plans of Athena, leader of the war-host.

(319) She[18] gave birth to Chimaera, who breathed invincible fire, terrible and great and swift-footed and mighty. She had three heads: one was a fierce-eyed lion's, one a she-goat's, one a snake's, a mighty dragon's. [In front a lion, behind a dragon, in the middle a she-goat, breathing forth the terrible strength of burning fire.][19] Pegasus and noble Bellerophon killed her. Overpowered by Orthus, she[20] bore the deadly Sphinx, destruction for the Cadmeans, and the Nemean lion, which Hera, Zeus' illustrious

[18] Probably Echidna.
[19] These two lines are identical with *Il.* 6.181–82; they describe Chimaera in terms of what seems to be a very different anatomy from the one in the preceding lines, and are rejected by many editors as an interpolation.
[20] Probably Chimaera.

γουνοῖσιν κατένασσε Νεμείης, πῆμ᾽ ἀνθρώποις.
330 ἔνθ᾽ ἄρ᾽ ὅ γ᾽ οἰκείων ἐλεφαίρετο φῦλ᾽ ἀνθρώπων,
κοιρανέων Τρητοῖο Νεμείης ἠδ᾽ Ἀπέσαντος·
ἀλλά ἑ ἲς ἐδάμασσε βίης Ἡρακληείης.
   Κητὼ δ᾽ ὁπλότατον Φόρκυι φιλότητι μιγεῖσα
γείνατο δεινὸν ὄφιν, ὃς ἐρεμνῆς κεύθεσι γαίης
335 πείρασιν ἐν μεγάλοις παγχρύσεα μῆλα φυλάσσει.
τοῦτο μὲν ἐκ Κητοῦς καὶ Φόρκυνος γένος ἐστί.

   Τηθὺς δ᾽ Ὠκεανῷ ποταμοὺς τέκε δινήεντας,
Νεῖλόν τ᾽ Ἀλφειόν τε καὶ Ἠριδανὸν βαθυδίνην,
Στρυμόνα Μαίανδρόν τε καὶ Ἴστρον καλλιρέεθρον
340 Φᾶσίν τε Ῥῆσόν τ᾽ Ἀχελῷόν τ᾽ ἀργυροδίνην
Νέσσόν τε Ῥοδίον θ᾽ Ἁλιάκμονά θ᾽ Ἑπτάπορόν τε
Γρήνικόν τε καὶ Αἴσηπον θεῖόν τε Σιμοῦντα
Πηνειόν τε καὶ Ἕρμον ἐϋρρείτην τε Κάικον
Σαγγάριόν τε μέγαν Λάδωνά τε Παρθένιόν τε
345 Εὐηνόν τε καὶ Ἀλδῆσκον θεῖόν τε Σκάμανδρον.
τίκτε δὲ θυγατέρων ἱερὸν γένος, αἳ κατὰ γαῖαν
ἄνδρας κουρίζουσι σὺν Ἀπόλλωνι ἄνακτι
καὶ ποταμοῖς, ταύτην δὲ Διὸς πάρα μοῖραν ἔχουσι,
Πειθώ τ᾽ Ἀδμήτη τε Ἰάνθη τ᾽ Ἠλέκτρη τε
350 Δωρίς τε Πρυμνώ τε καὶ Οὐρανίη θεοειδὴς
Ἱππώ τε Κλυμένη τε Ῥόδειά τε Καλλιρόη τε
Ζευξώ τε Κλυτίη τε Ἰδυῖά τε Πασιθόη τε
Πληξαύρη τε Γαλαξαύρη τ᾽ ἐρατή τε Διώνη

346 θυγατέρων: Κουράων West

consort, raised and settled among the hills of Nemea, a woe for human beings. For dwelling there it destroyed the tribes of human beings and lorded over Tretus in Nemea and Apesas; but the strength of Heracles' force overpowered it.

(333) Ceto mingled in love with Phorcys and gave birth to her youngest offspring, a terrible snake, which guards the all-golden apples in the hidden places of the dark earth at its great limits. This, then, is the progeny of Ceto and Phorcys.

(337) Tethys bore to Ocean eddying rivers, the Nile and Alpheius and deep-eddying Eridanus, Strymon and Meander and beautiful-flowing Ister, and Phasis and Rhesus and silver-eddying Achelous, and Nessus and Rhodius and Haliacmon and Heptaporus, and Grenicus and Aesepus and divine Simois, and Peneius and Hermus and fairflowing Caïcus, and great Sangarius and Ladon and Parthenius, and Euenus and Aldescus and divine Scamander. And she gave birth to a holy race of daughters[21] who, together with lord Apollo and the rivers, raise boys so that they become men on the earth, for this is the lot they have from Zeus: Peitho and Admete and Ianthe and Electra, and Doris and Prymno and Ourania of godlike figure, and Hippo and Clymene and Rhodea and Callirhoe, and Zeuxo and Clytia and Idyia and Pasithoe, and Plexaura and Galaxaura and lovely Dione, and Melobosis and Thoe

---

[21] Many of the names of the Oceanids reflect their roles as nymphs of fountains and groves and as protectresses of youths.

Μηλόβοσίς τε Θόη τε καὶ εὐειδὴς Πολυδώρη
355 Κερκηίς τε φυὴν ἐρατὴ Πλουτώ τε βοῶπις
Περσηίς τ' Ἰάνειρά τ' Ἀκάστη τε Ξάνθη τε
Πετραίη τ' ἐρόεσσα Μενεσθώ τ' Εὐρώπη τε
Μῆτίς τ' Εὐρυνόμη τε Τελεστώ τε κροκόπεπλος
Χρυσηίς τ' Ἀσίη τε καὶ ἱμερόεσσα Καλυψὼ
360 Εὐδώρη τε Τύχη τε καὶ Ἀμφιρὼ Ὠκυρόη τε
καὶ Στύξ, ἣ δή σφεων προφερεστάτη ἐστὶν ἀπασέων.
αὗται ἄρ' Ὠκεανοῦ καὶ Τηθύος ἐξεγένοντο
πρεσβύταται κοῦραι· πολλαί γε μέν εἰσι καὶ ἄλλαι·
τρὶς γὰρ χίλιαί εἰσι τανίσφυροι Ὠκεανῖναι,
365 αἵ ῥα πολυσπερέες γαῖαν καὶ βένθεα λίμνης
πάντη ὁμῶς ἐφέπουσι, θεάων ἀγλαὰ τέκνα.
τόσσοι δ' αὖθ' ἕτεροι ποταμοὶ καναχηδὰ ῥέοντες,
υἱέες Ὠκεανοῦ, τοὺς γείνατο πότνια Τηθύς·
τῶν ὄνομ' ἀργαλέον πάντων βροτὸν ἄνδρα ἐνισπεῖν,
370 οἱ δὲ ἕκαστοι ἴσασιν, ὅσοι περιναιετάουσι.

Θεία δ' Ἡέλιόν τε μέγαν λαμπράν τε Σελήνην
Ἠῶ θ', ἣ πάντεσσιν ἐπιχθονίοισι φαείνει
ἀθανάτοις τε θεοῖσι τοὶ οὐρανὸν εὐρὺν ἔχουσι,
γείναθ' ὑποδμηθεῖσ' Ὑπερίονος ἐν φιλότητι.
375 Κρείῳ δ' Εὐρυβίη τέκεν ἐν φιλότητι μιγεῖσα
Ἀστραῖόν τε μέγαν Πάλλαντά τε δῖα θεάων
Πέρσην θ', ὃς καὶ πᾶσι μετέπρεπεν ἰδμοσύνῃσιν.
Ἀστραίῳ δ' Ἠὼς ἀνέμους τέκε καρτεροθύμους,
ἀργεστὴν Ζέφυρον Βορέην τ' αἰψηροκέλευθον
380 καὶ Νότον, ἐν φιλότητι θεὰ θεῷ εὐνηθεῖσα.
τοὺς δὲ μέτ' ἀστέρα τίκτεν Ἑωσφόρον Ἠριγένεια

and Polydora of fair figure, and Cerceis, lovely of form, and cow-eyed Pluto, and Perseis and Ianeira and Acaste and Xanthe, and lovely Petraea and Menestho and Europa, and Metis and Eurynome and saffron-robed Telesto, and Chryseis and Asia and lovely Calypso, and Eudora and Tyche and Amphiro and Ocyrhoe, and Styx, who indeed is the greatest of them all. These came forth from Ocean and Tethys as the oldest maidens; but there are many others as well. For there are three thousand long-ankled daughters of Ocean who are widely dispersed and hold fast to the earth and the depths of the waters, everywhere in the same way, splendid children of goddesses; and there are just as many other loud-flowing rivers, sons of Ocean, to whom queenly Tethys gave birth. The names of them all it is difficult for a mortal man to tell, but each of those who dwell around them knows them.

(371) Theia, overpowered in love by Hyperion, gave birth to great Helius (Sun) and gleaming Selene (Moon) and Eos (Dawn), who shines for all those on the earth and for the immortal gods who possess the broad sky. Eurybia, revered among goddesses, mingling in love, bore to Crius great Astraeus and Pallas and Perses, who was conspicuous among all for his intelligence. Eos, a goddess bedded in love with a god, bore to Astraeus the strong-spirited winds, clear Zephyrus and swift-pathed Boreas and Notus; and after these the Early-born one[22] bore the star, Dawn-

---

[22] The Dawn.

---

358 Τελευτώ υΔ: Τελεσθώ      362 ἄρ' West: δ' codd.
370 ἕκαστα Σ (?) Eustathius: -οι codd.
379 ἀργεστὴν Jacoby: ἀργέστην codd.

ἄστρά τε λαμπετόωντα, τά τ' οὐρανὸς ἐστεφάνωται.

Στὺξ δ' ἔτεκ' Ὠκεανοῦ θυγάτηρ Πάλλαντι μιγεῖσα
Ζῆλον καὶ Νίκην καλλίσφυρον ἐν μεγάροισι
385 καὶ Κράτος ἠδὲ Βίην ἀριδείκετα γείνατο τέκνα.
τῶν οὐκ ἔστ' ἀπάνευθε Διὸς δόμος, οὐδέ τις ἕδρη,
οὐδ' ὁδός, ὅππη μὴ κείνοις θεὸς ἡγεμονεύει,
ἀλλ' αἰεὶ πὰρ Ζηνὶ βαρυκτύπῳ ἑδριόωνται.
ὣς γὰρ ἐβούλευσε Στὺξ ἄφθιτος Ὠκεανίνη
390 ἤματι τῷ, ὅτε πάντας Ὀλύμπιος ἀστεροπητὴς
ἀθανάτους ἐκάλεσσε θεοὺς ἐς μακρὸν Ὄλυμπον,
εἶπε δ', ὃς ἂν μετὰ εἷο θεῶν Τιτῆσι μάχοιτο,
μή τιν' ἀπορραίσειν γεράων, τιμὴν δὲ ἕκαστον
ἑξέμεν ἣν τὸ πάρος γε μετ' ἀθανάτοισι θεοῖσι.
395 τὸν δ' ἔφαθ', ὅστις ἄτιμος ὑπὸ Κρόνου ἠδ'
          ἀγέραστος,
τιμῆς καὶ γεράων ἐπιβησέμεν, ἧ θέμις ἐστίν.
ἦλθε δ' ἄρα πρώτη Στὺξ ἄφθιτος Οὐλυμπόνδε
σὺν σφοῖσιν παίδεσσι φίλου διὰ μήδεα πατρός·
τὴν δὲ Ζεὺς τίμησε, περισσὰ δὲ δῶρα ἔδωκεν.
400 αὐτὴν μὲν γὰρ ἔθηκε θεῶν μέγαν ἔμμεναι ὅρκον,
παῖδας δ' ἤματα πάντα ἑοῦ μεταναιέτας εἶναι.
ὣς δ' αὕτως πάντεσσι διαμπερές, ὥς περ ὑπέστη,
ἐξετέλεσσ'· αὐτὸς δὲ μέγα κρατεῖ ἠδὲ ἀνάσσει.

Φοίβη δ' αὖ Κοίου πολυήρατον ἦλθεν ἐς εὐνήν·
405 κυσαμένη δἤπειτα θεὰ θεοῦ ἐν φιλότητι
Λητὼ κυανόπεπλον ἐγείνατο, μείλιχον αἰεί,
ἤπιον ἀνθρώποισι καὶ ἀθανάτοισι θεοῖσι,
μείλιχον ἐξ ἀρχῆς, ἀγανώτατον ἐντὸς Ὀλύμπου.

bringer, and the shining stars with which the sky is crowned.

(383) Styx, Ocean's daughter, mingling with Pallas, bore Zelus (Rivalry) and beautiful-ankled Nike (Victory) in her house, and she gave birth to Cratos (Supremacy) and Bia (Force), eminent children. These have no house apart from Zeus nor any seat, nor any path except that on which the god leads them, but they are always seated next to deep-thundering Zeus. For this is what Styx, Ocean's eternal daughter, planned on the day when the Olympian lightener[23] summoned all the immortal gods to high Olympus and said that, whoever of the gods would fight together with him against the Titans, him he would not strip of his privileges, but that every one would have the honor he had had before among the immortal gods; and that whoever had been without honor and without privilege because of Cronus, him he would raise to honor and privileges, as is established right. So eternal Styx came first of all to Olympus with her own children, through the plans of her dear father; and Zeus honored her and gave her exceptional gifts. For he set her to be the great oath of the gods, and her sons to dwell with him for all their days. Just as he promised, so too he fulfilled for all, through and through; and he himself rules mightily and reigns.

(404) Phoebe came to the lovely bed of Coeus; and the goddess, pregnant in the love of a god, gave birth to dark-robed Leto, always soothing, gentle to human beings and to the immortal gods, soothing from the beginning, the kindliest one within Olympus. She also gave birth to fair-

[23] Zeus.

γείνατο δ' Ἀστερίην εὐώνυμον, ἥν ποτε Πέρσης
410 ἠγάγετ' ἐς μέγα δῶμα φίλην κεκλῆσθαι ἄκοιτιν.
ἡ δ' ὑποκυσαμένη Ἑκάτην τέκε, τὴν περὶ πάντων
Ζεὺς Κρονίδης τίμησε· πόρεν δέ οἱ ἀγλαὰ δῶρα,
μοῖραν ἔχειν γαίης τε καὶ ἀτρυγέτοιο θαλάσσης.
ἡ δὲ καὶ ἀστερόεντος ἀπ' οὐρανοῦ ἔμμορε τιμῆς,
415 ἀθανάτοις τε θεοῖσι τετιμένη ἐστὶ μάλιστα.
καὶ γὰρ νῦν, ὅτε πού τις ἐπιχθονίων ἀνθρώπων
ἔρδων ἱερὰ καλὰ κατὰ νόμον ἱλάσκηται,
κικλήσκει Ἑκάτην· πολλή τέ οἱ ἕσπετο τιμὴ
ῥεῖα μάλ', ᾧ πρόφρων γε θεὰ ὑποδέξεται εὐχάς,
420 καί τέ οἱ ὄλβον ὀπάζει, ἐπεὶ δύναμίς γε πάρεστιν.
ὅσσοι γὰρ Γαίης τε καὶ Οὐρανοῦ ἐξεγένοντο
καὶ τιμὴν ἔλαχον, τούτων ἔχει αἶσαν ἁπάντων·
οὐδέ τί μιν Κρονίδης ἐβιήσατο οὐδέ τ' ἀπηύρα,
ὅσσ' ἔλαχεν Τιτῆσι μέτα προτέροισι θεοῖσιν,
425 ἀλλ' ἔχει, ὡς τὸ πρῶτον ἀπ' ἀρχῆς ἔπλετο δασμός.
οὐδ', ὅτι μουνογενής, ἧσσον θεὰ ἔμμορε τιμῆς
καὶ γεράων γαίη τε καὶ οὐρανῷ ἠδὲ θαλάσσῃ,
ἀλλ' ἔτι καὶ πολὺ μᾶλλον, ἐπεὶ Ζεὺς τίεται αὐτήν.
ᾧ δ' ἐθέλῃ, μεγάλως παραγίνεται ἠδ' ὀνίνησιν·
430 ἔν τ' ἀγορῇ λαοῖσι μεταπρέπει, ὅν κ' ἐθέλῃσιν·
ἠδ' ὁπότ' ἐς πόλεμον φθισήνορα θωρήσσωνται
ἀνέρες, ἔνθα θεὰ παραγίνεται, οἷς κ' ἐθέλῃσι
νίκην προφρονέως ὀπάσαι καὶ κῦδος ὀρέξαι.
ἔν τε δίκῃ βασιλεῦσι παρ' αἰδοίοισι καθίζει,

427 γεράων van Lennep: γέρ]ας ἐν Π²⁵ak

named Asteria, whom Perses once led to his great house to be called his dear wife.

(411) And she became pregnant and bore Hecate, whom Zeus, Cronus' son, honored above all others: he gave her splendid gifts—to have a share of the earth and of the barren sea, and from the starry sky as well she has a share in honor, and is honored most of all by the immortal gods. For even now, whenever any human on the earth seeks propitiation by performing fine sacrifices according to custom, he invokes Hecate; and much honor very easily stays with that man whose prayers the goddess accepts with gladness, and she bestows happiness upon him, for this power she certainly has. For of all those who came forth from Earth and Sky and received honor, among all of these she has her due share; and neither did Cronus' son use force against her nor did he deprive her of anything that she had received as her portion among the Titans, the earlier gods, but she is still in possession according to the division as it was made at first from the beginning. Nor does the goddess, just because she is an only child, have a lesser share of honor and privileges on earth and in sky and sea, but instead she has far more, since Zeus honors her. She stands mightily at the side of whomever she wishes and helps him. In the assembly, whoever she wishes is conspicuous among the people; and when men arm themselves for man-destroying war, the goddess stands there by the side of whomever she wishes, zealously to grant victory and to stretch forth glory. She sits in judgment beside reverend kings; and again, she is good whenever men

---

434 ante 433 Π²⁵, ante (sive post) 430 Schoemann

435 ἐσθλὴ δ' αὖθ' ὁπότ' ἄνδρες ἀεθλεύωσ' ἐν ἀγῶνι·
   ἔνθα θεὰ καὶ τοῖς παραγίνεται ἠδ' ὀνίνησι,
   νικήσας δὲ βίῃ καὶ κάρτει, καλὸν ἄεθλον
   ῥεῖα φέρει χαίρων τε, τοκεῦσι δὲ κῦδος ὀπάζει.
   ἐσθλὴ δ' ἱππήεσσι παρεστάμεν, οἷς κ' ἐθέλῃσιν

440 καὶ τοῖς, οἳ γλαυκὴν δυσπέμφελον ἐργάζονται,
   εὔχονται δ' Ἑκάτῃ καὶ ἐρικτύπῳ Ἐννοσιγαίῳ,
   ῥηιδίως ἄγρην κυδρὴ θεὸς ὤπασε πολλήν,
   ῥεῖα δ' ἀφείλετο φαινομένην, ἐθέλουσά γε θυμῷ.
   ἐσθλὴ δ' ἐν σταθμοῖσι σὺν Ἑρμῇ ληίδ' ἀέξειν·

445 βουκολίας τ' ἀγέλας τε καὶ αἰπόλια πλατέ' αἰγῶν
   ποίμνας τ' εἰροπόκων ὀίων, θυμῷ γ' ἐθέλουσα,
   ἐξ ὀλίγων βριάει κἀκ πολλῶν μείονα θῆκεν.
   οὕτω τοι καὶ μουνογενὴς ἐκ μητρὸς ἐοῦσα
   πᾶσι μετ' ἀθανάτοισι τετίμηται γεράεσσι.

450 θῆκε δέ μιν Κρονίδης κουροτρόφον, οἳ μετ' ἐκείνην
   ὀφθαλμοῖσιν ἴδοντο φάος πολυδερκέος Ἠοῦς.
   οὕτως ἐξ ἀρχῆς κουροτρόφος, αἱ δέ τε τιμαί.

   Ῥείη δὲ δμηθεῖσα Κρόνῳ τέκε φαίδιμα τέκνα,
   Ἱστίην Δήμητρα καὶ Ἥρην χρυσοπέδιλον,

455 ἴφθιμόν τ' Ἀίδην, ὃς ὑπὸ χθονὶ δώματα ναίει
   νηλεὲς ἦτορ ἔχων, καὶ ἐρίκτυπον Ἐννοσίγαιον,
   Ζῆνά τε μητιόεντα, θεῶν πατέρ' ἠδὲ καὶ ἀνδρῶν,
   τοῦ καὶ ὑπὸ βροντῆς πελεμίζεται εὐρεῖα χθών.

   435 ἀεθλεύωσ' ἐν ἀ. West (-ωσιν ἀ. Koechly): ἐν ἀγῶνι
   ἀθλεύωσι(ν) b: αγωνι α[ Π25: ἀγ. ἀ(ε)θλ. kS(a)

are competing in an athletic contest—there the goddess stands by their side too and helps them, and when someone has gained victory by force and supremacy he easily and joyfully carries off a fine prize and grants glory to his parents; and she is good at standing by the side of horsemen, whomever she wishes. And upon those who work the bright, storm-tossed sea and pray to Hecate and the loud-sounding Earth-shaker,[24] the illustrious goddess easily bestows a big haul of fish, and easily she takes it away once it has been seen, if she so wishes in her spirit. And she is good in the stables at increasing the livestock together with Hermes; and the herds and droves of cattle, and the broad flocks of goats and the flocks of woolly sheep, if in her spirit she so wishes, from a few she strengthens them and from many she makes them fewer. And so, even though she is an only child from her mother, she is honored with privileges among all the immortals. And Cronus' son made her the nurse of all the children who after her see with their eyes the light of much-seeing Dawn. Thus since the beginning she is a nurse, and these are her honors.

(453) Rhea, overpowered by Cronus, bore him splendid children, Hestia, Demeter, and golden-sandaled Hera, and powerful Hades, who dwells in mansions beneath the earth and has a pitiless heart, and the loud-sounding Earth-shaker and the counsellor Zeus, the father of gods and of men, by whose thunder the broad earth is shaken.

[24] Poseidon.

---

445 τ᾽ ἀγέλας: δὲ βοῶν West

καὶ τοὺς μὲν κατέπινε μέγας Κρόνος, ὥς τις ἕκαστος
460 νηδύος ἐξ ἱερῆς μητρὸς πρὸς γούναθ᾽ ἵκοιτο,
τὰ φρονέων, ἵνα μή τις ἀγαυῶν Οὐρανιώνων
ἄλλος ἐν ἀθανάτοισιν ἔχοι βασιληίδα τιμήν.
πεύθετο γὰρ Γαίης τε καὶ Οὐρανοῦ ἀστερόεντος
οὕνεκά οἱ πέπρωτο ἑῷ ὑπὸ παιδὶ δαμῆναι,
465 καὶ κρατερῷ περ ἐόντι, Διὸς μεγάλου διὰ βουλάς.
τῷ ὅ γ᾽ ἄρ᾽ οὐκ ἀλαοσκοπιὴν ἔχεν, ἀλλὰ δοκεύων
παῖδας ἑοὺς κατέπινε· Ῥέην δ᾽ ἔχε πένθος ἄλαστον.
ἀλλ᾽ ὅτε δὴ Δί᾽ ἔμελλε θεῶν πατέρ᾽ ἠδὲ καὶ ἀνδρῶν
τέξεσθαι, τότ᾽ ἔπειτα φίλους λιτάνευε τοκῆας
470 τοὺς αὐτῆς, Γαῖάν τε καὶ Οὐρανὸν ἀστερόεντα,
μῆτιν συμφράσσασθαι, ὅπως λελάθοιτο τεκοῦσα
παῖδα φίλον, τείσαιτο δ᾽ ἐρινῦς πατρὸς ἑοῖο
παίδων ⟨θ᾽⟩ οὓς κατέπινε μέγας Κρόνος
        ἀγκυλομήτης.
οἳ δὲ θυγατρὶ φίλῃ μάλα μὲν κλύον ἠδ᾽ ἐπίθοντο,
475 καί οἱ πεφραδέτην, ὅσα περ πέπρωτο γενέσθαι
ἀμφὶ Κρόνῳ βασιλῆι καὶ υἱέι καρτεροθύμῳ·
πέμψαν δ᾽ ἐς Λύκτον, Κρήτης ἐς πίονα δῆμον,
ὁππότ᾽ ἄρ᾽ ὁπλότατον παίδων ἤμελλε τεκέσθαι,
Ζῆνα μέγαν· τὸν μέν οἱ ἐδέξατο Γαῖα πελώρη
480 Κρήτῃ ἐν εὐρείῃ τρεφέμεν ἀτιταλλέμεναί τε.
ἔνθά μιν ἷκτο φέρουσα θοὴν διὰ νύκτα μέλαιναν
πρώτην ἐς Λύκτον· κρύψεν δέ ἑ χερσὶ λαβοῦσα
ἄντρῳ ἐν ἠλιβάτῳ, ζαθέης ὑπὸ κεύθεσι γαίης,
Αἰγαίῳ ἐν ὄρει πεπυκασμένῳ ὑλήεντι.
485 τῷ δὲ σπαργανίσασα μέγαν λίθον ἐγγυάλιξεν

Great Cronus would swallow these down as each one came
from his mother's holy womb to her knees, mindful lest
anyone else of Sky's illustrious children should have the
honor of kingship among the immortals. For he had heard
from Earth and starry Sky that, mighty though he was, he
was destined to be overpowered by a child of his, through
the plans of great Zeus. For this reason, then, he held no
unseeing watch, but observed closely, and swallowed down
his children; and unremitting grief gripped Rhea. But
when she was about to bear Zeus, the father of gods and of
men, she beseeched her own dear parents, Earth and
starry Sky, to contrive some scheme so that she could bear
her dear son without being noticed, and take retribution
for the avenging deities of her father and of her children,
whom great crooked-counseled Cronus had swallowed
down. They listened well to their dear daughter and
obeyed her, and they revealed to her everything that was
fated to come about concerning Cronus the king and his
strong-spirited son. They told her to go to Lyctus, to the
rich land of Crete, when she was about to bear the youn-
gest of her children, great Zeus; and huge Earth received
him in broad Crete to nurse him and rear him up. There
she came first to Lyctus, carrying him through the swift
black night; taking him in her hands she concealed him in a
deep cave, under the hidden places of the holy earth, in
the Aegean mountain, abounding with forests. And she
wrapped a great stone in swaddling-clothes and put it into

---

477–84 exp. Goettling; duas recensiones 477, 481–4; 478–80
dist. Hermann

Οὐρανίδῃ μέγ᾽ ἄνακτι, θεῶν προτέρων βασιλῆι.
τὸν τόθ᾽ ἑλὼν χείρεσσιν ἑὴν ἐσκάτθετο νηδύν,
σχέτλιος, οὐδ᾽ ἐνόησε μετὰ φρεσίν, ὥς οἱ ὀπίσσω
ἀντὶ λίθου ἑὸς υἱὸς ἀνίκητος καὶ ἀκηδὴς
490 λείπεθ᾽, ὅ μιν τάχ᾽ ἔμελλε βίῃ καὶ χερσὶ δαμάσσας
τιμῆς ἐξελάαν, ὁ δ᾽ ἐν ἀθανάτοισιν ἀνάξειν.
    καρπαλίμως δ᾽ ἄρ᾽ ἔπειτα μένος καὶ φαίδιμα
        γυῖα
ηὔξετο τοῖο ἄνακτος· ἐπιπλομένου δ᾽ ἐνιαυτοῦ,
Γαίης ἐννεσίῃσι πολυφραδέεσσι δολωθείς,
495 ὃν γόνον ἂψ ἀνέηκε μέγας Κρόνος ἀγκυλομήτης,
νικηθεὶς τέχνῃσι βίηφί τε παιδὸς ἑοῖο.
πρῶτον δ᾽ ἐξήμησε λίθον, πύματον καταπίνων·
τὸν μὲν Ζεὺς στήριξε κατὰ χθονὸς εὐρυοδείης
Πυθοῖ ἐν ἠγαθέῃ, γυάλοις ὕπο Παρνησσοῖο,
500 σῆμ᾽ ἔμεν ἐξοπίσω, θαῦμα θνητοῖσι βροτοῖσι.
    λῦσε δὲ πατροκασιγνήτους ὀλοῶν ὑπὸ δεσμῶν,
Οὐρανίδας, οὓς δῆσε πατὴρ ἀεσιφροσύνῃσιν·
οἵ οἱ ἀπεμνήσαντο χάριν εὐεργεσιάων,
δῶκαν δὲ βροντὴν ἠδ᾽ αἰθαλόεντα κεραυνὸν
505 καὶ στεροπήν· τὸ πρὶν δὲ πελώρη Γαῖα κεκεύθει·
τοῖς πίσυνος θνητοῖσι καὶ ἀθανάτοισιν ἀνάσσει.

    κούρην δ᾽ Ἰαπετὸς καλλίσφυρον Ὠκεανίνην
ἠγάγετο Κλυμένην καὶ ὁμὸν λέχος εἰσανέβαινεν.
ἡ δέ οἱ Ἄτλαντα κρατερόφρονα γείνατο παῖδα,

---

486 προτέρων West: -ῳ codd.

the hand of Sky's son, the great ruler, the king of the earlier gods.[25] He seized this with his hands and put it down into his belly—cruel one, nor did he know in his spirit that in place of the stone his son remained hereafter, unconquered and untroubled, who would overpower him with force and his own hands, and would soon drive him out from his honor and be king among the immortals.

(492) Swiftly then the king's strength and his splendid limbs grew; and when a year had revolved, great crooked-counselled Cronus, deceived by Earth's very clever suggestions, brought his offspring up again, overcome by his son's devices and force. First he vomited up the stone, since he had swallowed it down last of all; Zeus set it fast in the broad-pathed earth in sacred Pytho, down in the valleys of Parnassus, to be a sign thereafter, a marvel for mortal human beings.

(501) And he freed from their deadly bonds his father's brothers, Sky's sons, whom their father had bound in his folly.[26] And they repaid him in gratitude for his kind deed, giving him the thunder and the blazing thunderbolt and the lightning, which huge Earth had concealed before. Relying on these, he rules over mortals and immortals.

(507) Iapetus married Clymene, Ocean's beautiful-ankled daughter, and went up into the same bed with her. She bore him Atlas, a strong-hearted son, and gave birth to

---

[25] The Titans.    [26] The Cyclopes.

---

492–506 secl. Arth. Meyer, Jacoby (492–500 Guyet, 501–6 Wolf)

493 ἐπιπλομένου δ' ἐνιαυτοῦ BkΣ: ἐπιπλομένων δ' ἐνιαυτῶν a

510 τίκτε δ᾽ ὑπερκύδαντα Μενοίτιον ἠδὲ Προμηθέα,
ποικίλον αἰολόμητιν, ἁμαρτίνοόν τ᾽ Ἐπιμηθέα·
ὃς κακὸν ἐξ ἀρχῆς γένετ᾽ ἀνδράσιν ἀλφηστῇσι·
πρῶτος γάρ ῥα Διὸς πλαστὴν ὑπέδεκτο γυναῖκα
παρθένον. ὑβριστὴν δὲ Μενοίτιον εὐρύοπα Ζεὺς

515 εἰς ἔρεβος κατέπεμψε βαλὼν ψολόεντι κεραυνῷ
εἵνεκ᾽ ἀτασθαλίης τε καὶ ἠνορέης ὑπερόπλου.
Ἄτλας δ᾽ οὐρανὸν εὐρὺν ἔχει κρατερῆς ὑπ᾽ ἀνάγκης,
πείρασιν ἐν γαίης πρόπαρ᾽ Ἑσπερίδων λιγυφώνων
ἑστηώς, κεφαλῇ τε καὶ ἀκαμάτῃσι χέρεσσι·

520 ταύτην γάρ οἱ μοῖραν ἐδάσσατο μητίετα Ζεύς.
δῆσε δ᾽ ἀλυκτοπέδῃσι Προμηθέα ποικιλόβουλον,
δεσμοῖς ἀργαλέοισι, μέσον διὰ κίον᾽ ἐλάσσας·
καί οἱ ἐπ᾽ αἰετὸν ὦρσε τανύπτερον· αὐτὰρ ὅ γ᾽ ἧπαρ
ἤσθιεν ἀθάνατον, τὸ δ᾽ ἀέξετο ἶσον ἁπάντῃ

525 νυκτός, ὅσον πρόπαν ἦμαρ ἔδοι τανυσίπτερος ὄρνις.
τὸν μὲν ἄρ᾽ Ἀλκμήνης καλλισφύρου ἄλκιμος υἱὸς
Ἡρακλέης ἔκτεινε, κακὴν δ᾽ ἀπὸ νοῦσον ἄλαλκεν
Ἰαπετιονίδῃ καὶ ἐλύσατο δυσφροσυνάων,
οὐκ ἀέκητι Ζηνὸς Ὀλυμπίου ὕψι μέδοντος,

530 ὄφρ᾽ Ἡρακλῆος Θηβαγενέος κλέος εἴη
πλεῖον ἔτ᾽ ἢ τὸ πάροιθεν ἐπὶ χθόνα πουλυβότειραν.
ταῦτ᾽ ἄρα ἀζόμενος τίμα ἀρίδεικετον υἱόν·
καί περ χωόμενος παύθη χόλου, ὃν πρὶν ἔχεσκεν,
οὕνεκ᾽ ἐρίζετο βουλὰς ὑπερμενέι Κρονίωνι.

535   καὶ γὰρ ὅτ᾽ ἐκρίνοντο θεοὶ θνητοί τ᾽ ἄνθρωποι

519 (=747) exp. Guyet      526–34 exp. Paley

44

the very renowned Menoetius and to Prometheus (Fore-thought), shifty, quick-scheming, and to mistaken-minded Epimetheus (Afterthought)—he who turned out to be an evil from the beginning for men who live on bread, for he was the one who first accepted Zeus' fabricated woman, the maiden. Far-seeing Zeus hurled down outrageous Menoetius into Erebus, striking him with a smoking thunderbolt because of his wickedness and defiant manhood. And by mighty necessity Atlas holds up the sky with his head and with his tireless hands, standing at the limits of the earth in front of the clear-voiced Hesperides; for this is the portion which the counsellor Zeus assigned him. And with painful fetters he bound shifty-planning Prometheus, with distressful bonds, driving them through the middle of a pillar; and he set upon him a long-winged eagle which ate his immortal liver, but this grew again on all sides at night just as much as the long-winged bird would eat during the whole day. It was killed by Heracles, the strong son of beautiful-ankled Alcmene, who warded off the evil plague from Iapetus' son and released him from distress—not against the will of Olympian Zeus, who rules on high, so that the glory of Theban-born Heracles would become even greater than before upon the bounteous earth. With this in mind, he honored his eminent son; and although he was angry with Prometheus, he ceased from the anger which he had had before because Prometheus had contended in counsels with Cronus' very strong son.

(535) For when the gods and mortal men were reaching

Μηκώνῃ, τότ᾿ ἔπειτα μέγαν βοῦν πρόφρονι θυμῷ
δασσάμενος προύθηκε, Διὸς νόον ἐξαπαφίσκων.
τῷ μὲν γὰρ σάρκάς τε καὶ ἔγκατα πίονα δημῷ
ἐν ῥινῷ κατέθηκε, καλύψας γαστρὶ βοείῃ,
540   τῷ δ᾿ αὖτ᾿ ὀστέα λευκὰ βοὸς δολίῃ ἐπὶ τέχνῃ
εὐθετίσας κατέθηκε, καλύψας ἀργέτι δημῷ.
   δὴ τότε μιν προσέειπε πατὴρ ἀνδρῶν τε θεῶν τε·
" Ἰαπετιονίδη, πάντων ἀριδείκετ᾿ ἀνάκτων,
ὦ πέπον, ὡς ἑτεροζήλως διεδάσσαο μοίρας."
545   ὣς φάτο κερτομέων Ζεὺς ἄφθιτα μήδεα εἰδώς·
τὸν δ᾿ αὖτε προσέειπε Προμηθεὺς ἀγκυλομήτης,
ἦκ᾿ ἐπιμειδήσας, δολίης δ᾿ οὐ λήθετο τέχνης·
"Ζεῦ κύδιστε μέγιστε θεῶν αἰειγενετάων,
τῶν δ᾿ ἕλευ ὁπποτέρην σε ἐνὶ φρεσὶ θυμὸς ἀνώγει".
550   φῆ ῥα δολοφρονέων· Ζεὺς δ᾿ ἄφθιτα μήδεα εἰδὼς
γνῶ ῥ᾿ οὐδ᾿ ἠγνοίησε δόλον· κακὰ δ᾿ ὄσσετο θυμῷ
θνητοῖς ἀνθρώποισι, τὰ καὶ τελέεσθαι ἔμελλε.
χερσὶ δ᾿ ὅ γ᾿ ἀμφοτέρῃσιν ἀνείλετο λευκὸν ἄλειφαρ,
χώσατο δὲ φρένας ἀμφί, χόλος δέ μιν ἵκετο θυμόν,
555   ὡς ἴδεν ὀστέα λευκὰ βοὸς δολίῃ ἐπὶ τέχνῃ.

537 διὸς Tr. (Lᵖᶜ in ras.): ζηνὸς codd.
538 τῷ codd.: τοῖς Byz. Schoemann: τῇ Guyet
540 τῷ codd.: τῇ Guyet: τοῖς West

27 The precise meaning of the verb Hesiod uses is obscure; it
seems to indicate that gods and men were now being separated
definitively from one another, presumably after a time when they
had been together.

a settlement[27] in Mecone, with eager spirit he divided up a great ox and, trying to deceive Zeus' mind, set it before him. For he set down on the skin before him the meat and the innards, rich with fat, hiding them in the ox's stomach; and then he set down before him in turn the ox's white bones, arranging them with deceptive craft, hiding them with gleaming fat.[28]

(542) Then the father of men and of gods addressed him: "Son of Iapetus, eminent among all rulers, my fine fellow, how unfairly you have divided up the portions!"

(545) So spoke in mockery Zeus, who knows eternal counsels; but crooked-counseled Prometheus addressed him in turn, smiling slightly, and he did not forget his deceptive craft: "Zeus, most renowned, greatest of the eternally living gods, choose from these whichever your spirit in your breast bids you."

(550) So he spoke, plotting deception. But Zeus, who knows eternal counsels, recognized the deception and did not fail to perceive it; and he saw in his spirit evils for mortal human beings—ones that were going to be fulfilled, too. With both hands he grasped the white fat, and he became enraged in his breast and wrath came upon his spirit when he saw the ox's white bones, the result of the decep-

---

[28] This passage has been much misunderstood and often emended. But the transmitted text makes excellent sense, so long as we recall that in epic usage, μέν and δέ can distinguish not only two persons but also two actions directed towards the same person (cf. *Il.* 4.415–17, 8.257–59, 8.323–35, 17.193–96, 18.438–42). Prometheus sets both portions before Zeus and lets him choose freely between them.

ἐκ τοῦ δ' ἀθανάτοισιν ἐπὶ χθονὶ φῦλ' ἀνθρώπων
καίουσ' ὀστέα λευκὰ θυηέντων ἐπὶ βωμῶν.
   τὸν δὲ μέγ' ὀχθήσας προσέφη νεφεληγερέτα Ζεύς·
" Ἰαπετιονίδη, πάντων πέρι μήδεα εἰδώς,
560 ὦ πέπον, οὐκ ἄρα πω δολίης ἐπελήθεο τέχνης".
   ὣς φάτο χωόμενος Ζεὺς ἄφθιτα μήδεα εἰδώς.
ἐκ τούτου δήπειτα χόλου μεμνημένος αἰεὶ
οὐκ ἐδίδου μελίῃσι πυρὸς μένος ἀκαμάτοιο
θνητοῖς ἀνθρώποις οἳ ἐπὶ χθονὶ ναιετάουσιν·
565 ἀλλά μιν ἐξαπάτησεν ἐὺς πάις Ἰαπετοῖο
κλέψας ἀκαμάτοιο πυρὸς τηλέσκοπον αὐγὴν
ἐν κοίλῳ νάρθηκι· δάκεν δ' ἄρα νειόθι θυμὸν
Ζῆν' ὑψιβρεμέτην, ἐχόλωσε δέ μιν φίλον ἦτορ,
ὡς ἴδ' ἐν ἀνθρώποισι πυρὸς τηλέσκοπον αὐγήν.
570 αὐτίκα δ' ἀντὶ πυρὸς τεῦξεν κακὸν ἀνθρώποισι·
γαίης γὰρ σύμπλασσε περικλυτὸς Ἀμφιγυήεις
παρθένῳ αἰδοίῃ ἴκελον Κρονίδεω διὰ βουλάς·
ζῶσε δὲ καὶ κόσμησε θεὰ γλαυκῶπις Ἀθήνη
ἀργυφέῃ ἐσθῆτι· κατὰ κρῆθεν δὲ καλύπτρην
575 δαιδαλέην χείρεσσι κατέσχεθε, θαῦμα ἰδέσθαι·
ἀμφὶ δέ οἱ στεφάνους νεοθηλέας, ἄνθεα ποίης,
ἱμερτοὺς περίθηκε καρήατι Παλλὰς Ἀθήνη·
ἀμφὶ δέ οἱ στεφάνην χρυσέην κεφαλῆφιν ἔθηκε,
τὴν αὐτὸς ποίησε περικλυτὸς Ἀμφιγυήεις
580 ἀσκήσας παλάμῃσι, χαριζόμενος Διὶ πατρί.

562 χόλου S<sup>ac</sup>: δόλου cett.
563 μελίῃσι kLSΣ: -οισι am

tive craft. And ever since then the tribes of human beings upon the earth burn white bones upon smoking altars for the immortals.

(558) Greatly angered, the cloud-gatherer Zeus addressed him: "Son of Iapetus, you who know counsels beyond all others, my fine fellow, so you did not forget your deceptive craft after all!"

(561) So spoke in rage Zeus, who knows eternal counsels. And from then on, constantly mindful of his wrath after that, he did not give the strength of tireless fire to the ash trees[29] for the mortal human beings who live upon the earth. But the good son of Iapetus fooled him by stealing the far-seen gleam of tireless fire in a hollow fennel stalk. It gnawed deeply at high-thundering Zeus' spirit and enraged his dear heart, when he saw the far-seen gleam of fire among human beings. Immediately he contrived an evil for human beings in exchange for fire. For the much-renowned Lame One[30] forged from earth the semblance of a reverend maiden by the plans of Cronus' son; and the goddess, bright-eyed Athena, girdled and adorned her with silvery clothing, and with her hands she hung a highly wrought veil from her head, a wonder to see; and around her head Pallas Athena placed freshly budding garlands that arouse desire, the flowers of the meadow; and around her head she placed a golden headband, which the much-renowned Lame One made himself, working it with his skilled hands, to do a favor for Zeus the father. On this

---

[29] See note on *Theogony* 187.     [30] Hephaestus.

573–84 exp. Seleucus
576–77 damn. Wolf

τῇ δ' ἔνι δαίδαλα πολλὰ τετεύχατο, θαῦμα ἰδέσθαι,
κνώδαλ' ὅσ' ἤπειρος δεινὰ τρέφει ἠδὲ θάλασσα·
τῶν ὅ γε πόλλ' ἐνέθηκε, χάρις δ' ἐπὶ πᾶσιν ἄητο,
θαυμάσια, ζωοῖσιν ἐοικότα φωνήεσσιν.

585   αὐτὰρ ἐπεὶ δὴ τεῦξε καλὸν κακὸν ἀντ' ἀγαθοῖο,
ἐξάγαγ' ἔνθά περ ἄλλοι ἔσαν θεοὶ ἠδ' ἄνθρωποι,
κόσμῳ ἀγαλλομένην γλαυκώπιδος Ὀβριμοπάτρης·
θαῦμα δ' ἔχ' ἀθανάτους τε θεοὺς θνητούς τ'
    ἀνθρώπους,
ὡς εἶδον δόλον αἰπύν, ἀμήχανον ἀνθρώποισιν.

590 ἐκ τῆς γὰρ γένος ἐστὶ γυναικῶν θηλυτεράων,
τῆς γὰρ ὀλοίόν ἐστι γένος καὶ φῦλα γυναικῶν,
πῆμα μέγα θνητοῖσι, μετ' ἀνδράσι ναιετάουσαι,
οὐλομένης πενίης οὐ σύμφοροι, ἀλλὰ κόροιο.
ὡς δ' ὁπότ' ἐν σμήνεσσι κατηρεφέεσσι μέλισσαι

595 κηφῆνας βόσκωσι, κακῶν ξυνήονας ἔργων·
αἱ μέν τε πρόπαν ἦμαρ ἐς ἠέλιον καταδύντα
ἠμάτιαι σπεύδουσι τιθεῖσί τε κηρία λευκά,
οἱ δ' ἔντοσθε μένοντες ἐπηρεφέας κατὰ σίμβλους
ἀλλότριον κάματον σφετέρην ἐς γαστέρ' ἀμῶνται·

600 ὡς δ' αὔτως ἄνδρεσσι κακὸν θνητοῖσι γυναῖκας
Ζεὺς ὑψιβρεμέτης θῆκε, ξυνήονας ἔργων
ἀργαλέων. ἕτερον δὲ πόρεν κακὸν ἀντ' ἀγαθοῖο,
ὅς κε γάμον φεύγων καὶ μέρμερα ἔργα γυναικῶν
μὴ γῆμαι ἐθέλῃ, ὀλοὸν δ' ἐπὶ γῆρας ἵκηται

---

582 δεινα Π[13]: πολλὰ ak Etym.     590 damn. Heyne
591 om. Par. 2833, damn. Schoemann

were contrived many designs, highly wrought, a wonder to
see, all the terrible monsters the land and the sea nourish;
he put many of these into it, wondrous, similar to living an-
imals endowed with speech, and gracefulness breathed
upon them all.

(585) Then, when he had contrived this beautiful evil
thing in exchange for that good one,[31] he led her out to
where the other gods and the human beings were, while
she exulted in the adornment of the mighty father's bright-
eyed daughter[32]; and wonder gripped the immortal gods
and the mortal human beings when they saw the steep de-
ception, intractable for human beings. For from her comes
the race of female women: for of her is the deadly race and
tribe of women,[33] a great woe for mortals, dwelling with
men, no companions of baneful poverty but only of luxury.
As when bees in vaulted beehives nourish the drones, part-
ners in evil works—all day long until the sun goes down,
every day, the bees hasten and set up the white honey-
combs, while the drones remain inside among the vaulted
beehives and gather into their own stomachs the labor of
others—in just the same way high-thundering Zeus set up
women as an evil for mortal men, as partners in distressful
works. And he bestowed another evil thing in exchange for
that good one: whoever flees marriage and the dire works
of women and chooses not to marry arrives at deadly old

[31] Fire.    [32] Athena.

[33] Many editors consider the two preceding lines to be alter-
native versions of one another, and reject one or the other.

592 μετ' codd.: σὺν Stobaeus
597 ἡμάτιον b: ἀκάματοι Hermann (-αι Goettling)

605 χήτει γηροκόμοιο· ὁ δ' οὐ βιότου γ' ἐπιδευὴς
ζώει, ἀποφθιμένου δὲ διὰ ζωὴν δατέονται
χηρωσταί. ᾧ δ' αὖτε γάμου μετὰ μοῖρα γένηται,
κεδνὴν δ' ἔσχεν ἄκοιτιν, ἀρηρυῖαν πραπίδεσσι,
τῷ δέ τ' ἀπ' αἰῶνος κακὸν ἐσθλῷ ἀντιφερίζει
610 ἐμμενές· ὃς δέ κε τέτμῃ ἀταρτηροῖο γενέθλης,
ζώει ἐνὶ στήθεσσιν ἔχων ἀλίαστον ἀνίην
θυμῷ καὶ κραδίῃ, καὶ ἀνήκεστον κακόν ἐστιν.

    ὣς οὐκ ἔστι Διὸς κλέψαι νόον οὐδὲ παρελθεῖν.
οὐδὲ γὰρ Ἰαπετιονίδης ἀκάκητα Προμηθεὺς
615 τοῖό γ' ὑπεξήλυξε βαρὺν χόλον, ἀλλ' ὑπ' ἀνάγκης
καὶ πολύιδριν ἐόντα μέγας κατὰ δεσμὸς ἐρύκει.

    Ὀβριάρεῳ δ' ὡς πρῶτα πατὴρ ὠδύσσατο θυμῷ
Κόττῳ τ' ἠδὲ Γύγῃ, δῆσε κρατερῷ ἐνὶ δεσμῷ,
ἠνορέην ὑπέροπλον ἀγώμενος ἠδὲ καὶ εἶδος
620 καὶ μέγεθος· κατένασσε δ' ὑπὸ χθονὸς εὐρυοδείης.
ἔνθ' οἵ γ' ἄλγε' ἔχοντες ὑπὸ χθονὶ ναιετάοντες
εἵατ' ἐπ' ἐσχατιῇ μεγάλης ἐν πείρασι γαίης
δηθὰ μάλ' ἀχνύμενοι, κραδίῃ μέγα πένθος ἔχοντες.
ἀλλά σφεας Κρονίδης τε καὶ ἀθάνατοι θεοὶ ἄλλοι
625 οὓς τέκεν ἠύκομος Ῥείη Κρόνου ἐν φιλότητι
Γαίης φραδμοσύνῃσιν ἀνήγαγον ἐς φάος αὖτις·
αὐτὴ γάρ σφιν ἅπαντα διηνεκέως κατέλεξε,
σὺν κείνοις νίκην τε καὶ ἀγλαὸν εὖχος ἀρέσθαι.

606 ζωὴν Π14 k Stobaeus: κτῆσιν abS
610 ἔμμεναι codd., Σ: corr. Wopkens

52

age deprived of assistance; while he lives he does not lack the means of sustenance, but when he has died his distant relatives divide up his substance. On the other hand, that man to whom the portion of marriage falls as a share, and who acquires a cherished wife, well-fitted in her thoughts, for him evil is balanced continually with good during his whole life. But he who obtains the baneful species lives with incessant woe in his breast, in his spirit and heart, and his evil is incurable.

(613) Thus it is not possible to deceive or elude the mind of Zeus. For not even Iapetus' son, guileful[34] Prometheus, escaped his heavy wrath, but by necessity a great bond holds him down, shrewd though he be.

(617) When first their father[35] became angry in his spirit with Obriareus[36] and Cottus and Gyges, he bound them with a mighty bond, for he was indignant at their defiant manhood and their form and size; and he settled them under the broad-pathed earth. Dwelling there, under the earth, in pain, they sat at the edge, at the limits of the great earth, suffering greatly for a long time, with much grief in their hearts. But Cronus' son and the other immortal gods whom beautiful-haired Rhea bore in love with Cronus brought them back up to the light once again, by the prophecies of Earth: for she told the gods everything from beginning to end, that it was together with these that they would carry off victory and their splendid

[34] The meaning of this epithet, which is also applied to Hermes, is obscure.

[35] Sky.

[36] An alternative form for the name Briareus.

δηρὸν γὰρ μάρναντο πόνον θυμαλγέ' ἔχοντες
631 ἀντίον ἀλλήλοισι διὰ κρατερὰς ὑσμίνας
630 Τιτῆνές τε θεοὶ καὶ ὅσοι Κρόνου ἐξεγένοντο,
632 οἱ μὲν ἀφ' ὑψηλῆς Ὄθρυος Τιτῆνες ἀγαυοί,
οἱ δ' ἄρ' ἀπ' Οὐλύμποιο θεοὶ δωτῆρες ἐάων
οὓς τέκεν ἠύκομος Ῥείη Κρόνῳ εὐνηθεῖσα.
635 οἵ ῥα τότ' ἀλλήλοισιν ἄχη θυμαλγέ' ἔχοντες
συνεχέως ἐμάχοντο δέκα πλείους ἐνιαυτούς·
οὐδέ τις ἦν ἔριδος χαλεπῆς λύσις οὐδὲ τελευτὴ
οὐδετέροις, ἶσον δὲ τέλος τέτατο πτολέμοιο.
    ἀλλ' ὅτε δὴ κείνοισι παρέσχεθεν ἄρμενα πάντα,
640 νέκταρ τ' ἀμβροσίην τε, τά περ θεοὶ αὐτοὶ ἔδουσι,
πάντων <τ'> ἐν στήθεσσιν ἀέξετο θυμὸς ἀγήνωρ,
ὡς νέκταρ τ' ἐπάσαντο καὶ ἀμβροσίην ἐρατεινήν,
δὴ τότε τοῖς μετέειπε πατὴρ ἀνδρῶν τε θεῶν τε·
"κέκλυτέ μευ Γαίης τε καὶ Οὐρανοῦ ἀγλαὰ τέκνα,
645 ὄφρ' εἴπω τά με θυμὸς ἐνὶ στήθεσσι κελεύει.
ἤδη γὰρ μάλα δηρὸν ἐναντίοι ἀλλήλοισι
νίκης καὶ κάρτευς πέρι μαρνάμεθ' ἤματα πάντα,
Τιτῆνές τε θεοὶ καὶ ὅσοι Κρόνου ἐκγενόμεσθα.
ὑμεῖς δὲ μεγάλην τε βίην καὶ χεῖρας ἀάπτους
650 φαίνετε Τιτήνεσσιν ἐναντίον ἐν δαῒ λυγρῇ,
μνησάμενοι φιλότητος ἐνηέος, ὅσσα παθόντες
ἐς φάος ἂψ ἀφίκεσθε δυσηλεγέος ὑπὸ δεσμοῦ
ἡμετέρας διὰ βουλὰς ὑπὸ ζόφου ἠερόεντος."

631, 630 hoc ordine Π⁵, inverso codd.

54

vaunt. For they battled for a long time, their spirits pained
with toil, opposing one another in mighty combats, the Ti-
tan gods and all those who were born from Cronus—from
lofty Othrys the illustrious Titans, and from Olympus the
gods, the givers of good things, those whom beautiful-
haired Rhea bore after she had bedded with Cronus. They
battled continually with one another, their spirits pained
with distress, for ten full years; nor was there any resolu-
tion for their grievous strife nor an end for either side, but
the outcome of the war was evenly balanced.

(639) But when he had offered them[37] all things fitting,
nectar and ambrosia, which the gods themselves eat, and
in the breasts of them all their manly spirit was strength-
ened once they received nectar and lovely ambrosia, the
father of men and of gods spoke among them: "Listen to
me, splendid children of Earth and Sky, so that I can say
what the spirit in my breast bids me. We have already been
fighting every day for a very long time, facing one another
for the sake of victory and supremacy, the Titan gods and
all of us who were born from Cronus. So manifest your
great strength and your untouchable hands, facing the Ti-
tans in baleful conflict, mindful of our kind friendship,
how after so many sufferings you have come up to the light
once again out from under a deadly bond, by our plans, out
from under the murky gloom."

[37] Obriareus, Cottus, and Gyges.

---

635 μα]χην Π5au: μάχη||| K: χόλον r: πόνον Schoemann: -ν,
ἄχη Wieseler
642 ante 641 habet k, damn. Guyet
647 κα[ Π6: κράτεος codd.: κάρτευς West

ὣς φάτο· τὸν δ' αἶψ' αὖτις ἀμείβετο Κόττος
    ἀμύμων·
655 "δαιμόνι', οὐκ ἀδάητα πιφαύσκεαι, ἀλλὰ καὶ αὐτοὶ
    ἴδμεν ὅ τοι περὶ μὲν πραπίδες, περὶ δ' ἐστὶ νόημα,
    ἀλκτὴρ δ' ἀθανάτοισιν ἀρῆς γένεο κρυεροῖο,
    σῇσι δ' ἐπιφροσύνῃσιν ὑπὸ ζόφου ἠερόεντος
    ἄψορρον ἐξαῦτις ἀμειλίκτων ὑπὸ δεσμῶν
660 ἠλύθομεν, Κρόνου υἱὲ ἄναξ, ἀνάελπτα παθόντες.
    τῷ καὶ νῦν ἀτενεῖ τε νόῳ καὶ πρόφρονι θυμῷ
    ῥυσόμεθα κράτος ὑμὸν ἐν αἰνῇ δηιοτῆτι,
    μαρνάμενοι Τιτῆσιν ἀνὰ κρατερὰς ὑσμίνας."
    ὣς φάτ'· ἐπήνησαν δὲ θεοὶ δωτῆρες ἐάων
665 μῦθον ἀκούσαντες· πολέμου δ' ἐλιλαίετο θυμὸς
    μᾶλλον ἔτ' ἢ τὸ πάροιθε· μάχην δ' ἀμέγαρτον
        ἔγειραν
    πάντες, θήλειαί τε καὶ ἄρσενες, ἤματι κείνῳ,
    Τιτῆνές τε θεοὶ καὶ ὅσοι Κρόνου ἐξεγένοντο,
    οὕς τε Ζεὺς ἐρέβεσφιν ὑπὸ χθονὸς ἧκε φόωσδε,
670 δεινοί τε κρατεροί τε, βίην ὑπέροπλον ἔχοντες.
    τῶν ἑκατὸν μὲν χεῖρες ἀπ' ὤμων ἀίσσοντο
    πᾶσιν ὁμῶς, κεφαλαὶ δὲ ἑκάστῳ πεντήκοντα
    ἐξ ὤμων ἐπέφυκον ἐπὶ στιβαροῖσι μέλεσσιν.
    οἳ τότε Τιτήνεσσι κατέσταθεν ἐν δαῒ λυγρῇ
675 πέτρας ἠλιβάτους στιβαρῇς ἐν χερσὶν ἔχοντες·
    Τιτῆνες δ' ἑτέρωθεν ἐκαρτύναντο φάλαγγας
    προφρονέως· χειρῶν τε βίης θ' ἅμα ἔργον ἔφαινον
    ἀμφότεροι, δεινὸν δὲ περίαχε πόντος ἀπείρων,
    γῇ δὲ μέγ' ἐσμαράγησεν, ἐπέστενε δ' οὐρανὸς εὐρὺς

(654) So he spoke. And at once excellent Cottus answered him in turn: "Really, Sir, it is not something unknown you are telling us. We too know ourselves that your thoughts are supreme and your mind is supreme, and that you have revealed yourself as a protector for the immortals against chilly ruin. It is by your prudent plans that we have once again come back out from under the murky gloom, from implacable bonds—something, Lord, Cronus' son, that we no longer hoped to experience. For that reason, with ardent thought and eager spirit we in turn shall now rescue your supremacy in the dread battle-strife, fighting against the Titans in mighty combats."

(664) So he spoke, and the gods, the givers of good things, praised his speech when they heard it. Their spirit craved war even more than before, and they all roused up dismal battle, the females and the males, on that day, both the Titan gods and those who were born from Cronus, and those whom Zeus sent up towards the light from Erebus, out from under the earth, terrible and mighty, with defiant strength. A hundred arms sprang forth from their shoulders, in the same way for all of them, and upon their massive limbs grew fifty heads out of each one's shoulders. They took up their positions against the Titans in baleful conflict, holding enormous boulders in their massive hands; and on the other side the Titans zealously reinforced their battle-ranks. Both sides manifested the deed of hands and of strength together. The boundless ocean echoed terribly around them, and the great earth crashed, and the broad sky groaned in response as it was shaken,

---

661 ]φρονι θυμω[ Π[13], unde πρόφρονι θ. West: ἐπίφρονι βουλῇ codd.

680  σειόμενος, πεδόθεν δὲ τινάσσετο μακρὸς Ὄλυμπος
ῥιπῇ ὑπ᾽ ἀθανάτων, ἔνοσις δ᾽ ἵκανε βαρεῖα
τάρταρον ἠερόεντα ποδῶν αἰπεῖά τ᾽ ἰωὴ
ἀσπέτου ἰωχμοῖο βολάων τε κρατεράων.
ὣς ἄρ᾽ ἐπ᾽ ἀλλήλοις ἵεσαν βέλεα στονόεντα·
685  φωνὴ δ᾽ ἀμφοτέρων ἵκετ᾽ οὐρανὸν ἀστερόεντα
κεκλομένων· οἱ δὲ ξύνισαν μεγάλῳ ἀλαλητῷ.

οὐδ᾽ ἄρ᾽ ἔτι Ζεὺς ἴσχεν ἑὸν μένος, ἀλλά νυ τοῦ γε
εἶθαρ μὲν μένεος πλῆντο φρένες, ἐκ δέ τε πᾶσαν
φαῖνε βίην· ἄμυδις δ᾽ ἄρ᾽ ἀπ᾽ οὐρανοῦ ἠδ᾽ ἀπ᾽
Ὀλύμπου
690  ἀστράπτων ἔστειχε συνωχαδόν, οἱ δὲ κεραυνοὶ
ἴκταρ ἅμα βροντῇ τε καὶ ἀστεροπῇ ποτέοντο
χειρὸς ἄπο στιβαρῆς, ἱερὴν φλόγα εἰλυφόωντες,
ταρφέες· ἀμφὶ δὲ γαῖα φερέσβιος ἐσμαράγιζε
καιομένη, λάκε δ᾽ ἀμφὶ περὶ μεγάλ᾽ ἄσπετος ὕλη·
695  ἔζεε δὲ χθὼν πᾶσα καὶ Ὠκεανοῖο ῥέεθρα
πόντός τ᾽ ἀτρύγετος· τοὺς δ᾽ ἄμφεπε θερμὸς ἀυτμὴ
Τιτῆνας χθονίους, φλὸξ δ᾽ αἰθέρα δῖαν ἵκανεν
ἄσπετος, ὄσσε δ᾽ ἄμερδε καὶ ἰφθίμων περ ἐόντων
αὐγὴ μαρμαίρουσα κεραυνοῦ τε στεροπῆς τε.
700  καῦμα δὲ θεσπέσιον κάτεχεν Χάος· εἴσατο δ᾽ ἄντα
ὀφθαλμοῖσιν ἰδεῖν ἠδ᾽ οὔασιν ὄσσαν ἀκοῦσαι
αὔτως, ὡς ὅτε Γαῖα καὶ Οὐρανὸς εὐρὺς ὕπερθε
πίλνατο· τοῖος γάρ κε μέγας ὑπὸ δοῦπος ὀρώρει,

694 περὶ West: πυρὶ Π²⁹ codd.
697 αἰθέρα Naber: ἠέρα codd. Σ

and high Olympus trembled from its very bottom under the rush of the immortals, and a deep shuddering from their feet reached murky Tartarus, and the shrill sound of the immense charge and of the mighty casts. And in this way they hurled their painful shafts against one another; and the noise of both sides reached the starry sky as they shouted encouragement, and they ran towards one another with a great war-cry.

(687) Then Zeus no longer held back his strength, but at once his breast was filled with strength and he manifested his full force. He strode at the same time from the sky and from Olympus, relentlessly hurling lightning bolts, and the thunderbolts, driving forward a sacred flame, flew densely packed, together with the thunder and lightning, all at once from his massive hand. All around, the life-giving earth roared as it burned, and all around the great immense forest crackled; the whole earth boiled, and the streams of Ocean and the barren sea. The hot blast encompassed the earthly Titans, and an immense blaze reached the divine aether, and the brilliant gleam of the lightning bolt and flash blinded their eyes, powerful though they were. A prodigious conflagration took possession of Chasm; and to look upon it with eyes and to hear its sound with ears, it seemed just as when Earth and broad Sky approached from above:[38] for this was the kind of great sound

[38] Despite some uncertainty about the Greek text, the meaning is clear: the analogy is not to some cataclysmic final collapse of the sky onto the earth, but instead to the primordial sexual union between Sky and Earth.

703 πίλναντο a

τῆς μὲν ἐρειπομένης, τοῦ δ' ὑψόθεν ἐξεριπόντος·
705 τόσσος δοῦπος ἔγεντο θεῶν ἔριδι ξυνιόντων.
σὺν δ' ἄνεμοι ἔνοσίν τε κονίην τ' ἐσφαράγιζον
βροντήν τε στεροπήν τε καὶ αἰθαλόεντα κεραυνόν,
κῆλα Διὸς μεγάλοιο, φέρον δ' ἰαχήν τ' ἐνοπήν τε
ἐς μέσον ἀμφοτέρων· ὄτοβος δ' ἄπλητος ὀρώρει
710 σμερδαλέης ἔριδος, κάρτευς δ' ἀνεφαίνετο ἔργον.
    ἐκλίνθη δὲ μάχη· πρὶν δ' ἀλλήλοις ἐπέχοντες
ἐμμενέως ἐμάχοντο διὰ κρατερὰς ὑσμίνας.
οἱ δ' ἄρ' ἐνὶ πρώτοισι μάχην δριμεῖαν ἔγειραν,
Κόττος τε Βριάρεώς τε Γύγης τ' ἄατος πολέμοιο·
715 οἵ ῥα τριηκοσίας πέτρας στιβαρέων ἀπὸ χειρῶν
πέμπον ἐπασσυτέρας, κατὰ δ' ἐσκίασαν βελέεσσι
Τιτῆνας· καὶ τοὺς μὲν ὑπὸ χθονὸς εὐρυοδείης
πέμψαν καὶ δεσμοῖσιν ἐν ἀργαλέοισιν ἔδησαν,
νικήσαντες χερσὶν ὑπερθύμους περ ἐόντας,
720 τόσσον ἔνερθ' ὑπὸ γῆς ὅσον οὐρανός ἐστ' ἀπὸ γαίης.

    τόσσον γάρ τ' ἀπὸ γῆς ἐς τάρταρον ἠερόεντα.
ἐννέα γὰρ νύκτας τε καὶ ἤματα χάλκεος ἄκμων
οὐρανόθεν κατιών, δεκάτῃ κ' ἐς γαῖαν ἵκοιτο·
723a [ἶσον δ' αὖτ' ἀπὸ γῆς ἐς τάρταρον ἠερόεντα·]
    ἐννέα δ' αὖ νύκτας τε καὶ ἤματα χάλκεος ἄκμων
725 ἐκ γαίης κατιών, δεκάτῃ κ' ἐς τάρταρον ἵκοι.

    710 κάρτευς . . . ἔργον West: κάρτος . . . ἔργ|γων Π19, codd.
    720–819 interpolatoribus pluribus trib. L. Dindorf, Her-
mann, alii

that would rise up as she was pressed down and as he pressed her down from on high—so great a sound was produced as the gods ran together in strife. At the same time, the winds noisily stirred up shuddering and dust and thunder and lightning and the blazing thunderbolt, the shafts of great Zeus, and they brought shouting and screaming into the middle between both sides. A dreadful din of terrifying strife rose up, and the deed of supremacy was made manifest.

(711) And the battle inclined to one side. For earlier, advancing against one another they had battled incessantly in mighty combats. But then among the foremost Cottus and Briareus and Gyges, insatiable of war, roused up bitter battle; and they hurled three hundred boulders from their massive hands one after another and overshadowed the Titans with their missiles. They sent them down under the broad-pathed earth and bound them in distressful bonds after they had gained victory over them with their hands, high-spirited though they were, as far down beneath the earth as the sky is above the earth.

(721) For it is just as far from the earth to murky Tartarus: for a bronze anvil, falling down from the sky for nine nights and days, on the tenth day would arrive at the earth; [and in turn it is the same distance from the earth to murky Tartarus;][39] and again, a bronze anvil, falling down from the earth for nine nights and days, on the tenth would

[39] This line is rejected as an interpolation by many editors.

___

723a om. (sed verbis suis reddit) *Isagoge in Aratum*

τὸν πέρι χάλκεον ἕρκος ἐλήλαται· ἀμφὶ δέ μιν νὺξ
τριστοιχὶ κέχυται περὶ δειρήν· αὐτὰρ ὕπερθε
γῆς ῥίζαι πεφύασι καὶ ἀτρυγέτοιο θαλάσσης.
ἔνθα θεοὶ Τιτῆνες ὑπὸ ζόφῳ ἠερόεντι
730 κεκρύφαται βουλῇσι Διὸς νεφεληγερέταο,
χώρῳ ἐν εὐρώεντι, πελώρης ἔσχατα γαίης.
τοῖς οὐκ ἐξιτόν ἐστι, θύρας δ' ἐπέθηκε Ποσειδέων
χαλκείας, τεῖχος δ' ἐπελήλαται ἀμφοτέρωθεν.
ἔνθα Γύγης Κόττος τε καὶ Ὀβριάρεως
μεγάθυμος
735 ναίουσιν, φύλακες πιστοὶ Διὸς αἰγιόχοιο.
ἔνθα δὲ γῆς δνοφερῆς καὶ Ταρτάρου ἠερόεντος
πόντου τ' ἀτρυγέτοιο καὶ οὐρανοῦ ἀστερόεντος
ἐξείης πάντων πηγαὶ καὶ πείρατ' ἔασιν,
ἀργαλέ' εὐρώεντα, τά τε στυγέουσι θεοί περ·
740 χάσμα μέγ', οὐδέ κε πάντα τελεσφόρον εἰς ἐνιαυτὸν
οὖδας ἵκοιτ', εἰ πρῶτα πυλέων ἔντοσθε γένοιτο,
ἀλλά κεν ἔνθα καὶ ἔνθα φέροι πρὸ θύελλα θυέλλης
ἀργαλέη· δεινὸν δὲ καὶ ἀθανάτοισι θεοῖσι
τοῦτο τέρας· καὶ Νυκτὸς ἐρεμνῆς οἰκία δεινὰ
745 ἕστηκεν νεφέλης κεκαλυμμένα κυανέῃσι.
τῶν πρόσθ' Ἰαπετοῖο πάις ἔχει οὐρανὸν εὐρὺν
ἑστηὼς κεφαλῇ τε καὶ ἀκαμάτῃσι χέρεσσιν
ἀστεμφέως, ὅθι Νύξ τε καὶ Ἡμέρη ἆσσον ἰοῦσαι
ἀλλήλας προσέειπον ἀμειβόμεναι μέγαν οὐδὸν
750 χάλκεον· ἡ μὲν ἔσω καταβήσεται, ἡ δὲ θύραζε

731 ἔσχατα Π¹⁹Π³⁰ a: κεύθεσι k

arrive at Tartarus. Around this a bronze barricade is extended, and on both sides of it night is poured out threefold around its neck; and above it grow the roots of the earth and of the barren sea.

(729) That is where the Titan gods are hidden under murky gloom by the plans of the cloud-gatherer Zeus, in a dank place, at the farthest part of huge earth. They cannot get out, for Poseidon has set bronze gates upon it, and a wall is extended on both sides.

(734) That is where Gyges, Cottus, and great-spirited Obriareus dwell, the trusted guards of aegis-holding Zeus.

(736) That is where the sources and limits of the dark earth are, and of murky Tartarus, of the barren sea, and of the starry sky, of everything, one after another, distressful, dank, things which even the gods hate: a great chasm, whose bottom one would not reach in a whole long year, once one was inside the gates, but one would be borne hither and thither by one distressful blast after another—it is terrible for the immortal gods as well, this monstrosity; and the terrible houses of dark Night stand here, shrouded in black clouds.

(746) In front of these, Iapetus' son[40] holds the broad sky with his head and tireless hands, standing immovable, where Night and Day passing near greet one another as they cross the great bronze threshold. The one is about to go in and the other is going out the door, and never does

[40] Atlas.

---

734–45 secl. West
742 θυέλλης Wakefield: θυέλλη Π²⁸ codd.

ἔρχεται, οὐδέ ποτ' ἀμφοτέρας δόμος ἐντὸς ἐέργει,
ἀλλ' αἰεὶ ἑτέρη γε δόμων ἔκτοσθεν ἐοῦσα
γαῖαν ἐπιστρέφεται, ἡ δ' αὖ δόμου ἐντὸς ἐοῦσα
μίμνει τὴν αὑτῆς ὥρην ὁδοῦ, ἔστ' ἂν ἵκηται·
755  ἡ μὲν ἐπιχθονίοισι φάος πολυδερκὲς ἔχουσα,
ἡ δ' Ὕπνον μετὰ χερσί, κασίγνητον Θανάτοιο,
Νὺξ ὀλοή, νεφέλῃ κεκαλυμμένη ἠεροειδεῖ.

ἔνθα δὲ Νυκτὸς παῖδες ἐρεμνῆς οἰκί' ἔχουσιν,
Ὕπνος καὶ Θάνατος, δεινοὶ θεοί· οὐδέ ποτ' αὐτοὺς
760  Ἥλιος φαέθων ἐπιδέρκεται ἀκτίνεσσιν
οὐρανὸν εἰσανιὼν οὐδ' οὐρανόθεν καταβαίνων.
τῶν ἕτερος μὲν γῆν τε καὶ εὐρέα νῶτα θαλάσσης
ἥσυχος ἀνστρέφεται καὶ μείλιχος ἀνθρώποισι,
τοῦ δὲ σιδηρέη μὲν κραδίη, χάλκεον δέ οἱ ἦτορ
765  νηλεὲς ἐν στήθεσσιν· ἔχει δ' ὃν πρῶτα λάβῃσιν
ἀνθρώπων· ἐχθρὸς δὲ καὶ ἀθανάτοισι θεοῖσιν.

ἔνθα θεοῦ χθονίου πρόσθεν δόμοι ἠχήεντες
ἰφθίμου τ' Ἀίδεω καὶ ἐπαινῆς Περσεφονείης
ἑστᾶσιν, δεινὸς δὲ κύων προπάροιθε φυλάσσει,
770  νηλειής, τέχνην δὲ κακὴν ἔχει· ἐς μὲν ἰόντας
σαίνει ὁμῶς οὐρῇ τε καὶ οὔασιν ἀμφοτέροισιν,
ἐξελθεῖν δ' οὐκ αὖτις ἐᾷ πάλιν, ἀλλὰ δοκεύων
ἐσθίει, ὅν κε λάβῃσι πυλέων ἔκτοσθεν ἰόντα.
ἰφθίμου τ' Ἀίδεω καὶ ἐπαινῆς Περσεφονείης.
775  ἔνθα δὲ ναιετάει στυγερὴ θεὸς ἀθανάτοισι,
δεινὴ Στύξ, θυγάτηρ ἀψορρόου Ὠκεανοῖο

768 om. Π²⁹, Par. 2772: susp. Wolf

the house hold them both inside, but always the one goes out from the house and passes over the earth, while the other in turn remaining inside the house waits for the time of her own departure, until it comes. The one holds much-seeing light for those on the earth, but the other holds Sleep in her hands, the brother of Death—deadly Night, shrouded in murky cloud.

(758) That is where the children of dark Night have their houses, Sleep and Death, terrible gods; never does the bright Sun look upon them with his rays when he goes up into the sky nor when he comes back down from the sky. One of them passes gently over the earth and the broad back of the sea and is soothing for human beings. But the other one's temper is of iron, and the bronze heart in his chest is pitiless: once he takes hold of any human, he owns him; and he is hateful even for the immortal gods.

(767) That is where, in front, stand the echoing houses of the earthly god, of powerful Hades and of dread Persephone, and a terrible dog guards them in front, pitiless. He has an evil trick: upon those going in he fawns alike with his tail and with both ears, but he does not let them leave again: instead, observing them closely he devours whomever he catches trying to go out from the gates of powerful Hades and dread Persephone.

(775) That is where the goddess dwells who is loathsome for the immortals, terrible Styx,[41] the oldest daugh-

---

[41] Hesiod connects the name Styx with her being loathsome, στυγερή, to the gods.

774 habet *r*, om. *ak*

πρεσβυτάτη· νόσφιν δὲ θεῶν κλυτὰ δώματα ναίει
μακρῇσιν πέτρῃσι κατηρεφέ· ἀμφὶ δὲ πάντῃ
κίοσιν ἀργυρέοισι πρὸς οὐρανὸν ἐστήρικται.
780 παῦρα δὲ Θαύμαντος θυγάτηρ πόδας ὠκέα Ἶρις
ἀγγελίη πωλεῖται ἐπ' εὐρέα νῶτα θαλάσσης.
ὁππότ' ἔρις καὶ νεῖκος ἐν ἀθανάτοισιν ὄρηται,
καί ῥ' ὅστις ψεύδηται Ὀλύμπια δώματ' ἐχόντων,
Ζεὺς δέ τε Ἶριν ἔπεμψε θεῶν μέγαν ὅρκον ἐνεῖκαι
785 τηλόθεν ἐν χρυσέῃ προχόῳ πολυώνυμον ὕδωρ,
ψυχρόν, ὅ τ' ἐκ πέτρης καταλείβεται ἠλιβάτοιο
ὑψηλῆς· πολλὸν δὲ ὑπὸ χθονὸς εὐρυοδείης
ἐξ ἱεροῦ ποταμοῖο ῥέει διὰ νύκτα μέλαιναν·
Ὠκεανοῖο κέρας, δεκάτη δ' ἐπὶ μοῖρα δέδασται·
790 ἐννέα μὲν περὶ γῆν τε καὶ εὐρέα νῶτα θαλάσσης
δίνῃς ἀργυρέῃς εἱλιγμένος εἰς ἅλα πίπτει,
ἡ δὲ μί' ἐκ πέτρης προρέει, μέγα πῆμα θεοῖσιν.
ὅς κεν τὴν ἐπίορκον ἀπολλείψας ἐπομόσσῃ
ἀθανάτων οἳ ἔχουσι κάρη νιφόεντος Ὀλύμπου,
795 κεῖται νήυτμος τετελεσμένον εἰς ἐνιαυτόν·
οὐδέ ποτ' ἀμβροσίης καὶ νέκταρος ἔρχεται ἆσσον
βρώσιος, ἀλλά τε κεῖται ἀνάπνευστος καὶ ἄναυδος
στρωτοῖς ἐν λεχέεσσι, κακὸν δ' ἐπὶ κῶμα καλύπτει.
αὐτὰρ ἐπὴν νοῦσον τελέσει μέγαν εἰς ἐνιαυτόν,
800 ἄλλος δ' ἐξ ἄλλου δέχεται χαλεπώτερος ἆθλος·
εἰνάετες δὲ θεῶν ἀπαμείρεται αἰὲν ἐόντων,
οὐδέ ποτ' ἐς βουλὴν ἐπιμίσγεται οὐδ' ἐπὶ δαῖτας
ἐννέα πάντ' ἔτεα· δεκάτῳ δ' ἐπιμίσγεται αὖτις

ter of backward-flowing Ocean. She lives apart from the gods in a famous mansion vaulted with great crags; it is set fast upon silver pillars on every side reaching towards the sky all around. Seldom does Thaumas' daughter, swift-footed Iris, travel to her with a message upon the broad back of the sea: whenever strife and quarrel arise among the immortals and one of those who have their mansions on Olympus tells a lie, Zeus sends Iris to bring from afar in a golden jug the great oath of the gods, the much-renowned water, icy, which pours down from a great, lofty crag. It flows abundantly from under the broad-pathed earth, from the holy river through the black night—a branch of Ocean, and a tenth portion has been assigned to her. For nine-fold around the earth and the broad back of the sea he whirls in silver eddies and falls into the sea, and she as one portion flows forth from the crag, a great woe for the gods. For whoever of the immortals, who possess the peak of snowy Olympus, swears a false oath after having poured a libation from her, he lies breathless for one full year; and he does not go near to ambrosia and nectar for nourishment, but lies there without breath and without voice on a covered bed, and an evil stupor shrouds him. And when he has completed this sickness for a long year, another, even worse trial follows upon this one: for nine years he is cut off from participation with the gods that always are, nor does he mingle with them in their assembly or their feasts for all of nine years; but in the tenth he mingles once again in the meetings of the immortals who have

---

781 ἀγγελίη Guyet: -ίη Π⁵?a Δ: ἀγγελίην Scorial. Φ III 16: -ίης U² Vat. 2185m²: -ίης Stephanus

εἴρας ἐς ἀθανάτων οἳ Ὀλύμπια δώματ' ἔχουσι.
805 τοῖον ἄρ' ὅρκον ἔθεντο θεοὶ Στυγὸς ἄφθιτον ὕδωρ,
ὠγύγιον· τὸ δ' ἵησι καταστυφέλου διὰ χώρου.
ἔνθα δὲ γῆς δνοφερῆς καὶ ταρτάρου ἠερόεντος
πόντου τ' ἀτρυγέτοιο καὶ οὐρανοῦ ἀστερόεντος
ἑξείης πάντων πηγαὶ καὶ πείρατ' ἔασιν,
810 ἀργαλέ' εὐρώεντα, τά τε στυγέουσι θεοί περ.

ἔνθα δὲ μαρμάρεαί τε πύλαι καὶ χάλκεος οὐδός,
ἀστεμφὲς ῥίζῃσι διηνεκέεσσιν ἀρηρώς,
αὐτοφυής· πρόσθεν δὲ θεῶν ἔκτοσθεν ἁπάντων
Τιτῆνες ναίουσι, πέρην χάεος ζοφεροῖο.
815 αὐτὰρ ἐρισμαράγοιο Διὸς κλειτοὶ ἐπίκουροι
δώματα ναιετάουσιν ἐπ' Ὠκεανοῖο θεμέθλοις,
Κόττος τ' ἠδὲ Γύγης· Βριάρεών γε μὲν ἠὺν ἐόντα
γαμβρὸν ἑὸν ποίησε βαρύκτυπος Ἐννοσίγαιος,
δῶκε δὲ Κυμοπόλειαν ὀπυίειν, θυγατέρα ἥν.

820 αὐτὰρ ἐπεὶ Τιτῆνας ἀπ' οὐρανοῦ ἐξέλασε Ζεύς,
ὁπλότατον τέκε παῖδα Τυφωέα Γαῖα πελώρη
Ταρτάρου ἐν φιλότητι διὰ χρυσῆν Ἀφροδίτην·
οὗ χεῖρες †μὲν ἔασιν ἐπ' ἰσχύι ἔργματ' ἔχουσαι,†
καὶ πόδες ἀκάματοι κρατεροῦ θεοῦ· ἐκ δέ οἱ ὤμων
825 ἦν ἑκατὸν κεφαλαὶ ὄφιος δεινοῖο δράκοντος,
γλώσσῃσι δνοφερῇσι λελιχμότες· ἐκ δέ οἱ ὄσσων
θεσπεσίης κεφαλῇσιν ὑπ' ὀφρύσι πῦρ ἀμάρυσσεν·
πασέων δ' ἐκ κεφαλέων πῦρ καίετο δερκομένοιο·

804 εἴρας ἐς Hermann: εἰρέας codd.: εἴραις Ruhnken

their mansions on Olympus. It is as this sort of oath that the gods have established the eternal water of Styx, primeval; and it pours out through a rugged place.

(807) That is where the sources and limits of the dark earth are, and of murky Tartarus, of the barren sea, and of the starry sky, of everything, one after another, distressful, dank, things which even the gods hate.

(811) That is where the marble gates are and the bronze threshold, fitted together immovably upon continuous roots, self-generated; and in front, apart from all the gods, live the Titans, on the far side of the gloomy chasm. The celebrated helpers of loud-thundering Zeus live in mansions upon the foundations of Ocean, Cottus and Gyges; but the deep-sounding Earth-shaker made Briareus, since he was good, his son-in-law, and he gave him Cymopolea, his daughter, to wed.

(820) When Zeus had driven the Titans from the sky, huge Earth bore as her youngest son Typhoeus, in love with Tartarus, because of golden Aphrodite. His hands †are holding deeds upon strength,†[42] and tireless the strong god's feet; and from his shoulders there were a hundred heads of a snake, a terrible dragon's, licking with their dark tongues; and on his prodigious heads fire sparkled from his eyes under the eyebrows, and from all of his heads

---

[42] Line 823 seems to be corrupt; no convincing defense or remedy for it has yet been found.

---

826 ἐκ δέ οἱ ὄσσων fere codd.: ἐν δέ οἱ ὄσσε West
828 damn. Ruhnken

φωναὶ δ᾽ ἐν πάσῃσιν ἔσαν δεινῆς κεφαλῇσι,
830 παντοίην ὄπ᾽ ἰεῖσαι ἀθέσφατον· ἄλλοτε μὲν γὰρ
φθέγγονθ᾽ ὥς τε θεοῖσι συνιέμεν, ἄλλοτε δ᾽ αὖτε
ταύρου ἐριβρύχεω μένος ἀσχέτου ὄσσαν ἀγαύρου,
ἄλλοτε δ᾽ αὖτε λέοντος ἀναιδέα θυμὸν ἔχοντος,
ἄλλοτε δ᾽ αὖ σκυλάκεσσιν ἐοικότα, θαύματ᾽ ἀκοῦσαι,
835 ἄλλοτε δ᾽ αὖ ῥοίζεσχ᾽, ὑπὸ δ᾽ ἤχεεν οὔρεα μακρά.
καί νύ κεν ἔπλετο ἔργον ἀμήχανον ἤματι κείνῳ,
καί κεν ὅ γε θνητοῖσι καὶ ἀθανάτοισιν ἄναξεν,
εἰ μὴ ἄρ᾽ ὀξὺ νόησε πατὴρ ἀνδρῶν τε θεῶν τε·
σκληρὸν δ᾽ ἐβρόντησε καὶ ὄβριμον, ἀμφὶ δὲ γαῖα
840 σμερδαλέον κονάβησε καὶ οὐρανὸς εὐρὺς ὕπερθε
πόντός τ᾽ Ὠκεανοῦ τε ῥοαὶ καὶ Τάρταρα γαίης.
ποσσὶ δ᾽ ὕπ᾽ ἀθανάτοισι μέγας πελεμίζετ᾽ Ὄλυμπος
ὀρνυμένοιο ἄνακτος· ἐπεστονάχιζε δὲ γαῖα.
καῦμα δ᾽ ὑπ᾽ ἀμφοτέρων κάτεχεν ἰοειδέα πόντον
845 βροντῆς τε στεροπῆς τε πυρός τ᾽ ἀπὸ τοῖο πελώρου
πρηστήρων ἀνέμων τε κεραυνοῦ τε φλεγέθοντος·
ἔζεε δὲ χθὼν πᾶσα καὶ οὐρανὸς ἠδὲ θάλασσα·
θυῖε δ᾽ ἄρ᾽ ἀμφ᾽ ἀκτὰς περί τ᾽ ἀμφί τε κύματα μακρὰ
ῥιπῇ ὕπ᾽ ἀθανάτων, ἔνοσις δ᾽ ἄσβεστος ὀρώρει·
850 τρέε δ᾽ Ἀίδης ἐνέροισι καταφθιμένοισιν ἀνάσσων
Τιτῆνές θ᾽ ὑποταρτάριοι Κρόνον ἀμφὶς ἐόντες
ἀσβέστου κελάδοιο καὶ αἰνῆς δηιοτῆτος.
    Ζεὺς δ᾽ ἐπεὶ οὖν κόρθυνεν ἑὸν μένος, εἵλετο δ᾽
        ὅπλα,

832 ἄσχετον codd.: corr. Winterton

fire burned as he glared. And there were voices in all his terrible heads, sending forth all kinds of sounds, inconceivable: for sometimes they would utter sounds as though for the gods to understand, and at other times the sound of a loud-bellowing, majestic bull, unstoppable in its strength, at other times that of a lion, with a ruthless spirit, at other times like young dogs, a wonder to hear, and at other times he hissed, and the high mountains echoed from below. And on that very day an intractable deed would have been accomplished, and he would have ruled over mortals and immortals, if the father of men and of gods had not taken sharp notice: he thundered hard and strong, and all around the earth echoed terrifyingly, and the broad sky above, and the sea, and the streams of Ocean, and Tartarus in the earth. As the lord rushed forward, great Olympus trembled under his immortal feet, and the earth groaned in response. The violet-dark sea was enveloped by a conflagration from both of them—of thunder and lightning, and fire from that monster of typhoons and winds, and the blazing thunder-bolt. And all the earth seethed, and the sky and sea; and long waves raged around the shores, around and about, under the rush of the immortals, and an inextinguishable shuddering arose. And Hades, who rules over the dead below, was afraid, and the Titans under Tartarus, gathered around Cronus, at the inextinguishable din and dread battle-strife.

(853) Then when Zeus had lifted up his strength and grasped his weapons, the thunder and lightning and the

---

846 exp. Heyne
852 damn. Hermann: habent $\Pi^{12}\Pi^{15}\Pi^{31}$

βροντήν τε στεροπήν τε καὶ αἰθαλόεντα κεραυνόν,
855 πλῆξεν ἀπ' Οὐλύμποιο ἐπάλμενος· ἀμφὶ δὲ πάσας
ἔπρεσε θεσπεσίας κεφαλὰς δεινοῖο πελώρου.
αὐτὰρ ἐπεὶ δή μιν δάμασε πληγῇσιν ἱμάσσας,
ἤριπε γυιωθείς, στονάχιζε δὲ γαῖα πελώρη·
φλὸξ δὲ κεραυνωθέντος ἀπέσσυτο τοῖο ἄνακτος
860 οὔρεος ἐν βήσσῃσιν ἀιδνῆς παιπαλοέσσης
πληγέντος, πολλὴ δὲ πελώρη καίετο γαῖα
αὐτμῇ θεσπεσίῃ, καὶ ἐτήκετο κασσίτερος ὣς
τέχνῃ ὑπ' αἰζηῶν ἐν ἐυτρήτοις χοάνοισι
θαλφθείς, ἠὲ σίδηρος, ὅ περ κρατερώτατός ἐστιν,
865 οὔρεος ἐν βήσσῃσι δαμαζόμενος πυρὶ κηλέῳ
τήκεται ἐν χθονὶ δίῃ ὑφ' Ἡφαίστου παλάμῃσιν·
ὣς ἄρα τήκετο γαῖα σέλαι πυρὸς αἰθομένοιο.
ῥῖψε δέ μιν θυμῷ ἀκαχὼν ἐς τάρταρον εὐρύν.

ἐκ δὲ Τυφωέος ἔστ' ἀνέμων μένος ὑγρὸν ἀέντων,
870 νόσφι Νότου Βορέω τε καὶ ἀργεστέω Ζεφύροιο·
οἵ γε μὲν ἐκ θεόφιν γενεήν, θνητοῖς μέγ' ὄνειαρ.
αἱ δ' ἄλλαι μὰψ αὖραι ἐπιπνείουσι θάλασσαν·
αἱ δή τοι πίπτουσαι ἐς ἠεροειδέα πόντον,
πῆμα μέγα θνητοῖσι, κακῇ θυίουσιν ἀέλλῃ·
875 ἄλλοτε δ' ἄλλαι ἄεισι διασκιδνᾶσί τε νῆας
ναύτας τε φθείρουσι· κακοῦ δ' οὐ γίνεται ἀλκὴ
ἀνδράσιν, οἳ κείνῃσι συνάντωνται κατὰ πόντον.
αἱ δ' αὖ καὶ κατὰ γαῖαν ἀπείριτον ἀνθεμόεσσαν
ἔργ' ἐρατὰ φθείρουσι χαμαιγενέων ἀνθρώπων,
880 πιμπλεῖσαι κόνιός τε καὶ ἀργαλέου κολοσυρτοῦ.

blazing thunderbolt, he struck him, leaping upon him from Olympus; and all around he scorched all the prodigious heads of the terrible monster. And when he had overpowered him, scourging him with blows, he fell down lamed, and the huge earth groaned; a flame shot forth from that thunderbolted lord in the mountain's dark, rugged dales, as he was struck, and the huge earth was much burned by the prodigious blast, and it melted like tin when it is heated with skill by young men in well-perforated melting-pots, or as iron, although it is the strongest thing, melts in the divine earth by the skilled hands of Hephaestus when it is overpowered in a mountain's dales by burning fire. In the same way, the earth melted in the blaze of the burning fire. And he hurled Typhoeus into broad Tartarus, grieving him in his spirit.

(869) From Typhoeus comes the strength of moist-blowing winds—apart from Notus and Boreas and clear Zephyrus, for these are from the gods by descent, a great boon for mortals. But the other breezes blow at random upon the sea: falling upon the murky sea, a great woe for mortals, they rage with an evil blast; they blow now one way, now another, and scatter the boats, and destroy the sailors; and there is no safeguard against this evil for men who encounter them upon the sea. And on the boundless, flowering earth too, they destroy the lovely works of earth-born human beings, filling them with dust and with distressful confusion.

---

860 ἀϊδνῆς vel –ῆς Π12akΣ Etym.: Ἀϊδνῆς Wilamowitz: ἀϊτνῆς anon. in ed. Iunt. exempl. Bodl.: Αἴτνης Tzetzes v. l., qui Aetnam utique intellexit
874 θύουσι(ν) codd.: πνείουσ[ι Π15

αὐτὰρ ἐπεί ῥα πόνον μάκαρες θεοὶ ἐξετέλεσσαν,
Τιτήνεσσι δὲ τιμάων κρίναντο βίηφι,
δή ῥα τότ' ὤτρυνον βασιλευέμεν ἠδὲ ἀνάσσειν
Γαίης φραδμοσύνῃσιν Ὀλύμπιον εὐρύοπα Ζῆν
885 ἀθανάτων· ὁ δὲ τοῖσιν ἐὺ διεδάσσατο τιμάς.
    Ζεὺς δὲ θεῶν βασιλεὺς πρώτην ἄλοχον θέτο
        Μῆτιν,
πλεῖστα θεῶν εἰδυῖαν ἰδὲ θνητῶν ἀνθρώπων.
ἀλλ' ὅτε δὴ ἄρ' ἔμελλε θεὰν γλαυκῶπιν Ἀθήνην
τέξεσθαι, τότ' ἔπειτα δόλῳ φρένας ἐξαπατήσας
890 αἱμυλίοισι λόγοισιν ἑὴν ἐσκάτθετο νηδύν,
Γαίης φραδμοσύνῃσι καὶ Οὐρανοῦ ἀστερόεντος·
τὼς γάρ οἱ φρασάτην, ἵνα μὴ βασιληίδα τιμὴν
ἄλλος ἔχοι Διὸς ἀντὶ θεῶν αἰειγενετάων.
ἐκ γὰρ τῆς εἵμαρτο περίφρονα τέκνα γενέσθαι·
895 πρώτην μὲν κούρην γλαυκώπιδα Τριτογένειαν,
ἶσον ἔχουσαν πατρὶ μένος καὶ ἐπίφρονα βουλήν,
αὐτὰρ ἔπειτ' ἄρα παῖδα θεῶν βασιλῆα καὶ ἀνδρῶν
ἤμελλεν τέξεσθαι, ὑπέρβιον ἦτορ ἔχοντα·
ἀλλ' ἄρα μιν Ζεὺς πρόσθεν ἑὴν ἐσκάτθετο νηδύν,
900 ὥς οἱ συμφράσσαιτο θεὰ ἀγαθόν τε κακόν τε.
    δεύτερον ἠγάγετο λιπαρὴν Θέμιν, ἣ τέκεν Ὥρας,
Εὐνομίην τε Δίκην τε καὶ Εἰρήνην τεθαλυῖαν,
αἵ τ' ἔργ' ὠρεύουσι καταθνητοῖσι βροτοῖσι,
Μοίρας θ', ἧς πλείστην τιμὴν πόρε μητίετα Ζεύς,
905 Κλωθώ τε Λάχεσίν τε καὶ Ἄτροπον, αἵ τε διδοῦσι
θνητοῖς ἀνθρώποισιν ἔχειν ἀγαθόν τε κακόν τε.

(881) When the blessed gods had completed their toil, and by force had reached a settlement with the Titans regarding honors, then by the prophecies of Earth they urged far-seeing Zeus to become king and to rule over the immortals; and he divided their honors well for them.

(886) Zeus, king of the gods, took as his first wife Metis (Wisdom), she who of the gods and mortal human beings knows the most. But when she was about to give birth to the goddess, bright-eyed Athena, he deceived her mind by craft and with guileful words he put her into his belly, by the prophecies of Earth and of starry Sky: for this was how they had prophesied to him, lest some other one of the eternally living gods hold the kingly honor instead of Zeus. For it was destined that exceedingly wise children would come to be from her: first she would give birth to a maiden, bright-eyed Tritogeneia,[43] possessing strength equal to her father's and wise counsel, and then to a son, a king of gods and of men, possessing a very violent heart. But before that could happen Zeus put her into his belly, so that the goddess would advise him about good and evil.

(901) Second, he married bright Themis, who gave birth to the Horae (Seasons), Eunomia (Lawfulness) and Dike (Justice) and blooming Eirene (Peace), who care for the works of mortal human beings, and the Destinies, upon whom the counsellor Zeus bestowed the greatest honor, Clotho and Lachesis and Atropos, who give to mortal human beings both good and evil to have.

[43] Athena.

---

900 οἱ συμφρ. Chrysippus: δή οἱ φρ. codd.
901–1022 Hesiodo abiud. West

τρεῖς δέ οἱ Εὐρυνόμη Χάριτας τέκε καλλιπαρήους,
Ὠκεανοῦ κούρη πολυήρατον εἶδος ἔχουσα,
Ἀγλαΐην τε καὶ Εὐφροσύνην Θαλίην τ' ἐρατεινήν·
910  τῶν καὶ ἀπὸ βλεφάρων ἔρος εἴβετο δερκομενάων
λυσιμελής· καλὸν δέ θ' ὑπ' ὀφρύσι δερκιόωνται.
αὐτὰρ ὁ Δήμητρος πολυφόρβης ἐς λέχος ἦλθεν·
ἣ τέκε Περσεφόνην λευκώλενον, ἣν Ἀιδωνεὺς
ἥρπασεν ἧς παρὰ μητρός, ἔδωκε δὲ μητίετα Ζεύς.
915  Μνημοσύνης δ' ἐξαῦτις ἐράσσατο καλλικόμοιο,
ἐξ ἧς οἱ Μοῦσαι χρυσάμπυκες ἐξεγένοντο
ἐννέα, τῇσιν ἄδον θαλίαι καὶ τέρψις ἀοιδῆς.
Λητὼ δ' Ἀπόλλωνα καὶ Ἄρτεμιν ἰοχέαιραν
ἱμερόεντα γόνον περὶ πάντων Οὐρανιώνων
920  γείνατ' ἄρ' αἰγιόχοιο Διὸς φιλότητι μιγεῖσα.
λοισθοτάτην δ' Ἥρην θαλερὴν ποιήσατ' ἄκοιτιν·
ἣ δ' Ἥβην καὶ Ἄρεα καὶ Εἰλείθυιαν ἔτικτε
μιχθεῖσ' ἐν φιλότητι θεῶν βασιλῆι καὶ ἀνδρῶν.
αὐτὸς δ' ἐκ κεφαλῆς γλαυκώπιδα γείνατ' Ἀθήνην,
925  δεινὴν ἐγρεκύδοιμον ἀγέστρατον ἀτρυτώνην,
πότνιαν, ᾗ κέλαδοί τε ἄδον πόλεμοί τε μάχαι τε·
Ἥρη δ' Ἥφαιστον κλυτὸν οὐ φιλότητι μιγεῖσα
γείνατο, καὶ ζαμένησε καὶ ἤρισεν ᾧ παρακοίτῃ,
ἐκ πάντων τέχνῃσι κεκασμένον Οὐρανιώνων.
930  ἐκ δ' Ἀμφιτρίτης καὶ ἐρικτύπου Ἐννοσιγαίου

908 εἶδος: ἦτορ a    924 γείνατ' Ἀ. Q Chrysippus:
τριτογένειαν abkS    930–1022 Hesiodo abiud. Jacoby, 930–
7, 940–62 Wilamowitz, alios alii

(907) Eurynome, Ocean's daughter, possessing lovely beauty, bore him three beautiful-cheeked Graces, Aglaea (Splendor) and Euphrosyne (Joy) and lovely Thalia (Good Cheer). From their eyes desire, the limb-melter, trickles down when they look; and they look beautifully from under their eyebrows.

(912) Then bounteous Demeter came to his bed; she bore white-armed Persephone, whom Aïdoneus[44] snatched away from her mother—but the counsellor Zeus gave her to him.

(915) Then he desired beautiful-haired Mnemosyne, from whom the Muses with golden headbands came to be, nine of them, who delight in festivities and the pleasure of song.

(918) Leto, mingling in love with aegis-holding Zeus, gave birth to Apollo and arrow-shooting Artemis, children lovely beyond all Sky's descendants.

(921) Last of all he made Hera his vigorous wife; and she, mingling in love with the king of gods and of men, gave birth to Hebe and Ares and Eileithyia.

(924) He himself gave birth from his head to bright-eyed Athena, terrible, battle-rouser, army-leader, indefatigable, queenly, who delights in din and wars and battles; but Hera was furious and contended with her husband, and without mingling in love gave birth to famous Hephaestus, expert with his skilled hands beyond all of Sky's descendants.

(930) From Amphitrite and the loud-sounding Earth-

---

[44] Hades.

Τρίτων εὐρυβίης γένετο μέγας, ὅς τε θαλάσσης
πυθμέν' ἔχων παρὰ μητρὶ φίλῃ καὶ πατρὶ ἄνακτι
ναίει χρύσεα δῶ, δεινὸς θεός. αὐτὰρ Ἄρηι
ῥινοτόρῳ Κυθέρεια Φόβον καὶ Δεῖμον ἔτικτε,

935 δεινούς, οἵ τ' ἀνδρῶν πυκινὰς κλονέουσι φάλαγγας
ἐν πολέμῳ κρυόεντι σὺν Ἄρηι πτολιπόρθῳ,
Ἁρμονίην θ', ἣν Κάδμος ὑπέρθυμος θέτ' ἄκοιτιν.

Ζηνὶ δ' ἄρ' Ἀτλαντὶς Μαίη τέκε κύδιμον Ἑρμῆν,
κήρυκ' ἀθανάτων, ἱερὸν λέχος εἰσαναβᾶσα.

940 Καδμηὶς δ' ἄρα οἱ Σεμέλη τέκε φαίδιμον υἱὸν
μιχθεῖσ' ἐν φιλότητι, Διώνυσον πολυγηθέα,
ἀθάνατον θνητή· νῦν δ' ἀμφότεροι θεοί εἰσιν.

Ἀλκμήνη δ' ἄρ' ἔτικτε βίην Ἡρακληείην
μιχθεῖσ' ἐν φιλότητι Διὸς νεφεληγερέταο.

945 Ἀγλαΐην δ' Ἥφαιστος ἀγακλυτὸς ἀμφιγυήεις
ὁπλοτάτην Χαρίτων θαλερὴν ποιήσατ' ἄκοιτιν.

χρυσοκόμης δὲ Διώνυσος ξανθὴν Ἀριάδνην,
κούρην Μίνωος, θαλερὴν ποιήσατ' ἄκοιτιν·
τὴν δέ οἱ ἀθάνατον καὶ ἀγήρων θῆκε Κρονίων.

950 Ἥβην δ' Ἀλκμήνης καλλισφύρου ἄλκιμος υἱός,
ἲς Ἡρακλῆος, τελέσας στονόεντας ἀέθλους,
παῖδα Διὸς μεγάλοιο καὶ Ἥρης χρυσοπεδίλου,
αἰδοίην θέτ' ἄκοιτιν ἐν Οὐλύμπῳ νιφόεντι·
ὄλβιος, ὃς μέγα ἔργον ἐν ἀθανάτοισιν ἀνύσσας

955 ναίει ἀπήμαντος καὶ ἀγήραος ἤματα πάντα.

Ἡελίῳ δ' ἀκάμαντι τέκε κλυτὸς Ὠκεανίνη
Περσηὶς Κίρκην τε καὶ Αἰήτην βασιλῆα.
Αἰήτης δ' υἱὸς φαεσιμβρότου Ἠελίοιο

shaker was born great, mighty Triton, who possesses the foundations of the sea and dwells in golden mansions beside his dear mother and his lordly father, a terrible god.

(933) To shield-piercing Ares Cytherea bore Fear and Terror, terrible, who rout the compact battle-lines of men in chilling war together with city-sacking Ares, and also Harmonia, whom high-spirited Cadmus made his wife.

(938) Maia, Atlas' daughter, going up into the holy bed, bore Zeus renowned Hermes, the messenger of the immortals.

(940) Semele, Cadmus' daughter, mingling in love, bore him a splendid son, much-cheering Dionysus, a mortal woman giving birth to an immortal son; and now both of them are gods.

(943) Alcmene, mingling in love with the cloud-gatherer Zeus, gave birth to Heracles' force.

(945) Hephaestus, the very renowned Lame One, made Aglaea, youngest of the Graces, his vigorous wife.

(947) Golden-haired Dionysus made blonde Ariadne, Minos' daughter, his vigorous wife; Cronus' son made her immortal and ageless for his sake.

(950) The strong son of beautiful-ankled Alcmene, Heracles' strength, made Hebe, the daughter of great Zeus and of golden-sandaled Hera, his reverend wife on snowy Olympus, after he had completed his painful tasks—happy he, for after having accomplished his great work among the immortals he dwells unharmed and ageless for all his days.

(956) Perseis, Ocean's renowned daughter, bore Circe and king Aeetes to tireless Helius. Aeetes, the son of

---

940–44 ἀθετοῦνται Σᶻ       947–55 ἀθετοῦνται Σᶻ

κούρην Ὠκεανοῖο τελήεντος ποταμοῖο
960 γῆμε θεῶν βουλῇσιν, Ἰδυῖαν καλλιπάρηον·
ἣ δή οἱ Μήδειαν εὔσφυρον ἐν φιλότητι
γείναθ' ὑποδμηθεῖσα διὰ χρυσῆν Ἀφροδίτην.

    ὑμεῖς μὲν νῦν χαίρετ', Ὀλύμπια δώματ' ἔχοντες,
νῆσοί τ' ἤπειροί τε καὶ ἁλμυρὸς ἔνδοθι πόντος·
965 νῦν δὲ θεάων φῦλον ἀείσατε, ἡδυέπειαι
Μοῦσαι Ὀλυμπιάδες, κοῦραι Διὸς αἰγιόχοιο,
ὅσσαι δὴ θνητοῖσι παρ' ἀνδράσιν εὐνηθεῖσαι
ἀθάναται γείναντο θεοῖς ἐπιείκελα τέκνα.
    Δημήτηρ μὲν Πλοῦτον ἐγείνατο δῖα θεάων,
970 Ἰασίῳ ἥρωι μιγεῖσ' ἐρατῇ φιλότητι
νειῷ ἔνι τριπόλῳ, Κρήτης ἐν πίονι δήμῳ,
ἐσθλόν, ὃς εἶσ' ἐπὶ γῆν τε καὶ εὐρέα νῶτα θαλάσσης
πᾶσαν· τῷ δὲ τυχόντι καὶ οὗ κ' ἐς χεῖρας ἵκηται,
τὸν δὴ ἀφνειὸν ἔθηκε, πολὺν δέ οἱ ὤπασεν ὄλβον.
975 Κάδμῳ δ' Ἁρμονίη, θυγάτηρ χρυσῆς Ἀφροδίτης,
Ἰνὼ καὶ Σεμέλην καὶ Ἀγαυὴν καλλιπάρηον
Αὐτονόην θ', ἣν γῆμεν Ἀρισταῖος βαθυχαίτης,
γείνατο καὶ Πολύδωρον ἐυστεφάνῳ ἐνὶ Θήβῃ.
    κούρη δ' Ὠκεανοῦ Χρυσάορι καρτεροθύμῳ
980 μιχθεῖσ' ἐν φιλότητι πολυχρύσου Ἀφροδίτης
Καλλιρόη τέκε παῖδα βροτῶν κάρτιστον ἀπάντων,
Γηρυονέα, τὸν κτεῖνε βίη Ἡρακληείη
βοῶν ἕνεκ' εἰλιπόδων ἀμφιρρύτῳ εἰν Ἐρυθείῃ.
    Τιθωνῷ δ' Ἠὼς τέκε Μέμνονα χαλκοκορυστήν,
985 Αἰθιόπων βασιλῆα, καὶ Ἠμαθίωνα ἄνακτα.

mortal-illumining Helius, married beautiful-cheeked Idyia, the daughter of the perfect river Ocean, by the plans of the gods; and she, overpowered in love because of golden Aphrodite, gave birth to fair-ankled Medea.

(963) Farewell now to you who dwell in Olympian mansions, and you islands and continents and the salty sea within. And now, sweet-voiced Olympian Muses, daughters of aegis-holding Zeus, sing of the tribe of goddesses, all those who bedded beside mortal men and, immortal themselves, gave birth to children equal to the gods.

(969) Demeter, divine among goddesses, gave birth to Plutus (Wealth), mingling in lovely desire with the hero Iasius in thrice-plowed fallow land in the rich land of Crete—fine Plutus, who goes upon the whole earth and the broad back of the sea, and whoever meets him and comes into his hands, that man he makes rich, and he bestows much wealth upon him.

(975) To Cadmus, Harmonia, golden Aphrodite's daughter, bore Ino and Semele and beautiful-cheeked Agave and Autonoe, whom deep-haired Aristaeus married, and Polydorus, in well-garlanded Thebes.

(979) Callirhoe, Ocean's daughter, mingling in golden Aphrodite's love with strong-spirited Chrysaor, bore a son, the strongest of all mortals, Geryoneus, whom Heracles' force killed on account of rolling-footed cattle in sea-girt Erythea.

(984) To Tithonus, Eos bore bronze-helmeted Memnon, the king of the Ethiopians, and lord Emathion. And to

---

961 δή Guyet: δέ codd.

αὐτάρ τοι Κεφάλῳ φιτύσατο φαίδιμον υἱόν,
ἴφθιμον Φαέθοντα, θεοῖς ἐπιείκελον ἄνδρα·
τόν ῥα νέον τέρεν ἄνθος ἔχοντ' ἐρικυδέος ἥβης
παῖδ' ἀταλὰ φρονέοντα φιλομμειδὴς Ἀφροδίτη
990 ὦρτ' ἀνερειψαμένη, καί μιν ζαθέοις ἐνὶ νηοῖς
νηοπόλον μύχιον ποιήσατο, δαίμονα δῖον.
    κούρην δ' Αἰήταο διοτρεφέος βασιλῆος
Αἰσονίδης βουλῇσι θεῶν αἰειγενετάων
ἦγε παρ' Αἰήτεω, τελέσας στονόεντας ἀέθλους,
995 τοὺς πολλοὺς ἐπέτελλε μέγας βασιλεὺς ὑπερήνωρ,
ὑβριστὴς Πελίης καὶ ἀτάσθαλος ὀβριμοεργός·
τοὺς τελέσας ἐς Ἰωλκὸν ἀφίκετο πολλὰ μογήσας
ὠκείης ἐπὶ νηὸς ἄγων ἑλικώπιδα κούρην
Αἰσονίδης, καί μιν θαλερὴν ποιήσατ' ἄκοιτιν.
1000 καί ῥ' ἥ γε δμηθεῖσ' ὑπ' Ἰήσονι ποιμένι λαῶν
Μήδειον τέκε παῖδα, τὸν οὔρεσιν ἔτρεφε Χείρων
Φιλλυρίδης· μεγάλου δὲ Διὸς νόος ἐξετελεῖτο.
    αὐτὰρ Νηρῆος κοῦραι ἁλίοιο γέροντος,
ἤτοι μὲν Φῶκον Ψαμάθη τέκε δῖα θεάων
1005 Αἰακοῦ ἐν φιλότητι διὰ χρυσῆν Ἀφροδίτην·
Πηλεῖ δὲ δμηθεῖσα θεὰ Θέτις ἀργυρόπεζα
γείνατ' Ἀχιλλῆα ῥηξήνορα θυμολέοντα.
    Αἰνείαν δ' ἄρ' ἔτικτεν ἐυστέφανος Κυθέρεια,
Ἀγχίσῃ ἥρωι μιγεῖσ' ἐρατῇ φιλότητι
1010 Ἴδης ἐν κορυφῇσι πολυπτύχου ἠνεμοέσσης.

986–91 *Catalogo* tribuit Pausanias
991 μύχιον Aristarchus: νύχιον ak

Cephalus she bore a splendid son, powerful Phaethon, a man equal to the gods. While he was young, a delicate-spirited child, and still possessed the tender flower of glorious youth, smile-loving Aphrodite snatched him away, and made him her innermost temple-keeper in her holy temples, a divine spirit.

(992) By the plans of the eternally living gods, Aeson's son[45] led away from Aeetes, that Zeus-nurtured king, Aeetes' daughter,[46] after completing the many painful tasks imposed upon him by the great overweening king, arrogant and wicked, violent-working Pelias. When Aeson's son had completed these he came to Iolcus, after enduring much toil, upon a swift ship, leading Aeetes' quick-eyed daughter, and he made her his vigorous wife. After she had been overpowered by Jason, the shepherd of the people, she gave birth to a son, Medeus, whom Chiron, Philyra's son, raised upon the mountains—and great Zeus' intention was fulfilled.

(1003) As for the daughters of Nereus, the old man of the sea, Psamathe, divine among goddesses, bore Phocus in love with Aeacus because of golden Aphrodite; while Thetis, the silver-footed goddess, overpowered by Peleus, gave birth to Achilles, man-breaker, lion-spirited.

(1008) Well-garlanded Cytherea bore Aeneas, mingling in lovely desire with the hero Anchises on the peaks of many-valleyed, windy Ida.

[45] Jason.
[46] Medea.

---

1010 ἤνεμ. Q: ὑληέσσης abkS

Κίρκη δ' Ἠελίου θυγάτηρ Ὑπεριονίδαο
γείνατ' Ὀδυσσῆος ταλασίφρονος ἐν φιλότητι
Ἄγριον ἠδὲ Λατῖνον ἀμύμονά τε κρατερόν τε·
Τηλέγονον δὲ ἔτικτε διὰ χρυσῆν Ἀφροδίτην·
1015  οἳ δή τοι μάλα τῆλε μυχῷ νήσων ἱεράων
πᾶσιν Τυρσηνοῖσιν ἀγακλειτοῖσιν ἄνασσον.
    Ναυσίθοον δ' Ὀδυσῆι Καλυψὼ δῖα θεάων
γείνατο Ναυσίνοόν τε μιγεῖσ' ἐρατῇ φιλότητι.

    αὗται μὲν θνητοῖσι παρ' ἀνδράσιν εὐνηθεῖσαι
1020  ἀθάναται γείναντο θεοῖς ἐπιείκελα τέκνα.
νῦν δὲ γυναικῶν φῦλον ἀείσατε, ἡδυέπειαι
Μοῦσαι Ὀλυμπιάδες, κοῦραι Διὸς αἰγιόχοιο.

1014 deest in *k*S sch. in Apollonium Rhodium, negl. Eustathius
1021–22 *Catalogi* initium om. Π¹³*ak*: habet Q, post add. L⁴ U²

(1011) Circe, the daughter of Hyperion's son Helius, in love with patient-minded Odysseus, gave birth to Agrius and Latinus, excellent and strong; and she bore Telegonus because of golden Aphrodite. These ruled over all the much-renowned Tyrrhenians, far away, in the innermost part of holy islands.

(1017) Calypso, divine among goddesses, bore Nausithous to Odysseus, and Nausinous, mingling in lovely desire.

(1019) These are the goddesses who bedded beside mortal men and, immortal themselves, gave birth to children equal to the gods. And now sing of the tribe of women, sweet-voiced Olympian Muses, daughters of aegis-holding Zeus.[47]

---

[47] These two lines are also the first two lines of the *Catalogue of Women*, cf. Fr. 1.

# ΕΡΓΑ ΚΑΙ ΗΜΕΡΑΙ

Μοῦσαι Πιερίηθεν, ἀοιδῇσι κλείουσαι,
δεῦτε, Δί᾽ ἐννέπετε σφέτερον πατέρ᾽ ὑμνείουσαι,
ὅν τε διὰ βροτοὶ ἄνδρες ὁμῶς ἄφατοί τε φατοί τε
ῥητοί τ᾽ ἄρρητοί τε Διὸς μεγάλοιο ἕκητι.
5 ῥέα μὲν γὰρ βριάει, ῥέα δὲ βριάοντα χαλέπτει,
ῥεῖα δ᾽ ἀρίζηλον μινύθει καὶ ἄδηλον ἀέξει,
ῥεῖα δέ τ᾽ ἰθύνει σκολιὸν καὶ ἀγήνορα κάρφει
Ζεὺς ὑψιβρεμέτης ὃς ὑπέρτατα δώματα ναίει.
κλῦθι ἰδὼν ἀιών τε, δίκῃ δ᾽ ἴθυνε θέμιστας
10 τύνη· ἐγὼ δέ κε Πέρσῃ ἐτήτυμα μυθησαίμην.

οὐκ ἄρα μοῦνον ἔην Ἐρίδων γένος, ἀλλ᾽ ἐπὶ
    γαῖαν
εἰσὶ δύω· τὴν μέν κεν ἐπαινήσειε νοήσας,
ἡ δ᾽ ἐπιμωμητή· διὰ δ᾽ ἄνδιχα θυμὸν ἔχουσιν.
ἡ μὲν γὰρ πόλεμόν τε κακὸν καὶ δῆριν ὀφέλλει,

1–16 deest C, 1–42 deest ω₄          1–10 ath.  Praxi-
phanes Aristarchus Crates, om. libri a Praxiphane Pausania visi

86

# WORKS AND DAYS

(1) Muses, from Pieria, glorifying in songs, come here, tell in hymns of your father Zeus, through whom mortal men are unfamed and famed alike, and named and unnamed, by the will of great Zeus. For easily he strengthens, and easily he crushes the strong, easily he diminishes the conspicuous and increases the inconspicuous, and easily he straightens the crooked and withers the manly—high-thundering Zeus, who dwells in the loftiest mansions. Give ear to me, watching and listening, and straighten the verdicts with justice yourself[1]; as for me, I will proclaim truths to Perses.

(11) So there was not just one birth of Strifes after all,[2] but upon the earth there are two Strifes. One of these a man would praise once he got to know it, but the other is blameworthy; and they have thoroughly opposed spirits. For the one fosters evil war and conflict—cruel one, no

---

[1] These requests are addressed to Zeus.

[2] This statement corrects the genealogy of Strife in *Theogony* 225.

15 σχετλίη· οὔ τις τήν γε φιλεῖ βροτός, ἀλλ᾽ ὑπ᾽
    ἀνάγκης
ἀθανάτων βουλῇσιν Ἔριν τιμῶσι βαρεῖαν.
τὴν δ᾽ ἑτέρην προτέρην μὲν ἐγείνατο Νὺξ ἐρεβεννή,
θῆκε δέ μιν Κρονίδης ὑψίζυγος, αἰθέρι ναίων
γαίης τ᾽ ἐν ῥίζῃσι καὶ ἀνδράσι πολλὸν ἀμείνω·
20 ἥ τε καὶ ἀπάλαμόν περ ὁμῶς ἐπὶ ἔργον ἔγειρεν.
εἰς ἕτερον γάρ τίς τε ἰδὼν ἔργοιο χατίζων
πλούσιον, ὃς σπεύδει μὲν ἀρώμεναι ἠδὲ φυτεύειν
οἶκόν τ᾽ εὖ θέσθαι, ζηλοῖ δέ τε γείτονα γείτων
εἰς ἄφενος σπεύδοντ᾽· ἀγαθὴ δ᾽ Ἔρις ἥδε βροτοῖσιν.
25 καὶ κεραμεὺς κεραμεῖ κοτέει καὶ τέκτονι τέκτων,
καὶ πτωχὸς πτωχῷ φθονέει καὶ ἀοιδὸς ἀοιδῷ.
    ὦ Πέρση, σὺ δὲ ταῦτα τεῷ ἐνικάτθεο θυμῷ,
μηδέ σ᾽ Ἔρις κακόχαρτος ἀπ᾽ ἔργου θυμὸν ἐρύκοι
νείκε᾽ ὀπιπεύοντ᾽ ἀγορῆς ἐπακουὸν ἐόντα.
30 ὥρη γάρ τ᾽ ὀλίγη πέλεται νεικέων τ᾽ ἀγορέων τε,
ᾧτινι μὴ βίος ἔνδον ἐπηετανὸς κατάκειται
ὡραῖος, τὸν γαῖα φέρει, Δήμητρος ἀκτήν.
τοῦ κε κορεσσάμενος νείκεα καὶ δῆριν ὀφέλλοις
κτήμασ᾽ ἐπ᾽ ἀλλοτρίοις. σοὶ δ᾽ οὐκέτι δεύτερον ἔσται
35 ὧδ᾽ ἔρδειν, ἀλλ᾽ αὖθι διακρινώμεθα νεῖκος
ἰθείῃσι δίκῃς, αἵ τ᾽ ἐκ Διός εἰσιν ἄρισται.
ἤδη μὲν γὰρ κλῆρον ἐδασσάμεθ᾽, ἄλλά τε πολλὰ
ἁρπάζων ἐφόρεις μέγα κυδαίνων βασιλῆας
δωροφάγους, οἳ τήνδε δίκην ἐθέλουσι δικάσσαι,
40 νήπιοι, οὐδὲ ἴσασιν ὅσῳ πλέον ἥμισυ παντός,

mortal loves that one, but it is by necessity that they honor
the oppressive Strife, by the plans of the immortals. But
the other one gloomy Night bore first; and Cronus' high-
throned son, who dwells in the aether, set it in the roots of
the earth, and it is much better for men. It rouses even the
helpless man to work. For a man who is not working but
who looks at some other man, a rich one who is hastening
to plow and plant and set his house in order, he envies
him, one neighbor envying his neighbor who is hastening
towards wealth: and this Strife is good for mortals. And
potter is angry with potter, and builder with builder, and
beggar begrudges beggar, and poet poet.

(27) Perses, do store this up in your spirit, lest gloating
Strife keep your spirit away from work, while you gawk
at quarrels and listen to the assembly. For he has little care
for quarrels and assemblies, whoever does not have plenti-
ful means of life stored up indoors in good season, what the
earth bears, Demeter's grain. When you can take your fill
of that, then you might foster quarrels and conflict for
the sake of another man's wealth. But you will not have a
second chance to act this way—no, let us decide our quar-
rel right here with straight judgments, which come from
Zeus, the best ones. For already we had divided up our al-
lotment, but you snatched much more besides and went
carrying it off, greatly honoring the kings, those gift-eaters,
who want to pass this judgment—fools, they do not know

---

19 τ' om. Par. 2763, del. Guyet
21 χατίζων DΦGalenus al.: χατίζει C

οὐδ᾽ ὅσον ἐν μαλάχῃ τε καὶ ἀσφοδέλῳ μέγ᾽ ὄνειαρ.

κρύψαντες γὰρ ἔχουσι θεοὶ βίον ἀνθρώποισιν·
ῥηιδίως γάρ κεν καὶ ἐπ᾽ ἤματι ἐργάσσαιο
ὥστέ σε κεἰς ἐνιαυτὸν ἔχειν καὶ ἀεργὸν ἐόντα·
45 αἶψά κε πηδάλιον μὲν ὑπὲρ καπνοῦ καταθεῖο,
ἔργα βοῶν δ᾽ ἀπόλοιτο καὶ ἡμιόνων ταλαεργῶν.
ἀλλὰ Ζεὺς ἔκρυψε χολωσάμενος φρεσὶν ᾗσιν,
ὅττί μιν ἐξαπάτησε Προμηθεὺς ἀγκυλομήτης.
τοὔνεκ᾽ ἄρ᾽ ἀνθρώποισιν ἐμήσατο κήδεα λυγρά·
50 κρύψε δὲ πῦρ· τὸ μὲν αὖτις ἐὺς πάις Ἰαπετοῖο
ἔκλεψ᾽ ἀνθρώποισι Διὸς παρὰ μητιόεντος
ἐν κοίλῳ νάρθηκι, λαθὼν Δία τερπικέραυνον.
τὸν δὲ χολωσάμενος προσέφη νεφεληγερέτα
Ζεύς·
" Ἰαπετιονίδη, πάντων πέρι μήδεα εἰδώς,
55 χαίρεις πῦρ κλέψας καὶ ἐμὰς φρένας ἠπεροπεύσας,
σοί τ᾽ αὐτῷ μέγα πῆμα καὶ ἀνδράσιν ἐσσομένοισιν.
τοῖς δ᾽ ἐγὼ ἀντὶ πυρὸς δώσω κακόν, ᾧ κεν ἅπαντες
τέρπωνται κατὰ θυμόν, ἑὸν κακὸν ἀμφαγαπῶντες."
ὣς ἔφατ᾽, ἐκ δ᾽ ἐγέλασσε πατὴρ ἀνδρῶν τε θεῶν
τε.
60 Ἥφαιστον δ᾽ ἐκέλευσε περικλυτὸν ὅττι τάχιστα
γαῖαν ὕδει φύρειν, ἐν δ᾽ ἀνθρώπου θέμεν αὐδὴν
καὶ σθένος, ἀθανάτῃς δὲ θεῇς εἰς ὦπα ἐίσκειν,
παρθενικῆς καλὸν εἶδος ἐπήρατον· αὐτὰρ Ἀθήνην

59 ἐτέλεσε Origenes

how much more the half is than the whole, nor how great
the boon is in mallow and asphodel![3]

(42) For the gods keep the means of life concealed from
human beings. Otherwise you would easily be able to work
in just one day so as to have enough for a whole year even
without working, and quickly you would store the rudder
above the smoke, and the work of the cattle and of the
hard-working mules would be ended.

(47) But Zeus concealed it, angry in his heart because
crooked-counseled Prometheus (Forethought) had de-
ceived him.[4] For that reason he devised baneful evils for
human beings, and he concealed fire; but the good son of
Iapetus[5] stole it back from the counsellor Zeus in a hollow
fennel-stalk for human beings, escaping the notice of Zeus
who delights in the thunderbolt.

(53) But the cloud-gatherer Zeus spoke to him in anger:
"Son of Iapetus, you who know counsels beyond all others,
you are pleased that you have stolen fire and beguiled my
mind—a great grief for you yourself, and for men to come.
To them I shall give in exchange for fire an evil in which
they may all take pleasure in their spirit, embracing their
own evil."

(59) So he spoke, and he laughed out loud, the father of
men and of gods. He commanded renowned Hephaestus
to mix earth with water as quickly as possible, and to put
the voice and strength of a human into it, and to make a
beautiful, lovely form of a maiden similar in her face to the

[3] Traditionally, the poor man's fare.
[4] See *Th* 535–57.
[5] Prometheus.

# HESIOD

ἔργα διδασκῆσαι, πολυδαίδαλον ἱστὸν ὑφαίνειν·
65  καὶ χάριν ἀμφιχέαι κεφαλῇ χρυσῆν Ἀφροδίτην,
καὶ πόθον ἀργαλέον καὶ γυιοβόρους μελεδώνας·
ἐν δὲ θέμεν κύνεόν τε νόον καὶ ἐπίκλοπον ἦθος
Ἑρμείην ἤνωγε, διάκτορον ἀργειφόντην.
    ὣς ἔφαθ᾽, οἱ δ᾽ ἐπίθοντο Διὶ Κρονίωνι ἄνακτι.
70  αὐτίκα δ᾽ ἐκ γαίης πλάσσε κλυτὸς Ἀμφιγυήεις
παρθένῳ αἰδοίῃ ἴκελον Κρονίδεω διὰ βουλάς·
ζῶσε δὲ καὶ κόσμησε θεὰ γλαυκῶπις Ἀθήνη·
ἀμφὶ δέ οἱ Χάριτές τε θεαὶ καὶ πότνια Πειθὼ
ὅρμους χρυσείους ἔθεσαν χροΐ, ἀμφὶ δὲ τήν γε
75  Ὧραι καλλίκομοι στέφον ἄνθεσιν εἰαρινοῖσιν·
πάντα δέ οἱ χροΐ κόσμον ἐφήρμοσε Παλλὰς Ἀθήνη.
ἐν δ᾽ ἄρα οἱ στήθεσσι διάκτορος Ἀργειφόντης
ψεύδεά θ᾽ αἱμυλίους τε λόγους καὶ ἐπίκλοπον ἦθος
τεῦξε Διὸς βουλῇσι βαρυκτύπου· ἐν δ᾽ ἄρα φωνὴν
80  θῆκε θεῶν κῆρυξ, ὀνόμηνε δὲ τήνδε γυναῖκα
Πανδώρην, ὅτι πάντες Ὀλύμπια δώματ᾽ ἔχοντες
δῶρον ἐδώρησαν, πῆμ᾽ ἀνδράσιν ἀλφηστῇσιν.
    αὐτὰρ ἐπεὶ δόλον αἰπὺν ἀμήχανον ἐξετέλεσσεν,
εἰς Ἐπιμηθέα πέμπε πατὴρ κλυτὸν Ἀργειφόντην
85  δῶρον ἄγοντα, θεῶν ταχὺν ἄγγελον· οὐδ᾽ Ἐπιμηθεὺς
ἐφράσαθ᾽, ὥς οἱ ἔειπε Προμηθεὺς μή ποτε δῶρον
δέξασθαι πὰρ Ζηνὸς Ὀλυμπίου, ἀλλ᾽ ἀποπέμπειν

66 γυιοβόρους Σ<sup>vet.</sup> (ci. Guyet): γυιοκόρους codd. Proclus
Σ<sup>vet</sup> Origenes al.
    70–2 (=Theog. 571–3) om. Origenes

92

immortal goddesses. He told Athena to teach her crafts, to weave richly worked cloth, and golden Aphrodite to shed grace and painful desire and limb-devouring cares around her head; and he ordered Hermes, the intermediary, the killer of Argus, to put a dog's mind and a thievish character into her.

(69) So he spoke, and they obeyed Zeus, the lord, Cronus' son. Immediately the famous Lame One fabricated out of earth a likeness of a modest maiden, by the plans of Cronus' son; the goddess, bright-eyed Athena, gave her a girdle and ornaments; the goddesses Graces and queenly Persuasion placed golden jewelry all around on her body; the beautiful-haired Seasons crowned her all around with spring flowers; and Pallas Athena fitted the whole ornamentation to her body. Then into her breast the intermediary, the killer of Argus, set lies and guileful words and a thievish character, by the plans of deep-thundering Zeus; and the messenger of the gods placed a voice in her and named this woman Pandora (All-Gift), since all those who have their mansions on Olympus had given her a gift—a woe for men who live on bread.

(83) When he had completed the sheer, intractable deception, the father sent the famous killer of Argus, the swift messenger of the gods, to take her as a gift to Epimetheus (Afterthought). And Epimetheus did not consider that Prometheus had told him never to accept a gift from Olympian Zeus, but to send it back again, lest some-

---

76 damn. Bentley
79 'περιττόν' dixerunt quidam ap. Proclum, exp. Bentley
82 ἐσ‹σ›ομένοισιν Philodemus

ἐξοπίσω, μή πού τι κακὸν θνητοῖσι γένηται.
αὐτὰρ ὁ δεξάμενος, ὅτε δὴ κακὸν εἶχ᾽ ἐνόησεν.

90 πρὶν μὲν γὰρ ζώεσκον ἐπὶ χθονὶ φῦλ᾽ ἀνθρώπων
νόσφιν ἄτερ τε κακῶν καὶ ἄτερ χαλεποῖο πόνοιο
νούσων τ᾽ ἀργαλέων αἵ τ᾽ ἀνδράσι κῆρας ἔδωκαν·
[αἶψα γὰρ ἐν κακότητι βροτοὶ καταγηράσκουσιν.]
ἀλλὰ γυνὴ χείρεσσι πίθου μέγα πῶμ᾽ ἀφελοῦσα
95 ἐσκέδασ᾽· ἀνθρώποισι δ᾽ ἐμήσατο κήδεα λυγρά.
μούνη δ᾽ αὐτόθι Ἐλπὶς ἐν ἀρρήκτοισι δόμοισιν
ἔνδον ἔμιμνε πίθου ὑπὸ χείλεσιν, οὐδὲ θύραζε
ἐξέπτη· πρόσθεν γὰρ ἐπέμβαλε πῶμα πίθοιο
αἰγιόχου βουλῇσι Διὸς νεφεληγερέταο.
100 ἄλλα δὲ μυρία λυγρὰ κατ᾽ ἀνθρώπους ἀλάληται·
πλείη μὲν γὰρ γαῖα κακῶν, πλείη δὲ θάλασσα·
νοῦσοι δ᾽ ἀνθρώποισιν ἐφ᾽ ἡμέρῃ, αἱ δ᾽ ἐπὶ νυκτὶ
αὐτόμαται φοιτῶσι κακὰ θνητοῖσι φέρουσαι
σιγῇ, ἐπεὶ φωνὴν ἐξείλετο μητίετα Ζεύς.
105 οὕτως οὔ τί πη ἔστι Διὸς νόον ἐξαλέασθαι.

εἰ δ᾽ ἐθέλεις, ἕτερόν τοι ἐγὼ λόγον ἐκκορυφώσω,
εὖ καὶ ἐπισταμένως, σὺ δ᾽ ἐνὶ φρεσὶ βάλλεο σῇσιν,
ὡς ὁμόθεν γεγάασι θεοὶ θνητοί τ᾽ ἄνθρωποι.

93 solus E in textu, in mg. H (deest et in Origene, non respic.
Proclus Σ^vet)      96 δόμοι[σιν Π₄₁codd., testt.: μυχοῖσιν
Seleucus ap. Σ (ubi πίθοισι, μύθοισι male codd. quidam)
98 ἐπέμβαλε Φ: ἐπέβαλε Origenes (alterutrum et Σ^vet):
ἐπέλ(λ)αβε CDΣ^vet (ἔνιοι) Plutarchus Stobaeus
99 habent Π₄₁ codd.: non habet Plutarchus (qui 94–8, 100–4),
non respic. Proclus Σ^vet

thing evil happen to mortals; it was only after he accepted her, when he already had the evil, that he understood.

(90) For previously the tribes of men used to live upon the earth entirely apart from evils, and without grievous toil and distressful diseases, which give death to men. [For in misery mortals grow old at once.][6] But the woman removed the great lid from the storage jar with her hands and scattered all its contents abroad—she wrought baneful evils for human beings. Only Anticipation[7] remained there in its unbreakable home under the mouth of the storage jar, and did not fly out; for before that could happen she closed the lid of the storage jar, by the plans of the aegis-holder, the cloud-gatherer, Zeus. But countless other miseries roam among mankind; for the earth is full of evils, and the sea is full; and some sicknesses come upon men by day, and others by night, of their own accord, bearing evils to mortals in silence, since the counsellor Zeus took their voice away. Thus it is not possible in any way to evade the mind of Zeus.

(106) If you wish, I shall recapitulate[8] another story, correctly and skillfully, and you lay it up in your spirit: how the gods and mortal human beings came about from the same origin.

---

[6] This line is found in the margin or text of very few manuscripts; it is identical with *Od.* 19.360 and is generally rejected here as an intrusive gloss. [7] Often translated "Hope"; but the Greek word can mean anticipation of bad as well as of good things. [8] The precise meaning of the verb is unclear.

---

104 ἀθετεῖται Σ<sup>vet</sup> (extat in Plutarcho)
108 exp. Lehrs (leg. Proclus Σ<sup>vet</sup>)

χρύσεον μὲν πρώτιστα γένος μερόπων ἀνθρώπων
110 ἀθάνατοι ποίησαν Ὀλύμπια δώματ᾽ ἔχοντες.
οἱ μὲν ἐπὶ Κρόνου ἦσαν, ὅτ᾽ οὐρανῷ ἐμβασίλευεν·
ὥστε θεοὶ δ᾽ ἔζωον ἀκηδέα θυμὸν ἔχοντες,
νόσφιν ἄτερ τε πόνου καὶ ὀιζύος· οὐδέ τι δειλὸν
γῆρας ἐπῆν, αἰεὶ δὲ πόδας καὶ χεῖρας ὁμοῖοι
115 τέρποντ᾽ ἐν θαλίῃσι κακῶν ἔκτοσθεν ἁπάντων·
θνῆσκον δ᾽ ὥσθ᾽ ὕπνῳ δεδμημένοι· ἐσθλὰ δὲ πάντα
τοῖσιν ἔην· καρπὸν δ᾽ ἔφερε ζείδωρος ἄρουρα
αὐτομάτη πολλόν τε καὶ ἄφθονον· οἱ δ᾽ ἐθελημοὶ
ἥσυχοι ἔργ᾽ ἐνέμοντο σὺν ἐσθλοῖσιν πολέεσσιν.
120 ἀφνειοὶ μήλοισι, φίλοι μακάρεσσι θεοῖσιν.
αὐτὰρ ἐπεὶ δὴ τοῦτο γένος κατὰ γαῖα κάλυψεν,
τοὶ μὲν δαίμονές εἰσι Διὸς μεγάλου διὰ βουλὰς
ἐσθλοί, ἐπιχθόνιοι, φύλακες θνητῶν ἀνθρώπων,
οἵ ῥα φυλάσσουσίν τε δίκας καὶ σχέτλια ἔργα
125 ἠέρα ἑσσάμενοι, πάντῃ φοιτῶντες ἐπ᾽ αἶαν,
πλουτοδόται· καὶ τοῦτο γέρας βασιλήιον ἔσχον.

δεύτερον αὖτε γένος πολὺ χειρότερον μετόπισθεν
ἀργύρεον ποίησαν Ὀλύμπια δώματ᾽ ἔχοντες,
χρυσέῳ οὔτε φυὴν ἐναλίγκιον οὔτε νόημα.
130 ἀλλ᾽ ἑκατὸν μὲν παῖς ἔτεα παρὰ μητέρι κεδνῇ
ἐτρέφετ᾽ ἀτάλλων μέγα νήπιος ᾧ ἐνὶ οἴκῳ·
ἀλλ᾽ ὅτ᾽ ἄρ᾽ ἡβήσαι τε καὶ ἥβης μέτρον ἵκοιτο,

113 πόνο]ν Π₈ Herodianus rhetor: πόνων codd. Eustathius
120 solus praebet Diodorus: om. Π₃₈ut vid., prorsus neglexit
Dicaearchus

96

(109) Golden was the race of speech-endowed human beings which the immortals, who have their mansions on Olympus, made first of all. They lived at the time of Cronus, when he was king in the sky; just like gods they spent their lives, with a spirit free from care, entirely apart from toil and distress. Worthless old age did not oppress them, but they were always the same in their feet and hands, and delighted in festivities, lacking in all evils; and they died as if overpowered by sleep. They had all good things: the grain-giving field bore crops of its own accord, much and unstinting, and they themselves, willing, mild-mannered, shared out the fruits of their labors together with many good things, wealthy in sheep, dear to the blessed gods. But since the earth covered up this race, by the plans of great Zeus they are fine spirits upon the earth, guardians of mortal human beings: they watch over judgments and cruel deeds, clad in invisibility, walking everywhere upon the earth, givers of wealth; and this kingly honor they received.

(127) Afterwards those who have their mansions on Olympus made a second race, much worse, of silver, like the golden one neither in body nor in mind. A boy would be nurtured for a hundred years at the side of his cherished mother, playing in his own house, a great fool. But when they reached adolescence and arrived at the full measure

---

122 εἰσι Διὸς μεγάλου διὰ βουλὰς ἐσθλοὶ ἐπιχθόνιοι codd. Proclus Lactantius: ἁγνοὶ (hoc et Plutarchus) ἐπιχθόνιοι τελέθουσι (καλέονται Plato *Crat.*) ἐσθλοὶ ἀλεξίκακοι Plato *Crat. Resp.* ἐπιχθόνιοι et Σ[vet] al.: ὑποχθ. Plato *Crat.* codd.
124–5 (=254–5) om. Π[38]ut vid. Π[40] Proclus Plutarchus Macrobius: habent codd. Σ[c]

παυρίδιον ζώεσκον ἐπὶ χρόνον, ἄλγε' ἔχοντες
ἀφραδίης· ὕβριν γὰρ ἀτάσθαλον οὐκ ἐδύναντο
135  ἀλλήλων ἀπέχειν, οὐδ' ἀθανάτους θεραπεύειν
ἤθελον οὐδ' ἔρδειν μακάρων ἱεροῖς ἐπὶ βωμοῖς,
ἢ θέμις ἀνθρώποισι κατ' ἤθεα. τοὺς μὲν ἔπειτα
Ζεὺς Κρονίδης ἔκρυψε χολούμενος, οὕνεκα τιμὰς
οὐκ ἔδιδον μακάρεσσι θεοῖς οἳ Ὄλυμπον ἔχουσιν.
140  αὐτὰρ ἐπεὶ καὶ τοῦτο γένος κατὰ γαῖα κάλυψεν,
τοὶ μὲν ὑποχθόνιοι μάκαρες θνητοὶ καλέονται,
δεύτεροι, ἀλλ' ἔμπης τιμὴ καὶ τοῖσιν ὀπηδεῖ.
    Ζεὺς δὲ πατὴρ τρίτον ἄλλο γένος μερόπων
        ἀνθρώπων
χάλκειον ποίησ', οὐκ ἀργυρέῳ οὐδὲν ὁμοῖον,
145  ἐκ μελιᾶν, δεινόν τε καὶ ὄβριμον, οἷσιν Ἄρηος
ἔργ' ἔμελε στονόεντα καὶ ὕβριες· οὐδέ τι σῖτον
ἤσθιον, ἀλλ' ἀδάμαντος ἔχον κρατερόφρονα θυμόν·
ἄπλαστοι· μεγάλη δὲ βίη καὶ χεῖρες ἄαπτοι
ἐξ ὤμων ἐπέφυκον ἐπὶ στιβαροῖσι μέλεσσιν.
150  τῶν δ' ἦν χάλκεα μὲν τεύχεα, χάλκεοι δέ τε οἶκοι,
χαλκῷ δ' εἰργάζοντο· μέλας δ' οὐκ ἔσκε σίδηρος.
καὶ τοὶ μὲν χείρεσσιν ὑπὸ σφετέρῃσι δαμέντες
βῆσαν ἐς εὐρώεντα δόμον κρυεροῦ Ἀίδαο,
νώνυμνοι· θάνατος δὲ καὶ ἐκπάγλους περ ἐόντας
155  εἷλε μέλας, λαμπρὸν δ' ἔλιπον φάος ἠελίοιο.

141 ὑποχθόνιοι ProclusC^rasD, reicit Tzetzes: ἐπιχθ-
ΣTzetzesψ: τοὶ χθ- Φ μάκαρες Σcodd.: φύλακες Proclus θνητοὶ
E: θεοὶ D^rasφ₇ + ψ₁₅: θνητοῖς Peppmüller

of puberty, they would live for a short time only, suffering pains because of their acts of folly. For they could not restrain themselves from wicked outrage against each other, nor were they willing to honor the immortals or to sacrifice upon the holy altars of the blessed ones, as is established right for human beings in each community. Then Zeus, Cronus' son, concealed these in anger, because they did not give honors to the blessed gods who dwell on Olympus. But since the earth covered up this race too, they are called blessed mortals under the earth—in second place, but all the same honor attends upon these as well.

(143) Zeus the father made another race of speech-endowed human beings, a third one, of bronze, not similar to the silver one at all, out of ash trees[9]—terrible and strong they were, and they cared only for the painful works of Ares and for acts of violence. They did not eat bread, but had a strong-hearted spirit of adamant—unapproachable they were, and upon their massive limbs grew great strength and untouchable hands out of their shoulders. Their weapons were of bronze, bronze were their houses, with bronze they worked; there was not any black iron. And these, overpowered by one another's hands, went down nameless into the dank house of chilly Hades: black death seized them, frightful though they were, and they left behind the bright light of the sun.

[9] Or from the Melian nymphs—which may just be another way of saying the same thing. See note on *Theogony* 187.

---

146 ὕβριος West
148 ἄπλατοι C Proclus

αὐτὰρ ἐπεὶ καὶ τοῦτο γένος κατὰ γαῖα κάλυψεν,
αὖτις ἔτ' ἄλλο τέταρτον ἐπὶ χθονὶ πουλυβοτείρῃ
Ζεὺς Κρονίδης ποίησε, δικαιότερον καὶ ἄρειον,
ἀνδρῶν ἡρώων θεῖον γένος, οἳ καλέονται

160  ἡμίθεοι, προτέρη γενεὴ κατ' ἀπείρονα γαῖαν.
καὶ τοὺς μὲν πόλεμός τε κακὸς καὶ φύλοπις αἰνὴ
τοὺς μὲν ὑφ' ἑπταπύλῳ Θήβῃ, Καδμηίδι γαίῃ,
ὤλεσε μαρναμένους μήλων ἕνεκ' Οἰδιπόδαο,
τοὺς δὲ καὶ ἐν νήεσσιν ὑπὲρ μέγα λαῖτμα
    θαλάσσης

165  ἐς Τροίην ἀγαγὼν Ἑλένης ἕνεκ' ἠυκόμοιο.
ἔνθ' ἦ τοι τοὺς μὲν θανάτου τέλος ἀμφεκάλυψεν,
τοῖς δὲ δίχ' ἀνθρώπων βίοτον καὶ ἤθε' ὀπάσσας

168  Ζεὺς Κρονίδης κατένασσε πατὴρ ἐς πείρατα γαίης,

170  καὶ τοὶ μὲν ναίουσιν ἀκηδέα θυμὸν ἔχοντες
ἐν μακάρων νήσοισι παρ' Ὠκεανὸν βαθυδίνην·
ὄλβιοι ἥρωες, τοῖσιν μελιηδέα καρπὸν
τρὶς ἔτεος θάλλοντα φέρει ζείδωρος ἄρουρα.

μηκέτ' ἔπειτ' ὤφελλον ἐγὼ πέμπτοισι μετεῖναι

175  ἀνδράσιν, ἀλλ' ἢ πρόσθε θανεῖν ἢ ἔπειτα γενέσθαι.

173 a–e τηλοῦ ἀπ' ἀθανάτων· τοῖσιν Κρόνος ἐμβασιλεύει.
    αὐτὸς γάρ μ]ιν ἔλυσε πατ[ὴρ ἀνδρῶ]ν τε θε[ῶν τε·
    νῦν δ' αἰεὶ] μετὰ τοῖς τιμὴ[ν ἔ]χει ὡς ἐ[πιεικές.
    Ζεὺς δ' αὖτ' ἄ]λλο γένος θῆκ[εν μερόπων
        ἀνθρώπων
    ὅσσοι νῦ]ν γεγάασιν ἐπὶ [χθονὶ πουλυβοτείρῃ.
  173 a (olim 169) post 160 memorat Σ; ante b-c habet Π₃₈, b-e
autem ante 174 Π₈
  173 a ἐβασίλευε Σ: ἐν[ Π₃₈: -ει Buttmann    b init. suppl.
West, cetera Weil    c init. suppl. Maehler: νῦν δ' ἤδη West τοῖσι

(156) When the earth covered up this race too, Zeus, Cronus' son, made another one in turn upon the bounteous earth, a fourth one, more just and superior, the godly race of men-heroes, who are called demigods, the generation before our own upon the boundless earth. Evil war and dread battle destroyed these, some under seven-gated Thebes in the land of Cadmus while they fought for the sake of Oedipus' sheep, others brought in boats over the great gulf of the sea to Troy for the sake of fair-haired Helen. There the end of death shrouded some of them, but upon others Zeus the father, Cronus' son, bestowed life and habitations far from human beings and settled them at the limits of the earth; and these dwell with a spirit free of care on the Islands of the Blessed beside deep-eddying Ocean—happy heroes, for whom the grain-giving field bears honey-sweet fruit flourishing three times a year.[10]

(174) If only then I did not have to live among the fifth men, but could have either died first or been born after-

---

[10] After this line, two papyri transmit the following lines, 173a-e (line 173a is also found in a few other sources): "far from human beings. Among these Cronus is king. For the father of men and of gods freed him himself; and now among these he always has honor, as is fitting. Zeus established another race of mortal human beings in turn, those who have now come into being upon the bounteous earth." This passage is most likely a very late interpolation, designed to reconcile Zeus with Cronus and to provide the fifth race with an introduction similar to that of the first four.

---

Π₈: corr. Weil τιμὴ[ν Weil, cetera Maehler    d init. suppl. West, exit. Wilam.    e init. supplevit Solmsen: τῶν οἱ νῦ]ν Kuiper: οἱ καὶ νῦ]ν Wilamowitz, exit. Weil

νῦν γὰρ δὴ γένος ἐστὶ σιδήρεον· οὐδέ ποτ᾽ ἦμαρ
παύσονται καμάτου καὶ ὀιζύος οὐδέ τι νύκτωρ
τειρόμενοι· χαλεπὰς δὲ θεοὶ δώσουσι μερίμνας.
ἀλλ᾽ ἔμπης καὶ τοῖσι μεμείξεται ἐσθλὰ κακοῖσιν.
180 Ζεὺς δ᾽ ὀλέσει καὶ τοῦτο γένος μερόπων ἀνθρώπων,
εὖτ᾽ ἂν γεινόμενοι πολιοκρόταφοι τελέθωσιν.
οὐδὲ πατὴρ παίδεσσιν ὁμοίιος οὐδέ τι παῖδες,
οὐδὲ ξεῖνος ξεινοδόκῳ καὶ ἑταῖρος ἑταίρῳ,
οὐδὲ κασίγνητος φίλος ἔσσεται, ὡς τὸ πάρος περ.
185 αἶψα δὲ γηράσκοντας ἀτιμήσουσι τοκῆας·
μέμψονται δ᾽ ἄρα τοὺς χαλεποῖς βάζοντες ἔπεσσιν,
σχέτλιοι, οὐδὲ θεῶν ὄπιν εἰδότες· οὐδὲ μὲν οἵ γε
γηράντεσσι τοκεῦσιν ἀπὸ θρεπτήρια δοῖεν.
χειροδίκαι· ἕτερος δ᾽ ἑτέρου πόλιν ἐξαλαπάξει·
190 οὐδέ τις εὐόρκου χάρις ἔσσεται οὐδὲ δικαίου
οὔτ᾽ ἀγαθοῦ, μᾶλλον δὲ κακῶν ῥεκτῆρα καὶ ὕβριν
ἀνέρα τιμήσουσι· δίκη δ᾽ ἐν χερσὶ καὶ αἰδὼς
οὐκ ἔσται· βλάψει δ᾽ ὁ κακὸς τὸν ἀρείονα φῶτα
μύθοισι σκολιοῖς ἐνέπων, ἐπὶ δ᾽ ὅρκον ὀμεῖται.
195 Ζῆλος δ᾽ ἀνθρώποισιν ὀιζυροῖσιν ἅπασιν
δυσκέλαδος κακόχαρτος ὁμαρτήσει, στυγερώπης.
καὶ τότε δὴ πρὸς Ὄλυμπον ἀπὸ χθονὸς εὐρυοδείης
λευκοῖσιν φάρεσσι καλυψαμένω χρόα καλὸν
ἀθανάτων μετὰ φῦλον ἴτον προλιπόντ᾽ ἀνθρώπους
200 Αἰδὼς καὶ Νέμεσις· τὰ δὲ λείψεται ἄλγεα λυγρὰ

177 π]αύονται Π₈
178 τ]ειρόμενοι e Π₃₈ West: φθειρόμενοι codd.

wards! For now the race is indeed one of iron. And they will not cease from toil and distress by day, nor from being worn out by suffering at night, and the gods will give them grievous cares. Yet all the same, for these people too good things will be mingled with evil ones. But Zeus will destroy this race of speech-endowed human beings too, when at their birth the hair on their temples will be quite gray. Father will not be like-minded with sons, nor sons at all,[11] nor guest with host, nor comrade with comrade, nor will the brother be dear, as he once was. They will dishonor their aging parents at once; they will reproach them, addressing them with grievous words—cruel men, who do not know of the gods' retribution!—nor would they repay their aged parents for their rearing. Their hands will be their justice, and one man will destroy the other's city. Nor will there be any grace for the man who keeps his oath, nor for the just man or the good one, but they will give more honor to the doer of evil and the outrage man. Justice will be in their hands, and reverence will not exist, but the bad man will harm the superior one, speaking with crooked discourses, and he will swear an oath upon them. And Envy, evil-sounding, gloating, loathsome-faced, will accompany all wretched human beings. Then indeed will Reverence and Indignation cover their beautiful skin with white mantles, leave human beings behind and go from the broad-pathed earth to the race of the immortals, to Olympus. Baleful

[11] I.e. with their father.

---

189 exp. Hagen: post 181 traiec. Pertusi
192 post χερσί interpunxit Heinsius

θνητοῖς ἀνθρώποισι, κακοῦ δ᾽ οὐκ ἔσσεται ἀλκή.

νῦν δ᾽ αἶνον βασιλεῦσ᾽ ἐρέω, φρονέουσι καὶ
   αὐτοῖς.
ὧδ᾽ ἴρηξ προσέειπεν ἀηδόνα ποικιλόδειρον,
ὕψι μάλ᾽ ἐν νεφέεσσι φέρων, ὀνύχεσσι μεμαρπώς·
205  ἡ δ᾽ ἐλεόν, γναμπτοῖσι πεπαρμένη ἀμφ᾽ ὀνύχεσσιν,
μύρετο· τὴν ὅ γ᾽ ἐπικρατέως πρὸς μῦθον ἔειπεν·
"δαιμονίη, τί λέληκας; ἔχει νύ σε πολλὸν ἀρείων·
τῇ δ᾽ εἶς ᾗ σ᾽ ἂν ἐγώ περ ἄγω καὶ ἀοιδὸν ἐοῦσαν·
δεῖπνον δ᾽ αἴ κ᾽ ἐθέλω ποιήσομαι ἠὲ μεθήσω.
210  ἄφρων δ᾽ ὅς κ᾽ ἐθέλῃ πρὸς κρείσσονας ἀντιφερίζειν·
νίκης τε στέρεται πρός τ᾽ αἴσχεσιν ἄλγεα πάσχει."
ὣς ἔφατ᾽ ὠκυπέτης ἴρηξ, τανυσίπτερος ὄρνις.

ὦ Πέρση, σὺ δ᾽ ἄκουε Δίκης, μηδ᾽ Ὕβριν
   ὄφελλε·
Ὕβρις γάρ τε κακὴ δειλῷ βροτῷ· οὐδὲ μὲν ἐσθλὸς
215  ῥηιδίως φερέμεν δύναται, βαρύθει δέ θ᾽ ὑπ᾽ αὐτῆς
ἐγκύρσας ἄτῃσιν· ὁδὸς δ᾽ ἑτέρηφι παρελθεῖν
κρείσσων ἐς τὰ δίκαια· Δίκη δ᾽ ὑπὲρ Ὕβριος ἴσχει
ἐς τέλος ἐξελθοῦσα· παθὼν δέ τε νήπιος ἔγνω·
αὐτίκα γὰρ τρέχει Ὅρκος ἅμα σκολιῇσι δίκῃσιν,
220  τῆς δὲ Δίκης ῥόθος ἑλκομένης ᾗ κ᾽ ἄνδρες ἄγωσιν
δωροφάγοι, σκολιῇς δὲ δίκῃς κρίνωσι θέμιστας.
ἡ δ᾽ ἕπεται κλαίουσα πόλιν καὶ ἤθεα λαῶν,

210–11 ath. Aristarchus, habent Π₅ Π₈ Π₃₈ etc.: post 212
transp. Graevius

pains will be left for mortal human beings, and there will be no safeguard against evil.

(202) And now I will tell a fable to kings who themselves too have understanding. This is how the hawk addressed the colorful-necked nightingale, carrying her high up among the clouds, grasping her with its claws, while she wept piteously, pierced by the curved claws; he said to her forcefully, "Silly bird, why are you crying out? One far superior to you is holding you. You are going wherever I shall carry you, even if you are a singer; I shall make you my dinner if I wish, or I shall let you go. Stupid he who would wish to contend against those stronger than he is: for he is deprived of the victory, and suffers pains in addition to his humiliations." So spoke the swift-flying hawk, the long-winged bird.

(213) As for you, Perses, give heed to Justice and do not foster Outrageousness. For Outrageousness is evil in a worthless mortal; and even a fine man cannot bear her easily, but encounters calamities and then is weighed down under her. The better road is the one towards what is just, passing her by on the other side. Justice wins out over Outrageousness when she arrives at the end; but the fool only knows this after he has suffered. For at once Oath starts to run along beside crooked judgments, and there is a clamor when Justice is dragged where men, gift-eaters, carry her off and pronounce verdicts with crooked judgments; but she stays, weeping, with the city and the people's abodes,

---

211 αἴσχεσιν ἄλγεα Π₅ Π₈ Π₃₈ Etym.codd., testt.: ἄλγεσιν αἴσχεα Merkelbach

ἠέρα ἑσσαμένη, κακὸν ἀνθρώποισι φέρουσα
οἵ τέ μιν ἐξελάσουσι καὶ οὐκ ἰθεῖαν ἔνειμαν.

225    οἳ δὲ δίκας ξείνοισι καὶ ἐνδήμοισι διδοῦσιν
ἰθείας καὶ μή τι παρεκβαίνουσι δικαίου,
τοῖσι τέθηλε πόλις, λαοὶ δ᾽ ἀνθέουσιν ἐν αὐτῇ·
Εἰρήνη δ᾽ ἀνὰ γῆν κουροτρόφος, οὐδέ ποτ᾽ αὐτοῖς
ἀργαλέον πόλεμον τεκμαίρεται εὐρύοπα Ζεύς·

230    οὐδέ ποτ᾽ ἰθυδίκῃσι μετ᾽ ἀνδράσι λιμὸς ὀπηδεῖ
οὐδ᾽ ἄτη, θαλίῃς δὲ μεμηλότα ἔργα νέμονται.
τοῖσι φέρει μὲν γαῖα πολὺν βίον, οὔρεσι δὲ δρῦς
ἄκρη μέν τε φέρει βαλάνους, μέσση δὲ μελίσσας·
εἰροπόκοι δ᾽ ὄιες μαλλοῖς καταβεβρίθασι·

235    τίκτουσιν δὲ γυναῖκες ἐοικότα τέκνα γονεῦσιν·
θάλλουσιν δ᾽ ἀγαθοῖσι διαμπερές· οὐδ᾽ ἐπὶ νηῶν
νίσονται, καρπὸν δὲ φέρει ζείδωρος ἄρουρα.

οἷς δ᾽ ὕβρις τε μέμηλε κακὴ καὶ σχέτλια ἔργα,
τοῖς δὲ δίκην Κρονίδης τεκμαίρεται εὐρύοπα Ζεύς.

240    πολλάκι καὶ ξύμπασα πόλις κακοῦ ἀνδρὸς ἀπηύρα,
ὅστις ἀλιτραίνει καὶ ἀτάσθαλα μηχανάαται.
τοῖσιν δ᾽ οὐρανόθεν μέγ᾽ ἐπήγαγε πῆμα Κρονίων,
λιμὸν ὁμοῦ καὶ λοιμόν· ἀποφθινύθουσι δὲ λαοί·
οὐδὲ γυναῖκες τίκτουσιν, μινύθουσι δὲ οἶκοι

245    Ζηνὸς φραδμοσύνῃσιν Ὀλυμπίου· ἄλλοτε δ᾽ αὖτε
ἢ τῶν γε στρατὸν εὐρὺν ἀπώλεσεν ἢ ὅ γε τεῖχος
ἢ νέας ἐν πόντῳ Κρονίδης ἀποτείνυται αὐτῶν.

ὦ βασιλῆς, ὑμεῖς δὲ καταφράζεσθε καὶ αὐτοὶ
τήνδε δίκην· ἐγγὺς γὰρ ἐν ἀνθρώποισιν ἐόντες

250    ἀθάνατοι φράζονται, ὅσοι σκολιῇσι δίκῃσιν

clad in invisibility, bearing evil to the human beings who drive her out and do not deal straight.

(225) But those who give straight judgments to foreigners and fellow-citizens and do not turn aside from justice at all, their city blooms and the people in it flower. For them, Peace, the nurse of the young, is on the earth, and far-seeing Zeus never marks out painful war; nor does famine attend straight-judging men, nor calamity, but they share out in festivities the fruits of the labors they care for. For these the earth bears the means of life in abundance, and on the mountains the oak tree bears acorns on its surface, and bees in its center; their woolly sheep are weighed down by their fleeces; and their wives give birth to children who resemble their parents. They bloom with good things continuously. And they do not go onto ships, for the grain-giving field bears them crops.

(238) But to those who care only for evil outrageousness and cruel deeds, far-seeing Zeus, Cronus' son, marks out justice. Often even a whole city suffers because of an evil man who sins and devises wicked deeds. Upon them, Cronus' son brings forth woe from the sky, famine together with pestilence, and the people die away; the women do not give birth, and the households are diminished by the plans of Olympian Zeus. And at another time Cronus' son destroys their broad army or their wall, or he takes vengeance upon their ships on the sea.

(248) As for you kings, too, ponder this justice yourselves. For among human beings there are immortals nearby, who take notice of all those who grind one another

---

244–45 Π₅Π₉ codd.: in libris nonnullis defuisse testatur Plutarchus (ap. Proclum), non laud. Aeschines

ἀλλήλους τρίβουσι θεῶν ὄπιν οὐκ ἀλέγοντες.
τρὶς γὰρ μύριοί εἰσιν ἐπὶ χθονὶ πουλυβοτείρῃ
ἀθάνατοι Ζηνὸς φύλακες θνητῶν ἀνθρώπων,
οἵ ῥα φυλάσσουσίν τε δίκας καὶ σχέτλια ἔργα,
255 ἠέρα ἑσσάμενοι, πάντῃ φοιτῶντες ἐπ' αἶαν.
ἡ δέ τε παρθένος ἐστὶ Δίκη, Διὸς ἐκγεγαυῖα,
κυδρή τ' αἰδοίη τε θεοῖς οἳ Ὄλυμπον ἔχουσιν·
καί ῥ' ὁπότ' ἄν τίς μιν βλάπτῃ σκολιῶς ὀνοτάζων,
αὐτίκα πὰρ Διὶ πατρὶ καθεζομένη Κρονίωνι
260 γηρύετ' ἀνθρώπων ἄδικον νόον, ὄφρ' ἀποτείσῃ
δῆμος ἀτασθαλίας βασιλέων, οἳ λυγρὰ νοέοντες
ἄλλῃ παρκλίνωσι δίκας σκολιῶς ἐνέποντες.
ταῦτα φυλασσόμενοι βασιλῆς ἰθύνετε μύθους
δωροφάγοι, σκολιῶν δὲ δικέων ἐπὶ πάγχυ λάθεσθε.
265 οἵ τ' αὐτῷ κακὰ τεύχει ἀνὴρ ἄλλῳ κακὰ τεύχων,
ἡ δὲ κακὴ βουλὴ τῷ βουλεύσαντι κακίστη.
πάντα ἰδὼν Διὸς ὀφθαλμὸς καὶ πάντα νοήσας
καί νυ τάδ' αἴ κ' ἐθέλῃσ' ἐπιδέρκεται, οὐδέ ἑ λήθει
οἵην δὴ καὶ τήνδε δίκην πόλις ἐντὸς ἐέργει.
270 νῦν δὴ ἐγὼ μήτ' αὐτὸς ἐν ἀνθρώποισι δίκαιος
εἴην μήτ' ἐμὸς υἱός, ἐπεὶ κακὸν ἄνδρα δίκαιον
ἔμμεναι, εἰ μείζω γε δίκην ἀδικώτερος ἕξει·
ἀλλὰ τά γ' οὔ πω ἔολπα τελεῖν Δία μητιόεντα.
    ὦ Πέρση, σὺ δὲ ταῦτα μετὰ φρεσὶ βάλλεο
        σῇσιν,
275 καί νυ Δίκης ἐπάκουε, βίης δ' ἐπιλήθεο πάμπαν.
τόνδε γὰρ ἀνθρώποισι νόμον διέταξε Κρονίων,
ἰχθύσι μὲν καὶ θηρσὶ καὶ οἰωνοῖς πετεηνοῖς

down with crooked judgments and have no care for the
gods' retribution. Thrice ten thousand are Zeus' immortal
guardians of mortal human beings upon the bounteous
earth, and they watch over judgments and cruel deeds,
clad in invisibility, walking everywhere upon the earth.
There is a maiden, Justice, born of Zeus, celebrated and
revered by the gods who dwell on Olympus, and whenever
someone harms her by crookedly scorning her, she sits
down at once beside her father Zeus, Cronus' son, and pro-
claims the unjust mind of human beings, so that he will
take vengeance upon the people for the wickedness of
their kings, who think baneful thoughts and bend judg-
ments to one side by pronouncing them crookedly. Bear
this in mind, kings, and straighten your discourses, you
gift-eaters, and put crooked judgments quite out of your
minds. A man contrives evil for himself when he contrives
evil for someone else, and an evil plan is most evil for the
planner. Zeus' eye, which sees all things and knows all
things, perceives this too, if he so wishes, and he is well
aware just what kind of justice this is which the city has
within it. Right now I myself would not want to be a just
man among human beings, neither I nor a son of mine,
since it is evil for a man to be just if the more unjust one will
receive greater justice. But I do not anticipate that the
counsellor Zeus will let things end up this way.

(274) Perses, lay these things in your heart and give
heed to Justice, and put violence entirely out of your mind.
This is the law that Cronus' son has established for human
beings: that fish and beasts and winged birds eat one an-

---

263 μύθους Φ: δίκας CD
267–73 damn. Plutarchus

ἔσθειν ἀλλήλους, ἐπεὶ οὐ Δίκη ἐστὶ μετ' αὐτοῖς·
ἀνθρώποισι δ' ἔδωκε Δίκην, ἣ πολλὸν ἀρίστη
280 γίνεται· εἰ γάρ τίς κ' ἐθέλῃ τὰ δίκαι' ἀγορεῦσαι
γινώσκων, τῷ μέν τ' ὄλβον διδοῖ εὐρύοπα Ζεύς·
ὃς δέ κε μαρτυρίῃσιν ἑκὼν ἐπίορκον ὀμόσσας
ψεύσεται, ἐν δὲ Δίκην βλάψας νήκεστον ἀάσθη,
τοῦ δέ τ' ἀμαυροτέρη γενεὴ μετόπισθε λέλειπται·
285 ἀνδρὸς δ' εὐόρκου γενεὴ μετόπισθεν ἀμείνων.

σοὶ δ' ἐγὼ ἐσθλὰ νοέων ἐρέω, μέγα νήπιε Πέρση.
τὴν μέν τοι Κακότητα καὶ ἰλαδὸν ἔστιν ἑλέσθαι
ῥηιδίως· λείη μὲν ὁδός, μάλα δ' ἐγγύθι ναίει·
τῆς δ' Ἀρετῆς ἱδρῶτα θεοὶ προπάροιθεν ἔθηκαν
290 ἀθάνατοι· μακρὸς δὲ καὶ ὄρθιος οἶμος ἐς αὐτὴν
καὶ τρηχὺς τὸ πρῶτον· ἐπὴν δ' εἰς ἄκρον ἵκηται,
ῥηιδίη δἤπειτα πέλει, χαλεπή περ ἐοῦσα.
οὗτος μὲν πανάριστος, ὃς αὐτῷ πάντα νοήσει,
φρασσάμενος τά κ' ἔπειτα καὶ ἐς τέλος ᾖσιν ἀμείνω·
295 ἐσθλὸς δ' αὖ καὶ κεῖνος, ὃς εὖ εἰπόντι πίθηται·
ὃς δέ κε μήτ' αὐτὸς νοέῃ μήτ' ἄλλου ἀκούων
ἐν θυμῷ βάλληται, ὁ δ' αὖτ' ἀχρήιος ἀνήρ.
ἀλλὰ σύ γ' ἡμετέρης μεμνημένος αἰὲν ἐφετμῆς
ἐργάζεο Πέρση, δῖον γένος, ὄφρα σε Λιμὸς
300 ἐχθαίρῃ, φιλέῃ δέ σ' ἐυστέφανος Δημήτηρ
αἰδοίη, βιότου δὲ τεὴν πιμπλῆσι καλιήν·
Λιμὸς γάρ τοι πάμπαν ἀεργῷ σύμφορος ἀνδρί.
τῷ δὲ θεοὶ νεμεσῶσι καὶ ἀνέρες, ὅς κεν ἀεργὸς

other, since Justice is not among them; but to human be-
ings he has given Justice, which is the best by far. For if
someone who recognizes what is just is willing to speak
it out publicly, then far-seeing Zeus gives him wealth.
But whoever willfully swears a false oath, telling a lie in his
testimony, he himself is incurably hurt at the same time as
he harms Justice, and in after times his family is left more
obscure; whereas the family of the man who keeps his oath
is better in after times.

(286) To you, Perses, you great fool, I will speak my fine
thoughts: Misery is there to be grabbed in abundance, eas-
ily, for smooth is the road, and she lives very nearby; but in
front of Excellence the immortal gods have set sweat, and
the path to her is long and steep, and rough at first—yet
when one arrives at the top, then it becomes easy, difficult
though it still is.
(293) The man who thinks of everything by himself,
considering what will be better, later and in the end—this
man is the best of all. That man is fine too, the one who is
persuaded by someone who speaks well. But whoever nei-
ther thinks by himself nor pays heed to what someone else
says and lays it to his heart—that man is good for nothing.
So, Perses, you of divine stock, keep working and always
bear in mind our behest, so that Famine will hate you and
well-garlanded reverend Demeter will love you and fill
your granary with the means of life. For Famine is ever the
companion of a man who does not work; and gods and men
feel resentment against that man, whoever lives without

288 λείη Plato Xenophon al.: ὀλίγη codd. Proclus

ζώῃ, κηφήνεσσι κοθούροις εἴκελος ὀργήν,
305 οἵ τε μελισσάων κάματον τρύχουσιν ἀεργοὶ
ἔσθοντες· σοὶ δ' ἔργα φίλ' ἔστω μέτρια κοσμεῖν,
ὥς κέ τοι ὡραίου βιότου πλήθωσι καλιαί.
ἐξ ἔργων δ' ἄνδρες πολύμηλοί τ' ἀφνειοί τε·
καί τ' ἐργαζόμενος πολὺ φίλτερος ἀθανάτοισιν
310 ἔσσεαι ἠδὲ βροτοῖς· μάλα γὰρ στυγέουσιν ἀεργούς.
ἔργον δ' οὐδὲν ὄνειδος, ἀεργίη δέ τ' ὄνειδος·
εἰ δέ κεν ἐργάζῃ, τάχα σε ζηλώσει ἀεργὸς
πλουτέοντα· πλούτῳ δ' ἀρετὴ καὶ κῦδος ὀπηδεῖ·
δαίμονι δ' οἷος ἔησθα, τὸ ἐργάζεσθαι ἄμεινον,
315 εἴ κεν ἀπ' ἀλλοτρίων κτεάνων ἀεσίφρονα θυμὸν
εἰς ἔργον τρέψας μελετᾷς βίου, ὥς σε κελεύω.
αἰδὼς δ' οὐκ ἀγαθὴ κεχρημένον ἄνδρα κομίζειν,
αἰδώς, ἥ τ' ἄνδρας μέγα σίνεται ἠδ' ὀνίνησιν·
αἰδώς τοι πρὸς ἀνολβίη, θάρσος δὲ πρὸς ὄλβῳ.
320 χρήματα δ' οὐχ ἁρπακτά· θεόσδοτα πολλὸν
ἀμείνω.
εἰ γάρ τις καὶ χερσὶ βίῃ μέγαν ὄλβον ἕληται,
ἢ ὅ γ' ἀπὸ γλώσσης ληίσσεται, οἷά τε πολλὰ
γίνεται, εὖτ' ἂν δὴ κέρδος νόον ἐξαπατήσει
ἀνθρώπων, Αἰδῶ δέ τ' Ἀναιδείη κατοπάζῃ,
325 ῥεῖα δέ μιν μαυροῦσι θεοί, μινύθουσι δὲ οἶκον

304 ὀργήν Π₃₃CᵃᶜDᵃᶜ sch. in Platonem al.: ὁρμήν CᵖᶜDᵖᶜ (m.
1) Φ sch. in Theocritum al.: ἀλκήν φ₉φ₁₁ψ₁₅
310 deest et in Π₅Π₁₁Π₃₃ D Proclo Stobaeo: hab. C (m. rec. in
mg.) Φ      317–18 ath. Plutarchus; 318 post 319 transp.
Peppmüller: 317 et 319 invicem transp. Mazon

working, in his temper like stingless drones that consume
the labor of the bees, eating it without working. But as for
you, be glad to organize your work properly, so that your
granaries will be filled with the means of life in good sea-
son. It is from working that men have many sheep and are
wealthy, and if you work you will be dearer by far to im-
mortals and to mortals: for they very much hate men who
do not work.[12] Work is not a disgrace at all, but not working
is a disgrace. And if you work, the man who does not work
will quickly envy you when you are rich; excellence and
fame attend upon riches. Whatever sort you are by for-
tune, working is better, if you turn your foolish spirit away
from other men's possessions towards work, taking care for
the means of life, as I bid you. Shame is not good at provid-
ing for a needy man—shame, which greatly harms men
and also benefits them: for shame goes along with poverty,
and self-confidence goes along with wealth.

(320) Property is not to be snatched: god-given is better
by far. For if someone grabs great wealth with his hands by
violence, or plunders it by means of his tongue, as often
happens when profit deceives the mind of human beings
and Shamelessness drives Shame away, then the gods eas-
ily make him obscure, and they diminish that man's house-

[12] Line 310, "you will be ... and to mortals: for they very much
hate men who do not work," is missing in papyri, scholia, and some
medieval manuscripts, and is excluded by many editors.

---

318 om. D, in marg. rest. m. al.
321 ὄλβον: ὅρκον Π₃₃ Byz. Etym. Genuinum A s. v.
μαυροῦσι

113

ἀνέρι τῷ, παῦρον δέ τ᾽ ἐπὶ χρόνον ὄλβος ὀπηδεῖ.
ἶσον δ᾽ ὅς θ᾽ ἱκέτην ὅς τε ξεῖνον κακὸν ἔρξει,
ὅς τε κασιγνήτοιο ἑοῦ ἀνὰ δέμνια βαίνῃ
κρυπταδίης εὐνῆς ἀλόχου, παρακαίρια ῥέζων,
330    ὅς τέ τεο ἀφραδίης ἀλιτήνεται ὀρφανὰ τέκνα,
ὅς τε γονῆα γέροντα κακῷ ἐπὶ γήραος οὐδῷ
νεικείῃ χαλεποῖσι καθαπτόμενος ἐπέεσσιν·
τῷ δ᾽ ἤτοι Ζεὺς αὐτὸς ἀγαίεται, ἐς δὲ τελευτὴν
ἔργων ἀντ᾽ ἀδίκων χαλεπὴν ἐπέθηκεν ἀμοιβήν.
335    ἀλλὰ σὺ τῶν μὲν πάμπαν ἔεργ᾽ ἀεσίφρονα θυμόν,
κὰδ δύναμιν δ᾽ ἔρδειν ἱέρ᾽ ἀθανάτοισι θεοῖσιν
ἁγνῶς καὶ καθαρῶς, ἐπὶ δ᾽ ἀγλαὰ μηρία καίειν·
ἄλλοτε δὲ σπονδῇσι θύεσσί τε ἱλάσκεσθαι,
ἠμὲν ὅτ᾽ εὐνάζῃ καὶ ὅτ᾽ ἂν φάος ἱερὸν ἔλθῃ,
340    ὥς κέ τοι ἵλαον κραδίην καὶ θυμὸν ἔχωσιν,
ὄφρ᾽ ἄλλων ὠνῇ κλῆρον, μὴ τὸν τεὸν ἄλλος.
τὸν φιλέοντ᾽ ἐπὶ δαῖτα καλεῖν, τὸν δ᾽ ἐχθρὸν
ἐᾶσαι·
τὸν δὲ μάλιστα καλεῖν ὅστις σέθεν ἐγγύθι ναίει·
εἰ γάρ τοι καὶ χρῆμ᾽ ἐγχώριον ἄλλο γένηται,
345    γείτονες ἄζωστοι ἔκιον, ζώσαντο δὲ πηοί.
πῆμα κακὸς γείτων, ὅσσόν τ᾽ ἀγαθὸς μέγ᾽ ὄνειαρ·
ἔμμορέ τοι τιμῆς, ὅς τ᾽ ἔμμορε γείτονος ἐσθλοῦ·
οὐδ᾽ ἂν βοῦς ἀπόλοιτ᾽, εἰ μὴ γείτων κακὸς εἴη.
εὖ μὲν μετρεῖσθαι παρὰ γείτονος, εὖ δ᾽ ἀποδοῦναι,
350    αὐτῷ τῷ μέτρῳ, καὶ λώιον, αἴ κε δύνηαι,
ὡς ἂν χρηίζων καὶ ἐς ὕστερον ἄρκιον εὕρῃς.
μὴ κακὰ κερδαίνειν· κακὰ κέρδεα ἶσ᾽ ἄτῃσιν.

hold, and wealth attends him for only a short time. It is the same if someone does evil to a suppliant or to a guest, or if he goes up to his own brother's bed, sleeping with his sister-in-law in secret, acting wrongly, or if in his folly he sins against orphaned children, or if he rebukes his aged father upon the evil threshold of old age, attacking him with grievous words: against such a man, Zeus himself is enraged, and in the end he imposes a grievous return for unjust works.

(335) But as for you, keep your foolish spirit entirely away from these things. According to your capability, make holy sacrifice to the immortal gods in a hallowed and pure manner, and burn splendid thigh-pieces on the altar; at other times, seek propitiation with libations and burnt-offerings, both when you go to bed and when the holy light returns, so that their heart and spirit will be propitious to you, so that you may barter for other people's allotment, not someone else for yours.

(342) Invite your friend to the feast, but let your enemy be; and above all call whoever lives near to you. For if something untoward happens on your estate, your neighbors come ungirt, but your in-laws gird themselves. A bad neighbor is a woe, just as much as a good one is a great boon: whoever has a share in a fine neighbor has a share in good value; not even a cow would be lost, if the neighbor were not bad. Measure out well from your neighbor, and pay him back well, with the very same measure, and better if you can, so that if you are in need again you will find him reliable later too. Do not seek profit evilly: evil profit is as

---

344 ἐγχώριον Etym.codd.: ἐγκώμιον Π₁₉ ΣProclus testt.

τὸν φιλέοντα φιλεῖν καὶ τῷ προσιόντι προσεῖναι,
καὶ δόμεν ὅς κεν δῷ, καὶ μὴ δόμεν ὅς κεν μὴ δῷ·
355 δώτῃ μέν τις ἔδωκεν, ἀδώτῃ δ' οὔ τις ἔδωκεν·
Δὼς ἀγαθή, Ἅρπαξ δὲ κακή, θανάτοιο δότειρα.
ὃς μὲν γάρ κεν ἀνὴρ ἐθέλων ὅ γε καὶ μέγα δώῃ,
χαίρει τῷ δώρῳ καὶ τέρπεται ὃν κατὰ θυμόν·
ὃς δέ κεν αὐτὸς ἕληται ἀναιδείηφι πιθήσας,
360 καί τε σμικρὸν ἐόν, τό γ' ἐπάχνωσεν φίλον ἦτορ.
364      οὐδὲ τό γ' εἰν οἴκῳ κατακείμενον ἀνέρα κήδει·
365 οἴκοι βέλτερον εἶναι, ἐπεὶ βλαβερὸν τὸ θύρηφιν.
366 ἐσθλὸν μὲν παρεόντος ἑλέσθαι, πῆμα δὲ θυμῷ
367 χρηίζειν ἀπεόντος· ἅ σε φράζεσθαι ἄνωγα.
361 εἰ γάρ κεν καὶ σμικρὸν ἐπὶ σμικρῷ καταθεῖο,
362 καὶ θαμὰ τοῦτ' ἔρδοις, τάχα κεν μέγα καὶ τὸ γένοιτο.
363 ὃς δ' ἐπ' ἐόντι φέρει, ὁ δ' ἀλέξεται αἴθοπα λιμόν·
368 ἀρχομένου δὲ πίθου καὶ λήγοντος κορέσασθαι,
μεσσόθι φείδεσθαι· δειλὴ δ' ἐν πυθμένι φειδώ.
370 μισθὸς δ' ἀνδρὶ φίλῳ εἰρημένος ἄρκιος ἔστω·
καί τε κασιγνήτῳ γελάσας ἐπὶ μάρτυρα θέσθαι·
πίστεις †δ' ἄρ' ὁμῶς καὶ ἀπιστίαι ὤλεσαν ἄνδρας.

354–55 proscr. Plutarchus
361–363 post 367 transp. Most
363 post 360 traiec. Evelyn-White
370–72 eiecerunt aliqui, om. Π₁₁Π₃₃ (et fort. Π₁₉Π₃₈)
CDTzetzesΦψ: novit Plutarchus sed incertum ubi (e. g. post 352):
in textu hic habent MoschopulusTr, ante 369 ψ₁₁ (traiecit
corrector), in marg. m. al. C⁴ω₂ω₃Nφ₃ψ₉ψ₁₃: 370 solum post 382
φ₇φ₈  370 Pittheo tribuit Aristoteles, Hesiodo Plutarchus

bad as calamities. Be friendly to your friend, and go visit those who visit you. And give to him who gives and do not give to him who does not give: for one gives to a giver, but no one gives to a non-giver—Give is good, Grab is bad, a giver of death. For whatever a man gives willingly, even if it is much, he rejoices in the gift and takes pleasure in his spirit; but whoever snatches, relying upon shamelessness, this congeals his own heart, even if it is little.

(364) What lies stored up in the household does not cause a man grief: it is better for things to be at home, for what is outdoors is at risk. It is fine to take from what you have, but it is woe for the spirit to have need of what you do not have. I bid you take notice of this. For if you put down even a little upon a little and do this often, then this too will quickly become a lot; whoever adds to what is already there wards off fiery famine.[13] Take your fill when the storage-jar is just opened or nearly empty, be thrifty in the middle: thrift in the lees is worthless. Let the payment agreed for a man who is your friend be reliable; and smile upon your brother—but add a witness too: for both trust and distrust have destroyed men. Do not let an arse-fancy

---

[13] Lines 361–63 discuss the accumulation of domestic stores and are out of place after 360, which concludes the advice to give to others rather than snatching from them; they fit much better after 367, and so, against all the manuscripts, I have transposed them here. The traditional order may have arisen from the similarity between σμικρόν in line 360 and σμικρὸν ἐπὶ σμικρῷ in 361.

Heliodorus Michael
372 δ' ἄρα C⁴ω₃φ₃ψ₉ψ₁₃, δ' ἄρα N: γάρ τοι Bentley: δή ῥα Reiz: γάρ ῥα Allen

μηδὲ γυνή σε νόον πυγοστόλος ἐξαπατάτω
αἱμύλα κωτίλλουσα, τεὴν διφῶσα καλιήν·
375 ὃς δὲ γυναικὶ πέποιθε, πέποιθ᾽ ὅ γε φιλήτῃσιν.
μουνογενὴς δὲ πάις εἴη πατρώιον οἶκον
φερβέμεν· ὣς γὰρ πλοῦτος ἀέξεται ἐν μεγάροισιν·
γηραιὸς δὲ θάνοι ἕτερον παῖδ᾽ ἐγκαταλείπων.
ῥεῖα δέ κεν πλεόνεσσι πόροι Ζεὺς ἄσπετον ὄλβον·
380 πλείων μὲν πλεόνων μελέτη, μείζων δ᾽ ἐπιθήκη.

σοὶ δ᾽ εἰ πλούτου θυμὸς ἐέλδεται ἐν φρεσὶν ᾗσιν,
ὧδ᾽ ἔρδειν, καὶ ἔργον ἐπ᾽ ἔργῳ ἐργάζεσθαι.
Πληιάδων Ἀτλαγενέων ἐπιτελλομενάων
ἄρχεσθ᾽ ἀμήτου, ἀρότοιο δὲ δυσομενάων·
385 αἳ δή τοι νύκτας τε καὶ ἤματα τεσσαράκοντα
κεκρύφαται, αὖτις δὲ περιπλομένου ἐνιαυτοῦ
φαίνονται τὰ πρῶτα χαρασσομένοιο σιδήρου.
οὗτός τοι πεδίων πέλεται νόμος, οἵ τε θαλάσσης
ἐγγύθι ναιετάουσ᾽ οἵ τ᾽ ἄγκεα βησσήεντα
390 πόντου κυμαίνοντος ἀπόπροθι, πίονα χῶρον
ναίουσιν· γυμνὸν σπείρειν, γυμνὸν δὲ βοωτεῖν,
γυμνὸν δ᾽ ἀμάειν, εἴ χ᾽ ὥρια πάντ᾽ ἐθέλῃσθα
ἔργα κομίζεσθαι Δημήτερος, ὥς τοι ἕκαστα
ὥρι᾽ ἀέξηται, μή πως τὰ μέταζε χατίζων
395 πτώσσῃς ἀλλοτρίους οἴκους καὶ μηδὲν ἀνύσσεις—
ὡς καὶ νῦν ἐπ᾽ ἔμ᾽ ἦλθες· ἐγὼ δέ τοι οὐκ ἐπιδώσω

woman deceive your mind by guilefully cajoling you while she pokes into your granary: whoever trusts a woman, trusts swindlers. Let there be a single-born son to nourish the father's household: in this way wealth is increased in the halls; and may he die an old man, leaving behind one son in his turn. And yet Zeus could easily bestow immense wealth upon more people: more hands, more work, and the surplus is bigger.

(381) If the spirit in your breast longs for wealth, then act in this way, and work at work upon work.

(383) When the Atlas-born Pleiades rise,[14] start the harvest—the plowing, when they set.[15] They are concealed for forty nights and days,[16] but when the year has revolved they appear once more, when the iron is being sharpened. This is the rule for the plains, and for those who dwell near the sea and those far from the swelling sea in the valleys and glens, fertile land: sow naked, and plow naked, and harvest naked, if you want to bring in all of Demeter's works in due season, so that each crop may grow for you in its season, lest being in need later you go as a beggar to other people's houses and achieve nothing—just as now you have come to me. But I shall not give you anything

[14] In the first half of May.
[15] In late October or early November.
[16] From the end of March until the beginning of May.

---

375 et $\Pi_{19}$: damn. Plutarchus
378 ath. Σ (habent $\Pi_{11}$ $\Pi_{19}$ $\Pi_{33}$) θάνοι $\Pi_{19}$ Hermann: θάνοις codd. Σᵛᵉᵗ Proclus

οὐδ' ἐπιμετρήσω· ἐργάζεο, νήπιε Πέρση,
ἔργα, τά τ' ἀνθρώποισι θεοὶ διετεκμήραντο,
μή ποτε σὺν παίδεσσι γυναικί τε θυμὸν ἀχεύων
400 ζητεύῃς βίοτον κατὰ γείτονας, οἱ δ' ἀμελῶσιν.
δὶς μὲν γὰρ καὶ τρὶς τάχα τεύξεαι· ἢν δ' ἔτι λυπῇς,
χρῆμα μὲν οὐ πρήξεις, σὺ δ' ἐτώσια πόλλ'
    ἀγορεύσεις,
ἀχρεῖος δ' ἔσται ἐπέων νομός. ἀλλά σ' ἄνωγα
φράζεσθαι χρειῶν τε λύσιν λιμοῦ τ' ἀλεωρήν.
405 οἶκον μὲν πρώτιστα γυναῖκά τε βοῦν τ' ἀροτῆρα,
κτητήν, οὐ γαμετήν, ἥτις καὶ βουσὶν ἔποιτο.
χρήματα δ' εἰν οἴκῳ πάντ' ἄρμενα ποιήσασθαι,
μὴ σὺ μὲν αἰτῇς ἄλλον, ὁ δ' ἀρνῆται, σὺ δὲ τητᾷ,
ἡ δ' ὥρη παραμείβηται, μινύθῃ δέ τοι ἔργον.
410 μηδ' ἀναβάλλεσθαι ἔς τ' αὔριον ἔς τε ἔνηφιν·
οὐ γὰρ ἐτωσιοεργὸς ἀνὴρ πίμπλησι καλιὴν
οὐδ' ἀναβαλλόμενος· μελέτη δέ τοι ἔργον ὀφέλλει·
αἰεὶ δ' ἀμβολιεργὸς ἀνὴρ ἄτῃσι παλαίει.
    ἦμος δὴ λήγει μένος ὀξέος ἠελίοιο
415 καύματος εἰδαλίμου, μετοπωρινὸν ὀμβρήσαντος
Ζηνὸς ἐρισθενέος, μετὰ δὲ τρέπεται βρότεος χρὼς
πολλὸν ἐλαφρότερος· δὴ γὰρ τότε Σείριος ἀστὴρ
βαιὸν ὑπὲρ κεφαλῆς κηριτρεφέων ἀνθρώπων
ἔρχεται ἠμάτιος, πλεῖον δέ τε νυκτὸς ἐπαυρεῖ·
420 τῆμος ἀδηκτοτάτη πέλεται τμηθεῖσα σιδήρῳ
ὕλη, φύλλα δ' ἔραζε χέει πτόρθοιό τε λήγει·
τῆμος ἄρ' ὑλοτομεῖν μεμνημένος, ὥριον ἔργον.
ὅλμον μὲν τριπόδην τάμνειν, ὕπερον δὲ τρίπηχυ,

120

extra, nor measure out extra for you. Work, foolish Perses, at the works which the gods have marked out for human beings, lest someday, sorrowing in your spirit, together with your children and your wife you seek a livelihood among your neighbors, but they pay no attention to you. For two times maybe and three times you will succeed; but if you bother them again, you will accomplish nothing but will speak a lot in vain, and the rangeland of your words will be useless. I bid you take notice of how to clear your debts and how to ward off famine: a house first of all, a woman, and an ox for plowing—the woman one you purchase, not marry, one who can follow with the oxen—and arrange everything well in the house, lest you ask someone else and he refuse and you suffer want, and the season pass by, and the fruit of your work be diminished. Do not postpone until tomorrow and the next day: for the futilely working man does not fill his granary, nor does the postponer; industry fosters work, and the work-postponing man is always wrestling with calamities.

(414) When the strength of the sharp sun ceases from its sweaty heat, as mighty Zeus sends the autumn rain, and a mortal's skin changes with great relief—for that is when the star Sirius goes during the day only briefly above the heads of death-nurtured human beings and takes a greater share of the night—at that time,[17] wood that is cut with the iron is least bitten by worms, and its leaves fall to the ground and it ceases putting forth shoots. So at that time be mindful and cut wood, a seasonable work: cut a mortar three feet long, and a pestle three cubits long,[18] and an axle

---

[17] In late September and early October.
[18] About four and a half feet.

ἄξονα δ' ἑπταπόδην· μάλα γάρ νύ τοι ἅρμενον οὕτω·
425 εἰ δέ κεν ὀκταπόδη, ἀπὸ καὶ σφῦράν κε τάμοιο.
τρισπίθαμον δ' ἅψιν τάμνειν δεκαδώρῳ ἀμάξῃ.
πόλλ' ἐπικαμπύλα κᾶλα· φέρειν δὲ γύην ὅτ' ἂν εὕρῃς
εἰς οἶκον, κατ' ὄρος διζήμενος ἢ κατ' ἄρουραν,
πρίνινον· ὃς γὰρ βουσὶν ἀροῦν ὀχυρώτατός ἐστιν,
430 εὖτ' ἂν Ἀθηναίης δμωὸς ἐν ἐλύματι πήξας
γόμφοισιν πελάσας προσαρήρεται ἱστοβοῆϊ.
δοιὰ δὲ θέσθαι ἄροτρα πονησάμενος κατὰ οἶκον,
αὐτόγυον καὶ πηκτόν, ἐπεὶ πολὺ λώιον οὕτω·
εἴ χ' ἕτερον ἄξαις, ἕτερόν κ' ἐπὶ βουσὶ βάλοιο.
435 δάφνης ἢ πτελέης ἀκιώτατοι ἱστοβοῆες,
δρυὸς ⟨δ'⟩ ἔλυμα, πρίνου δὲ γύης. βόε δ' ἐννεαετήρω
ἄρσενε κεκτῆσθαι, τῶν γὰρ σθένος οὐκ ἀλαπαδνόν,
ἥβης μέτρον ἔχοντε· τὼ ἐργάζεσθαι ἀρίστω.
οὐκ ἂν τώ γ' ἐρίσαντε ἐν αὔλακι κὰμ μὲν ἄροτρον
440 ἄξειαν, τὸ δὲ ἔργον ἐτώσιον αὖθι λίποιεν.
τοῖς δ' ἅμα τεσσαρακονταετὴς αἰζηὸς ἕποιτο,
ἄρτον δειπνήσας τετράτρυφον ὀκτάβλωμον,
ὅς κ' ἔργου μελετῶν ἰθεῖάν κ' αὔλακ' ἐλαύνοι,
μηκέτι παπταίνων μεθ' ὁμήλικας, ἀλλ' ἐπὶ ἔργῳ
445 θυμὸν ἔχων· τοῦ δ' οὔ τι νεώτερος ἄλλος ἀμείνων
σπέρματα δάσσασθαι καὶ ἐπισπορίην ἀλέασθαι·
κουρότερος γὰρ ἀνὴρ μεθ' ὁμήλικας ἐπτόηται.
    φράζεσθαι δ' εὖτ' ἂν γεράνου φωνὴν ἐπακούσεις

436 δ' addidit West

seven feet long: for this way things will fit together very well. If you cut a length eight feet long, you could cut a mallet-head from it too. Cut a three-span broad[19] wheel for a ten-palm sized[20] cart. There are lots of bent timbers: search for one on the mountain or through the fields, and if you find one of holm-oak take it into your house as a plow-tree. For that wood stands up most strongly for plowing with oxen, when Athena's servant has drawn it near and attached it to the yoke-pole after having fastened it with pegs to the plow-stock. Toil hard to lay up a pair of plows in your house, one of a single piece and one put together, since it is much better this way: if you broke one, you could set the other one upon your oxen. Yoke-poles of laurel or of elm are the least wormy, of oak the plow-stock, of holm-oak the plow-tree. Acquire two oxen, nine years old, male, that have reached the measure of puberty, for their strength has not been drained away yet: they are best at working. They will not break the plow by contending with one another in the furrow, leaving the work futile right there. Together with these, a strong forty-year-old man should follow with the plow, after he has breakfasted on a four-piece,[21] eight-part loaf, someone who puts care into his work and will drive a straight furrow, no longer gaping after his age-mates, but keeping his mind on his work. And another man, not a bit younger than him, is better for scattering the seeds and avoiding over-seeding: for a younger man is all aflutter for his age-mates.

(448) Take notice, when you hear the voice of the crane

---

[19] About two feet three inches.
[20] About two and a half feet.     [21] It is unclear what exactly is meant; another suggestion is "four-times kneaded."

ὑψόθεν ἐκ νεφέων ἐνιαύσια κεκληγυίης,
450 ἥ τ' ἀρότοιό τε σῆμα φέρει καὶ χείματος ὥρην
δεικνύει ὀμβρηροῦ· κραδίην δ' ἔδακ' ἀνδρὸς ἀβούτεω·
δὴ τότε χορτάζειν ἕλικας βόας ἔνδον ἐόντας.
ῥηίδιον γὰρ ἔπος εἰπεῖν· "βόε δὸς καὶ ἅμαξαν"
ῥηίδιον δ' ἀπανήνασθαι· "πάρα δ' ἔργα βόεσσιν."
455 φησὶ δ' ἀνὴρ φρένας ἀφνειὸς πήξασθαι ἅμαξαν·
νήπιος, οὐδὲ τὸ οἶδ'· ἑκατὸν δέ τε δούρατ' ἀμάξης,
τῶν πρόσθεν μελέτην ἐχέμεν οἰκήια θέσθαι.

εὖτ' ἂν δὴ πρώτιστ' ἄροτος θνητοῖσι φανήῃ,
δὴ τότ' ἐφορμηθῆναι, ὁμῶς δμῶές τε καὶ αὐτός,
460 αὔην καὶ διερὴν ἀρόων ἀρότοιο καθ' ὥρην,
πρωὶ μάλα σπεύδων, ἵνα τοι πλήθωσιν ἄρουραι.
ἔαρι πολεῖν· θέρεος δὲ νεωμένη οὔ σ' ἀπατήσει·
νειὸν δὲ σπείρειν ἔτι κουφίζουσαν ἄρουραν.
νειὸς ἀλεξιάρη παίδων εὐκηλήτειρα.

465 εὔχεσθαι δὲ Διὶ χθονίῳ Δημήτερί θ' ἁγνῇ
ἐκτελέα βρίθειν Δημήτερος ἱερὸν ἀκτὴν
ἀρχόμενος τὰ πρῶτ' ἀρότου, ὅτ' ἂν ἄκρον ἐχέτλης
χειρὶ λαβὼν ὅρπηκι βοῶν ἐπὶ νῶτον ἵκηαι
ἔνδρυον ἑλκόντων μεσάβῳ. ὁ δὲ τυτθὸν ὄπισθεν
470 δμῳὸς ἔχων μακέλην πόνον ὀρνίθεσσι τιθείη
σπέρμα κατακρύπτων· εὐθημοσύνη γὰρ ἀρίστη
θνητοῖς ἀνθρώποις, κακοθημοσύνη δὲ κακίστη.
ὧδέ κεν ἁδροσύνη στάχυες νεύοιεν ἔραζε,

464 ἀλεξιάρη παίδων εὐκηλ- ΣProclus Etym.codd. test.:
ἀλεξιάρης Ἀιδωνέος κηλ- West

every year calling from above out of the clouds[22]: she brings the sign for plowing and indicates the season of winter rain, and this gnaws the heart of the man without oxen. That is the time to fatten the curving-horned oxen indoors: for it is easy to say, "Give me a pair of oxen and a cart," but it is also easy to refuse, saying, "There is already work at hand for my oxen." The man who is wealthy only in his mind says that he will put together his cart—the fool, he does not know this: one hundred are the boards of a cart, take care to lay them up in your house beforehand.

(458) When the plowing-time first shows itself to mortals, set out for it, both your slaves and yourself, plowing by dry and by wet in the plowing-season, hastening very early, so that your fields will be filled. Turn the soil over in the spring; land left fallow in the summer will not disappoint you; sow the fallow land while the field is still brittle. Fallow land is an averter of death, a soother of children.

(465) Pray to Zeus of the land and to hallowed Demeter to make Demeter's holy grain ripen heavy, as you begin plowing at the very start, when you have taken the end of the plow-tail in your hand and have come down with the goad upon the oxen's backs while they draw the yoke-pole by its leather strap. Just a little behind, let another man, a slave holding a mattock, make toil for the birds by covering up the seed: for good management is the best for mortal human beings, bad management the worst. In this way the ears of corn will bend towards the ground in their ripeness,

---

[22] In late October or early November.

εἰ τέλος αὐτὸς ὄπισθεν Ὀλύμπιος ἐσθλὸν ὀπάζοι,
475 ἐκ δ' ἀγγέων ἐλάσειας ἀράχνια· καί σε ἔολπα
γηθήσειν βιότου αἱρεόμενον ἔνδον ἐόντος·
εὐοχθέων δ' ἵξεαι πολιὸν ἔαρ, οὐδὲ πρὸς ἄλλους
αὐγάσεαι, σέο δ' ἄλλος ἀνὴρ κεχρημένος ἔσται.

εἰ δέ κεν ἠελίοιο τροπῇς ἀρόῳς χθόνα δῖαν,
480 ἥμενος ἀμήσεις, ὀλίγον περὶ χειρὸς ἐέργων,
ἀντία δεσμεύων, κεκονιμένος, οὐ μάλα χαίρων,
οἴσεις δ' ἐν φορμῷ· παῦροι δέ σε θηήσονται.
ἄλλοτε δ' ἀλλοῖος Ζηνὸς νόος αἰγιόχοιο,
ἀργαλέος δ' ἄνδρεσσι καταθνητοῖσι νοῆσαι.

485 εἰ δέ κεν ὄψ' ἀρόσεις, τόδε κέν τοι φάρμακον εἴη·
ἦμος κόκκυξ κοκκύζει δρυὸς ἐν πετάλοισιν
τὸ πρῶτον, τέρπει δὲ βροτοὺς ἐπ' ἀπείρονα γαῖαν,
τῆμος Ζεὺς ὕοι τρίτῳ ἤματι μηδ' ἀπολήγοι,
μήτ' ἄρ' ὑπερβάλλων βοὸς ὁπλὴν μήτ' ἀπολείπων·
490 οὕτω κ' ὀψαρότης πρωιηρότῃ ἰσοφαρίζοι.
ἐν θυμῷ δ' εὖ πάντα φυλάσσεο, μηδέ σε λήθοι
μήτ' ἔαρ γινόμενον πολιὸν μήθ' ὥριος ὄμβρος.

πὰρ δ' ἴθι χάλκειον θῶκον καὶ ἐπαλέα λέσχην
ὥρῃ χειμερίῃ, ὁπότε κρύος ἀνέρας ἔργων
495 ἰσχάνει· ἔνθά κ' ἄοκνος ἀνὴρ μέγα οἶκον ὀφέλλοι·
μή σε κακοῦ χειμῶνος ἀμηχανίη καταμάρψῃ
σὺν Πενίῃ, λεπτῇ δὲ παχὺν πόδα χειρὶ πιέζῃς.
πολλὰ δ' ἀεργὸς ἀνήρ, κενεὴν ἐπὶ ἐλπίδα μίμνων,

490 πρωιη- Kirchhoff: προηρότῃ C, (η in ras.) D: -αρηρότῃ
(-τι) Φ: -αρότῃ Proclus ut vid.: πρωτηρότῃ Byz. (S) Ammonius

126

if afterwards the Olympian himself grants them a fine result; you will drive the spider-webs away from the storage-vessels, and I anticipate that you will rejoice as you draw on the means of life that are indoors. You will arrive at bright spring in good shape and will not gape at other people; but some other man will stand in need of you.

(479) If you plow the divine earth first at the winter solstice,[23] you will harvest sitting down, covered in dust, grasping only a little with your hand and tying it together in opposite directions, not at all pleased, and you will carry it off in a basket; few will admire you. But the mind of aegis-holding Zeus is different at different times, and it is difficult for mortal men to know it. If you do plow late, this will be a remedy for you: when the cuckoo in the leaves of the oak tree first calls and gives pleasure to mortals on the boundless earth,[24] if at that time Zeus rains for three days without ceasing, neither exceeding the hoof-print of an ox nor falling short of it—in this way the late plower will vie with the early plower. Bear everything well in mind: mark well the bright spring when it comes, and the rain in good season.

(493) Pass by the bronze-worker's bench and his warm lounge in the wintry season, when the cold holds men back from fieldwork but an unhesitating man could greatly foster his household—lest a bad, intractable winter catch you up together with Poverty, and you rub a swollen foot with a skinny hand.[25] A man who does not work, waiting upon an

[23] About 20 December.
[24] In March.
[25] Symptoms of malnutrition.

127

χρηίζων βιότοιο, κακὰ προσελέξατο θυμῷ.
500 ἐλπὶς δ' οὐκ ἀγαθὴ κεχρημένον ἄνδρα κομίζειν,
ἥμενον ἐν λέσχῃ, τῷ μὴ βίος ἄρκιος εἴη.
δείκνυε δὲ δμώεσσι θέρεος ἔτι μέσσου ἐόντος·
"οὐκ αἰεὶ θέρος ἐσσεῖται· ποιεῖσθε καλιάς."

μῆνα δὲ Ληναιῶνα, κάκ' ἤματα, βουδόρα πάντα,
505 τοῦτον ἀλεύασθαι, καὶ πηγάδας, αἵ τ' ἐπὶ γαῖαν
πνεύσαντος Βορέαο δυσηλεγέες τελέθουσιν,
ὅς τε διὰ Θρήκης ἱπποτρόφου εὐρέι πόντῳ
ἐμπνεύσας ὤρινε· μέμυκε δὲ γαῖα καὶ ὕλη·
πολλὰς δὲ δρῦς ὑψικόμους ἐλάτας τε παχείας
510 οὔρεος ἐν βήσσῃς πιλνᾷ χθονὶ πουλυβοτείρῃ
ἐμπίπτων, καὶ πᾶσα βοᾷ τότε νήριτος ὕλη·
θῆρες δὲ φρίσσουσ', οὐρὰς δ' ὑπὸ μέζε' ἔθεντο,
τῶν καὶ λάχνῃ δέρμα κατάσκιον· ἀλλά νυ καὶ τῶν
ψυχρὸς ἐὼν διάησι δασυστέρνων περ ἐόντων.
515 καί τε διὰ ῥινοῦ βοὸς ἔρχεται οὐδέ μιν ἴσχει,
καί τε δι' αἶγα ἄησι τανύτριχα· πώεα δ' οὔ τι,
οὕνεκ' ἐπηετανοὶ τρίχες αὐτῶν, οὐ διάησιν
ἲς ἀνέμου Βορέω· τροχαλὸν δὲ γέροντα τίθησιν
καὶ διὰ παρθενικῆς ἁπαλόχροος οὐ διάησιν,
520 ἥ τε δόμων ἔντοσθε φίλῃ παρὰ μητέρι μίμνει
οὔ πω ἔργ' εἰδυῖα πολυχρύσου Ἀφροδίτης·
εὖ τε λοεσσαμένη τέρενα χρόα καὶ λίπ' ἐλαίῳ
χρισαμένη μυχίη καταλέξεται ἔνδοθι οἴκου,
ἤματι χειμερίῳ, ὅτ' ἀνόστεος ὃν πόδα τένδει

523 μυχίη Φ Proclus: νυχίη CD

128

empty hope, in need of the means of life, says many evil things to his spirit. Hope is not good at providing for a man in need who sits in the lounge and does not have enough of the means of life. Point out to the slaves while it is still midsummer: "It will not always be summer, make huts for yourselves."

(504) The month of Lenaion,[26] evil days, ox-flayers all of them—avoid it, and the frosts that are deadly upon the earth when Boreas blows, which stirs up the broad sea through horse-raising Thrace when it blows upon it, and the earth and the forest bellow. It falls upon many lofty-leaved oaks and sturdy firs in the mountain's dales and bends them down to the bounteous earth, and the whole immense forest groans aloud. The wild animals shiver and stick their tails under their genitals, even those whose skin is shadowed by fur; but, chilly as it is, it blows through them although their breasts are shaggy, and it goes through the hide of an ox, and this does not stop it, and it blows through the long-haired goat—but not at all through sheep does the force of the wind Boreas blow, for their fleece is plentiful. It makes the old man curved like a wheel, but it does not blow through the soft-skinned maiden who stays at the side of her dear mother inside the house, still ignorant of the works of golden Aphrodite; after washing her tender skin well and anointing herself richly with oil she lies down in the innermost recess inside the house—on a wintry day, when the boneless one[27] gnaws its foot in its

---

[26] The second half of January and the beginning of February.

[27] Probably the octopus is meant, but other suggestions include the cuttlefish and the snail.

525 ἔν τ' ἀπύρῳ οἴκῳ καὶ ἤθεσι λευγαλέοισιν·
οὐ γάρ οἱ ἠέλιος δείκνυ νομὸν ὁρμηθῆναι,
ἀλλ' ἐπὶ κυανέων ἀνδρῶν δῆμόν τε πόλιν τε
στρωφᾶται, βράδιον δὲ Πανελλήνεσσι φαείνει.
καὶ τότε δὴ κεραοὶ καὶ νήκεροι ὑληκοῖται

530 λυγρὸν μυλιόωντες ἀνὰ δρία βησσήεντα
φεύγουσιν, καὶ πᾶσιν ἐνὶ φρεσὶ τοῦτο μέμηλεν,
οἳ σκέπα μαιόμενοι πυκινοὺς κευθμῶνας ἔχουσιν
κὰκ γλάφυ πετρῆεν. τότε δὴ τρίποδι βροτῷ ἶσοι,
οὗ τ' ἐπὶ νῶτα ἔαγε, κάρη δ' εἰς οὖδας ὁρᾶται·

535 τῷ ἴκελοι φοιτῶσιν ἀλευόμενοι νίφα λευκήν.

καὶ τότε ἕσσασθαι ἔρυμα χροός, ὥς σε κελεύω,
χλαῖνάν τε μαλακὴν καὶ τερμιόεντα χιτῶνα·
στήμονι δ' ἐν παύρῳ πολλὴν κρόκα μηρύσασθαι·
τὴν περιέσσασθαι, ἵνα τοι τρίχες ἀτρεμέωσιν

540 μηδ' ὀρθαὶ φρίσσωσιν ἀειρόμεναι κατὰ σῶμα.
ἀμφὶ δὲ ποσσὶ πέδιλα βοὸς ἶφι κταμένοιο
ἄρμενα δήσασθαι, πίλοις ἔντοσθε πυκάσσας·
πρωτογόνων δ' ἐρίφων, ὁπότ' ἂν κρύος ὥριον ἔλθῃ,
δέρματα συρράπτειν νεύρῳ βοός, ὄφρ' ἐπὶ νώτῳ

545 ὑετοῦ ἀμφιβάλῃ ἀλέην· κεφαλῆφι δ' ὕπερθεν
πῖλον ἔχειν ἀσκητόν, ἵν' οὔατα μὴ καταδεύῃ.
ψυχρὴ γάρ τ' ἠὼς πέλεται Βορέαο πεσόντος·
ἠῶος δ' ἐπὶ γαῖαν ἀπ' οὐρανοῦ ἀστερόεντος
ἀὴρ πυροφόρος τέταται μακάρων ἐπὶ ἔργοις,

533 κὰκ West: κὰγ Wilamowitz: καὶ Proclus Etym.codd.
549 πυροφόροις ψ$_{10}$ (cum gl. σιτοφόροις), ci. Hermann:

fireless house and dismal abodes, for the sun does not show it a rangeland towards which it can set out but instead roams to the dark men's people and city,[28] and shines more tardily for all the Greeks. And that is when the forest dwellers, horned and hornless alike, gnash their teeth miserably and flee through the wooded thickets, caring in their spirit only for searching for shelter and finding sturdy hiding-places down in the hollow of a stone; that is when they avoid the white snow and stalk about like a three-footed mortal[29] whose back is broken and whose head looks down to the ground.

(536) And that is when you should put on a defense for your skin, as I bid you: a soft cloak and a tunic that reaches your feet. Wind plenty of woof on a puny warp: put this around you, so that your hairs do not tremble nor stand up straight shivering along your body. Bind around your feet well-fitting boots from the leather of a slaughtered ox, padded inside with felt; when the seasonable cold comes, stitch the skins of newly born kids together with the sinew of an ox, so that you can put it around your back as protection against the rain; wear a well-made felt cap upon your head, so that you do not get your ears wet. For the dawn is chilly when Boreas comes down, and a dawn mist is stretched out upon the earth from the starry sky onto the wheat-bearing works of the blessed ones—a mist which is

---

[28] According to the early Greeks, the sun spent more time in Africa in the winter.

[29] An old man, walking with a stick.

---

πυροφ˴όρος Π₅ΣProclus codd., πυρφόρος testt.: ὀμβροφόρος ci. Seleucus

550 ὅς τε ἀρυσσάμενος ποταμῶν ἀπὸ αἰεναόντων,
ὑψοῦ ὑπὲρ γαίης ἀρθεὶς ἀνέμοιο θυέλλῃ
ἄλλοτε μέν θ᾽ ὕει ποτὶ ἕσπερον, ἄλλοτ᾽ ἄησιν
πυκνὰ Θρηικίου Βορέω νέφεα κλονέοντος.
τὸν φθάμενος ἔργον τελέσας οἶκόνδε νέεσθαι,
555 μή ποτέ σ᾽ οὐρανόθεν σκοτόεν νέφος ἀμφικαλύψει.
χρῶτα δὲ μυδαλέον θήῃ κατά θ᾽ εἵματα δεύσει·
ἀλλ᾽ ὑπαλεύασθαι· μεὶς γὰρ χαλεπώτατος οὗτος
χειμέριος, χαλεπὸς προβάτοις, χαλεπὸς δ᾽
ἀνθρώποις.
τῆμος τώμισυ βοῦσ᾽, ἐπὶ δ᾽ ἀνέρι τὸ πλέον εἴη
560 ἁρμαλιῆς· μακραὶ γὰρ ἐπίρροθοι εὐφρόναι εἰσίν.
ταῦτα φυλασσόμενος τετελεσμένον εἰς ἐνιαυτὸν
ἰσοῦσθαι νύκτας τε καὶ ἤματα, εἰς ὅ κεν αὗτις
Γῆ πάντων μήτηρ καρπὸν σύμμικτον ἐνείκῃ.
εὖτ᾽ ἂν δ᾽ ἑξήκοντα μετὰ τροπὰς ἠελίοιο
565 χειμέρι᾽ ἐκτελέσει Ζεὺς ἤματα, δή ῥα τότ᾽ ἀστὴρ
Ἀρκτοῦρος προλιπὼν ἱερὸν ῥόον Ὠκεανοῖο
πρῶτον παμφαίνων ἐπιτέλλεται ἀκροκνέφαιος·
τὸν δὲ μέτ᾽ ὀρθρογόη Πανδιονὶς ὦρτο χελιδὼν
ἐς φάος ἀνθρώποις, ἔαρος νέον ἱσταμένοιο.
570 τὴν φθάμενος οἴνας περιταμνέμεν· ὡς γὰρ ἄμεινον.
ἀλλ᾽ ὁπότ᾽ ἂν φερέοικος ἀπὸ χθονὸς ἂμ φυτὰ
βαίνῃ
Πληιάδας φεύγων, τότε δὴ σκάφος οὐκέτι οἰνέων,
ἀλλ᾽ ἅρπας τε χαρασσέμεναι καὶ δμῶας ἐγείρειν.
φεύγειν δὲ σκιεροὺς θώκους καὶ ἐπ᾽ ἠῶ κοῖτον

drawn up from ever-flowing rivers and is raised up on high above the earth by a blast of wind; and sometimes it rains towards evening, at other times it blows, when Thracian Boreas drives thick clouds in rout. Forestall him, finish your work and get home ahead of him, lest a shadowy cloud from heaven cover you round, and make your skin wet and drench your clothes. Avoid this: for this is the most difficult month, wintry, difficult for livestock, and difficult for human beings. At this time give half the usual rations to the oxen, but more[30] to a man: for the long nights are a help. Bear these things in mind and balance the nights and days[31] until the end of the year, when Earth, mother of all, brings forth her various fruit once again.

(564) When Zeus has completed sixty wintry days after the solstice, the star Arcturus is first seen rising, shining brightly just at dusk, leaving behind the holy stream of Oceanus.[32] After this, Pandion's daughter, the dawn-lamenting swallow, rises into the light for human beings, and the spring begins anew. Forestall her, prune the vines first: for that way it is better.

(571) But when the house-carrier[33] climbs up from the ground on the plants, fleeing the Pleiades,[34] there is no longer any digging for vines: sharpen the scythes and rouse your slaves. Avoid shadowy seats and sleeping until dawn

---

[30] I.e. than half his normal ration.
[31] I.e. against each other.
[32] The second half of February.          [33] The snail.

---

561–63 damn. Plutarchus

568 ὀρθρογ. Byz. (S) Σ<sup>vet</sup>: ὀρθογόη codd. Proclus Hesychius al.: ὀρθοβόη quidam teste Proclo

575 ὥρῃ ἐν ἀμήτου, ὅτε τ᾽ ἠέλιος χρόα κάρφει·
τημοῦτος σπεύδειν καὶ οἴκαδε καρπὸν ἀγινεῖν
ὄρθρου ἀνιστάμενος, ἵνα τοι βίος ἄρκιος εἴη.
ἠὼς γάρ τ᾽ ἔργοιο τρίτην ἀπομείρεται αἶσαν·
ἠώς τοι προφέρει μὲν ὁδοῦ, προφέρει δὲ καὶ ἔργου,
580 ἠώς, ἥ τε φανεῖσα πολέας ἐπέβησε κελεύθου
ἀνθρώπους, πολλοῖσι δ᾽ ἐπὶ ζυγὰ βουσὶ τίθησιν.

ἦμος δὲ σκόλυμός τ᾽ ἀνθεῖ καὶ ἠχέτα τέττιξ
δενδρέῳ ἐφεζόμενος λιγυρὴν καταχεύετ᾽ ἀοιδὴν
πυκνὸν ὑπὸ πτερύγων θέρεος καματώδεος ὥρῃ,
585 τῆμος πιόταταί τ᾽ αἶγες καὶ οἶνος ἄριστος,
μαχλόταται δὲ γυναῖκες, ἀφαυρότατοι δέ τοι ἄνδρες
εἰσίν, ἐπεὶ κεφαλὴν καὶ γούνατα Σείριος ἄζει,
αὐαλέος δέ τε χρὼς ὑπὸ καύματος· ἀλλὰ τότ᾽ ἤδη
εἴη πετραίη τε σκιὴ καὶ Βίβλινος οἶνος
590 μᾶζά τ᾽ ἀμολγαίη γάλα τ᾽ αἰγῶν σβεννυμενάων
καὶ βοὸς ὑλοφάγοιο κρέας μή πω τετοκυίης
πρωτογόνων τ᾽ ἐρίφων· ἐπὶ δ᾽ αἴθοπα πινέμεν οἶνον
ἐν σκιῇ ἑζόμενον, κεκορημένον ἦτορ ἐδωδῆς,
ἀντίον ἀκραέος Ζεφύρου τρέψαντα πρόσωπα·
595 κρήνης δ᾽ αἰενάου καὶ ἀπορρύτου, ἥ τ᾽ ἀθόλωτος,
τρὶς ὕδατος προχέειν, τὸ δὲ τέτρατον ἱέμεν οἴνου.

δμωσὶ δ᾽ ἐποτρύνειν Δήμητερος ἱερὸν ἀκτὴν
δινέμεν, εὖτ᾽ ἂν πρῶτα φανῇ σθένος Ὠρίωνος,
χώρῳ ἐν εὐαεῖ καὶ εὐτροχάλῳ ἐν ἀλωῇ·
600 μέτρῳ δ᾽ εὖ κομίσασθαι ἐν ἄγγεσιν. αὐτὰρ ἐπὴν δὴ

578 ἀπαμείρ. C^ac (?) D^ac(?) Eustathius

134

in the harvest season, when the sun withers the skin: make haste at that time and carry home the crops, getting up at sunrise, so that your means of life will be sufficient. For dawn claims as its portion a third of the work, dawn gives you a head start on the road, gives you a head start on your work too—dawn, which when it shows itself sets many men on their way and puts the yoke on many oxen.

(582) When the golden thistle blooms and the chirping cicada, sitting in a tree, incessantly pours out its clear-sounding song from under its wings in the season of toil-some summer, at that time[35] goats are fattest, and wine is best, and women are most lascivious—and men are weak-est, for Sirius parches their head and knees, and their skin is dry from the heat. At that time let there be a rock's shadow and Bibline wine,[36] bread made with milk, cheese from goats that are just drying up, and the meat of a forest-grazing cow that has not yet calved and of newly born kids. Drink some gleaming wine too, sitting in the shade, when you have eaten to your heart's content, with your face turned towards fresh-blowing Zephyrus; first pour three portions from the water of an ever-flowing spring, running and unmuddied, then put in a fourth part of wine.

(597) Urge your slaves to winnow Demeter's holy grain when Orion's strength first shows itself,[37] in a well-aired place and on a well-rolled threshing-floor. Bring it in prop-erly, with a measure in storage-vessels. When you have laid

[34] In mid-May.
[35] In mid-July.
[36] A celebrated Thracian wine.
[37] About 20 June.

πάντα βίον κατάθηαι ἐπάρμενον ἔνδοθι οἴκου,
θῆτά τ᾽ ἄοικον ποιεῖσθαι καὶ ἄτεκνον ἔριθον
δίζησθαι κέλομαι· χαλεπὴ δ᾽ ὑπόπορτις ἔριθος·
καὶ κύνα καρχαρόδοντα κομεῖν—μὴ φείδεο σίτου—
605 μή ποτέ σ᾽ ἡμερόκοιτος ἀνὴρ ἀπὸ χρήμαθ᾽ ἕληται.
χόρτον δ᾽ ἐσκομίσαι καὶ συρφετόν, ὄφρα τοι εἴη
βουσὶ καὶ ἡμιόνοισιν ἐπηετανόν. αὐτὰρ ἔπειτα
δμῶας ἀναψῦξαι φίλα γούνατα καὶ βόε λῦσαι.
   εὖτ᾽ ἂν δ᾽ Ὠρίων καὶ Σείριος ἐς μέσον ἔλθῃ
610 οὐρανόν, Ἀρκτοῦρον δ᾽ ἐσίδῃ ῥοδοδάκτυλος Ἠώς,
ὦ Πέρση, τότε πάντας ἀπόδρεπε οἴκαδε βότρυς·
δεῖξαι δ᾽ ἠελίῳ δέκα τ᾽ ἤματα καὶ δέκα νύκτας,
πέντε δὲ συσκιάσαι, ἕκτῳ δ᾽ εἰς ἄγγε᾽ ἀφύσσαι
δῶρα Διωνύσου πολυγηθέος. αὐτὰρ ἐπὴν δὴ
615 Πληιάδες θ᾽ Ὑάδες τε τό τε σθένος Ὠρίωνος
δύνωσιν, τότ᾽ ἔπειτ᾽ ἀρότου μεμνημένος εἶναι
ὡραίου· πλειὼν δὲ κατὰ χθονὸς ἄρμενος εἴη.

   εἰ δέ σε ναυτιλίης δυσπεμφέλου ἵμερος αἱρεῖ·
εὖτ᾽ ἂν Πληιάδες σθένος ὄβριμον Ὠρίωνος
620 φεύγουσαι πίπτωσιν ἐς ἠεροειδέα πόντον,
δὴ τότε παντοίων ἀνέμων θυίουσιν ἀῆται·
καὶ τότε μηκέτι νῆας ἔχειν ἐνὶ οἴνοπι πόντῳ,
γῆν δ᾽ ἐργάζεσθαι μεμνημένος ὥς σε κελεύω.
νῆα δ᾽ ἐπ᾽ ἠπείρου ἐρύσαι πυκάσαι τε λίθοισιν
625 πάντοθεν, ὄφρ᾽ ἴσχωσ᾽ ἀνέμων μένος ὑγρὸν ἀέντων,

622 νῆα Solmsen

up all the means of life well prepared inside your house, then I bid you turn your hired man out of your house and look for a serving-girl without her own child; for a serving-girl with a baby under her flank is a difficult thing. And get a jagged-toothed dog—do not be sparing with its food, lest some day-sleeping man[38] steal your things from you. Bring in fodder and sweepings, so that there is plenty for the oxen and mules. Then let the slaves relax their knees, and unyoke the pair of oxen.

(609) When Orion and Sirius come into the middle of the sky, and rosy-fingered Dawn sees Arcturus,[39] then, Perses, pluck off all the grapes and take them home. Set them out in the sun for ten days and ten nights, then cover them up in the shade for five, and on the sixth draw out the gift of much-cheering Dionysus into storage-vessels. When the Pleiades and Hyades and the strength of Orion set,[40] that is the time to be mindful of plowing in good season. May the whole year be well-fitting in the earth.

(618) But if desire for storm-tossed seafaring seize you: when the Pleiades, fleeing Orion's mighty strength, fall into the murky sea, at that time[41] blasts of all sorts of winds rage; do not keep your boat any longer in the wine-dark sea at that time, but work the earth, mindful, as I bid you. Draw up your boat onto the land and prop it up with stones, surrounding it on all sides, so that they can resist the strength of the winds that blow moist, and draw out the

[38] A thief.
[39] In mid-September.
[40] In October.
[41] In November.

χείμαρον ἐξερύσας, ἵνα μὴ πύθῃ Διὸς ὄμβρος.
ὅπλα δ' ἐπάρμενα πάντα τεῷ ἐγκάτθεο οἴκῳ,
εὐκόσμως στολίσας νηὸς πτερὰ ποντοπόροιο·
πηδάλιον δ' εὐεργὲς ὑπὲρ καπνοῦ κρεμάσασθαι·
630 αὐτὸς δ' ὡραῖον μίμνειν πλόον, εἰς ὅ κεν ἔλθῃ·
καὶ τότε νῆα θοὴν ἅλαδ' ἑλκέμεν, ἐν δέ τε φόρτον
ἄρμενον ἐντύνασθαι, ἵν' οἴκαδε κέρδος ἄρηαι·
ὥς περ ἐμός τε πατὴρ καὶ σὸς μέγα νήπιε Πέρση
πλωΐζεσκ' ἐν νηυσὶ βίου κεχρημένος ἐσθλοῦ.
635 ὅς ποτε καὶ τυῖδ' ἦλθε πολὺν διὰ πόντον ἀνύσσας
Κύμην Αἰολίδα προλιπὼν ἐν νηὶ μελαίνῃ,
οὐκ ἄφενος φεύγων οὐδὲ πλοῦτόν τε καὶ ὄλβον,
ἀλλὰ κακὴν πενίην, τὴν Ζεὺς ἄνδρεσσι δίδωσιν·
νάσσατο δ' ἄγχ' Ἑλικῶνος ὀιζυρῇ ἐνὶ κώμῃ,
640 Ἄσκρῃ, χεῖμα κακῇ, θέρει ἀργαλέῃ, οὐδέ ποτ'
ἐσθλῇ.

τύνη δ', ὦ Πέρση, ἔργων μεμνημένος εἶναι
ὡραίων πάντων, περὶ ναυτιλίης δὲ μάλιστα.
νῆ' ὀλίγην αἰνεῖν, μεγάλῃ δ' ἐνὶ φορτία θέσθαι·
μείζων μὲν φόρτος, μεῖζον δ' ἐπὶ κέρδεϊ κέρδος
645 ἔσσεται, εἴ κ' ἄνεμοί γε κακὰς ἀπέχωσιν ἀήτας.

εὖτ' ἂν ἐπ' ἐμπορίην τρέψας ἀεσίφρονα θυμὸν
βούληαι χρέα τε προφυγεῖν καὶ λιμὸν ἀτερπέα,
δείξω δή τοι μέτρα πολυφλοίσβοιο θαλάσσης,
οὔτέ τι ναυτιλίης σεσοφισμένος οὔτέ τι νηῶν·
650 οὐ γάρ πώ ποτε νηί γ' ἐπέπλων εὐρέα πόντον,
εἰ μὴ ἐς Εὔβοιαν ἐξ Αὐλίδος, ᾗ ποτ' Ἀχαιοὶ

bilge-plug, so that Zeus' rain does not rot it. Lay up all the gear well prepared in your house after you have folded the sea-crossing boat's wings in good order; and hang up the well-worked rudder above the smoke. You yourself wait until the sailing season arrives, and then drag your swift boat down to the sea, arrange the cargo in it and get it ready so that you can bring the profit home, just as my father and yours, Perses, you great fool, used to sail in boats, deprived as he was of a fine means of life. Once he came here too, after he had crossed over a big sea, leaving behind Aeolian Cyme in a black boat, fleeing not wealth nor riches nor prosperity, but evil poverty, which Zeus gives to men. And he settled near Helicon in a wretched village, Ascra, evil in winter, distressful in summer, not ever fine.

(641) As for you, Perses, be mindful of all kinds of work in good season, but above all regarding seafaring. Praise a small boat, but place your load in a big one: for the cargo will be bigger, and your profit will be bigger, profit on profit—if the winds hold back their evil blasts.

(646) If you turn your foolish spirit to commerce and decide to flee debts and joyless hunger, I shall show you the measures of the much-roaring sea, I who have no expertise at all in either seafaring or boats. For never yet did I sail the broad sea in a boat, except to Euboea from Aulis,

---

632 ἄγηαι Peppmüller
649 σημειοῦται Σ[vet]
650–62 proscr. Plutarchus, 651–60 alii

μείναντες χειμῶνα πολὺν σὺν λαὸν ἄγειραν
Ἑλλάδος ἐξ ἱερῆς Τροίην ἐς καλλιγύναικα.
ἔνθα δ' ἐγὼν ἐπ' ἄεθλα δαΐφρονος Ἀμφιδάμαντος
655 Χαλκίδα τ' εἰς ἐπέρησα· τὰ δὲ προπεφραδμένα
πολλὰ
ἆθλ' ἔθεσαν παῖδες μεγαλήτορος· ἔνθά μέ φημι
ὕμνῳ νικήσαντα φέρειν τρίποδ' ὠτώεντα.
τὸν μὲν ἐγὼ Μούσῃς Ἑλικωνιάδεσσ' ἀνέθηκα,
ἔνθά με τὸ πρῶτον λιγυρῆς ἐπέβησαν ἀοιδῆς.
660 τόσσόν τοι νηῶν γε πεπείρημαι πολυγόμφων·
ἀλλὰ καὶ ὣς ἐρέω Ζηνὸς νόον αἰγιόχοιο·
Μοῦσαι γάρ μ' ἐδίδαξαν ἀθέσφατον ὕμνον ἀείδειν.
ἤματα πεντήκοντα μετὰ τροπὰς ἠελίοιο,
ἐς τέλος ἐλθόντος θέρεος, καματώδεος ὥρης,
665 ὡραῖος πέλεται θνητοῖς πλόος· οὔτε κε νῆα
καυάξαις οὔτ' ἄνδρας ἀποφθείσειε θάλασσα,
εἰ δὴ μὴ πρόφρων γε Ποσειδάων ἐνοσίχθων
ἢ Ζεὺς ἀθανάτων βασιλεὺς ἐθέλῃσιν ὀλέσσαι·
ἐν τοῖς γὰρ τέλος ἐστὶν ὁμῶς ἀγαθῶν τε κακῶν τε.
670 τῆμος δ' εὐκρινέες τ' αὖραι καὶ πόντος ἀπήμων·
εὔκηλος τότε νῆα θοὴν ἀνέμοισι πιθήσας
ἑλκέμεν ἐς πόντον φόρτον τ' ἐς πάντα τίθεσθαι.
σπεύδειν δ' ὅττι τάχιστα πάλιν οἰκόνδε νέεσθαι,
μηδὲ μένειν οἶνόν τε νέον καὶ ὀπωρινὸν ὄμβρον
675 καὶ χειμῶν' ἐπιόντα Νότοιό τε δεινὰς ἀήτας,
ὅς τ' ὤρινε θάλασσαν ὁμαρτήσας Διὸς ὄμβρῳ
πολλῷ ὀπωρινῷ, χαλεπὸν δέ τε πόντον ἔθηκεν.
ἄλλος δ' εἰαρινὸς πέλεται πλόος ἀνθρώποισιν·

where once the Achaeans, waiting through the winter, gathered together a great host to sail from holy Greece to Troy with its beautiful women. There I myself crossed over into Chalcis for the games of valorous Amphidamas—that great-hearted man's sons had announced and established many prizes—and there, I declare, I gained victory with a hymn, and carried off a tripod with handles. This I dedicated to the Heliconian Muses, where they first set me upon the path of clear-sounding song. This is as much experience of many-bolted ships as I have acquired; yet even so I shall speak forth the mind of aegis-holding Zeus, for the Muses taught me to sing an inconceivable hymn.

(663) Sailing is in good season for mortals for fifty days after the solstice,[42] when the summer goes to its end, during the toilsome season. You will not wreck your boat then nor will the sea drown your men—so long as Poseidon, the earth-shaker, or Zeus, king of the immortals, does not wish to destroy them: for in these gods is the fulfillment, both of good and of evil alike. That is when breezes are easy to distinguish and the sea is painless: at that time entrust your swift boat confidently to the winds, drag it down to the sea and put all your cargo into it. But make haste to sail back home again as quickly as possible, and do not wait for the new wine and the autumn rain and the approaching winter and the terrible blasts of Notus, which stirs up the sea, accompanying Zeus' heavy autumn rain, and makes the sea difficult.[43] There is also another sailing for human beings,

[42] From the end of June until August.
[43] Late September.

657 ἄλλοι γράφουσιν· ὕ. ν. ἐν Χαλκίδι θεῖον Ὅμηρον Σ^vet

ἦμος δὴ τὸ πρῶτον, ὅσον τ' ἐπιβᾶσα κορώνη
680 ἴχνος ἐποίησεν, τόσσον πέταλ' ἀνδρὶ φανήῃ
ἐν κράδῃ ἀκροτάτῃ, τότε δ' ἄμβατός ἐστι θάλασσα·
εἰαρινὸς δ' οὗτος πέλεται πλόος. οὔ μιν ἔγωγε
αἴνημ'· οὐ γὰρ ἐμῷ θυμῷ κεχαρισμένος ἐστίν·
ἁρπακτός· χαλεπῶς κε φύγοις κακόν· ἀλλά νυ καὶ τὰ
685 ἄνθρωποι ῥέζουσιν ἀιδρίῃσι νόοιο·
χρήματα γὰρ ψυχὴ πέλεται δειλοῖσι βροτοῖσιν.
δεινὸν δ' ἐστὶ θανεῖν μετὰ κύμασιν· ἀλλά σ' ἄνωγα
φράζεσθαι τάδε πάντα μετὰ φρεσὶν ὡς ἀγορεύω.
μηδ' ἐν νηυσὶν ἅπαντα βίον κοίλῃσι τίθεσθαι,
690 ἀλλὰ πλέω λείπειν, τὰ δὲ μείονα φορτίζεσθαι·
δεινὸν γὰρ πόντου μετὰ κύμασι πήματι κύρσαι,
δεινὸν δ' εἴ κ' ἐπ' ἄμαξαν ὑπέρβιον ἄχθος ἀείρας
ἄξονα καυάξαις καὶ φορτία μαυρωθείη.

μέτρα φυλάσσεσθαι· καιρὸς δ' ἐπὶ πᾶσιν ἄριστος.
695 ὡραῖος δὲ γυναῖκα τεὸν ποτὶ οἶκον ἄγεσθαι,
μήτε τριηκόντων ἐτέων μάλα πόλλ' ἀπολείπων
μήτ' ἐπιθεὶς μάλα πολλά· γάμος δέ τοι ὥριος οὗτος.
ἡ δὲ γυνὴ τέτορ' ἡβώοι, πέμπτῳ δὲ γαμοῖτο.
παρθενικὴν δὲ γαμεῖν, ὥς κ' ἤθεα κεδνὰ διδάξεις·
700 τὴν δὲ μάλιστα γαμεῖν, ἥτις σέθεν ἐγγύθι ναίει,
πάντα μάλ' ἀμφὶς ἰδών, μὴ γείτοσι χάρματα γήμῃς.
οὐ μὲν γάρ τι γυναικὸς ἀνὴρ ληίζετ' ἄμεινον
τῆς ἀγαθῆς, τῆς δ' αὖτε κακῆς οὐ ῥίγιον ἄλλο,

700 om. Π₅ Stobaeus, non respic. Proclus Σᵛᵉᵗ

in the spring-time: at that time[44]—when a man thinks that the leaves at the top of the fig-tree are as big as the foot-print a crow leaves as it goes—the sea can first be embarked upon: this is the spring-time sailing. As for me, I do not praise it, for it is not pleasing to my spirit: it is snatched, only with difficulty would you escape evil. And yet human beings do this too in the ignorance of their mind: for property is life for worthless mortals; yet it is a terrible thing to die among the waves. I bid you take notice of all these things in your spirit as I speak them out publicly: do not put all your means of life in hollow boats, but leave aside more, and load the lesser part: for it is a terrible thing to encounter grief among the waves of the sea—terrible too if by lifting an excessive weight onto your cart you wreck its axle and the load is ruined.

(694) Bear in mind measures; rightness is the best in all things. Lead a wife to your house when you are in good season, neither falling very many years short of thirty nor having added very many: this is a marriage in good season for you. The woman should have reached puberty four years earlier, and in the fifth she should marry. Marry a virgin so that you can teach her cherished usages: and above all marry one who lives near to you, after you have looked around carefully in all directions, lest your marriage cause your neighbors merriment. For a man acquires nothing better than a good wife, but nothing more chilling than a

44 The end of April.

143

δειπνολόχης, ἥ τ' ἄνδρα καὶ ἴφθιμόν περ ἐόντα
705 εὕει ἄτερ δαλοῖο καὶ ὠμῷ γήραϊ δῶκεν.
    εὖ δ' ὄπιν ἀθανάτων μακάρων πεφυλαγμένος
    εἶναι.
    μηδὲ κασιγνήτῳ ἶσον ποιεῖσθαι ἑταῖρον·
    εἰ δέ κε ποιήσῃς, μή μιν πρότερος κακὸν ἔρξεις,
    μηδὲ ψεύδεσθαι γλώσσης χάριν· εἰ δέ σέ γ' ἄρχῃ
710 ἤ τι ἔπος εἰπὼν ἀποθύμιον ἠὲ καὶ ἔρξας,
    δὶς τόσα τείννυσθαι μεμνημένος· εἰ δέ κεν αὖτις
    ἡγῆτ' ἐς φιλότητα, δίκην δ' ἐθέλῃσι παρασχεῖν,
    δέξασθαι· δειλός τοι ἀνὴρ φίλον ἄλλοτε ἄλλον
    ποιεῖται· σὲ δὲ μή τι νόος κατελεγχέτω εἶδος.
715   μηδὲ πολύξεινον μηδ' ἄξεινον καλέεσθαι,
    μηδὲ κακῶν ἕταρον μηδ' ἐσθλῶν νεικεστῆρα.
    μηδέ ποτ' οὐλομένην πενίην θυμοφθόρον ἀνδρὶ
    τέτλαθ' ὀνειδίζειν, μακάρων δόσιν αἰὲν ἐόντων.
    γλώσσης τοι θησαυρὸς ἐν ἀνθρώποισιν ἄριστος
720 φειδωλῆς, πλείστη δὲ χάρις κατὰ μέτρον ἰούσης·
    εἰ δὲ κακὸν εἴπῃς, τάχα κ' αὐτὸς μεῖζον ἀκούσαις.
    μηδὲ πολυξείνου δαιτὸς δυσπέμφελος εἶναι·
    ἐκ κοινοῦ πλείστη τε χάρις δαπάνη τ' ὀλιγίστη.

    μηδέ ποτ' ἐξ ἠοῦς Διὶ λείβειν αἴθοπα οἶνον
725 χερσὶν ἀνίπτοισιν μηδ' ἄλλοις ἀθανάτοισιν·
    οὐ γὰρ τοί γε κλύουσιν, ἀποπτύουσι δέ τ' ἀράς.
    μηδ' ἄντ' ἠελίου τετραμμένος ὀρθὸς ὀμείχειν·

706 susp. Lehrs: post 723 transp. Steitz

bad one, a dinner-ambusher, one who singes her husband without a torch, powerful though he be, and gives him over to a raw old age.

(706) Bear well in mind the retribution of the blessed immortals. Do not treat a comrade in the same way as your brother: but if you do, then do not harm him first, nor give him a lying grace with your tongue; but if he begins, telling you some word contrary to your spirit or even doing some such thing, then be mindful to pay him back twice as much. But if he is led once again towards friendship and decides to offer requital, accept it: for worthless is the man who makes now one man his friend, now another. Do not let your mind at all put to shame your outward appearance.

(715) Do not acquire the reputation of having many guests or of having none at all, neither that of being the companion of base men nor a reviler of fine ones. Do not ever dare to reproach a man with baneful, spirit-destroying poverty, the gift of the blessed ones that always are. Among men, the tongue that is the best treasure is a sparing one, and the most pleasure comes from a tongue that goes according to measure: if you say evil, soon you yourself will hear it more. And do not be storm-tossed in your mood at a dinner with many guests: when things are shared in common, the pleasure is the most and the expense is the least.

(724) And do not ever pour a libation of gleaming wine at dawn to Zeus or the other immortals with unwashed hands; for they do not listen, but spurn the prayers. And do not urinate standing up facing the sun; but be mindful to

---

708 ἔρξαι Solmsen
724–59 Hesiodo abiud. Wilamowitz, alii

αὐτὰρ ἐπεί κε δύῃ, μεμνημένος, ἔς τ' ἀνιόντα,
730 μηδ' ἀπογυμνωθείς· μακάρων τοι νύκτες ἔασιν·
729 μήτ' ἐν ὁδῷ μήτ' ἐκτὸς ὁδοῦ προβάδην οὐρήσεις·
731 ἑζόμενος δ' ὅ γε θεῖος ἀνήρ, πεπνυμένα εἰδώς,
ἤ ὅ γε πρὸς τοῖχον πελάσας εὐερκέος αὐλῆς.
μηδ' αἰδοῖα γονῇ πεπαλαγμένος ἔνδοθι οἴκου
ἱστίῃ ἐμπελαδὸν παραφαινέμεν, ἀλλ' ἀλέασθαι.
735 μηδ' ἀπὸ δυσφήμοιο τάφου ἀπονοστήσαντα
σπερμαίνειν γενεήν, ἀλλ' ἀθανάτων ἀπὸ δαιτός.
757 μηδέ ποτ' ἐν προχοῇς ποταμῶν ἅλαδε προρεόντων
758 μηδ' ἐπὶ κρηνάων οὐρεῖν, μάλα δ' ἐξαλέασθαι,
759 μηδ' ἐναποψύχειν· τὸ γὰρ οὔ τοι λώιόν ἐστιν.
737 μηδέ ποτ' αἰενάων ποταμῶν καλλίρροον ὕδωρ
ποσσὶ περᾶν πρίν γ' εὔξῃ ἰδὼν ἐς καλὰ ῥέεθρα,
χεῖρας νιψάμενος πολυηράτῳ ὕδατι λευκῷ·
740 ὃς ποταμὸν διαβῇ κακότητ' ἰδὲ χεῖρας ἄνιπτος,
τῷ δὲ θεοὶ νεμεσῶσι καὶ ἄλγεα δῶκαν ὀπίσσω.
μηδ' ἀπὸ πεντόζοιο θεῶν ἐν δαιτὶ θαλείῃ
αὖον ἀπὸ χλωροῦ τάμνειν αἴθωνι σιδήρῳ.
μηδέ ποτ' οἰνοχόην τιθέμεν κρητῆρος ὕπερθεν
745 πινόντων· ὀλοὴ γὰρ ἐπ' αὐτῷ μοῖρα τέτυκται.
μηδὲ δόμον ποιῶν ἀνεπίξεστον καταλείπειν,
μή τοι ἐφεζομένη κρώξει λακέρυζα κορώνη.
μηδ' ἀπὸ χυτροπόδων ἀνεπιρρέκτων ἀνελόντα
ἔσθειν μηδὲ λόεσθαι, ἐπεὶ καὶ τοῖς ἔπι ποινή.
750 μηδ' ἐπ' ἀκινήτοισι καθίζειν, οὐ γὰρ ἄμεινον,

729 post 730 traiecit Solmsen
757–59 damn. Plutarchus: post 756 ferunt Π₅codd., sed 758

146

do so after it sets, and before it rises, but even so do not completely bare yourself: for the nights belong to the blessed ones. And do not urinate while you are walking, on the road or off the road: it is crouching that the god-fearing man, who knows wisdom, does it, or after he has approached towards the wall of a well-fenced courtyard. And inside the house do not reveal your genitals besmirched with intercourse near the hearth, but avoid this. And do not sow offspring when you come home from an ill-spoken funeral, but from a dinner of the immortals. And do not ever urinate into the streams of rivers that flow down towards the sea nor onto fountains—avoid this entirely—and do not defecate into them: for that is not better. And do not cross on foot the fair-pouring water of ever-flowing rivers before you have prayed, looking into the beautiful stream, and washed your hands with lovely, clear water: whoever crosses a river, unwashed in evil and in his hands, against him the gods feel resentment, and they give him pains afterwards. And during the festival, the dinner of the gods, do not cut the dry from the living from the five-brancher with the gleaming iron.[45] And do not ever put the ladle on top of the wine-bowl while people are drinking; for a baneful fate is established for this. And do not leave a house unfinished when you make it, lest a screaming crow sit upon it and croak. And do not take from undedicated cauldrons to eat or wash yourself, since upon these things too there is punishment. And do not seat a twelve-day-old

---

[45] Do not cut your nails.

---

et hic ('736 a') CDTzetzesΦψ (at non Π₅Π₃₉Proclus MoschopulusTrω₂): omnes huc transtulit West

740 ath. Aristarchus

παῖδα δυωδεκαταῖον, ὅ τ᾽ ἀνέρ᾽ ἀνήνορα ποιεῖ,
μηδὲ δυωδεκάμηνον· ἴσον καὶ τοῦτο τέτυκται.
μηδὲ γυναικείῳ λουτρῷ χρόα φαιδρύνεσθαι
ἀνέρα· λευγαλέη γὰρ ἐπὶ χρόνον ἔστ᾽ ἐπὶ καὶ τῷ
755 ποινή. μηδ᾽ ἱεροῖσιν ἐπ᾽ αἰθομένοισι κυρήσας
756 μωμεύειν ἀίδηλα· θεός νύ τε καὶ τὰ νεμεσσᾷ.
760  ὧδ᾽ ἔρδειν· δειλὴν δὲ βροτῶν ὑπαλεύεο φήμην·
φήμη γάρ τε κακὴ πέλεται, κούφη μὲν ἀεῖραι
ῥεῖα μάλ᾽, ἀργαλέη δὲ φέρειν, χαλεπὴ δ᾽ ἀποθέσθαι.
φήμη δ᾽ οὔ τις πάμπαν ἀπόλλυται, ἥντινα πολλοὶ
λαοὶ φημίξουσι· θεός νύ τίς ἐστι καὶ αὐτή.

765  ἤματα δ᾽ ἐκ Διόθεν πεφυλαγμένος εὖ κατὰ μοῖραν
πεφραδέμεν δμώεσσι· τριηκάδα μηνὸς ἀρίστην
ἔργά τ᾽ ἐποπτεύειν ἠδ᾽ ἁρμαλιὴν δατέασθαι,
εὖτ᾽ ἂν ἀληθείην λαοὶ κρίνοντες ἄγωσιν.
αἵδε γὰρ ἡμέραι εἰσὶ Διὸς παρὰ μητιόεντος·
770 πρῶτον ἔνη τετράς τε καὶ ἑβδόμη ἱερὸν ἦμαρ·
(τῇ γὰρ Ἀπόλλωνα χρυσάορα γείνατο Λητώ)
ὀγδοάτη δ᾽ ἐνάτη τε. δύω γε μὲν ἤματα μηνὸς
ἔξοχ᾽ ἀεξομένοιο βροτήσια ἔργα πένεσθαι,
ἑνδεκάτη δὲ δυωδεκάτη τ᾽ ἄμφω γε μὲν ἐσθλαί,
775 ἠμὲν ὄις πείκειν ἠδ᾽ εὔφρονα καρπὸν ἀμᾶσθαι,
ἡ δὲ δυωδεκάτη τῆς ἑνδεκάτης μέγ᾽ ἀμείνων·
τῇ γάρ τοι νῇ νήματ᾽ ἀερσιπότητος ἀράχνης

boy upon things that cannot be moved,[46] for that is not
better—it makes a man unmanly—nor a twelve-month-
old one: this too is established in the same way. And do not
clean a man's skin in a woman's wash-water: for there is a
dismal punishment upon this too, for a time. And do not
carp destructively at burning sacrifices when you encoun-
ter them: for a god feels resentment against this too.

(760) Act this way. Avoid the wretched talk of mortals.
For talk is evil: it is light to raise up quite easily, but it is
difficult to bear, and hard to put down. No talk is ever en-
tirely gotten rid of, once many people talk it up: it too is
some god.

(765) Bear well in mind the days that come from Zeus
and point them out according to their portion to the slaves.
The thirtieth of the month is the best for watching over the
works and distributing the rations: people celebrate it be-
cause they distinguish the truth. These are the days that
come from counsellor Zeus: to begin with, the first, the
fourth, and the seventh, a holy day (for on this last, Leto
gave birth to Apollo with his golden sword), and the eighth
and the ninth. Two days of the waxing month are outstand-
ing for toiling at a mortal's works, the eleventh and the
twelfth. Both of them are fine, for shearing sheep and for
gathering together the gladdening corn, but the twelfth is
much better than the eleventh. It is on that day that the
high-flying spider spins its webs in the fullness of the day

---

[46] E.g., tombs.

---

765–828 Dies Hesiodo post alios abiud. Nilsson

ἤματος ἐκ πλείου, ὅτε τ' ἴδρις σωρὸν ἀμᾶται·
τῇ δ' ἱστὸν στήσαιτο γυνὴ προβάλοιτό τε ἔργον.
780  μηνὸς δ' ἱσταμένου τρεισκαιδεκάτην ἀλέασθαι
σπέρματος ἄρξασθαι· φυτὰ δ' ἐνθρέψασθαι ἀρίστη.
ἕκτη δ' ἡ μέσση μάλ' ἀσύμφορός ἐστι φυτοῖσιν,
ἀνδρογόνος δ' ἀγαθή· κούρῃ δ' οὐ σύμφορός ἐστιν,
οὔτε γενέσθαι πρῶτ' οὔτ' ἄρ γάμου ἀντιβολῆσαι.
785  οὐδὲ μὲν ἡ πρώτη ἕκτη κούρῃ γε γενέσθαι
ἄρμενος, ἀλλ' ἐρίφους τάμνειν καὶ πώεα μήλων,
σηκόν τ' ἀμφιβαλεῖν ποιμνήιον ἤπιον ἦμαρ·
ἐσθλὴ δ' ἀνδρογόνος· φιλέοι δέ κε κέρτομα βάζειν
ψεύδεά θ' αἱμυλίους τε λόγους κρυφίους τ'
        ὀαρισμούς.
790  μηνὸς δ' ὀγδοάτῃ κάπρον καὶ βοῦν ἐρίμυκον
ταμνέμεν, οὐρῆας δὲ δυωδεκάτῃ ταλαεργούς.
εἰκάδι δ' ἐν μεγάλῃ πλέῳ ἤματι ἴστορα φῶτα
γείνασθαι· μάλα γάρ τε νόον πεπυκασμένος ἔσται.
ἐσθλὴ δ' ἀνδρογόνος δεκάτη, κούρῃ δέ τε τετρὰς
795  μέσσῃ· τῇ δέ τε μῆλα καὶ εἰλίποδας ἕλικας βοῦς
καὶ κύνα καρχαρόδοντα καὶ οὐρῆας ταλαεργοὺς
πρηΰνειν ἐπὶ χεῖρα τιθείς. πεφύλαξο δὲ θυμῷ
τετράδ' ἀλεύασθαι φθίνοντός θ' ἱσταμένου τε
ἄλγεα θυμοβόρα· μάλα τοι τετελεσμένον ἦμαρ.
800  ἐν δὲ τετάρτῃ μηνὸς ἄγεσθ' εἰς οἶκον ἄκοιτιν,
οἰωνοὺς κρίνας οἳ ἐπ' ἔργματι τούτῳ ἄριστοι.

785 κούρῃ γε Rzach: κ]ούρῃ τε Π₅D: κούρῃσι CH
792–96 om. Plutarchus (homoeotel.)

and the canny one[47] gathers together its heap. On that day a woman should raise her loom and set up her work.

(780) For beginning with the sowing, avoid the thirteenth day after the month begins; and yet it is the best one for getting your plants bedded in. The middle sixth day is very unfavorable for plants, but good for a man to be born; but it is not favorable for a maiden, neither to be born in the first place nor to get married. Nor is the first sixth day fitting for a maiden to be born, but it is a kind day for castrating kids and rams and for fencing in an enclosure for the flocks. And it is fine for a man to be born: such men are fond of speaking mockery and lies and guileful words and hidden whispers. On the eighth day of the month castrate a boar and a loud-bellowing bull, hard-working mules on the twelfth. On the great twentieth, in the fullness of the day, a wise man is born: his mind will be very sagacious. The tenth is fine for a man to be born, for a maiden the middle fourth: on that day place your hand upon sheep and rolling-footed curving-horned oxen and a jagged-toothed dog and hard-working mules, and tame them. Bear in mind to avoid the fourth day, both of the waning month and of the beginning one, spirit-devouring pains: this is a particularly authorized day. On the fourth day of the month lead a wife to your house, after you have distinguished the bird-omens that are the best for this kind of work. Avoid the fifth days,

---

[47] The ant.

---

796 οὐρῆας: ἡμιόνους Φ
799 αλγεα θυμοβορ[ Π₅, ἄλγεα θυμοβόρα Schoemann: ἄλγεα θυμοβορεῖν codd.: ἄλγε᾽ ἃ θυμοβορεῖ (servato 798) Rzach: ἄλγεσι θυμοβορεῖν West

πέμπτας δ' ἐξαλέασθαι, ἐπεὶ χαλεπαί τε καὶ αἰναί·
ἐν πέμπτῃ γάρ φασιν Ἐρινύας ἀμφιπολεύειν
Ὅρκον γεινόμενον, τὸν Ἔρις τέκε πῆμ' ἐπιόρκοις.
805    μέσσῃ δ' ἑβδομάτῃ Δημήτερος ἱερὸν ἀκτὴν
εὖ μάλ' ὀπιπεύοντα ἐυτροχάλῳ ἐν ἀλωῇ
βάλλειν, ὑλοτόμον τε ταμεῖν θαλαμήια δοῦρα
νήιά τε ξύλα πολλά, τά τ' ἄρμενα νηυσὶ πέλονται·
τετράδι δ' ἄρχεσθαι νῆας πήγνυσθαι ἀραιάς.
810    εἰνὰς δ' ἡ μέσση ἐπὶ δείελα λώιον ἦμαρ·
πρωτίστη δ' εἰνὰς παναπήμων ἀνθρώποισιν·
ἐσθλὴ μὲν γάρ θ' ἥ γε φυτευέμεν ἠδὲ γενέσθαι
ἀνέρι τ' ἠδὲ γυναικί, καὶ οὔ ποτε πάγκακον ἦμαρ.
παῦροι δ' αὖτε ἴσασι τρισεινάδα μηνὸς ἀρίστην
815    ἄρξασθαί τε πίθου καὶ ἐπὶ ζυγὸν αὐχένι θεῖναι
βουσὶ καὶ ἡμιόνοισι καὶ ἵπποις ὠκυπόδεσσι
νῆα ‹τε› πολυκλήιδα θοὴν εἰς οἴνοπα πόντον
εἰρύμεναι· παῦροι δέ τ' ἀληθέα κικλήσκουσιν.
τετράδι δ' οἶγε πίθον—περὶ πάντων ἱερὸν ἦμαρ—
820    μέσσῃ. παῦροι δ' αὖτε μετεικάδα μηνὸς ἀρίστην
ἠοῦς γεινομένης· ἐπὶ δείελα δ' ἐστὶ χερείων.

   αἵδε μὲν ἡμέραι εἰσὶν ἐπιχθονίοις μέγ' ὄνειαρ·
αἱ δ' ἄλλαι μετάδουποι, ἀκήριοι, οὔ τι φέρουσαι,
ἄλλος δ' ἀλλοίην αἰνεῖ, παῦροι δέ τ' ἴσασιν·
825    ἄλλοτε μητρυιὴ πέλει ἡμέρη, ἄλλοτε μήτηρ
τάων. εὐδαίμων τε καὶ ὄλβιος, ὃς τάδε πάντα
εἰδὼς ἐργάζηται ἀναίτιος ἀθανάτοισιν,
ὄρνιθας κρίνων καὶ ὑπερβασίας ἀλεείνων.

815 αὐχένα codd.: corr. Hermann

since they are difficult and dread: for they say that it was on the fifth that the Erinyes attended upon Oath as it was born—Oath, which Strife bore as a woe to those who break their oath.

(805) On the middle seventh day inspect Demeter's holy grain very well and winnow it on a well-rolled threshing-floor, and the woodcutter should cut boards for a bedchamber and many planks for a boat, ones which are well fitting for boats. On the fourth begin to build narrow boats.

(810) The middle ninth is a better day towards evening, but the first ninth is entirely harmless for human beings: it is a fine day for both a man and a woman to be conceived and to be born, and never is that day entirely evil. Then again, few know that the thrice-ninth day is the best of the month for starting in on a storage-jar and for placing a yoke on the neck of oxen and mules and swift-footed horses, and for drawing a swift, many-benched boat down to the wine-dark sea—few call things truthfully. On the middle fourth, open a storage-jar—beyond all others it is a holy day. Then again, few know that the twenty-first is the best of the month at daybreak; towards evening it is worse.

(822) These days are a great boon for those on the earth. But the others are random, doomless, they bring nothing. One man praises one kind of day, another another; but few are the ones who know. One time one of these days is a mother-in-law, another time a mother. Happy and blessed is he who knows all these things and does his work without giving offense to the immortals, distinguishing the birds and avoiding trespasses.

153

# TESTIMONIA

## LIFE

### BIOGRAPHIES

**T1**  *Suda* η 583 (II p. 592 Adler)

Ἡσίοδος, Κυμαῖος· νέος δὲ κομισθεὶς ὑπὸ τοῦ πατρὸς
Δίου καὶ μητρὸς Πυκιμήδης ἐν Ἄσκρῃ τῆς Βοιωτίας.
γενεαλογεῖται δὲ εἶναι τοῦ Δίου, τοῦ Ἀπελλίδος, τοῦ
Μελανώπου· ὅν φασί τινες τοῦ Ὁμήρου προπάτορος
εἶναι πάππον, ὡς ἀνεψιαδοῦν εἶναι Ἡσιόδου τὸν
Ὅμηρον, ἑκάτερον δὲ ἀπὸ τοῦ Ἄτλαντος κατάγεσθαι.
ποιήματα δὲ αὐτοῦ ταῦτα· Θεογονία, Ἔργα καὶ Ἡμέ-
ραι, Ἀσπίς, Γυναικῶν ἡρωϊνῶν κατάλογος ἐν βιβλίοις
ε', Ἐπικήδειον εἰς Βάτραχόν τινα, ἐρώμενον αὐτοῦ,
περὶ τῶν Ἰδαίων Δακτύλων· καὶ ἄλλα πολλά. ἐτε-
λεύτησε δὲ ἐπιξενωθεὶς παρ' Ἀντίφῳ καὶ Κτιμένῳ, οἳ

# TESTIMONIA

## LIFE

### BIOGRAPHIES

**T1** The *Suda*

Hesiod: From Cyme. As a youth he was cared for by his father Dius and his mother Pycimede in Ascra in Boeotia. His genealogy: he is said to be the son of Dius, the son of Apelles, the son of Melanopus, who some say is the grandfather of the founding father Homer, so that Homer would be Hesiod's second cousin and their lines of descent would both derive from Atlas. His poems are the following: *Theogony*; *Works and Days*; *Shield*; *Catalogue of Women Heroines* in 5 books; *Dirge,* for a certain Batrachus, his beloved; *On the Idaean Dactyls*; and many others. He died while staying as a guest with Antiphus and Ctimenus: at

HESIOD

νύκτωρ δόξαντες ἀναιρεῖν φθορέα ἀδελφῆς αὐτῶν,
ἀνεῖλον τὸν Ἡσίοδον ἄκοντες. ἦν δὲ Ὁμήρου κατά
τινας πρεσβύτερος, κατὰ δὲ ἄλλους σύγχρονος· Πορ-
φύριος (FGrHist 260 F 20a) καὶ ἄλλοι πλεῖστοι νεώτε-
ρον ἑκατὸν ἐνιαυτοῖς ὁρίζουσιν, ὡς λβ′ μόνους ἐνιαυ-
τοὺς συμπροτερεῖν τῆς πρώτης Ὀλυμπιάδος.

**T2** Tzetzes Schol. Hes. *Op.* pp. 87–92 Colonna (A.
Colonna, ed., *Hesiodi Op.*, Milano-Varese 1959)

ὁ Ἡσίοδος σὺν ἀδελφῷ Πέρσῃ παῖς ἐγεγόνει Δίου καὶ
Πυκιμήδης, Κυμαίων Αἰολέων, πενήτων ἀνθρώπων, οἳ
διὰ τὸ ἄπορον καὶ τὰ χρέα τὴν ἑαυτῶν πατρίδα Κύμην
φυγόντες μεταναστεύουσι περὶ τὴν Ἄσκρην, χωρίον
τῶν Βοιωτῶν δυσχείμερόν τε καὶ κακοθέρειον, περὶ
τοὺς πρόποδας κειμένην τοῦ Ἑλικῶνος κἀκεῖ κατοι-
κοῦσι. τοιαύτη δὲ τῶν ἀνθρώπων πενίᾳ συνεσχημέ-
νων, συνέβαινε τὸν Ἡσίοδον τοῦτον ἄρνας ἐν τῷ
Ἑλικῶνι ποιμαίνειν. φασὶ δὲ ὡς ἐννέα τινὲς ἐλθοῦσαι
γυναῖκες Μοῦσαι καὶ δρεψάμεναι κλῶνας δάφνης
Ἑλικωνίτιδος αὐτὸν ἐπεσίτισαν, καὶ οὕτω σοφίας καὶ
ποιητικῆς ἐμπεφόρητο. . . . συνηκμακέναι δ' αὐτὸν οἱ
μὲν Ὁμήρῳ φασίν, οἱ δὲ καὶ Ὁμήρου προγενέστερον
εἶναι διισχυρίζονται. καὶ οἱ μὲν προγενέστερον εἶναι
Ὁμήρου τοῦτον διισχυριζόμενοι ἐν ἀρχαῖς εἶναί φασι
τῆς Ἀρχίππου ἀρχῆς, Ὅμηρον δὲ ἐν τῷ τέλει—ὁ δ'
Ἄρχιππος οὗτος υἱὸς ἦν Ἀκάστου, ἄρξας Ἀθηναίων
ἔτη τριάκοντα καὶ πέντε –· οἱ δὲ συγχρόνους εἶναι

156

night they thought that they were killing the seducer of their sister, but unintentionally they killed Hesiod. According to some he was older than Homer, according to others contemporary with him; Porphyry and most others define him as being younger by a hundred years, and if so he would be earlier than the first Olympiad by only 32 years (i.e. ca. 807/6 BC).

**T2**  Tzetzes, Scholium on Hesiod's *Works and Days*

Hesiod, together with his brother Perses, was born as son of Dius and Pycimede, who were from Aeolian Cyme, poor people who because of their lack of resources and their debts abandoned their native Cyme and emigrated to Ascra, a little town in Boeotia, bad in winter and evil in summer, lying at the foot of Mount Helicon, and they settled there. While the human beings were afflicted by such poverty, it happened that this Hesiod was pasturing his flocks on Helicon. They say that some women, nine of them, came and plucked twigs from the Heliconian laurel and fed him with them, and in this way he took his fill of wisdom and poetry. . . . Some say that he flourished at the same time as Homer, others maintain that he was even older than Homer. And those who maintain that he was older than Homer say that he lived at the beginning of the reign of Archippus, and Homer at its end; this Archippus was the son of Acastus and ruled over the Athenians for 35 years. Those who say they were contemporaries say that they competed with one another upon the

# HESIOD

λέγοντες ἐπὶ τῇ τελευτῇ Ἀμφιδάμαντος τοῦ βασιλέως
Εὐβοίας φασὶν αὐτοὺς ἀγωνίσασθαι, καὶ νενικηκέναι
Ἡσίοδον, ἀγωνοθετοῦντος καὶ κρίνοντος τὰ μέτρα
Πανείδου τοῦ βασιλέως τοῦ ἀδελφοῦ Ἀμφιδάμαντος
καὶ τῶν υἱῶν Ἀμφιδάμαντος Γανύκτορός τε καὶ τῶν
λοιπῶν. . .ἀλλὰ ταῦτα μὲν ληρήματα τῶν νεωτέρων
εἰσί. . .Ὅμηρος γὰρ ὁ χρυσοῦς, ὡς ἐγῷμαι, μᾶλλον δὲ
ἀκριβεστάτως ἐπίσταμαι, πολύ τε παλαιότερος Ἡσιό-
δου ὑπῆρχε. . .ἀλλ' ἴσως ἕτερος Ὅμηρος ἦν τῷ Ἡσιό-
δῳ ἰσόχρονος ὁ τοῦ Εὔφρονος παῖς ὁ Φωκεύς. . .τὸν
παλαιὸν δὲ Ὅμηρον Διονύσιος ὁ κυκλογράφος φησὶν
(FGrHist 15 F 8) ἐπ' ἀμφωτέρων ὑπάρχειν τῶν Θη-
βαϊκῶν στρατειῶν καὶ τῆς Ἰλίου ἁλώσεως. ἐκ τούτου
γοῦν λογίζομαι τοῦτον τοῦ Ἡσιόδου εἶναι τετρακο-
σίων ἐτῶν προγενέστερον. Ἀριστοτέλης γάρ, ἢ ὁ
φιλόσοφος, μᾶλλον δὲ οἶμαι ὁ τοὺς πέπλους συν-
τάξας, ἐν τῇ Ὀρχομενίων πολιτείᾳ (Fr. 565 Rose)
Στησίχορον τὸν μελοποιὸν εἶναί φησιν υἱὸν Ἡσιόδου
ἐκ τῆς Κτιμένης αὐτῷ γεννηθέντα τῆς Ἀμφιφάνους
καὶ Γανύκτορος ἀδελφῆς, θυγατρὸς δὲ Φηγέως. . .οἱ δὲ
Ὁμήρου τετρακοσίοις ὑστέριζον ἔτεσι, καθά φησι καὶ
Ἡρόδοτος. . .βίβλους μὲν οὗτος ἑκκαίδεκα συνεγρά-
ψατο, Ὅμηρος δὲ ὁ παλαιὸς ιγ΄. τελευτᾷ δὲ ὁ ῥηθεὶς
οὗτος Ἡσίοδος ἐν Λοκρίδι τοιουτοτρόπως. μετὰ τὴν
νίκην, ἣν αὐτὸν νενικηκέναι φασὶν ἐπὶ τῇ τελευτῇ
Ἀμφιδάμαντος εἰς Δελφοὺς ἐπορεύθη, καὶ ἐδόθη αὐτῷ
οὑτοσὶ ὁ χρησμός·

death of King Amphidamas of Euboea and that Hesiod won at the contest established and judged by King Panedes, Amphidamas' brother, and by Amphidamas' sons, Ganyctor and the rest of them. . . . But that is all nonsense invented by more recent writers . . . For golden Homer, as I believe—no, as I know with absolute precision—was much more ancient than Hesiod . . . But perhaps there was another Homer who was contemporary with Hesiod, the Phocian, son of Euphron . . . Dionysius (i.e. of Samos), who wrote on the cycle, says that the ancient Homer lived at the same time as the Theban wars and also as the capture of Troy. For this reason I calculate that he was four hundred years earlier than Hesiod. For Aristotle the philosopher, or rather I suppose the author of the *Peploi*,[1] says in *The Constitution of Orchomenus* that the lyric poet Stesichorus was the son of Hesiod, born to him from Ctimene, the sister of Amphiphanes and Ganyctor, and the daughter of Phegeus. . . . Others say that he was later than Homer by four hundred years, as Herodotus too says.[2]. . .This Hesiod composed 16 books, the ancient Homer 13. Hesiod died in Locris, in the following way: after the victory which they say he won upon the death of Amphidamas, he traveled to Delphi where he received this oracle:

[1] A pseudo-Aristotelian mythographical treatise.
[2] But cf. T10.

ὄλβιος οὗτος ἀνὴρ ὃς ἐμὸν δόμον ἀμφιπολεύει,
Ἡσίοδος, Μούσῃσι τετιμένος ἀθανάτῃσι·
τοῦ δή τοι κλέος ἔσται ὅσον τ' ἐπικίδναται Ἠώς.
ἀλλὰ Διὸς πεφύλαξο Νεμείου κάλλιμον ἄλσος·
καὶ γάρ τοι θανάτοιο τέλος πεπρωμένον ἐστίν.

ὁ δὲ τὴν ἐν Πελοποννήσῳ Νεμέαν φυγὼν ἐν Οἰνόῃ τῆς
Λοκρίδος ὑπὸ Ἀμφιφάνους καὶ Γανύκτορος, τῶν Φη-
γέως παίδων, ἀναιρεῖται καὶ ῥίπτεται εἰς τὴν θάλασ-
σαν, ὡς φθείρας τὴν ἀδελφὴν αὐτῶν Κτιμένην, ἐξ ἧς
ἐγεννήθη Στησίχορος· ἐκαλεῖτο δὲ Οἰνόη Διὸς Νεμεί-
ου ἱερόν. μετὰ δὲ τρίτην ἡμέραν ὑπὸ δελφίνων πρὸς
αἰγιαλὸν ἐξήχθη τὸ σῶμα μεταξὺ Λοκρίδος καὶ Εὐ-
βοίας, καὶ ἔθαψαν αὐτὸν Λοκροὶ ἐν Νεμέᾳ τῆς Οἰνόης.
οἱ δὲ φονεῖς τούτου νηὸς ἐπιβάντες ἐπειρῶντο φυγεῖν,
χειμῶνι δὲ διεφθάρησαν. Ὀρχομένιοι δὲ ὕστερον
κατὰ χρησμὸν ἐνεγκόντες τὰ Ἡσιόδου ὀστᾶ θάπτου-
σιν ἐν μέσῃ τῇ ἀγορᾷ καὶ ἐπέγραψαν τάδε·

Ἄσκρα μὲν πατρὶς πολυλάϊος, ἀλλὰ θανόντος
    ὀστέα πληξίππου γῆ Μινύης κατέχει
Ἡσιόδου, τοῦ πλεῖστον ἐν ἀνθρώποις κλέος
    ἐστίν,
ἀνδρῶν κρινομένων ἐν βασάνοις σοφίης.

ἐπέγραψε δὲ καὶ Πίνδαρος·

χαῖρε δὶς ἡβήσας καὶ δὶς τάφου ἀντιβολήσας,
    Ἡσίοδ', ἀνθρώποις μέτρον ἔχων σοφίης.

Happy this man, who is visiting my house,
Hesiod, honored by the immortal Muses;
indeed, his glory will reach as far as the dawn is
    outspread.
But beware the beautiful grove of Nemean Zeus:
for there the end of death is fated for you.

So he fled from the Peloponnesian Nemea; but in Locrian
Oenoe he was killed and thrown into the sea by Amphi-
phanes and Ganyctor, the sons of Phegeus, for having se-
duced their sister Ctimene, from whom Stesichorus was
born. For Oenoe was called the temple of Nemean Zeus.
Three days later his body was carried by dolphins to the
shore between Locris and Euboea, and the Locrians bur-
ied him in Oenoan Nemea. His murderers boarded a ship
and tried to flee, but they died in a storm. Later, according
to an oracle, the Orchomenians transported Hesiod's
bones and buried them in the middle of the market-place,
and they set up the following inscription:

Ascra with its many cornfields (was) my homeland,
      but now that I have died
    the land of the horse-smiting Minyan holds my
    bones,
Hesiod's, whose glory among human beings is the
      greatest
    when men are judged in the trials of wisdom.

Pindar too wrote an inscription:

Hail, you who twice were young and twice received a
      tomb,
    Hesiod, you who hold the measure of wisdom for
    human beings.

161

# DATE AND RELATION TO HOMER
# AND OTHER POETS

**T3** Aul. Gell. 3.11.1–5

super aetate Homeri atque Hesiodi non consentitur. alii
Homerum quam Hesiodum maiorem natu fuisse scripse-
runt, in quis Philochorus (*FGrHist* 328 F 210) et Xeno-
phanes (11 B 13 DK), alii minorem, in quis L. Accius
poeta (Fr. 1 Funaioli = p. 578 Warmington) et Ephorus
(*FGrHist* 70 F 101) historiae scriptor. M. autem Varro in
primo *de imaginibus* (Fr. 68 Funaioli), uter prior sit natus,
parum constare dicit, sed non esse dubium, quin aliquo
tempore eodem vixerint, idque ex epigrammate ostendi,
quod in tripode scriptum est, qui in monte Helicone ab
Hesiodo positus traditur. Accius autem in primo *didasca-
lico* (Fr. 1 Funaioli = p. 578 Warmington) levibus admo-
dum argumentis utitur, per quae ostendi putat Hesiodum
natu priorem: "quod Homerus", inquit, "cum in principio
carminis Achillem esse filium Pelei diceret, quis esset Pe-
leus, non addidit; quam rem procul," inquit, "dubio dixis-
set, nisi ab Hesiodo iam dictum videret (*Theog.* 1006–7).
de Cyclope itidem," inquit, "vel maxime quod unoculus
fuit, rem tam insignem non praeterisset, nisi aeque prioris
Hesiodi carminibus involgatum esset (*Theog.* 139–46)".

# DATE AND RELATION TO HOMER AND OTHER POETS

*The Scholarly Controversy*

**T3** Aulus Gellius, *Attic Nights*

Regarding the age of Homer and of Hesiod there is no consensus. Some, including Philochorus and Xenophanes, have written that Homer was born before Hesiod; others, including the poet Lucius Accius and the historian Ephorus, that he was younger. But Varro says in book 1 of his *Portraits* that it is not at all certain which of the two was born first but that there can be no doubt that they were both alive at the same time for a while, and that this is demonstrated by the epigram which is engraved on a tripod which is said to have been set up on Mount Helicon by Hesiod.[3] Accius, however, in book 1 of his *Didascalica* makes use of quite feeble arguments which he supposes demonstrate that Hesiod was born first. "When Homer," he said, "stated in the beginning of his poem that Achilles was Peleus' son, he did not add who Peleus was"; but, he (i.e. Accius) says, "without a doubt he (i.e. Homer) would have said this if he had not seen that it had already been said by Hesiod (cf. *Theogony* 1006–7). In the same way," he (i.e. Accius) said, "concerning the Cyclops he (i.e. Homer) would certainly not have omitted to indicate so remarkable a fact as that he was one-eyed, unless in the same way it had already been made well known by the poems of his predecessor Hesiod (cf. *Theogony* 139–46)."

---

[3] Cf. *The Contest of Homer and Hesiod* 13, pp. 340–41 West; T40.

**T4**  Paus. 9.30.3

περὶ δὲ Ἡσιόδου τε ἡλικίας καὶ Ὁμήρου πολυ-
πραγμονήσαντι ἐς τὸ ἀκριβέστατον οὔ μοι γράφειν
ἡδὺ ἦν, ἐπισταμένῳ τὸ φιλαίτιον ἄλλων τε καὶ οὐχ
ἥκιστα ὅσοι κατ' ἐμὲ ἐπὶ ποιήσει τῶν ἐπῶν καθεστή-
κεσαν.

**T5**  Posidonius Fr. 459 Theiler (= Tzetzes, *Exeg. Il.*, p.
19.1–4 Hermann)

καὶ τοῦ Ποσειδωνίου οἶμαι μὴ ἀκηκοὼς λέγοντος
αὐτὸν τὸν Ἡσίοδον ὕστερον γενόμενον πολλὰ παρα-
φθεῖραι τῶν Ὁμήρου ἐπῶν.

**T6**  Cic. *Cato maior de senectute* 15.54

at Homerus, qui multis ut mihi videtur ante saeculis fuit. . .
(= T152)

**T7**  Vell. Paterc. 1.7.1

huius temporis aequalis Hesiodus fuit, circa CXX annos
distinctus ab Homeri aetate, vir perelegantis ingenii et
mollissima dulcedine carminum memorabilis, otii quietis-
que cupidissimus, ut tempore tanto viro, ita operis auc-
toritate proximus, qui vitavit ne in id quod Homerus
incideret, patriamque et parentes testatus est, sed patri-
am, quia multatus ab ea erat, contumeliosissime.

**T4**  Pausanias, *Description of Greece*

Although I investigated the ages of Hesiod and Homer as exactly as possible, I take no pleasure in writing about this, since I know that other people are captious, especially the appointed experts on epic poetry in my time.

Cf. T1, T2

### Homer Older Than Hesiod

**T5**  Posidonius, uncertain fragment

I believe that I have perhaps read Posidonius too saying that Hesiod himself was born much later and corrupted many of Homer's verses.

**T6**  Cicero, *Cato. On Old Age*

but Homer, who lived many generations, as I believe, before (scil. Hesiod) . . . (= T152)

**T7**  Velleius Paterculus, *Compendium of Roman History*

At this time (ca. 820 B.C.) lived Hesiod, who differed in age from Homer by about 120 years, a man of extremely refined talent and renowned for the extraordinarily gentle sweetness of his poems, greatly desirous of peace and quiet, second to such a great man (i.e. Homer) both in time and in the prestige of his work. He avoided making the same error as Homer did, and provided testimony concerning his homeland and parents—but in the case of his homeland he did so very abusively, since he had been punished by it.

**T8** Plut. *Consolatio ad Apollonium* 7 p. 105d

ὁ δὲ μετὰ τοῦτον καὶ τῇ δόξῃ καὶ τῷ χρόνῳ, καίτοι τῶν
Μουσῶν ἀναγορεύων ἑαυτὸν μαθητὴν Ἡσίοδος. . .

**T9** Solinus 40.17

inter quem et Hesiodum poetam, qui in auspiciis olympi-
adis primae obiit, centum triginta octo anni interfuerunt.

**T10** Hdt. 2.53.2

Ἡσίοδον γὰρ καὶ Ὅμηρον ἡλικίην τετρακοσίοισι
ἔτεσι δοκέω μέο πρεσβυτέρους γενέσθαι καὶ οὐ πλέ-
οσι.

**T11** Aul. Gell. 17.21.3

de Homero et Hesiodo inter omnes fere scriptores con-
stitit aetatem eos egisse vel isdem fere temporibus vel
Homerum aliquanto antiquiorem, utrumque tamen ante
Romam conditam vixisse Silviis Albae regnantibus annis
post bellum Troianum, ut Cassius in primo *annalium* de
Homero atque Hesiodo scriptum reliquit (Fr. 8 Peter),
plus centum atque sexaginta, ante Romam autem condi-
tam, ut Cornelius Nepos in primo *Chronicorum* de Home-
ro dixit (Fr. 2 Peter), annis circiter centum et sexaginta.

## TESTIMONIA

**T8**  Plutarch, *Letter of Condolence to Apollonius*

Hesiod, who comes after him (i.e. Homer) both in fame and in time, even though he proclaims himself a disciple of the Muses . . .

**T9**  Gaius Iulius Solinus, *Collection of Memorable Things*

Between him (i.e. Homer) and the poet Hesiod, who died at the beginning of the first Olympiad (777/76), 138 years went by.

Cf. T1, T2; and Proclus, *Chrestomathy I. Homer's Date, Life, Character, Catalogue of Poems* 6 (pp. 422–23 West), and Anonymus I, *Life of Homer* (Vita Romana) 4 (pp. 434–35 West)

### Homer and Hesiod as Contemporaries

**T10**  Herodotus, *History*

For I believe that Hesiod and Homer were born 400 years before me (ca. 885 BC) and not more.

**T11**  Aulus Gellius, *Attic Nights*

Concerning Homer and Hesiod almost all authors agree that they lived more or less at the same time, or that Homer was only a little bit older, and in any case that they both lived before the foundation of Rome, while the Silvii ruled in Alba, more than 160 years after the Trojan war, as Cassius wrote about Homer and Hesiod in book 1 of his *Annals*, but about 160 years before the founding of Rome, as Cornelius Nepos says about Homer in book 1 of his *Chronicles*.

**T12** Clem. Alex. *Strom.* 1.21.117.4, p. 74.5–7 Stählin

Εὐθυμένης δὲ ἐν τοῖς Χρονικοῖς (*FGrHist* 243 F 1)
συνακμάσαντα (scil. Ὅμηρον) Ἡσιόδῳ ἐπὶ Ἀκάστου
ἐν Χίῳ γενέσθαι περὶ τὸ διακοσιοστὸν ἔτος ὕστερον
τῆς Ἰλίου ἁλώσεως. ταύτης δέ ἐστι τῆς δόξης καὶ
Ἀρχέμαχος ἐν Εὐβοϊκῶν τρίτῳ (*FGrHist* 424 F 3).

**T13** Philostratus *Heroicus* 43.7, p. 56.4–6 De Lannoy

οἱ δὲ ἑξήκοντα καὶ ἑκατὸν ἔτη γεγονέναι μετὰ τὴν
Τροίαν ἐπὶ Ὅμηρόν τέ φασι καὶ Ἡσίοδον, ὅτε δὴ
ᾆσαι ἄμφω ἐν Χαλκίδι.

**T14** Syncellus *Chronographia*

**(a)** p. 202.21–22 Mosshammer

Ἡσίοδός τε ἐγνωρίζετο, ὃν Ἔφορος (*FGrHist* 70 F
101b) ἀνεψιὸν καὶ σύγχρονον Ὁμήρου φησί.

**(b)** p. 206.9 Mosshammer

ἐπ᾽ αὐτοῦ ὁ μέγας ποιητὴς Ὅμηρος παρ᾽ Ἕλλησι καὶ
Ἡσίοδος.

**T15** Marmor Parium *FGrHist* 239 A ep. 28–29

28 ἀφ᾽ οὗ [ Ἡσ]ίοδος ὁ ποιητὴς [ἐφάν]η, ἔτη ⌐ΗΓ⌐ΔΔ..,
  βασιλεύοντος Ἀθηνῶν. . |. . . . .

**T12** Clement of Alexandria, *Miscellanies*

Euthymenes says in his *Chronicles* that he (i.e. Homer) flourished at the same time as Hesiod and was born during the reign of Acastus on Chios, about 200 years after the capture of Troy. Archemachus too is of the same opinion in book 3 of his *Euboean History*.

**T13** Philostratus, *Heroicus*

Others say that 160 years went by from Troy to Homer and Hesiod, when they both sang in Chalcis.

**T14** Syncellus, *Chronography*

(a) Hesiod was becoming known, who Ephorus says was a first cousin and contemporary of Homer.
(b) During his (i.e. David's) reign (*anno mundi* ca. 4428–68), the great poet Homer among the Greeks, and Hesiod.

Cf. T2, T65; and *The Contest of Homer and Hesiod* 5–13 (pp. 322–45 West), Proclus, *Chrestomathy I. Homer's Date, Life, Character, Catalogue of Poems* 4 (pp. 420–21 West)

*Hesiod Older Than Homer*

**T15** The Parian Marble Inscription

28. From when the poet Hesiod appeared, 67[3?] years, when [      ] was king of the Athenians (937/5?).

29  ἀφ᾽ οὗ Ὅμηρος ὁ ποιητὴς ἐφάνη, ἔτη ⌐ΗΔΔΔΔΙΙΙ,
βασιλεύοντος Ἀθηνῶ[ν Δ]ιογνήτου.

**T16** Gnomologium Vaticanum Graecum 1144, f. 222ᵛ
Sternbach (L. Sternbach, "Gnomica," in *Commentationes
philologae . . . Ribbeck*, Lipsiae 1888, p. 358)

Σιμωνίδης τὸν Ἡσίοδον κηπουρὸν ἔλεγε, τὸν δὲ Ὅμη-
ρον στεφανηπλόκον, τὸν μὲν ὡς φυτεύσαντα τὰς περὶ
θεῶν καὶ ἡρώων μυθολογίας, τὸν δὲ ὡς ἐξ αὐτῶν
συμπλέξαντα τὸν Ἰλιάδος καὶ Ὀδυσσείας στέφανον.

**T17** Hippias 86 B 6 DK, *FGrHist* 6 F 4

τούτων ἴσως εἴρηται τὰ μὲν Ὀρφεῖ, τὰ δὲ Μουσαίῳ
κατὰ βραχὺ ἄλλῳ ἀλλαχοῦ, τὰ δὲ Ἡσιόδῳ, τὰ δὲ
Ὁμήρῳ, τὰ δὲ τοῖς ἄλλοις τῶν ποιητῶν, τὰ δὲ ἐν
συγγραφαῖς, τὰ μὲν Ἕλλησι, τὰ δὲ βαρβάροις.

**T18** Aristoph. *Ranae* 1030–36

σκέψαι γὰρ ἀπ᾽ ἀρχῆς
ὡς ὠφέλιμοι τῶν ποιητῶν οἱ γενναῖοι γεγένηνται.
Ὀρφεὺς μὲν γὰρ τελετάς θ᾽ ἡμῖν κατέδειξε
    φόνων τ᾽ ἀπέχεσθαι,
Μουσαῖος δ᾽ ἐξακέσεις τε νόσων καὶ χρησμούς,
    Ἡσίοδος δὲ
γῆς ἐργασίας, καρπῶν ὥρας, ἀρότους· ὁ δὲ θεῖος
    Ὅμηρος

29. From when the poet Homer appeared, 643 years, when Diognetus was king of the Athenians (907/5).

**T16**  Vatican Collection of Greek Sayings

Simonides said that Hesiod was a gardener and Homer a weaver of garlands, since the former planted the mythological stories about gods and heroes, while the latter wove together the garland of the *Iliad* and *Odyssey* out of them.

Cf. T2; and *The Contest of Homer and Hesiod* 4 (pp. 322–23 West), (Pseudo-) Plutarch, *On Homer* 2 (pp. 404–7 West), Anonymus I, *Life of Homer* (Vita Romana) 4 (pp. 434–35 West)

*The Sequence Orpheus-Musaeus-Hesiod-Homer*

**T17**  Hippias of Elis, fragment

Of these things, perhaps some have been said by Orpheus, others by Musaeus, briefly, here and there, some by Hesiod, others by Homer, some by other poets, others in prose writings, some by Greeks, others by barbarians.

**T18**  Aristophanes, *Frogs*

For look, starting from the very beginning,
how useful the noble poets have been.
For Orpheus taught us initiatory rites and refraining
    from slaughter,
Musaeus cures for illnesses and oracles, Hesiod
working the land, the seasons for harvesting and
    plowing; and godly Homer,

171

ἀπὸ τοῦ τιμὴν καὶ κλέος ἔσχεν πλὴν τοῦδ' ὅτι
χρήστ' ἐδίδαξεν,
τάξεις, ἀρετάς, ὁπλίσεις ἀνδρῶν;

**T19** Schol. Hes. *Op.* 271a Pertusi

ἰστέον δὲ ὅτι υἱὸς Ἡσιόδου Μνασέας ἐστί. Φιλόχορος
(*FGrHist* 328 F 213) δὲ Στησίχορόν φησι τὸν ἀπὸ
Κλυμένης· ἄλλοι δὲ Ἀρχιέπην.

**T20** Cic. *De republica* 2.20 (ed. Ziegler)

Stesichor〉us ne〈pos ei〉us, ut di〈xeru〉nt quid〈am, e〉x
filia. quo 〈vero〉 ille mor〈tuus, e〉odem 〈est an〉no
na〈tus Si〉moni〈des ol〉ympia〈de se〉xta et quin〈qua-
g〉esima.

Stesichor〉us: suppl. Mommsen

**T21** Cic. *Disp. Tusc.* 1.1.3

si quidem Homerus fuit et Hesiodus ante Romam con-
ditam. . .

**T22** Plin. *Hist. nat.* 14.1.3

ante milia annorum inter principia litterarum Hesiodo
praecepta agricolis pandere orso. . .

what did he receive honor and glory from, if not from
  teaching us useful things,
battle orderings and the virtues and arming of men?

Cf. T116a, T119bi, bii

*Hesiod as Stesichorus' Father or Grandfather*

**T19** Scholium on the *Works and Days*

You should know that Hesiod's son is Mnaseas. Philo-
chorus says he was Stesichorus, and the mother was
Clymene. Others say she was Archiepe.

**T20** Cicero, *On the Republic*

[Stesichorus], his (i.e. Hesiod's) grandson, as some have
said, from his daughter. [But] Simonides was born in the
same year in which he (i.e. Stesichorus) died, in the 56th
Olympiad (i.e. 556/5).

Cf. T2

*Miscellaneous*

**T21** Cicero, *Tusculan Disputations*

if indeed Homer and Hesiod lived before the foundation
of Rome . . .

**T22** Pliny the Elder, *Natural History*

a thousand years ago (i.e. about 920 BC), at the very begin-
ning of writing, Hesiod was the first to give precepts to
farmers . . .

**T23** Euseb. *Hier.*

**(a)** 119F, p. 71b.5 Helm

quidam Homerum et Hesiodum his temporibus fuisse se aiunt.

**(b)** 145F, p. 84b.2 Helm

Hesiodus insignis habetur, ut vult Porphyrius (*FGrHist* 260 F 20b).

**(c)** 151F, p. 87b.9 Helm

Hesiodus secundum quosdam clarus habetur.

**T24** Tzetzes *Chil.* 13.643–44 Leone

Ἡσίοδος δὲ ἤκμαζεν, ὡς εὗρον ἐν ἑτέροις, κατὰ τὴν ἑνδεκάτην μὲν αὐτὴν Ὀλυμπιάδα.

## BIRTH

**T25** Schol. Hes. *Op.* 635a Pertusi

Ἔφορος (*FGrHist* 70 F 100) δέ φησι τοῦτον εἰς Ἄσκρην ἐλθεῖν, οὐ δι᾿ ἐμπορίαν, ἀλλὰ φόνον ἐμφύλιον ἐργασάμενον.

**T23** Eusebius, *Chronicle of Jerome*

**(a)** Some say that Homer and Hesiod lived at this time (i.e. 1017/16 BC).

**(b)** Hesiod is considered renowned (i.e. 809/8 BC), according to Porphyry.

**(c)** According to some, Hesiod is considered famous (i.e. 767/6 BC).

**T24** Tzetzes, *Chiliads*

Hesiod flourished, as I have found in other authors (scil. other than Apollodorus), in the 11th Olympiad (736/3).

### BIRTH

**T25** Scholium on Hesiod's *Works and Days*

Ephorus says that he (i.e. Hesiod's father) came to Ascra not because of poverty but because he had murdered a kinsman.

**T26** Vacca *Vita Lucani* p. 403.21–26 Badalì

eventus . . . qui in Hesiodo refertur . . . cunas infantis,
quibus ferebatur, apes circumvolarunt osque insedere
conplures, aut dulcem iam tum spiritum eius haurientes
aut facundum et qualem nunc existimamus, futurum sig-
nificantes.

# NAME

**T27** *Etym. Gudianum* p. 249.49 Sturz (*Etym. Magnum* p.
438.20)

Ἡσίοδος, Αἰωλικῶς, ὁ τὴν αἰσίαν ὁδὸν πορευόμενος.
Ἔργα καὶ Ἡμέρας ἔγραψε πρὸς τὴν τοῦ βίου
ἐργασίαν καὶ νομοθεσίαν. ἢ ὅτι αἰσίως ἐβάδισε.
συνέτυχε γὰρ ταῖς Μούσαις, καὶ οὐχ ὡς Θάμυρις
διετέθη. ὅθεν καὶ ποιητὴς ἄριστος.

**T28** *Etym. Magnum* p. 438.24

Ἡσίοδος· παρὰ τὸν ἤσω μέλλοντα, καὶ τὸ ὁδός.

**T29** Schol. Hes. *Op.* 1 p. 22.1 Gaisford

Ἡσίοδος ἐκ τοῦ ἤσις ἡ εὐφροσύνη, καὶ τοῦ εἴδω τὸ
λέγω γίνεται.

**T26**  Vacca, *Life of Lucan*

An event . . . which is reported about Hesiod . . . bees swarmed around the infant's cradle, in which he was being carried about, and many came to sit upon his mouth, either drinking his breath, which was already sweet at that age, or signifying that he would be eloquent and such as we now recognize him to have been.

Cf. also *The Contest of Homer and Hesiod* 1 (pp. 318–19 West)

## NAME

**T27**  *Etymologicum Gudianum* and *Magnum*

Hesiod: in Aeolic, he who travels on an auspicious (*aisia*) road (*hodos*). He wrote the *Works and Days* with a view towards working for the means of life and towards legislation. Or because he walked auspiciously: for he encountered the Muses, and was not treated by them as Thamyris was; for this reason he is an excellent poet.

**T28**  *Etymologicum Magnum*

Hesiod: from the future *hêsô* "I will cast" and the word *hodos* "road."

**T29**  Scholium on Hesiod's *Works and Days*

"Hesiod" comes from *hêsis* "festivity" and *eidô* "I say."

# HESIOD

# DEATH

**T30**  Thuc. 3.96.1

αὐλισάμενος δὲ τῷ στρατῷ ἐν τοῦ Διὸς τοῦ Νεμείου τῷ ἱερῷ, ἐν ᾧ Ἡσίοδος ὁ ποιητὴς λέγεται ὑπὸ τῶν ταύτῃ ἀποθανεῖν, χρησθὲν αὐτῷ ἐν Νεμέᾳ τοῦτο παθεῖν.

**T31**  Paus. 9.31.6

ἐναντία δὲ καὶ ἐς τοῦ Ἡσιόδου τὴν τελευτήν ἐστιν εἰρημένα. ὅτι μὲν γὰρ οἱ παῖδες τοῦ Γανύκτορος Κτίμενος καὶ Ἄντιφος ἔφυγον ἐς Μολυκρίαν ἐκ Ναυπάκτου διὰ τοῦ Ἡσιόδου τὸν φόνον καὶ αὐτόθι ἀσεβήσασιν ἐς Ποσειδῶνα ἐγένετο τῇ Μολυκρίᾳ σφίσιν ἡ δίκη, τάδε μὲν καὶ οἱ πάντες κατὰ ταὐτὰ εἰρήκασι· τὴν δὲ ἀδελφὴν τῶν νεανίσκων οἱ μὲν ἄλλου τοῦ φασιν αἰσχύναντος Ἡσίοδον λαβεῖν οὐκ ἀληθῆ τὴν τοῦ ἀδικήματος δόξαν, οἱ δὲ ἐκείνου γενέσθαι τὸ ἔργον.

τῇ Μολυκρίᾳ Porson: τῇ μολυκρίδι codd.

**T32**  Plut. *Sept. sap. conv.* 19 p. 162c-e

Μιλησίου γάρ, ὡς ἔοικεν, ἀνδρός, ᾧ ξενίας ἐκοινώνει ὁ Ἡσίοδος καὶ διαίτης ἐν Λοκροῖς, τῇ τοῦ ξένου θυγατρὶ κρύφα συγγενομένου καὶ φωραθέντος ὑποψίαν ἔσχεν ὡς γνοὺς ἀπ᾽ ἀρχῆς καὶ συνεπικρύψας τὸ ἀδίκημα, μηδενὸς ὢν αἴτιος, ὀργῆς δὲ καιρῷ καὶ δια-

## DEATH

**T30**  Thucydides, *History*

He (i.e. Demosthenes) bivouacked with his army at the temple of Nemean Zeus, where the poet Hesiod is said by the locals to have died after he had received an oracle that this would happen to him in Nemea.

**T31**  Pausanias, *Description of Greece*

There are conflicting versions of the death of Hesiod. That the sons of Ganyctor, Ctimenus and Antiphus, fled to Molycria from Naupactus because of the murder of Hesiod and that they were punished there for their sacrileges against Poseidon—this is said by all in the same way. But some say that it was someone else who seduced the young men's sister and that Hesiod has undeservedly gotten a bad reputation for this crime, while others say that the deed was done by him.

**T32**  Plutarch, *The Dinner of the Seven Wise Men*

A man from Miletus, as it seems, with whom Hesiod was sharing room and board in Locris, had intercourse in secret with the host's daughter; and when he was caught, he (i.e. Hesiod) was suspected of having known about the crime from the beginning and having helped to conceal it, although in fact he was guilty of nothing but undeservedly

βολῆς περιπεσὼν ἀδίκως. ἀπέκτειναν γὰρ αὐτὸν οἱ
τῆς παιδίσκης ἀδελφοὶ περὶ τὸ Λοκρικὸν Νέμειον
ἐνεδρεύσαντες, καὶ μετ᾽ αὐτοῦ τὸν ἀκόλουθον, ᾧ Τρω-
ΐλος ἦν ὄνομα. τῶν δὲ σωμάτων εἰς τὴν θάλατταν
ὠσθέντων τὸ μὲν τοῦ Τρωΐλου, εἰς τὸν Δάφνον ποτα-
μὸν ἔξω φορούμενον, ἐπεσχέθη περικλύστῳ χοιράδι
μικρὸν ὑπὲρ τὴν θάλατταν ἀνεχούσῃ· καὶ μέχρι νῦν
Τρωΐλος ἡ χοιρὰς καλεῖται· τοῦ δ᾽ Ἡσιόδου τὸν
νεκρὸν εὐθὺς ἀπὸ γῆς ὑπολαβοῦσα δελφίνων ἀγέλη
πρὸς τὸ Ῥίον κατὰ τὴν Μολύκρειαν ἐκόμιζε. ἐτύγχανε
δὲ Λοκροῖς ἡ τῶν Ῥίων καθεστῶσα θυσία καὶ πανή-
γυρις, ἣν ἄγουσιν ἔτι νῦν ἐπιφανῶς περὶ τὸν τόπον
ἐκεῖνον. ὡς δ᾽ ὤφθη προσφερόμενον τὸ σῶμα, θαυμά-
σαντες ὡς εἰκὸς ἐπὶ τὴν ἀκτὴν κατέδραμον, καὶ γνωρί-
σαντες ἔτι πρόσφατον τὸν νεκρὸν ἅπαντα δεύτερα τοῦ
ζητεῖν τὸν φόνον ἐποιοῦντο διὰ τὴν δόξαν τοῦ Ἡσι-
όδου. καὶ τοῦτο μὲν ταχέως ἔπραξαν, εὑρόντες τοὺς
φονεῖς· αὐτούς τε γὰρ κατεπόντισαν ζῶντας καὶ τὴν
οἰκίαν κατέσκαψαν. ἐτάφη δ᾽ ὁ Ἡσίοδος πρὸς τῷ
Νεμείῳ· τὸν δὲ τάφον οἱ πολλοὶ τῶν ξένων οὐκ ἴσασιν,
ἀλλ᾽ ἀποκέκρυπται ζητούμενος ὑπ᾽ Ὀρχομενίων, ὥς
φασι, βουλομένων κατὰ χρησμὸν ἀνελέσθαι τὰ λεί-
ψανα καὶ θάψαι παρ᾽ αὐτοῖς.

fell foul of an angry accusation. For the girl's brothers lay in wait for him near the temple of Nemean Zeus in Locris and killed him, and together with him his attendant, whose name was Troilus. Their bodies were thrown into the sea. Troilus' was borne outwards by the river Daphnus and came to rest on a wave-swept rock that stuck out a little bit above the surface of the sea; and even today that rock is called Troilus. As for Hesiod's corpse, a school of dolphins took it up just off the land and brought it to Rhium in Molycreia. It happened that the customary Rhian sacrifice and festival was taking place in Locris; they celebrate it publicly even now around that place. When the body was seen being carried to land, they ran to the shore, understandably astonished, and when they recognized the body, which was still fresh, they made investigating the murder their first priority because of Hesiod's fame. And they quickly succeeded in discovering the murderers, and cast them living into the sea and tore down their house. Hesiod was buried near the temple of Nemean Zeus. Most outsiders do not know about his grave, for it has been hidden because the Orchomenians are looking for it, as they say, since in accordance with an oracle they want to remove his remains and bury him in their own land.

**T33** Plut. *De sollert. animal.*

**(a)** 13 p. 969d-e

ταὐτὰ δὲ καὶ τὸν Ἡσιόδου κύνα τοῦ σοφοῦ δρᾶσαι λέγουσι, τοὺς Γανύκτορος ἐξελέγξαντα τοῦ Ναυπακτίου παῖδας, ὑφ' ὧν ὁ Ἡσίοδος ἀπέθανεν.

**(b)** 36 p. 984d

ἔδει δὲ τὸν κύν' αἰτιασάμενον μὴ παραλιπεῖν τοὺς δελφῖνας· τυφλὸν γὰρ ἦν τὸ μήνυμα τοῦ κυνός, ὑλακτοῦντος καὶ μετὰ βοῆς ἐπιφερομένου τοῖς φονεῦσιν, ⟨εἰ μὴ τὸν νεκρὸν⟩ περὶ τὸ Νέμειον θαλάσσῃ διαφερόμενον ἀράμενοι δελφῖνες, ἕτεροι παρ' ἑτέρων ἐκδεχόμενοι προθύμως, εἰς τὸ Ῥίον ἐκθέντες ἔδειξαν ἐσφαγμένον.

⟨εἰ μὴ τὸν νεκρὸν⟩ add. Bachet de Meziriac

**T34** Pollux 5.42

κύνες δ' ἔνδοξοι· . . . οἱ δ' Ἡσιόδου παραμείναντες αὐτῷ ἀναιρεθέντι κατήλεγξαν ὑλακῇ τοὺς φονεύσαντας.

**T33**  Plutarch, *On the Cleverness of Animals*

**(a)** They say that wise Hesiod's dog did the same thing, convicting the sons of Ganyctor of Naupactus, who had killed Hesiod.

**(b)** While you were indicating the dog as the cause you should not have left out the dolphins. For the information provided by the dog, which was barking and rushing in full voice against the murderers, would have been quite futile if the dolphins had not picked up his body, which was drifting in the sea around the temple of Nemean Zeus, eagerly taking him up in turns, and then set him ashore at Rhium, revealing that he had been murdered.

**T34**  Pollux, *Lexicon*

Famous dogs: . . . those of Hesiod, which remained beside him after he had been killed and convicted the murderers by barking.

Cf. T1, T2; and also *The Contest of Homer and Hesiod* 14 (pp. 340–45 West)

## MISCELLANEOUS

**T35**  Paus. 1.2.3

Ἡσίοδος δὲ καὶ Ὅμηρος ἢ συγγενέσθαι βασιλεῦσιν
ἠτύχησαν ἢ καὶ ἑκόντες ὠλιγώρησαν, ὁ μὲν ἀγροικίᾳ
καὶ ὄκνῳ πλάνης. . .

# POEMS

## PERFORMANCES BY HESIOD

**T36**  Plato *Resp.* 10 600d

Ὅμηρον δ᾽ ἄρα οἱ ἐπ᾽ ἐκείνου, εἴπερ οἷός τ᾽ ἦν πρὸς
ἀρετὴν ὀνῆσαι ἀνθρώπους, ἢ Ἡσίοδον ῥαψῳδεῖν ἂν
περιιόντας εἴων. . .;

**T37**  Diog. Laert. 2.46

τούτῳ τις, καθά φησιν Ἀριστοτέλης ἐν τρίτῳ Περὶ
ποιητικῆς (Fr. 75 Rose), ἐφιλονείκει Ἀντίλοχος Λήμνι-
ος καὶ Ἀντιφῶν ὁ τερατοσκόπος, . . . καὶ Κέρκωψ
Ἡσιόδῳ ζῶντι, τελευτήσαντι δὲ. . .Ξενοφάνης (21 B 11
DK).

## MISCELLANEOUS

**T35**  Pausanias, *Description of Greece*

Hesiod and Homer either were not lucky enough to associate with kings or else deliberately looked down upon doing so, the former because he was rustic and reluctant to travel . . .

# POEMS

## PERFORMANCES BY HESIOD

**T36**  Plato, *Republic*

If Homer had been capable of benefiting men with regard to virtue, would his contemporaries have allowed him or Hesiod to wander around and perform as a rhapsode . . . ?

**T37**  Diogenes Laertius, *Lives of Eminent Philosophers*

As Aristotle says in book 3 of the *Poetics*, someone named Antilochus of Lemnus and Antiphon the seer vied with him (i.e. Socrates), just as . . . Cercops did with Hesiod when he was alive, and . . . Xenophanes after he had died.

HESIOD

**T38** Plut. *Sept. sap. conv.* 10 pp. 153f-154a

ἀκούομεν γὰρ ὅτι καὶ πρὸς τὰς Ἀμφιδάμαντος ταφὰς
εἰς Χαλκίδα τῶν τότε σοφῶν οἱ δοκιμώτατοι ποιηταὶ
συνῆλθον· . . . ἐπεὶ δὲ τὰ παρεσκευασμένα τοῖς ποιη-
ταῖς ἔπη χαλεπὴν καὶ δύσκολον ἐποίει τὴν κρίσιν διὰ
τὸ ἐφάμιλλον, ἥ τε δόξα τῶν ἀγωνιστῶν, Ὁμήρου καὶ
Ἡσιόδου, πολλὴν ἀπορίαν μετ᾽ αἰδοῦς τοῖς κρίνουσι
παρεῖχεν, ἐτράποντο πρὸς τοιαύτας ἐρωτήσεις, καὶ
πρόεβαλ᾽ ὁ μέν, ὥς φασι, Λέσχης·

  Μοῦσά μοι ἔννεπε κεῖνα, τὰ μήτ᾽ ἐγένοντο
    πάροιθε
  μήτ᾽ ἔσται μετόπισθεν. (*Parva Ilias* Fr. 1 Bernabè)

ἀπεκρίνατο δ᾽ Ἡσίοδος ἐκ τοῦ παρατυχόντος·

  ἀλλ᾽ ὅταν ἀμφὶ Διὸς τύμβῳ καναχήποδες ἵπποι
  ἅρματα συντρίψωσιν ἐπειγόμενοι περὶ νίκης.

καὶ διὰ τοῦτο λέγεται μάλιστα θαυμασθεὶς τοῦ τρίπο-
δος τυχεῖν.

**T39** Paus. 10.7.3

λέγεται δὲ καὶ Ἡσίοδον ἀπελαθῆναι τοῦ ἀγωνίσματος
.ἅτε οὐ κιθαρίζειν ὁμοῦ τῇ ᾠδῇ δεδιδαγμένον.

**T40** Paus. 9.31.3

ἐν δὲ τῷ Ἑλικῶνι καὶ ἄλλοι τρίποδες κεῖνται καὶ

186

**T38** Plutarch, *The Dinner of the Seven Wise Men*

For we are told that the most renowned poets among the wise men of that time came together in Chalcis for the funeral of Amphidamas.... Since the poems which the poets had prepared made the decision difficult and irksome because they were of matching quality, and the renown of the contestants Homer and Hesiod made the judges feel helpless and embarrassed, they turned to riddles of the following sort, and Lesches, as they say, proposed the following:

> Muse, tell me what has never happened earlier
> nor will ever come about later.

And Hesiod answered on the spot,

> When around the tomb of Zeus the loud-footed
>     horses
> make the chariots rub together, hastening for the
>     victory.

And he is said to have been very much admired because of this and to have won the tripod.

**T39** Pausanias, *Description of Greece*

Hesiod is said to have been expelled from the competition (i.e. in music at Delphi) since he had not learned to accompany himself on the lyre while he sang.

**T40** Pausanias, *Description of Greece*

In Helicon there are other tripods preserved as dedica-

ἀρχαιότατος, ὃν ἐν Χαλκίδι λαβεῖν τῇ ἐπ᾽ Εὐρίπῳ
λέγουσιν Ἡσίοδον νικήσαντα ᾠδῇ.

**T41** Schol. Pind. *Nem.* 2.1 (III p. 31.13 Drachmann)

ῥαψῳδῆσαι δέ φησι πρῶτον τὸν Ἡσίοδον Νικοκλῆς
(*FGrHist* 376 F 8).

## CATALOGUES OF POEMS

**T42** Paus. 9.31.4–5

Βοιωτῶν δὲ οἱ περὶ τὸν Ἑλικῶνα οἰκοῦντες παρειλημ-
μένα δόξῃ λέγουσιν ὡς ἄλλο Ἡσίοδος ποιήσειεν
οὐδὲν ἢ τὰ Ἔργα· καὶ τούτων δὲ τὸ ἐς τὰς Μούσας
ἀφαιροῦσι προοίμιον, ἀρχὴν τῆς ποιήσεως εἶναι τὸ ἐς
τὰς Ἔριδας λέγοντες (v.11)· καί μοι μόλυβδον ἐδεί-
κνυσαν, ἔνθα ἡ πηγή, τὰ πολλὰ ὑπὸ τοῦ χρόνου
λελυμασμένον· ἐγγέγραπται δὲ αὐτῷ τὰ Ἔργα. ἔστι
δὲ καὶ ἑτέρα κεχωρισμένη τῆς προτέρας, ὡς πολύν
τινα ἐπῶν ὁ Ἡσίοδος ἀριθμὸν ποιήσειεν, ἐς γυναῖκάς
τε ᾀδόμενα καὶ ἃς μεγάλας ἐπονομάζουσιν Ἠοίας, καὶ
Θεογονίαν τε καὶ ἐς τὸν μάντιν Μελάμποδα, καὶ ὡς
Θησεὺς ἐς τὸν Ἅιδην ὁμοῦ Πειρίθῳ καταβαίη παραι-
νέσεις τε Χίρωνος ἐπὶ διδασκαλίᾳ δὴ τῇ Ἀχιλλέως,
καὶ ὅσα ἐπὶ Ἔργοις τε καὶ Ἡμέραις. οἱ δὲ αὐτοὶ οὗτοι
λέγουσι καὶ ὡς μαντικὴν Ἡσίοδος διδαχθείη παρὰ
Ἀκαρνάνων· καὶ ἔστιν ἔπη Μαντικά, ὁπόσα τε ἐπελε-
ξάμεθα καὶ ἡμεῖς, καὶ ἐξηγήσεις ἐπὶ τέρασιν.

tions; the oldest is one that they say Hesiod received in Chalcis on the Euripus when he won a victory in song.

**T41**  Scholium on Pindar's *Nemeans*

Nicocles says that Hesiod was the first to perform as a rhapsode.

Cf. also *The Contest of Homer and Hesiod* 5–13 (pp. 322–41 West)

## CATALOGUES OF POEMS

### Many Poems

**T42**  Pausanias, *Description of Greece*

The Boeotians who live around Helicon say that of the poems commonly ascribed to him Hesiod composed nothing but the *Works*. And from this poem they remove the proem to the Muses, saying that it begins with the lines about the Strifes (i.e. line 11). And where the fountain is they showed me a lead tablet, very much damaged by the passage of time. On it was written the *Works*. But there is another opinion, different from the first one, according to which Hesiod composed a very great number of epic poems: the poem about women; and what they call the *Great Ehoiai*; *The Theogony*; the poem about the seer Melampous; the one about Theseus' descent into Hades together with Peirithous; and *The Precepts of Chiron* (the ones for teaching Achilles); and everything that follows after the *Works and Days*. These latter also say that Hesiod was taught the mantic art by the Acharnians; and in fact there is a poem on soothsaying, which we too have read, and explanations of prodigies.

189

**T43** 'Proclus' Proleg. ad Hes. *Op.*, p. 8 Gaisford

Ἡσιόδου Ἔργα καὶ Ἡμέραι τὸ βιβλίον ἐπιγέ-
γραπται. . . οὕτω δὲ ἐπιγέγραπται πρὸς ἀντιδιαστο-
λὴν τῶν ἑτέρων αὐτοῦ πεντεκαίδεκα βίβλων Ἀσπίδος,
Θεογονίας, Ἡρωογονίας, Γυναικῶν καταλόγου, καὶ
λοιπῶν ἁπασῶν.

**T44** [Asclepiades vel] Archias *Anth. Pal.* 9.64.7–8

οὗ σὺ κορεσσάμενος μακάρων γένος ἔργα τε
  μολπαῖς
καὶ γένος ἀρχαίων ἔγραφες ἡμιθέων.

**T45** Luc. *Hesiodus* 1

θεῶν τε γένεσεις διηγούμενος ἄχρι καὶ τῶν πρώτων
ἐκείνων, Χάους καὶ Γῆς καὶ Οὐρανοῦ καὶ Ἔρωτος—ἔτι
δὲ γυναικῶν ἀρετὰς καὶ παραινέσεις γεωργικάς, καὶ
ὅσα περὶ Πλειάδων καὶ ὅσα περὶ καιρῶν ἀρότου καὶ
ἀμήτου καὶ πλοῦ καὶ ὅλως τῶν ἄλλων ἁπάντων.

**T46** Max. Tyr. 26.4.89–93 Trapp = 26. IVa.78–82 Koniaris

καθάπερ ὁ Ἡσίοδος, χωρὶς μὲν τὰ γένη τῶν ἡρώων,
ἀπὸ γυναικῶν ἀρχόμενος καταλέγει {τὰ γένη} ὅστις
ἐξ ἧσ<τινος> ἔφυ, χωρὶς δὲ αὐτῶν πεποίηνται οἱ θεῖοι
λόγοι, ἅμα τοῖς λόγοις θεογονία· χωρὶς δ' αὖ ὠφελεῖ

**T43** 'Proclus', Prolegomena to Hesiod *Works and Days*

The book is entitled *Hesiod's Works and Days*. . . . And it is entitled in this way to set it apart from his fifteen other books, *Shield, Theogony, Heroogony, Catalogue of Women*, and all the others.

Cf. T1, T2

*Theogony, Works and Days, Catalogue of Women*

**T44** [Asclepiades or] Archias, epigram from the *Palatine Anthology*

> Having drunk your fill of this[4], the race of the blessed
>    ones and the works
>   you wrote in your songs, and the race of the
>    ancient half-gods.

**T45** Lucian, "Dialogue with Hesiod"

recounting the births of the gods going back to those very first ones, Chasm and Earth and Sky and Love, and also the virtues of women and agricultural precepts, about the Pleiades and the seasons for plowing and harvesting and sailing and everything else.

**T46** Maximus of Tyre, *Philosophical Orations*

Just as Hesiod catalogued separately the genealogies of the heroes, starting from the woman from which each one was born; and separately from these he composed discussions of divine matters, and together with these discussions a theogony; and again separately he provides useful

---

[4] The fountain of Helicon; T44 is the continuation and conclusion of T93.

191

τὰ εἰς τὸν βίον, ἔργα τε ἃ δραστέον, καὶ ἡμέραι ἐν αἷς δραστέον.

καταλέγει in app. Trapp: καταλέγων codd.        τὰ γένη susp.
Koniaris, del. Most        ἤσ‹τινος› Anon. Lond.        αὐτῶν
Paris. Reg. 1962: αὐτῷ Vatic. 1950 (apogr.)

**T47**  Manilius 2.11–25 ed. Housman

                    sed proximus illi
Hesiodus memorat divos divumque parentis
et Chaos enixum terras orbemque sub illo
infantem et primos titubantia sidera cursus
Titanasque senes, Iovis et cunabula magni
et sub fratre viri nomen, sine matre parentis,
atque iterum patrio nascentem corpore Bacchum,
silvarumque deos sacrataque numina nymphis.
quin etiam ruris cultus legesve notavit
militiamque soli, quod colles Bacchus amaret,
quod fecunda Ceres campos, quod Pallas utrumque,
atque arbusta vagis essent quod adultera pomis;
omniaque inmenso volitantia lumina mundo,
pacis opus, magnos naturae condit in usus.
astrorum quidam varias dixere figuras . . .

information regarding the means of life, the works to do and the days to do them.

*Theogony, Works and Days*

**T47** Manilius, *Astronomica*

But second after him (i.e. Homer),
Hesiod tells of the gods and the parents of gods,
and Chasm that gave birth to the earth, and the world
    as an infant
under its reign, and the stars wavering on their first
    pathways,
and the ancient Titans, and the cradle of great Zeus,
and the name of husband (i.e. Zeus) under the
    category of brother (scil. of Hera) and that of
    parent (scil. of Athena) without any mother,
and Dionysus being born a second time from his
    father's body,
and the gods of the forests, and the Nymphs,
    hallowed divinities.
He also noted down the cultivation of the countryside
    and laws
and the military service of the soil, that Dionysus
    loves the hills,
fertile Demeter the plains, Athena both of them,
that trees are adulterous with errant fruits.
And all the heavenly bodies flying in the immense
    universe—
a work of peace—he establishes for the great
    purposes of nature.
Some have spoken of the various figures of the
    stars . . .

**T48**  Schol. Hes. *Op*. Prolegomena B p. 3.9–10 Pertusi

μετὰ τὴν ἡρωϊκὴν γενεαλογίαν καὶ τοὺς καταλόγους
ἐπεζήτησε καινουργῆσαι πάλιν ἑτέραν ὑπόθεσιν.

## INDIVIDUAL POEMS

**T49**  Schol. Hes. *Op*. Prolegomena A.c p. 2.7–12 Pertusi

ὅτι δὲ τὸ προοίμιόν τινες διέγραψαν, ὥσπερ ἄλλοι τε
καὶ Ἀρίσταρχος ὀβελίζων τοὺς στίχους, καὶ Πραξι-
φάνης ὁ τοῦ Θεοφράστου μαθητὴς (Fr. 22 a Wehr-
li). . .οὗτος μέντοι καὶ ἐντυχεῖν φησιν ἀπροοιμιάστῳ
τῷ βιβλίῳ καὶ ἀρχομένῳ χωρὶς τῆς ἐπικλήσεως τῶν
Μουσῶν ἐντεῦθεν· "οὐκ ἄρα μοῦνον ἔην ἐρίδων γένος"
(v. 11).

**T50**  Vita Chigiana Dionys. Perieget. 72.58–60 Kassel

τὸ δὲ τῶν Ἔργων καὶ Ἡμερῶν Ἡσιόδου καὶ τῆς
Θεογονίας πάσης ἔστι προτάξαι ποιήσεως· διὸ καὶ ὁ
Κράτης (Fr. 78 Broggiato) αὐτὰ κατὰ λόγον ἠθέτει.

# TESTIMONIA

*Works and Days, Catalogue of Women*

**T48**  Scholia on Hesiod's *Works and Days*, Prolegomena

After the heroic genealogy and the *Catalogues*, he wanted to begin anew with a different subject matter.


## INDIVIDUAL POEMS

### *Theogony*

T1, T3, T8, T27, T42-T47, T86, T87, T93, T95, T97-T100, T109, T111, T116c, T117–20, T134–37, T139, T140, T142–44, T153, T154


### *Works and Days*

**T49**  Scholia on Hesiod's *Works and Days*, Prolegomena

Some have crossed out the proem, as for example Aristarchus among others, who obelizes the verses, and Theophrastus' student Praxiphanes. . . . This latter says that he encountered a copy without the proem, which lacked the invocation to the Muses and began with "So there was not just one birth of Strifes after all" (i.e. line 11).

**T50**  Chigi Life of Dionysius Periegetes

That (scil. proem) of Hesiod's *Works and Days* and of the *Theogony* is a prelude for his poetry as a whole; hence Crates (i.e. of Mallus) too athetized them, reasonably.

**T51** Titulus funerarius Prisci (C. Marek, *Stadt, Ära und Territorium in Pontus-Bithynia und Nord-Galatia*, Istanbuler Forschungen 39, Tübingen 1993, p. 207 no. 79, cf. pp. 100–16; *SEG* 43.911)

12  ὡς δ' ἐτέλεσσεν ἀγῶνα μέγαν κ' ἐπελήλυθε
  πάτρᾳ,
 φέγγος πᾶσιν ἔλ‹α›νψε, μάλιστα δ' ἐοῖσι
  γονεῦσιν,
 καὶ τότε νοῦν ἔστρεψεν ἀροτρεύειν πατρ‹ί›αν
  γῆν,
15  πάντα ποιῶν ἅμα καὶ θρεπτοῖς ἐπέτελλε
  γεωργοῖς
 ἄρμενα πάντα ποιεῖν, ὅσα Ἡσίοδος περὶ
  γεωργοὺς
 [ἐξα]μάειν καρποὺς μεγάλους ἐπεδείξατ' ἀφεὶς
  τώς.
 β[ρῖσε δ' ὅ]λοις ἀγαθοῖσι πολὺν χρόνον
  ἰσπαταλήσας,
19  ὄλβῳ καὶ πλούτῳ κεκορ‹ε›σμένος εἰς ἀνάπαυσιν.

**T52** Arg. *Scuti* I

Τῆς Ἀσπίδος ἡ ἀρχὴ ἐν τῷ τετάρτῳ Καταλόγῳ φέρεται μέχρι στίχων ν' καὶ ϛ' (= Hesiodus Fr. 139 Most).

---

[5] For a similar reference to Hesiod's *Works and Days* in another funerary epigram, this one from Claudiupolis in Bithynia (of uncertain date, after 130 AD), see S. Sahin, *Bithynische Studien*.

**T51**  Funerary epigram for the soldier and farmer
Priscus (Caesarea in Paphlagonia, after 138 AD)[5]

> When he had completed the great struggle[6] and      12
>     returned to his fatherland,
> he shone as a beacon to all, especially to his own
>     parents;
> and then he turned his mind to plowing his father's
>     land,
> and doing everything himself, at the same time he      15
>     also ordered his home-born peasants
> to do everything fitting that Hesiod indicated about
>     farmers,
> thereby allowing them to harvest crops in abundance.
> And he was laden with all good things and lived in
>     luxury for a long time,
> fully sated with bliss and wealth until his final repose.      19

cf. also T1, T7, T18, T22, T25, T27, T35, T42-T48, T80, T87a,
T89, T90b, T91, T92, T95, T96, T105-T107, T112, T113b, T120a,
T127, T143-T145, T147–48, T150-T155

*Shield*

**T52**  Argument to the *Shield*

The beginning of the *Shield* is transmitted in Book 4 of the
*Catalogue* up to line 56 (= Hesiod Fr. 139). For this reason,

Inschriften griechischer Städte aus Kleinasien 7 (Bonn 1978), pp.
50–52 no. 2; F. Becker-Bertau, *Inschriften von Klaudiu Polis*,
Inschriften griechischer Städte aus Kleinasien 31 (Bonn 1986),
pp. 81–83, no. 75; cf. *SEG* 28.982.
   6 Military service.

διὸ καὶ ὑπώπτευκεν Ἀριστοφάνης (Aristoph. Byz. Fr. 406 Slater) ὡς οὐκ οὖσαν αὐτὴν Ἡσιόδου, ἀλλ᾽ ἑτέρου τινὸς τὴν Ὁμηρικὴν ἀσπίδα μιμήσασθαι προαιρουμένου.

Μεγακλείδης ὁ Ἀθηναῖος (Fr. 7 Janko) γνήσιον μὲν οἶδε τὸ ποίημα, ἄλλως δὲ ἐπιτιμᾷ τῷ Ἡσιόδῳ· ἄλογον γάρ φησι ποιεῖν ὅπλα Ἥφαιστον τοῖς τῆς μητρὸς ἐχθροῖς. Ἀπολλώνιος δὲ ὁ Ῥόδιος ἐν τῷ τρίτῳ (Fr. XXI Michaelis) φησὶν αὐτοῦ εἶναι ἔκ τε τοῦ χαρακτῆρος καὶ ἐκ τοῦ πάλιν τὸν Ἰόλαον ἐν τῷ Καταλόγῳ εὑρίσκειν ἡνιοχοῦντα Ἡρακλεῖ (Hesiodus Fr. 141 Most). καὶ Στησίχορος (Fr. 92 Page) δέ φησιν Ἡσιόδου εἶναι τὸ ποίημα.

**T53** [Longin.] *De sublim.* 9.5

εἴγε Ἡσιόδου καὶ τὴν Ἀσπίδα θετέον. . .

**T54** Philostratus *Heroicus* 25.7, p. 29.18–21 De Lannoy

Ἡσίοδον μὲν ἐν ἄλλοις τε καὶ οὐκ ὀλίγοις καὶ νὴ Δί᾽ ἐν τοῖς ἐκτυπώμασι τῶν ἀσπίδων· ἑρμηνεύων γὰρ οὗτός ποτε τὴν τοῦ Κύκνου ἀσπίδα τὸ τῆς Γοργοῦς εἶδος (*Scut.* 223–25) ὑπτίως τε καὶ οὐ ποιητικῶς ᾖσεν.

**T55** Schol. Dion. Thrax p. 124.4 Hilgard

τὰ ψευδεπίγραφα τῶν βιβλίων, ὡς ἔχει ἡ Ἀσπὶς Ἡσιόδου· ἑτέρου γάρ ἐστιν, ἐπιγραφῇ δὲ καὶ ὀνομα-

Aristophanes (scil. of Byzantium) suspected that it did not belong to Hesiod but to someone else who had chosen to imitate the Homeric "Shield."

Megaclides of Athens considered the poem to be genuine but censured Hesiod: for he said it was illogical that Hephaestus should make weapons for his mother's enemies. Apollonius Rhodius says in Book 3 that it is his (i.e. Hesiod's), because of the style and because he finds Iolaus elsewhere in the *Catalogue* driving the chariot for Heracles (= Hesiod Fr. 141). And Stesichorus says that the poem is Hesiod's.

**T53** Pseudo-Longinus, *On the Sublime*

if indeed the *Shield* is also to be attributed to Hesiod . . .

**T54** Philostratus, *Heroicus*

(scil. Protesilaus criticizes) Hesiod regarding many passages, especially his depictions of shields. For when he described Cycnus'[7] shield, he sang of the appearance of the Gorgon (*Shield* 223–25) carelessly and not poetically.

**T55** Scholium on Dionysius Thrax

Falsely titled books, like for example Hesiod's *Shield*; for this was written by someone else who used the title and

---

[7] In fact, Heracles'.

σίᾳ ἐχρήσατο τῇ τοῦ Ἡσιόδου, ἵνα διὰ τῆς ἀξιοπιστί-
ας τοῦ ποιητοῦ ἄξιον κριθῇ ἀναγνώσεως.

**T56** Hermesianax Fr. 7.21–26 Powell

φημὶ δὲ καὶ Βοιωτὸν ἀποπρολιπόντα μέλαθρον
  Ἡσίοδον πάσης ἤρανον ἱστορίης
Ἀσκραίων ἐσικέσθαι ἐρῶνθ᾿ Ἑλικωνίδα κώμην·
  ἔνθεν ὅ γ᾿ Ἠοίην μνώμενος Ἀσκραϊκὴν
πόλλ᾿ ἔπαθεν, πάσας δὲ λόγων ἀνεγράψατο
    βίβλους
  ὑμνῶν, ἐκ πρώτης παιδὸς ἀνερχόμενος.

**T57** Dio Chrys. *Orat.* 2.13

"ὁ μέντοι Ἡσίοδος, ὦ πάτερ, δοκεῖ μοι οὐδὲ αὐτὸς
ἀγνοεῖν τὴν ἑαυτοῦ δύναμιν ὅσον ἐλείπετο Ὁμήρου."
"πῶς λέγεις;"
"ὅτι ἐκείνου περὶ τῶν ἡρώων ποιήσαντος αὐτὸς
ἐποίησε Γυναικῶν κατάλογον, καὶ τῷ ὄντι τὴν γυναι-
κωνῖτιν ὕμνησε, παραχωρήσας Ὁμήρῳ τοὺς ἄνδρας
ἐπαινέσαι."

**T58** [Luc.] *Erotes* 3.18

ἔναγχος γοῦν διηγουμένου σου τὸν πολύν, ὡς παρ᾿
Ἡσιόδῳ, κατάλογον ὧν ἀρχῆθεν ἠράσθης. . .

---

[8] Ehoie.

name of Hesiod, so that it would be judged worth reading because of our trust in the poet.

cf. also T1, T43, T144, T145

*Catalogue of Women*

**T56** Hermesianax, *Leontion*

And I say that after he left his home far behind,
    Boeotian Hesiod, the keeper of all of history,
he arrived full of love at the Heliconian village of the
        Ascraeans;
    and there, wooing the Ascraean girl Ehoie,
he suffered greatly, and he wrote down all those
        books of his discourses,
    singing hymns, starting from his first girlfriend.[8]

**T57** Dio Chrysostom, "On Kingship"

"But it seems to me, old man, that even Hesiod too is not unaware of how far his own power falls short of Homer's."

"What do you mean?"

"While that one (i.e. Homer) composed a poem about heroes, he himself composed a catalogue of women, and in fact he hymned the women's quarters, leaving it to Homer to praise men."

**T58** Pseudo-Lucian, "Loves"

while you are narrating the long catalogue, as is found in Hesiod too, of those with whom you have fallen in love since the beginning . . .

201

**T59** Max. Tyr. 18.9.231–233 Trapp = 18. IXa.201–202 Koniaris

Ἡσιόδῳ δὲ ἀείδουσιν αἱ Μοῦσαι τί ἄλλο ἢ γυναικῶν ἔρωτας, καὶ ἀνδρῶν καὶ ποταμῶν ἔρωτας καὶ βασιλέων καὶ φυτῶν;

**T60** Men. Rhet. περὶ ἐπιδεικτικῶν 6 (III p. 402.17–20 Spengel, p. 140 Russell-Wilson)

ἐπιφωνήσεις δὲ καὶ τῶν Σαπφοῦς ἐρωτικῶν καὶ τῶν Ὁμήρου καὶ Ἡσιόδου· πολλὰ δὲ αὐτῷ ἐν τοῖς Καταλόγοις τῶν γυναικῶν εἴρηται περὶ θεῶν συνουσίας καὶ γάμου.

**T61** Serv. ad Verg. *Aen.* 7.268 (II p. 147.11–14 Thilo)

antiquis semper mos fuit meliores generos rogare . . . Hesiodus etiam περὶ γυναικῶν inducit multas heroidas optasse nuptias virorum fortium.

**T62** Eunap. *Vitae sophist.* 6.10.1

τούτου δὲ τοῦ γένους, οὐ γὰρ τὰς Ἡσιόδου καλουμένας Ἠοίας ἔσπευδον γράφειν, ἀπόρροιαί τινες, ὥσπερ ἀστέρων περιελείφθησαν. . .

**T63** Diomedes *Grammatici Latini* I p. 482.33–483.1 Keil

historice est qua narrationes et genealogiae componuntur,

**T59**  Maximus of Tyre, *Philosophical Orations*

What else do the Muses sing to Hesiod besides the loves of women and men, and of rivers and kings and plants?

**T60**  Menander Rhetor, *On Epideictic Speeches*

You should also quote from Sappho's erotic poems, and from Homer's and Hesiod's; for much is said by him (i.e. Hesiod) in the *Catalogues of Women* about the gods' sexual unions and marriages.

**T61**  Servius on Virgil's *Aeneid*

It was always a custom among the ancients to ask for sons-in-law better (scil. than themselves). . . . And Hesiod *About Women* introduces many heroines wishing for marriages with brave men.

**T62**  Eunapius, *Lives of the Sophists*

From this family (i.e. that of the female philosopher Sosipatra)—for it has not been my intention to write Hesiod's so-called *Ehoiai*—there have survived some emanations as though from the stars . . .

**T63**  Diomedes, "On Poems"

a historical (scil. poem) is one in which narratives and

# HESIOD

ut est Hesiodi γυναικῶν κατάλογος et similia.

**T64** Hesych. η 650 Latte (cf. *Etym. Gudianum* p. 246.23 Sturz)

ἠοῖαι· ὁ κατάλογος Ἡσιόδου.

**T65** Eustath. in Hom. *Od.* 11.225, p. 1680.29

ὅτι πάνυ δεξιῶς ὁ ποιητὴς τὴν ῥαψῳδίαν ταύτην ἡρώων ἅμα καὶ ἡρωΐδων πεποίηκε κατάλογον, Ἡσιόδου μόνων γυναικῶν ποιησαμένου κατάλογον.

**T66** Athen. 8.66 p. 364b

ἐκ τῶν εἰς Ἡσίοδον ἀναφερομένων μεγάλων Ἠοίων καὶ μεγάλων Ἔργων.

**T67** Plut. *Quaest. conv.* 8.8.4 p. 730f

ὁ τὸν Κήυκος γάμον εἰς τὰ Ἡσιόδου παρεμβαλών (= Hesiodus Fr. 204e Most). . .

**T68** Athen. 2.32 p. 49b

Ἡσίοδος ἐν Κήυκος γάμῳ—κἂν γὰρ γραμματικῶν παῖδες ἀποξενῶσι τοῦ ποιητοῦ τὰ ἔπη ταῦτα, ἀλλ' ἐμοὶ δοκεῖ ἀρχαῖα εἶναι... (= Hesiodus Fr. 204b Most).

genealogies are composed, like Hesiod's *Catalogue of Women* and similar poems.

**T64** Hesychius, *Lexicon*

*Ehoiai*: the catalogue by Hesiod.

**T65** Eustathius on Homer's *Odyssey*

Quite cleverly the poet (i.e. Homer) composed this book (*Odyssey* 11) as a catalogue of heroes and heroines at the same time, since Hesiod had composed a catalogue exclusively of women.

cf. also T1, T42-T46, T48

## Great Ehoiai

**T66** Athenaeus, *Scholars at Dinner*

from the *Great Ehoiai* and the *Great Works* which are attributed to Hesiod.

cf. also T42

## The Wedding of Ceyx

**T67** Plutarch, *Table Talk*

the man who interpolated *The Wedding of Ceyx* into Hesiod's works (= Hesiod Fr. 204e) . . .

**T68** Athenaeus, *Scholars at Dinner*

Hesiod in *The Wedding of Ceyx*—for even if the grammarians' slaves banish this epic from the poet, nonetheless to me it seems to be ancient . . . (= Hesiod Fr. 204b)

**T69** Quintil. *Inst. orat.* 1.1.15

is primus (scil. Aristophanes Byzantinus, Fr. 407 Slater)
ὑποθήκας. . .νεγαϛιτ εσσε ηυιυσ ποεταε.

**T70** Schol. Pind. *Pyth.* 6.22 (II p. 197.9 Drachmann)

τὰς δὲ Χείρωνος ὑποθήκας Ἡσιόδῳ ἀνατιθέασιν, ὧν ἡ
ἀρχή· (Hesiodus Fr. 218 Most)

**T71** *Suda* χ 267 (IV p. 803.3 Adler)

Χείρων, Κένταυρος· ὃς πρῶτος εὗρεν ἰατρικὴν διὰ
βοτανῶν· Ὑποθήκας δι᾽ ἐπῶν, ἃς ποιεῖται πρὸς Ἀχιλ-
λέα· καὶ Ἱππιατρικόν· διὸ καὶ Κένταυρος ὠνομάσθη.

## The Melampodia

T42

## The Descent of Peirithous to Hades

T42

## The Idaean Dactyls

T1

## The Precepts of Chiron

**T69** Quintilian, *Institutions of Oratory*

He (i.e. Aristophanes of Byzantium) was the first to assert that the *Precepts* . . . are not by this poet (i.e. Hesiod).

**T70** Scholium on Pindar's *Pythians*

They attribute to Hesiod *The Precepts of Chiron*, of which this is the beginning: (Hesiod Fr. 218).

**T71** The *Suda*

Chiron: a Centaur, who was the first to discover medicine by means of herbs. ‹He wrote› *Precepts* in epic verses which are addressed to Achilles; and also *Veterinary Medicine*. For this reason he was also called Centaur.

cf. also T42

**T72** [Plato] *Epinomis* 990a

ὅτι σοφώτατον ἀνάγκη τὸν ἀληθῶς ἀστρονόμον εἶναι,
μὴ τὸν καθ᾽ Ἡσίοδον ἀστρονομοῦντα καὶ πάντας τοὺς
τοιούτους, οἷον δυσμάς τε καὶ ἀνατολὰς ἐπεσκεμμένον
. . .

**T73** Callim. *Epigram* 27

Ἡσιόδου τό τ᾽ ἄεισμα καὶ ὁ τρόπος· οὐ τὸν
    ἀοιδῶν
  ἔσχατον, ἀλλ᾽ ὀκνέω μὴ τὸ μελιχρότατον
τῶν ἐπέων ὁ Σολεὺς ἀπεμάξατο· χαίρετε λεπταὶ
  ῥήσιες, Ἀρήτου σύμβολον ἀγρυπνίης.

**T74** Plin. *Hist. nat.* 18.213

Hesiodus—nam huius quoque nomine exstat astrologia (=
Hesiodus Fr. 226 Most) . . .

**T75** Athen. 11.80 p. 491b

ὁ τὴν εἰς Ἡσίοδον δὲ ἀναφερομένην ποιήσας Ἀστρο-
νομίαν . . .

*The Great Works*

T66

*Astronomy or Astrology*

**T72**  Pseudo-Plato, *Epinomis*

that of necessity the true astronomer must be wisest of all,
not one who does astronomy according to Hesiod and all
who are like him, merely studying the settings and risings
. . .

**T73**  Callimachus, epigram

> Hesiod's is the song and the mode; it is not the very
>     last bit of the poet,
>   but rather, I do not doubt, his most honey-sweet
> epic verses, that the man from Soli[9] has taken as
>     model. Hail slender
>   discourses, token of Aratus' sleeplessness!

**T74**  Pliny the Elder, *Natural History*

Hesiod—for an *Astrology* in his name too is extant . . . (=
Hesiod Fr. 226)

**T75**  Athenaeus, *Scholars at Dinner*

and the author of the *Astronomy* which is attributed to
Hesiod . . .

[9] Aratus.

**T76** Plut. *De Pyth. orac.* 18 p. 402f

οὐδ' ἀστρολογίαν ἀδοξοτέραν ἐποίησαν οἱ περὶ Ἀρί-
σταρχον καὶ Τιμόχαριν καὶ Ἀρίστυλλον καὶ Ἵππαρ-
χον καταλογάδην γράφοντες, ἐν μέτροις πρότερον
Εὐδόξου καὶ Ἡσιόδου καὶ Θαλοῦ γραφόντων, εἴ γε
Θαλῆς ἐποίησεν, ὡς ἀληθῶς εἰπεῖν, τὴν εἰς αὐτὸν
ἀναφερομένην Ἀστρολογίαν.

**T77** Georg. Mon. (Hamartolus) *Chron.* 1.10 (1.40 de
Boor)

λέγει γὰρ Ἰώσηπος, ὅτι πρῶτος Ἀβραὰμ δημιουργὸν
τὸν θεὸν ἀνεκήρυξε καὶ πρῶτος κατελθὼν εἰς Αἴγυ-
πτον ἀριθμητικὴν καὶ ἀστρονομίαν Αἰγυπτίους ἐδίδα-
ξεν. πρῶτοι γὰρ εὑρεταὶ τούτων οἱ Χαλδαῖοι γεγένην-
ται, παρὰ δὲ τῶν Ἑβραίων ἔλαβον Φοίνικες, ἀφ' ὧν ὁ
μὲν Κάδμος ταῦτα μετήγαγεν εἰς τοὺς Ἕλληνας, ὁ δὲ
Ἡσίοδος εὖ μάλα συντάξας εὐφυῶς ἐξελλήνισεν.

**T78** Tzetzes *Chil.* 12.161–62 Leone

οὐ γράφει βίβλον ἀστρικήν, ἧς τὴν ἀρχὴν οὐκ οἶδα,
ἐν μέσῳ τοῦ βιβλίου δὲ τὰ ἔπη κεῖνται ταῦτα (Hesi-
odus Fr. 227 Most);

**T76**  Plutarch, *On the Pythian Oracles*

Nor was astronomy rendered less respectable by Aristarchus and Timocharis and Aristyllus and Hipparchus and their followers writing in prose, even if before them Eudoxus and Hesiod and Thales wrote in verse (if Thales really did write the *Astrology* which is attributed to him).

**T77**  Georgius Monachus (Hamartolus), *Chronicle*

Josephus says that Abraham was the first to proclaim that God was the creator[10] and the first to go down into Egypt and teach arithmetic and astronomy to the Egyptians. For the first discoverers of these disciplines were the Chaldaeans, and the Phoenicians took them from the Hebrews. From these, Cadmus transferred them to the Greeks, and Hesiod put them into order very well and with great talent hellenized them.

**T78**  Tzetzes, *Chiliads*

Did he (i.e. Hesiod) not write an astral book? I do not know its beginning; but in the middle of the book are found the following lines: (Hesiod Fr. 227)

---

[10] Cf. Josephus, *Jewish Antiquities* 1.155 (though Josephus seems nowhere to provide any warrant for the following claims).

**T79**  Athen. 11.109 p. 503d

ὁ τὸν Αἰγίμιον δὲ ποιήσας εἴθ' Ἡσίοδός ἐστιν ἢ
Κέρκωψ ὁ Μιλήσιος (= Hesiodus Fr. 238 Most). . .

**T80**  Schol. Hes. *Op.* 828 (p. 259.3–5 Pertusi)

τούτοις δὲ ἐπάγουσί τινες τὴν Ὀρνιθομαντείαν ἅτινα
Ἀπολλώνιος ὁ Ῥόδιος ἀθετεῖ (p. 42 Michaelis).

**T81**  Athen. 3.84 p. 116a-d

Εὐθύδημος ὁ Ἀθηναῖος (*SH* 455). . .ἐν τῷ περὶ ταρίχων
Ἡσίοδόν φησι περὶ πάντων τῶν ταριχευομένων τάδ'
εἰρηκέναι· . . .ταῦτα τὰ ἔπη ἐμοὶ δοκεῖ τινος μαγείρου
εἶναι μᾶλλον ἢ τοῦ μουσικωτάτου Ἡσιόδου. . .δοκεῖ
οὖν μοι αὐτοῦ τοῦ Εὐθυδήμου εἶναι τὰ ποιήματα.

## *Aegimius*

**T79** Athenaeus, *Scholars at Dinner*

the author of the *Aegimius*, whether it is Hesiod or Cercops of Miletus (= Hesiod Fr. 238) . . .

cf. T37

## *Bird Omens*

**T80** Scholium on Hesiod's *Works and Days*

At this point some people add the *Bird Omens*, which Apollonius Rhodius (p. 42 Michaelis) marks as spurious.

## *Dirge for Batrachus*

T1

## *On Preserved Foods*

**T81** Athenaeus, *Scholars at Dinner*

Euthydemus of Athens . . . says in his *On Preserved Foods* that Hesiod said the following about all preserved foods: . . . These verses seem to me to be the work of some cook rather than the highly refined Hesiod's. . . . So this poem seems to me to be the work of Euthydemus himself.

**T82** Pollux 10.85

τοῦ ποιήσαντος τοὺς Κεραμέας, οὕς τινες Ἡσιόδῳ προσνέμουσιν.

# INFLUENCE AND RECEPTION

## PERFORMANCES OF HESIOD'S POEMS

**T83** Plato *Ion* 531a

"νῦν δέ μοι τοσόνδε ἀπόκριναι· πότερον περὶ Ὁμήρου μόνον δεινὸς εἶ ἢ καὶ περὶ Ἡσιόδου καὶ Ἀρχιλόχου;"
"οὐδαμῶς, ἀλλὰ περὶ Ὁμήρου μόνον· ἱκανὸν γάρ μοι δοκεῖ εἶναι."

**T84** Diogenes Babyl. Fr. 80 SVF 3.231.8–13 apud Philodem. *De musica* 4.9 (XVII.2–13) pp. 60–61 Neubecker

κἀκεῖνο δὲ χρηστ[ο]μαθῶς εἴρηται τὸ σαίνε̣[σθαι] μὲν καὶ τοὺς ἰδιώτας ὑπὸ τῆς οἰκειότητος, παραλαμβάνειν [γ]ε τοι καὶ ἀκροάματ᾽ εἰς τὰ συμπόσια, διαπίπτειν δὲ τῷ μὴ τὸν Ὅμηρον καὶ τὸν Ἡσίοδον

---

[11] Plato represents Ion as a successful rhapsode who both per-

*The Potters*

**T82** Pollux, *Lexicon*

the author of *The Potters*, which some people attribute to Hesiod . . .

cf. (Pseudo-)Herodotus, *On Homer's Origins, Date, and Life* 32 (pp. 390–95 West)

# INFLUENCE AND RECEPTION

## PERFORMANCES OF HESIOD'S POEMS

**T83** Plato, *Ion*[11]

"Now answer me this much: are you only terribly clever about Homer or also about Hesiod and Archilochus?"

"Not at all, but only about Homer—that seems to me to be enough."

**T84** Diogenes of Babylon, *On Music*

The following statement too is quite correct: ordinary people too are pleased by the appropriateness (i.e. of music to drinking parties) and they bring what they have heard with them to drinking parties, but they make a mistake by not bringing with them Homer and Hesiod and the other

forms and explains archaic poetry in public competitions. For public performance of Hesiod cf. also Plato, *Laws* 2.658d.

καὶ τοὺς ἄλλους ποιητὰς τῶν μέτρων καὶ μελῶν·
βελτίω γὰρ ἔστω τὰ χρώμενα συμπόσια τοῖς τούτων.

**T85** Athen. 14.12 p. 620a-d

οὐκ ἀπελείποντο δὲ ἡμῶν τῶν συμποσίων οὐδὲ ῥαψῳ-
δοί. . .ὅτι δ᾽ ἐκαλοῦντο οἱ ῥαψῳδοὶ καὶ Ὁμηρισταὶ
Ἀριστοκλῆς ἐν τῷ περὶ Χορῶν (FHG 4.331). τοὺς δὲ
νῦν Ὁμηριστὰς ὀνομαζομένους πρῶτος εἰς τὰ θέατρα
παρήγαγε Δημήτριος ὁ Φαληρεύς (Fr. 55 a SOD=Fr. 33
Wehrli). Χαμαιλέων δὲ ἐν τῷ περὶ Στησιχόρου (Fr. 31
Giordano=Fr. 28 Wehrli) καὶ μελῳδηθῆναί φησιν οὐ
μόνον τὰ Ὁμήρου, ἀλλὰ καὶ Ἡσιόδου καὶ Ἀρχιλόχου,
ἔτι δὲ Μιμνέρμου (Test. 22 G-P²) καὶ Φωκυλίδου (Test.
10 G-P²). . .Ἰάσων δ᾽ ἐν τρίτῳ περὶ τῶν Ἀλεξάνδρου
Ἱερῶν (FGrHist 632 F 1) ἐν Ἀλεξανδρείᾳ φησὶν ἐν τῷ
μεγάλῳ θεάτρῳ ὑποκρίνασθαι Ἡγήσιαν τὸν κωμῳδὸν
τὰ Ἡσιόδου, Ἑρμόφαντον δὲ τὰ Ὁμήρου.

**T86** Plut. *Quaest. conv.* 9.14.1 p. 743c

ἐκ τούτου σπονδὰς ἐποιησάμεθα ταῖς Μούσαις, καὶ τῷ
Μουσηγέτῃ παιανίσαντες συνῄσαμεν τῷ Ἐράτωνι
πρὸς τὴν λύραν ἐκ τῶν Ἡσιόδου τὰ περὶ τὴν τῶν
Μουσῶν γένεσιν (*Theog.* 53ss.)

poets who composed verses and melodies: let us consider the better drinking parties to be the ones where the poems of these poets are performed.

**T85** Athenaeus, *Scholars at Dinner*

Rhapsodes were not lacking from our drinking parties either. . . . Aristocles said in his *On Choruses* that rhapsodes were also called Homerists. The first person to introduce those who are now called Homerists into theaters was Demetrius of Phalerum. Chamaeleon in *On Stesichorus* says that not only Homer's poems were set to music but also Hesiod's and Archilochus', and further Mimnermus' and Phocylides'. . . . Jason in book 3 *On the Divine Honors to Alexander* says that at the great theater in Alexandria the comic actor Hegesias performed Hesiod's poems, and Hermophantus Homer's.

**T86** Plutarch, *Table Talk*

After this we made libations to the Muses, we sang a paean to Apollo, the leader of the Muses, and then we sang to the lyre, together with Eraton, from among Hesiod's verses the ones about the birth of the Muses (i.e. *Theogony* 53ff.).

POETRY

**T87** Callimachus

**(a)** *Aetia* I Fr. 2.1–5 Pfeiffer

ποιμ]ένι μῆλα νέμ[οντι παρ᾽ ἴχνιον ὀξέος ἵππου
  Ἡσιόδ]ῳ Μουσέων ἑσμὸ[ς ὅτ᾽ ἠντίασεν
μ]έν οἱ Χάεος γενεσ[
    ]ἐπὶ πτέρνης ὑδα[
τεύχω]ν ὡς ἑτέρῳ τις ἑῷ [κακὸν ἥπατι τεύχει

**(b)** *Aetia* IV Fr. 112.3–6 Pfeiffer

...]τερης οὔ σε ψευδον[......]ματι
πάντ᾽ ἀγαθὴν καὶ πάντα τ[ελ]εσφόρον εἶπέν...[..].[
  κείν.. τῷ Μοῦσαι πολλὰ νέμοντι βοτὰ
σὺν μύθους ἐβάλοντο παρ᾽ ἴχν[ι]ον ὀξέος ἵππου.

**T88** Alcaeus Mess. *Anth. Pal.* 7.55

Λοκρίδος ἐν νέμεϊ σκιερῷ νέκυν Ἡσιόδοιο
  Νύμφαι κρηνίδων λοῦσαν ἀπὸ σφετέρων
καὶ τάφον ὑψώσαντο· γάλακτι δὲ ποιμένες αἰγῶν
  ἔρραναν ξανθῷ μιξάμενοι μέλιτι·
τοίην γὰρ καὶ γῆρυν ἀπέπνεεν ἐννέα Μουσέων
  ὁ πρέσβυς καθαρῶν γευσάμενος λιβάδων.

---

12 Cf. also T73.    13 Cf. *Works and Days* 265.

## POETRY

**T87** Callimachus[12]

**(a)** *Aetia* I, near the beginning

> To the shepherd who was pasturing his sheep by the
>        hoof-print of the swift horse,
>    to Hesiod, the swarm of Muses when they met
>        him
> ] him the birth of Chasm [
>                       ] at the water of the hoof [
> that in doing evil to someone else one does evil to
>        one's own heart.[13]

**(b)** *Aetia* IV, conclusion

>                  ] not falsely [
> did he say you were fully good and fully perfecting [
>    that man at whom the Muses, while he tended his
>        many sheep,
> cast stories beside the hoof-print of the swift horse.

**T88** Alcaeus of Messina, epigram

> In a shadowy glade of Locris, the nymphs
>    washed Hesiod's corpse with water from their
>        fountains
> and piled up a tomb, and onto it goatherds poured
>        libations of milk
>    mixing them with blond honey;
> for that was the kind of voice he had breathed forth,
>    the old man who had tasted of the pure streams of
>        the nine Muses.

# HESIOD

**T89**  Marcus Argent. *Anth. Pal.* 9.161

Ἡσιόδου ποτὲ βύβλον ἐμαῖς ὑπὸ χερσὶν
  ἑλίσσων
Πύρρην ἐξαπίνης εἶδον ἐπερχομένην·
βύβλον δὲ ῥίψας ἐπὶ γῆν χερί, τοῦτ' ἐβόησα·
  "Ἔργα τί μοι παρέχεις, ὦ γέρον Ἡσίοδε;"

**T90**  Verg.

**(a)** *Buc.* 6.64–73

tum canit, errantem Permessi ad flumina Gallum
Aonas in montis ut duxerit una sororum,
utque viro Phoebi chorus adsurrexerit omnis;
ut Linus haec illi divino carmine pastor,
floribus atque apio crinis ornatus amaro,
dixerit: «hos tibi dant calamos, en accipe, Musae,
Ascraeo quos ante seni, quibus ille solebat
cantando rigidas deducere montibus ornos;
his tibi Grynei nemoris dicatur origo,
ne quis sit lucus, quo se plus iactet Apollo»

---

14 The last line is a pun; it also means, "Why do you cause me trouble, old Hesiod?"
15 Silenus.

**T89**  Marcus Argentarius, epigram

> Once while I was unrolling a volume of Hesiod in my
>> hands
>> I suddenly saw Pyrrha coming towards me.
> I threw the book onto the ground with my hand and
>> cried out,
>> "Why do you bother me with 'Works,' old
>> Hesiod?"[14]

**T90**  Virgil

**(a)** *Eclogues*

> Then he[15] sings of Gallus wandering by the streams
>> of Permessus,
> how one of the sisters led him into the Aonian
>> mountains,
> and how the whole chorus of Apollo rose up to greet
>> him;
> how Linus, a shepherd of divine song,
> his hair adorned with flowers and bitter parsley,
> said this to him: "The Muses give you these reeds—
>> here, take them—
> which once they gave to the old man of Ascra, with
>> which he used
> to draw down the unbending ash-trees from the
>> mountains by singing.
> With these may you tell of the origin of the Grynaean
>> grove,
> so that there be no forest of which Apollo is prouder."

**(b)** *Georg.* 2.173–76

salve, magna parens frugum, Saturnia tellus,
magna virum: tibi res antiquae laudis et artem
ingredior sanctos ausus recludere fontis
Ascraeumque cano Romana per oppida carmen.

**T91** Prop. 2.34.77–80

tu canis Ascraei veteris praecepta poetae,
    quo seges in campo, quo viret uva iugo.
tale facis carmen docta testudine, quale
    Cynthius impositis temperat articulis.

**T92** Ov. *Amores* 1.15.11–12

vivet et Ascraeus, dum mustis uva tumebit,
    dum cadet incurva falce resecta Ceres.

**T93** [Asclepiades vel] Archias *Anth. Pal.* 9.64, 1–6

αὐταὶ ποιμαίνοντα μεσαμβρινὰ μῆλά σε Μοῦσαι
    ἔδρακον ἐν κραναοῖς οὔρεσιν, Ἡσίοδε,
καί σοι καλλιπέτηλον, ἐρυσσάμεναι περὶ πᾶσαι,
    ὤρεξαν δάφνας ἱερὸν ἀκρεμόνα,

---

16 Italy.
17 Virgil.
18 On the strings.
19 Like Homer.

## TESTIMONIA

**(b)** *Georgics*

Hail, great mother of fruits, land of Saturn,[16]
great mother of men: it is for your sake that I embark
    upon matters of ancient praise and art,
daring to open up holy fountains,
and I sing an Ascraean song through Roman towns.

**T91**  Propertius, elegy

You[17] sing the precepts of the ancient poet of Ascra,
    in which field the grain flourishes, on which hill
        the grape.
With your learned lyre you compose the kind of
        poem that
Cynthian Apollo moderates with his fingers set[18].

**T92**  Ovid, *Loves*

The Ascraean man too[19] will live as long as the grape
    swells for the must,
as long as the grain falls when it is cut by the curved
    sickle.

**T93**  [Asclepiades or] Archias, epigram

The Muses themselves, while you were pasturing
        your noon-time sheep,
    they saw you among the rugged mountains,
        Hesiod;
and all drawing around you they stretched out to you
        a beautiful-flowered
holy branch of laurel,

δῶκαν δὲ κράνας Ἑλικωνίδος ἔνθεον ὕδωρ,
τὸ πτανοῦ πώλου πρόσθεν ἔκοψεν ὄνυξ.

**T94** Demiurgus *Anth. Pal.* 7.52

Ἑλλάδος εὐρυχόρου στέφανον καὶ κόσμον
ἀοιδῆς,
Ἀσκραῖον γενεὴν Ἡσίοδον κατέχω.

**T95** P. Oxy. 3537 recto 3ff. [1]

τίνας ἂν λόγου[ς Ἡσίοδος εἴπο]ι ὑπὸ
τῶν Μουσῶν ε [        μ]ενος

Τίς με θεῶν ἐτίνα[ξε; τίς ἔνθεο]ν ἤγαγεν ἄσθμα
Οὔρεά τε προλιπόντ[ι καὶ ἄλσεα κ]αὶ βοτὰ μήλων
Νυκτὶ μιῇ; τίς ἐπίστ[ατ᾽ ἀπ᾽ ἐνδό]ξου Ἑλικῶνος
Δάφνης εὐπετάλο[ιο δρέπειν ἐρι]θηλέας ὄζους;
5 Αὐτή μοι γένος εἰπ[ὲ θεῶν πτολ]έμους τε γιγάντων
Πάντων θ᾽ ἡρώ[ων γενεήν, φῦλ]όν τε γυναικῶν.
Αὐτὴ κόσμον ἔνισπ[ε, τὸν οὐδέπο]τ᾽ ἔδρακον ὄσσοις.
Μάνδρη ἐμὴ τριτά[λαινα καὶ αὔλ]ιες αἱ πάρος
αἰγῶν
Ἔρχομαι ἐς πτολ ....[ c. 8        κ]ύκλον ἀγώνων.

[1] Cf. M.L. West, *ZPE* 57 (1984) 33–36; G. Agosti, *ZPE* 119 (1997) 1–5.

and they gave you the inspiring water of the
　　　Heliconian fountain,
　　which once the winged mare's hoof struck:

(T44 follows)

**T94**  Demiurgus, epigram

The crown of spacious Greece and the ornament of
　　　poetry,
　　I contain Hesiod, Ascraean by birth.

**T95**  Oxyrhynchus papyrus (third or early fourth
century AD)

　　　　　　　What Hesiod would have said
　　　　　when he was [　　　　　] by the Muses
Who of the gods has shaken me? [Who] has sent a
　　[divine] breath
to me as I leave behind the mountains [and groves] and
　　flocks of sheep
in one night? Who [knew how, from famous] Helicon,
[to pluck] the luxuriant branches of beautiful-leaved
　　laurel?
Tell me yourself the race [of the gods and the wars] of　　5
　　the Giants
and [the generation] of all the heroes and [the tribe] of
　　women;
yourself describe the universe, [which I have never] seen
　　with my eyes.
O my thrice-wretched cattle stables [and] my former
　　goat[-stalls,]
I am going to [　　　　　] the circle of contests.

10 Ἱερὸς οὐκέτι κιττὸ[ς ἐπαρκέσει] οὐδ' ἔτι ποίμνῃ·
Βαιὴ ἐμ[οὶ] σύμπασα λ[υγροῖς σὺν] δώμασιν
   Ἄσκρη,
Οὐδ' αὐτῆς Κύμης [ἀλεγίζω· χαίρ]ετε πάντες.
Μηλονόμον Μοῦσαι [καλήν μ' ἐδ]ίδαξαν ἀοιδήν,
Ἐκ δ' ἑλόμην πολὺ [χεῦμα θεοπν]εύστου
   Ἀγανίππης.

15 Νῦν μοι Δῖε πάτερ π[ολὺ φίλτατε, ] νῦν Πυκιμήδῃ
Ὀλβίστη μήτειρα καὶ[.....νήπιε] Πέρσῃ,
Σ̣τήσετ. ιεισαλ. οιο [        ο]ὐ γὰρ ἀοιδὴν
Παύρην βυκολικ[ὴν ἀναβάλλο]μαι, οὐδ' ὅσσ' ἀφαυροὶ
Ῥηιδίως μέλπουσι[   c. 6   ἀγρο]ιῶται,

20 Οὐδέ μοι αἰπολικὴ . [   c. 10 ]. εὔα‹δ›ε σῦριγξ·
Σὺν δ' αὐτοῖς καλά[μοισιν ἀπέσ]τυγον ἄγριον ἠχήν.
Ἐκ Διὸς ἐκ Μουσέων [   c. 10   ]ξ οὐράνιοί μοι
Φαίνονται πυλεῶν[ες, ὁρῶ δ' εἰς θ]εῖα μέλαθρα·
Ἤδη δ' ἀείδειν ἐθέλ[ω   c. 9   ]εοσδε.

v. 1 ἔνθεον, 4 δρέπειν , 8 αὔλιες suppl. Diggle apud Parsons
v. 1 τίς ἔνθεο]ν, v. 2 προλιπόντ[ι, 5 πτολ-, 7, 10, 11, 12, 15, 16, 17
Σ̣τήσετ, 18, 23 suppl. West      v. 2 καὶ ἄλσεα, 3, 4, 5, 6, 8, 13,
14, 18, 19, 21 suppl. Parsons        9 πτόλεμον vel πτολίε̣θ̣ρ[ον
Parsons, πτολέμοιο West       10 κῆπος Griffiths
13 μηλονόμον Most: μηλονόμοι pap.       20 εὔα‹δ›ε Bari-
gazzi, Di Benedetto apud Parsons

No longer will the holy ivy [be enough], nor any longer     10
   my flock:
too small for me is all Ascra [with its wretched] houses,
nor [do I care for] Cyme itself. [Farewell] to them all.
The Muses have taught me, a sheep-tender, [beautiful]
   song,
I have taken a big [swallow] from [god-inspired]
   Aganippe.
Now, Dius, my [dearly beloved] father; now, Pycimede,     15
most blessed mother; and [      foolish] Perses,
you will set up [          ]. For not a
small bucolic poem [do I begin to sing,] nor what the
   feeble
rustics easily sing [         ],
nor does the goatherd's pipe please me [      ]:     20
I have come to loathe its rustic sound together with [the
   reeds] themselves.
From Zeus, from the Muses [        ]. The heavenly
gates are revealed to me, [and I see into] the halls of the
   gods.
Now I begin to sing [            ].[20]

---

[20] As Agosti discovered, the Greek poem is an acrostic: the first letter of each line, taken together, yields the Homeric (not Hesiodic) tag phrase τὸν δ᾽ ἀπαμειβόμενος προσέφη, "and answering him he said." The poem seems to have ended here, as the acrostic is complete and the next line is vacant. For another poetic variation on Hesiod's *Theogony*, cf. P. Oxy. 2816 (beginning of the third century AD) = *SH* 938.

**T96**  Nonn. *Dionys.* 13.75

δυσπέμφελον Ἄσκρην,
πατρίδα δαφνήεσσαν ἀσιγήτοιο νομῆος.

## RELIGION

**T97**  Xenophanes 21 B 11 DK

πάντα θεοῖσ᾽ ἀνέθηκαν Ὅμηρός θ᾽ Ἡσίοδός τε,
ὅσσα παρ᾽ ἀνθρώποισιν ὀνείδεα καὶ ψόγος ἐστίν,
κλέπτειν μοιχεύειν τε καὶ ἀλλήλους ἀπατεύειν.

**T98**  Hdt. 2.53.2

οὗτοι δέ εἰσι οἱ ποιήσαντες θεογονίην Ἕλλησι καὶ
τοῖσι θεοῖσι τὰς ἐπωνυμίας δόντες καὶ τιμάς τε καὶ
τέχνας διελόντες καὶ εἴδεα αὐτῶν σημήναντες.

**T99**  Plato *Resp.* 2.377c-378c

" ὧν δὲ νῦν λέγουσι τοὺς πολλοὺς ἐκβλητέον. . . . οὓς
(scil. μύθους) Ἡσίοδός τε . . . καὶ Ὅμηρος ἡμῖν
ἐλεγέτην καὶ οἱ ἄλλοι ποιηταί. οὗτοι γάρ που μύθους
τοῖς ἀνθρώποις ψευδεῖς συντιθέντες ἔλεγόν τε καὶ
λέγουσι."
"ποίους δή . . . καὶ τί αὐτῶν μεμφόμενος λέγεις;"
". . .ὅταν εἰκάζῃ τις κακῶς τῷ λόγῳ, περὶ θεῶν τε καὶ

---

21 Cf. also *Euthyphro* 6a, *Symposium* 195c.

**T96**  Nonnus, *Dionysiaca*

bad-weather Ascra,
the laurelled homeland of the eloquent shepherd.

Cf. T56

## RELIGION

### Theology

**T97**  Xenophanes, *Silloi (Satirical Verses)*

Homer and Hesiod attributed all things to the gods
which are a shame and rebuke among human beings:
committing theft and adultery and deceiving each other.

**T98**  Herodotus, *History*

These (i.e. Hesiod and Homer) are the ones who estab-
lished a theogony for the Greeks and who gave the gods
their appellations and distributed their honors and skills
and explained their forms.

**T99**  Plato, *Republic* 2.377d–378c[21]

"Most of the ones (i.e. the stories) they now tell must be
thrown out. . . . The ones that Hesiod and Homer told us,
and the other poets. For it is these who have composed
false stories and told them, and tell them, to human be-
ings."

"What kinds of stories? . . . And what fault do you say
you find in them?"

". . . Whenever one creates a wrong image in language

ἡρώων οἷοί εἰσιν. . .πρῶτον μέν . . . τὸ μέγιστον καὶ
περὶ τῶν μεγίστων ψεῦδος ὁ εἰπὼν οὐ καλῶς ἐψεύσατο
ὡς Οὐρανός τε ἠργάσατο ἅ φησι δρᾶσαι αὐτὸν Ἡσί-
οδος, ὅ τε αὖ Κρόνος ὡς ἐτιμωρήσατο αὐτόν (Theog.
154–210). τὰ δὲ δὴ τοῦ Κρόνου ἔργα καὶ πάθη ὑπὸ τοῦ
ὑέος (Theog. 495–505), οὐδ᾽ ἂν εἰ ἦν ἀληθῆ ᾤμην δεῖν
ῥᾳδίως οὕτως λέγεσθαι πρὸς ἄφρονάς τε καὶ νέους. . .
οὐδέ γε. . .τὸ παράπαν ὡς θεοὶ θεοῖς πολεμοῦσί τε καὶ
ἐπιβουλεύουσι καὶ μάχονται—οὐδὲ γὰρ ἀληθῆ. . .
πολλοῦ δεῖ γιγαντομαχίας τε μυθολογητέον αὐτοῖς
καὶ ποικιλτέον, καὶ ἄλλας ἔχθρας πολλὰς καὶ παντο-
δαπὰς θεῶν τε καὶ ἡρώων πρὸς συγγενεῖς τε καὶ
οἰκείους αὐτῶν."

**T100**  Diog. Laert. 8.21

φησὶ δ᾽ Ἱερώνυμος (Fr. 42 Wehrli) κατελθόντα αὐτὸν
εἰς Ἅιδου τὴν μὲν Ἡσιόδου ψυχὴν ἰδεῖν πρὸς κίονι
χαλκῷ δεδεμένην καὶ τρίζουσαν, τὴν δ᾽ Ὁμήρου κρε-
μαμένην ἀπὸ δένδρου καὶ ὄφεις περὶ αὐτὴν ἀνθ᾽ ὧν
εἶπον περὶ θεῶν.

**T101**  Plut. *Numa* 4.9

ἀπέδωκε δέ τινα τιμὴν καὶ Ἀρχιλόχῳ καὶ Ἡσιόδῳ
τελευτήσασι διὰ τὰς Μούσας τὸ δαιμόνιον.

about what the gods and heroes are like. . . . First of all . . . the greatest falsehood and the one about the greatest matters was said falsely and wrongly by the person who said that Sky did what Hesiod said he did, and then that Cronus avenged himself on him (i.e. *Theogony* 154–210). Cronus' deeds and his sufferings at the hands of his son (i.e. *Theogony* 459–505) must not, I think, be told so easily to the foolish and young, even if they were true . . . And not . . . at all how gods war and plot and fight against gods—for they are not true either . . . and even less are the battles of Giants to be recounted and elaborated on for them, and the many and various other hatreds of gods and heroes against their relatives and friends."

**T100**  Diogenes Laertius, *Lives of Eminent Philosophers*[22]

Hieronymus (i.e. of Rhodes) says that when he (i.e. Pythagoras) descended to Hades he saw Hesiod's soul bound to a bronze pillar and screaming, and Homer's hung from a tree and surrounded by snakes, because of what they had said about the gods.

### Cults and Veneration of Hesiod

**T101**  Plutarch, *Life of Numa*

Because of their Muses, the divinity bestowed a certain honor upon both Archilochus and Hesiod after they had died.

[22] Cf. T114.

**T102**  Plut. Fr. 82 Sandbach = Schol. Hes. *Op.* 633–40 (p. 202 Pertusi)

ἀοίκητον δὲ αὐτὸ ὁ Πλούταρχος ἱστορεῖ καὶ τότε εἶναι, Θεσπιέων ἀνελόντων τοὺς οἰκοῦντας, Ὀρχομενίων δὲ τοὺς σωθέντας δεξαμένων· ὅθεν καὶ τὸν θεὸν Ὀρχομενίοις προστάξαι τὰ Ἡσιόδου λείψανα λαβεῖν, καὶ θάψαι παρ' αὐτοῖς, ὡς καὶ Ἀριστοτέλης φησί, γράφων τὴν Ὀρχομενίων πολιτείαν (Fr. 565 Rose).

**T103**  Paus. 9.38.3–4

τάφοι δὲ Μινύου τε καὶ Ἡσιόδου· καταδέξασθαι δέ φασιν οὕτω τοῦ Ἡσιόδου τὰ ὀστᾶ. νόσου καταλαμβανούσης λοιμώδους καὶ ἀνθρώπους καὶ τὰ βοσκήματα ἀποστέλλουσι θεωροὺς παρὰ τὸν θεόν· τούτοις δὲ ἀποκρίνασθαι λέγουσι τὴν Πυθίαν, Ἡσιόδου τὰ ὀστᾶ ἐκ τῆς Ναυπακτίας ἀγαγοῦσιν ἐς τὴν Ὀρχομενίαν, ἄλλο δὲ εἶναί σφισιν οὐδὲν ἴαμα. τότε δὲ ἐπερέσθαι δεύτερα, ὅπου τῆς Ναυπακτίας αὐτὰ ἐξευρήσουσι· καὶ αὖθις τὴν Πυθίαν εἰπεῖν ὡς μηνύσοι κορώνη σφίσιν. οὕτω τοῖς θεοπρόποις ἀποβᾶσιν ἐς τὴν γῆν πέτραν τε οὐ πόρρω τῆς ὁδοῦ καὶ τὴν ὄρνιθα ἐπὶ τῇ πέτρᾳ φασὶν ὀφθῆναι· καὶ τοῦ Ἡσιόδου δὲ τὰ ὀστᾶ εὗρον ἐν χηραμῷ τῆς πέτρας. καὶ ἐλεγεῖα ἐπὶ τῷ μνήματι ἐπεγέγραπτο·

Ἄσκρη μὲν πατρὶς πολυλήιος, ἀλλὰ θανόντος

**T102** Plutarch in a Scholium on Hesiod's *Works and Days*

Plutarch reports that it (i.e. Ascra) was uninhabited in his time too, because the Thespians killed the inhabitants and the Orchomenians took in the survivors. For this reason, he said, the god had ordered the Orchomenians to take Hesiod's mortal remains and bury them in their own city, as Aristotle too says in his treatise *On the Orchomenian Constitution*.[23]

**T103** Pausanias, *Description of Greece*

And there are tombs of Minyas and of Hesiod (i.e. at Orchomenus). They say that Hesiod's bones were brought there in the following way. Because a pestilential disease had befallen both men and livestock, they sent envoys to the god; they say that the Pythia replied to them that they were to bring Hesiod's bones from the region of Naupactus to that of Orchomenus, and that there was no other remedy for them. Then they asked a second time, where in the region of Naupactus they would find them; and the Pythia said that a crow would show them. And so, they say, when the emissaries were landing they saw a stone not far from the road, and the bird on the stone, and they found Hesiod's bones in a hole in the rock. And an elegy was engraved upon the memorial:

> Ascra with its many cornfields (was) my homeland,
>     but now that I have died

---

[23] Cf. T2.

ὀστέα πληξίππων γῆ Μινυῶν κατέχει
Ἡσιόδου, τοῦ πλεῖστον ἐν Ἑλλάδι κῦδος ὀρεῖται
ἀνδρῶν κρινομένων ἐν βασάνῳ σοφίης.

**T104** Inscriptiones Graecae VII 1785; cf. *SEG* 32.426, 506; 36.487

ὅρος τᾶς | γᾶς τᾶς [ία]|ρᾶς τῶν σ[υν]|θυτάων τᾶμ |
Μωσάων Εἰ|σιοδείων

**T105** Inscriptiones Graecae VII 4240a, b, c[2]

(a) 1  Εὐθυ[κλ]ῆς παῖς Ἀμφικρίτου Μούσαις ἀνέθηκε
     κοσμήσ[ας] ἔπεσιν, τῶν ἁ χάρις εἴη ἀείνως
  3  καὶ γένεος τὸ τέλος κείνου καὶ τοὔνομα σῴζοι.
(b) 1  οὕτως ἀντωποῖς ἀριγηρα[λ]έος βροτῷ ἶσα
     οὐκ ἀδ[α]ὴς Ἑλικὼν Μου[σ]άων χρησμὸν ἰαχέω·
     "πειθομένοι[σ]ι βροτοῖς ὑποθήκαις Ἡσιόδοιο
  4  εὐνομία χ[ώ]ρα τ' ἔσται καρποῖσι βρύουσα."
(c) 1  Ἡσίοδος Δίου Μούσας Ἑλικῶνά τε θεῖον
     καλ(λ)ίστοις ὕμνοις [

  3                 ]ν α[ . . ]ιον ἄνδρα.

(a)1 Εὐθυ[κλ]ῆς Peek     (b)1 οὕτως ἀντωποῖς Peek
(c)2–3 [κύδην', ὁ δ' ἄρ' Ἀμφικρίτοιο] / [παῖς κεῖνον τιμάει
εὔστομο]ν α[ἴσ]ιον Peek

   [2] Cf. W. Peek, *Philologus* 121 (1977) 173–75; A. Hurst, *Recherches et Rencontres* 7 (1996) 57–71.

   [24] Cf. T105.

> The land of the horse-smiting Minyans holds my
>     bones,
> Hesiod's, whose glory among human beings is the
>     greatest
> When men are judged in the trials of wisdom.

Cf. T2, T32

**T104**  Boundary stone (Thespiae; dated on epigraphic
grounds to the end of the third century BC)[24]

Boundary of the holy land of those who sacrifice together
to the Muses of Hesiod

**T105**  Stele with three dedicatory inscriptions
(Thespiae, third century BC)[25]

(a)      Euthycles, son of Amphicritus, has made a dedica-
            tion to the Muses,
         adorning it with epic verses. May their grace be ev-
            erlasting,
         and keep safe the fulfillment of his family and his
            name.
(b)      Like this, facing you, very aged, like a mortal,
         I, Helicon, not ignorant of the Muses, proclaim an
            oracle:
         "For mortals who obey Hesiod's injunctions
         there will be good laws and the land will be full of
            fruits."
(c)      Hesiod, son of Dius, the Muses and godly Helicon
         in most beautiful hymns [

                                                    ] man.

25 Cf. T104.

235

**T106**  *SEG* 44.1291, 47.1874; BE 1995.604[3]

Ἡσίοδός π[ο]τε κλεινός, | ἐπεὶ Πέρση[ν τὸν
    ἀδελφόν] |
χῶρος ἀπω.[        ] | τὰ πατρῷϊα [ - - - - - - - - -] |
ἀλλὰ δέ τοι πά[νυ πολλὰ] | παρήνεσεν ὡς ἐπιεικές, |
ὡς ἐπιεικὲς ὄν, | καὶ ταῦτα νεωτέρω[ι - - - - - - - -]

1 Πέρση[ν τὸν ἀδελφόν] Mahé: Πέρσ[ῃ τῷ ἀδελφῷ] Peek
2 ἀπώκ[νησεν] dubitanter Mahé: ἀπον[ήθη καὶ πάν] | τα Peek:
ἀπων[ήθη Hallof πατρῶϊ ἄ[μ᾽ ὄλεσσεν] Peek: τὰ πατρῷϊα [οὐκ
ἐπέδωκε] Hallof    3 ἀλλὰ Hallof    4 ὡς ἐπιεικὲς del.
Peek, qui post v. 3 versum excidisse suspicatus est ⟨καὶ πάλιν
ἐργάζεσθ᾽ ἐκέλευσ᾽· | ὁ δ᾽ ἄρ᾽ εἴκαθεν αὐτοῦ⟩ | ⟨εὐφρονέ⟩οντι
[κάσει], | καὶ ταῦτα νεωτέρω[ι ὄντι]⟩  in fine νεωτερι[κοῖσιν
Tybout   νεώτερο[ς ὤν dubitanter Richardson

**T107**  Inscriptiones Graecae X 2. 2. 1 (pars II, fasc. II,
sectio I), 55; cf. *SEG* 49.710

[οὐδέ ποτ᾽ ἰθυδίκῃσι μετ᾽ ἀ]νδράσι λειμὸς ὀπηδεῖ
[οὐδ᾽ ἀάτη, θαλίης δὲ μεμηλ]ότα ἔργα νέμονται.
                θεῷ
            Δικαιοσύνῃ

**T108**  Paus. 9.27.5

ἐνταῦθα Ἡσίοδος ἀνάκειται χαλκοῦς.

---

[3] Cf. J.-P. Mahé, *Topoi* 4 (1994) 567–86; K. Hallof, *Hyper-
boreus* 3.1 (1997) 2–3.

**T106**  Hexametric inscription (Armawir in Armenia, ca. 200 BC)

Once famous Hesiod, when Perses, [his brother,
the estate [          ] his father's [
But he gave [very many] injunctions, as was appropriate,
as was appropriate,[26] and these to a younger [

**T107**  Dedicatory inscription (Heraclea Lyncestis in Macedonia, 110–20 AD)

Nor does] famine attend [straight-judging] men,
nor calamity, but] they share out [in festivities] the
    fruits of the labors [they care for.[27]

To the Goddess
Justice

**T108**  Pausanias, *Description of Greece*

There (i.e. in the marketplace at Thespiae) stands a bronze statue of Hesiod.

[26] The repetition of these words in the inscription is almost certainly mistaken.

[27] *Works and Days* 230–31.

# HESIOD

**T109**  Paus. 9.30.3

κάθηται δὲ καὶ Ἡσίοδος κιθάραν ἐπὶ τοῖς γόνασιν
ἔχων, οὐδέν τι οἰκεῖον Ἡσιόδῳ φόρημα· δῆλα γὰρ δὴ
καὶ ἐξ αὐτῶν τῶν ἐπῶν (*Theog.* 30–31) ὅτι ἐπὶ ῥάβδου
δάφνης ᾖδε.

**T110**  Paus. 5.26.2

παρὰ δὲ τοῦ ναοῦ τοῦ μεγάλου τὴν ἐν ἀριστερᾷ
πλευράν. . . ποιητῶν δὲ Ὅμηρον καὶ Ἡσίοδον . . .

**T111**  Christodorus Theb. Aeg. *Anth. Pal.* 2.38–40

Ἡσίοδος δ' Ἀσκραῖος ὀρειάσιν εἴδετο Μούσαις
φθεγγόμενος, χαλκὸν δὲ βιάζετο θυιάδι λύσσῃ,
ἔνθεον ἱμείρων ἀνάγειν μέλος.


## PHILOSOPHY

**T112**  Plut. *Theseus* 3.3

ἦν δὲ τῆς σοφίας ἐκείνης τοιαύτη τις ὡς ἔοικεν ἰδέα
καὶ δύναμις, οἵᾳ χρησάμενος Ἡσίοδος εὐδοκιμεῖ μά-
λιστα περὶ τὰς ἐν τοῖς Ἔργοις γνωμολογίας.

**T109**  Pausanias, *Description of Greece*

And Hesiod (i.e. in Helicon) is seated holding a lyre on his knees—not at all an appropriate ornament for Hesiod: for it is clear from his epic poems themselves (i.e. *Theogony* 30–31) that he sang holding a staff of laurel.

**T110**  Pausanias, *Description of Greece*

(the dedications of Micythus at Olympia:) beside the great temple, on the left side . . . and of poets, Homer and Hesiod . . .

**T111**  Christodorus of Egyptian Thebes, epigram

(at Byzantium in the gymnasium of Zeuxippus:)

Ascraean Hesiod seemed to be speaking to the
    mountain Muses
and he was trying to burst the bronze in his divine
    frenzy,
desiring to give voice to an inspired song.

## PHILOSOPHY[28]

**T112**  Plutarch, *Life of Theseus*

That wisdom (i.e. in the age of Pittheus of Troezen) apparently had the same sort of form and power as the one that made Hesiod celebrated above all for the aphoristic maxims in the *Works*.

[28] Cf. also T97–T100 (Theology).

**T113** Heraclitus

**(a)** 22 B 40 DK

πολυμαθίη νόον ἔχειν οὐ διδάσκει· Ἡσίοδον γὰρ ἂν
ἐδίδαξε καὶ Πυθαγόρην αὖτίς τε Ξενοφάνεά τε καὶ
Ἑκαταῖον.

**(b)** 22 B 57 DK

διδάσκαλος δὲ πλείστων Ἡσίοδος· τοῦτον ἐπίστανται
πλεῖστα εἰδέναι, ὅστις ἡμέρην καὶ εὐφρόνην οὐκ ἐγί-
νωσκεν· ἔστι γὰρ ἕν.

**T114** Iambl. *Vita Pyth*. 164

χρῆσθαι δὲ καὶ Ὁμήρου καὶ Ἡσιόδου λέξεσιν ἐξει-
λεγμέναις πρὸς ἐπανόρθωσιν ψυχῆς.

**T115** Plato *Protagoras* 316d

ἐγὼ δὲ τὴν σοφιστικὴν τέχνην φημὶ μὲν εἶναι παλαι-
άν, τοὺς δὲ μεταχειριζομένους αὐτὴν τῶν παλαιῶν
ἀνδρῶν, φοβουμένους τὸ ἐπαχθὲς αὐτῆς, πρόσχημα
ποιεῖσθαι καὶ προκαλύπτεσθαι, τοὺς μὲν ποίησιν,
οἷον Ὅμηρόν τε καὶ Ἡσίοδον καὶ Σιμωνίδην, τοὺς δὲ
αὖ τελετάς τε καὶ χρησμῳδίας, τοὺς ἀμφί τε Ὀρφέα
καὶ Μουσαῖον . . .

**T113**  Heraclitus

**(a)** Learning many things does not teach one to have an intelligent mind; for otherwise it would have taught this to Hesiod and Pythagoras, and to Xenophanes and Hecataeus.

**(b)** The teacher of most people is Hesiod; they think that he knows the most—he who did not know what day and night are: for they are one.

**T114**  Iamblichus, *Life of Pythagoras*[29]

They (i.e. the Pythagoreans) employed expressions of both Homer and Hesiod in order to correct souls.

**T115**  Plato, *Protagoras*

I (i.e. Protagoras) claim that the sophistic art is ancient, but that those ancient men who applied it, fearing that it was annoying, made a pretence and concealed it, some using poetry as a screen, like Homer and Hesiod and Simonides, others doing so with rites and oracles, like Orpheus and Musaeus and their followers . . .

---

[29] Cf. T100.

**T116** Plato

**(a)** *Apologia* 41a

ἢ αὖ Ὀρφεῖ συγγενέσθαι καὶ Μουσαίῳ καὶ Ἡσιόδῳ καὶ Ὁμήρῳ ἐπὶ πόσῳ ἄν τις δέξαιτ᾽ ἂν ὑμῶν; ἐγὼ μὲν γὰρ πολλάκις ἐθέλω τεθνάναι εἰ ταῦτ᾽ ἔστιν ἀληθῆ.

**(b)** *Symposium* 209d

εἰς Ὅμηρον ἀποβλέψας καὶ Ἡσίοδον καὶ τοὺς ἄλλους ποιητὰς τοὺς ἀγαθοὺς ζηλῶν, οἷα ἔκγονα ἑαυτῶν καταλείπουσιν, ἃ ἐκείνοις ἀθάνατον κλέος καὶ μνήμην παρέχεται . . .

**(c)** *Timaeus* 40d-41a

περὶ δὲ τῶν ἄλλων δαιμόνων εἰπεῖν καὶ γνῶναι τὴν γένεσιν μεῖζον ἢ καθ᾽ ἡμᾶς, πειστέον δὲ τοῖς εἰρηκό-σιν ἔμπροσθεν, ἐκγόνοις μὲν θεῶν οὖσιν, ὡς ἔφασαν, σαφῶς δέ που τούς γε αὑτῶν προγόνους εἰδόσιν· ἀδύνατον οὖν θεῶν παισὶν ἀπιστεῖν, καίπερ ἄνευ τε εἰκότων καὶ ἀναγκαίων ἀποδείξεων λέγουσιν, ἀλλ᾽ ὡς οἰκεῖα φασκόντων ἀπαγγέλλειν ἑπομένους τῷ νόμῳ πιστευτέον. οὕτως οὖν κατ᾽ ἐκείνους ἡμῖν ἡ γένεσις περὶ τούτων τῶν θεῶν ἐχέτω καὶ λεγέσθω. Γῆς τε καὶ Οὐρανοῦ παῖδες Ὠκεανός τε καὶ Τηθὺς ἐγενέσθην, τούτων δὲ Φόρκυς Κρόνος τε καὶ Ῥέα καὶ ὅσοι μετὰ τούτων, ἐκ δὲ Κρόνου καὶ Ῥέας Ζεὺς Ἥρα τε καὶ

## T116  Plato[30]

### (a)  *Apology*

Or again, to converse with Orpheus and Musaeus and Hesiod and Homer—how much would any of you give to be able to do this? As for me, I would be willing to die many times if this is true.

### (b)  *Symposium*

considering Homer and Hesiod and the other good poets with envy for the kind of progeny of themselves they left behind, which provides them with immortal glory and remembrance . . .

### (c)  *Timaeus*

About the other divinities, to say and to know their origin is beyond us, and we must believe those who spoke in ancient times, themselves children of the gods, as they said, and surely they must have known their own ancestors. So it is impossible to distrust the children of gods, even though they speak without probable and necessary proofs, but since they say that they are reporting matters regarding their own families we must follow custom and believe them. So it is according to them that we must accept and declare the origin concerning these gods. Of Earth and Sky were born the children Ocean and Tethys, and of these Phorcys and Cronus and Rhea and all the others together with these, and from Cronus and Rhea were born Zeus and

---

[30] Cf. T36, T72, T83, T115, and Fr. 92, 274, 300.; and *Rep.* III 414b–415d. Plato is apparently the earliest author who cites from Hesiod exclusively the *Theogony* and the *Works and Days*.

πάντες ὅσους ἴσμεν ἀδελφοὺς λεγομένους αὐτῶν, ἔτι
τε τούτων ἄλλους ἐκγόνους.

**T117** Aristoteles

**(a)** *Phys.* 4.1 208b27–33

ὅτι μὲν οὖν ἐστί τι ὁ τόπος παρὰ τὰ σώματα, καὶ πᾶν
σῶμα αἰσθητὸν ἐν τόπῳ, διὰ τούτων ἄν τις ὑπολάβοι·
δόξειε δ' ἂν καὶ Ἡσίοδος ὀρθῶς λέγειν ποιήσας πρῶ-
τον τὸ Χάος. λέγει γοῦν πάντων μὲν "πρώτιστα Χάος
γένετ', αὐτὰρ ἔπειτα Γαῖ' εὐρύστερνος," (*Theog.* 116–
17) ὡς δέον πρῶτον ὑπάρξαι χώραν τοῖς οὖσι, διὰ τὸ
νομίζειν, ὥσπερ οἱ πολλοί, πάντα εἶναί που καὶ ἐν
τόπῳ.

**(b)** *De caelo* 3.1 298b28

εἰσὶ γάρ τινες οἵ φασιν οὐθὲν ἀγένητον εἶναι τῶν
πραγμάτων, ἀλλὰ πάντα γίγνεσθαι, γενόμενα δὲ τὰ
μὲν ἄφθαρτα διαμένειν, τὰ δὲ πάλιν φθείρεσθαι, μάλι-
στα μὲν οἱ περὶ Ἡσίοδον, εἶτα καὶ τῶν ἄλλων οἱ
πρῶτοι φυσιολογήσαντες.

**(c)** *Metaphys.*

**i.** A3 983b27–984a2

εἰσὶ δέ τινες οἳ καὶ τοὺς παμπαλαίους καὶ πολὺ πρὸ
τῆς νῦν γενέσεως καὶ πρώτους θεολογήσαντας οὕτως

Hera and all those we know of who are said to be their brothers and sisters, and then others who were the children of these.

**T117** Aristotle[31]

**(a)** *Physics*

That place is something aside from bodies, and that every perceivable body is in place, one might suppose on the basis of these considerations. Hesiod too would seem to have spoken correctly when he made Chasm first. At least he says, "In truth, first of all Chasm came to be, and then broad-breasted Earth" (*Theogony* 116–17), as though there had necessarily to be first a space for the things that are, thinking as he does, as most people do, that everything is somewhere and in place.

**(b)** *On the Heavens*

There are those who say that nothing is ungenerated but that all things are generated, and that once they have been generated some of them remain indestructible while the others are once again destroyed—above all Hesiod and his followers, and then later among other people the first natural philosophers.

**(c)** *Metaphysics*

**i.** There are those who think that the first theologians too, who were very ancient and lived long before the present

31 Cf. T2, T37, T102, T119c, T128, and Fr. 303.

οἴονται περὶ τῆς φύσεως ὑπολαβεῖν· Ὠκεανόν τε γὰρ
καὶ Τηθὺν ἐποίησαν τῆς γενέσεως πατέρας (*Theog.*
337–70), καὶ τὸν ὅρκον τῶν θεῶν ὕδωρ, τὴν
καλουμένην ὑπ᾽ αὐτῶν Στύγα (*Theog.* 775–806)·
τιμιώτατον μὲν γὰρ τὸ πρεσβύτατον, ὅρκος δὲ τὸ
τιμιώτατόν ἐστιν. εἰ μὲν οὖν ἀρχαία τις αὕτη καὶ
παλαιὰ τετύχηκεν οὖσα περὶ τῆς φύσεως ἡ δόξα, τάχ᾽
ἂν ἄδηλον εἴη, Θαλῆς μέντοι λέγεται οὕτως
ἀποφήνασθαι περὶ τῆς πρώτης αἰτίας . . .

**ii.** A4 984b23–32

ὑποπτεύσειε δ᾽ ἄν τις Ἡσίοδον πρῶτον ζητῆσαι τὸ
τοιοῦτον, κἂν εἴ τις ἄλλος ἔρωτα ἢ ἐπιθυμίαν ἐν τοῖς
οὖσιν ἔθηκεν ὡς ἀρχήν, οἷον καὶ Παρμενίδης· καὶ γὰρ
οὗτος κατασκευάζων τὴν τοῦ παντὸς γένεσιν "πρώτι-
στον μέν" φησιν "ἔρωτα θεῶν μητίσατο πάντων" (28 B
13 DK), Ἡσίοδος δὲ "πάντων μὲν πρώτιστα Χάος
γένετ᾽, αὐτὰρ ἔπειτα Γαῖ᾽ εὐρύστερνος . . . ἠδ᾽ Ἔρος,
ὃς πάντεσσι μεταπρέπει ἀθανάτοισιν" (*Theog.* 116–
20), ὡς δέον ἐν τοῖς οὖσιν ὑπάρχειν τιν᾽ αἰτίαν ἥτις
κινήσει καὶ συνάξει τὰ πράγματα. τούτους μὲν οὖν
πῶς χρὴ διανεῖμαι περὶ τοῦ τίς πρῶτος, ἐξέστω
κρίνειν ὕστερον . . .

**iii.** A8 989a8–12

καίτοι διὰ τί ποτ᾽ οὐ καὶ τὴν γῆν λέγουσιν, ὥσπερ οἱ

generation, had the same idea regarding nature (viz. that water is its origin). For they made Ocean and Tethys the parents of generation (*Theogony* 337–70[32]) and made water, which they called the Styx, the oath by which the gods swear (*Theogony* 775–806[33]); for what is oldest is most honorable, and what is most honorable is the oath by which one swears. Well, whether this opinion about nature really is primeval and ancient may well be unclear, but at any rate Thales is said to have spoken in this way about the first cause . . .

**ii.** Someone might suspect that Hesiod was the first to look for something of this sort (viz. a principle which is the cause of beauty and movement), and anyone else who placed love or desire as a principle among the things that are, like Parmenides too. For the latter as well, when he arranges the creation of the universe, says, "She planned love first of all the gods," and Hesiod says, "First of all Chasm came to be, and then broad-breasted Earth . . . and Eros, who is foremost among all the immortals" (*Theogony* 116–20), indicating they thought it necessary that there be among the things that are some cause which will move things and bring them together. Well, how we should classify these with regard to who came first, let us be permitted to decide later . . .

**iii.** And yet why do they (i.e. those who claim there is

[32] Cf. also *Il*. 14.201, 302.
[33] Cf. also *Il*. 15.37–38, *Od*. 5.185–86.

πολλοὶ τῶν ἀνθρώπων; πάντα γὰρ εἶναί φασι γῆν,
φησὶ δὲ καὶ Ἡσίοδος τὴν γῆν πρώτην γενέσθαι τῶν
σωμάτων (*Theog.* 116–17)· οὕτως ἀρχαίαν καὶ δημοτι-
κὴν συμβέβηκεν εἶναι τὴν ὑπόληψιν.

iv. B4 1000a5–19

οὐθενὸς δ᾽ ἐλάττων ἀπορία παραλέλειπται καὶ τοῖς
νῦν καὶ τοῖς πρότερον, πότερον αἱ αὐταὶ τῶν φθαρτῶν
καὶ τῶν ἀφθάρτων ἀρχαί εἰσιν ἢ ἔτεραι. εἰ μὲν γὰρ αἱ
αὐταί, πῶς τὰ μὲν φθαρτὰ τὰ δὲ ἄφθαρτα, καὶ διὰ τίν᾽
αἰτίαν; οἱ μὲν οὖν περὶ Ἡσίοδον καὶ πάντες ὅσοι
θεολόγοι μόνον ἐφρόντισαν τοῦ πιθανοῦ τοῦ πρὸς
αὑτούς, ἡμῶν δ᾽ ὠλιγώρησαν (θεοὺς γὰρ ποιοῦντες
τὰς ἀρχὰς καὶ ἐκ θεῶν γεγονέναι, τὰ μὴ γευσάμενα
τοῦ νέκταρος καὶ τῆς ἀμβροσίας θνητὰ γενέσθαι
φασίν, δῆλον ὡς ταῦτα τὰ ὀνόματα γνώριμα λέγοντες
αὑτοῖς· καίτοι περὶ αὐτῆς τῆς προσφορᾶς τῶν αἰτίων
τούτων ὑπὲρ ἡμᾶς εἰρήκασιν· εἰ μὲν γὰρ χάριν ἡδονῆς
αὐτῶν θιγγάνουσιν, οὐθὲν αἴτια τοῦ εἶναι τὸ νέκταρ
καὶ ἡ ἀμβροσία, εἰ δὲ τοῦ εἶναι, πῶς ἂν εἶεν ἀίδιοι
δεόμενοι τροφῆς;)—ἀλλὰ περὶ μὲν τῶν μυθικῶς σοφι-
ζομένων οὐκ ἄξιον μετὰ σπουδῆς σκοπεῖν.

**T118** Sext. Emp. *Adv. phys.* 2.18 = *Adv. math.* 10.18

ὁ μὲν γὰρ εἰπών·

ἤτοι μὲν πρώτιστα Χάος γένετ᾽, αὐτὰρ ἔπειτα

one material principle) not name earth too (i.e. besides fire, water, and air), like most men? For they say that all things are earth, and Hesiod too says that the earth was created first among bodies (*Theogony* 116–17), so ancient and popular has this notion been.

**iv.** A very great difficulty has been neglected both by contemporary philosophers and by earlier ones, whether the principles of destructible things and of indestructible ones are the same or different. For if they are the same, how is it that some things are destructible and others indestructible, and for what reason? Hesiod and his followers and all the theologians only thought of what was plausible for themselves, and paid no attention to us. For when they establish that the principles are gods and are born from gods, they say that what does not taste nectar and ambrosia becomes mortal. It is clear that they are saying words that are intelligible for themselves, and yet what they have said about the actual application of these causes is beyond us. For if they (i.e. the gods) take hold of nectar and ambrosia for the sake of pleasure, then these are not at all the cause of their being; but if it is for the sake of being, how can they be eternal if they are in need of nourishment? But about mythic sophistries it is not worth inquiring seriously.

**T118** Epicurus

Sextus Empiricus, *Against the Physicists*

For he who said, "In truth, first of all Chasm came to be,

# HESIOD

Γαῖ᾽ εὐρύστερνος, πάντων ἕδος (*Theog.* 116–117),

ἐξ αὐτοῦ περιτρέπεται· ἐρομένου γάρ τινος αὐτόν, ἐκ
τίνος γέγονε τὸ Χάος, οὐχ ἕξει λέγειν. καὶ τοῦτό
φασιν ἔνιοι αἴτιον γεγονέναι Ἐπικούρῳ τῆς ἐπὶ τὸ
φιλοσοφεῖν ὁρμῆς. κομιδῇ γὰρ μειρακίσκος ὢν ἤρετο
τὸν ἐπαναγινώσκοντα αὐτῷ γραμματιστήν· "ἤτοι μὲν
πρώτιστα Χάος γένετ᾽", ἐκ τίνος τὸ χάος ἐγένετο,
εἴπερ πρῶτον ἐγένετο. τούτου δὲ εἰπόντος μὴ ἑαυτοῦ
ἔργον εἶναι τὰ τοιαῦτα διδάσκειν, ἀλλὰ τῶν καλου-
μένων φιλοσόφων, "τοίνυν", ἔφησεν ὁ Ἐπίκουρος, "ἐπ᾽
ἐκείνους μοι βαδιστέον ἐστίν, εἴπερ αὐτοὶ τὴν τῶν
ὄντων ἀλήθειαν ἴσασιν".

**T119** Stoici

**(a)** Zeno Fr. 167, *SVF* I p. 43.20–24 = Cic. *De natura
deorum* 1.14.36

cum vero Hesiodi Theogoniam interpretatur, tollit omni-
no usitatas perceptasque cognitiones deorum; neque enim
Iovem neque Iunonem neque Vestam neque quemquam,
qui ita appelletur, in deorum habet numero, sed rebus
inanimis atque mutis per quandam significationem haec
docet tributa nomina.

and then broad-breasted Earth, the seat of all" (*Theogony* 116–17), is refuted by himself. For if someone asks him what Chasm came to be out of, he will not be able to say. And some say that this was the reason that Epicurus decided to study philosophy. For when he was still very young he asked his teacher, who was reading out to him the line, "In truth, first of all Chasm came to be," what Chasm came to be out of, if it came to be first. And when he (i.e. the teacher) replied that to teach things of that sort was not his job, but of those called philosophers, "Well then," Epicurus said, "I must go to them, if indeed they are the ones who know the truth of things."[34]

**T119**  Stoics[35]

**(a)**  Zeno

But when he (i.e. Zeno) interprets Hesiod's *Theogony*, he completely destroys the customary and perceived notions of the gods: for he does not reckon among the number of the gods either Zeus or Hera or Hestia or anyone named like this, but teaches that these names have been assigned to inanimate and mute things to signify something.[36]

[34] A shorter version of the same story is found in Diogenes Laertius 10.2, with the additional information that Epicurus was 14 years old at the time.

[35] Cf. also Crates of Mallus, T50 and T139.

[36] Cf. Zeno Fr. 100, *SVF*1.28.5–10; Fr. 103–5, *SVF* 1.29.6–24; Fr. 276, *SVF* 1.63.25–27.

# HESIOD

**(b)** Cleanthes et Chrysippus

**(i)** Cleanthes Fr. 539, *SVF* I p. 123.11–15 = Philodemus *De pietate* B 9970–80 Obbink

ἐν δὲ τῶι δευτέρ[ωι] τά τε εἰς Ὀρφέα κ[αὶ] Μουσαῖον ἀναφερόμενα καὶ τὰ παρ' Ὁμήρωι καὶ Ἡσιόδωι καὶ Εὐριπίδηι καὶ ποιηταῖς ἄλλοις γ' [ὡ]ς καὶ Κλεάνθης [π]ειρᾶται σ[υ]νοικειοῦν ταῖς δόξαις αὐτῶ[ν].

**(ii)** Chrysippus Fr. 1077, *SVF* II p. 316.13–15 = Cic. *De natura deorum* I 15.41

in secundo autem volt Orphei, Musaei, Hesiodi, Homerique fabellas accommodare ad ea, quae ipse primo libro de deis immortalibus dixerit, ut etiam veterrimi poetae, qui haec ne suspicati quidem sint, Stoici fuisse videantur.

**(iii)** Chrysippus Fr. 907, *SVF* II p. 255.30–34 = Galenus *De placitis Hippocr. et Plato.* III 4

ἐμπλήσας ὁ Χρύσιππος ὅλον τὸ βιβλίον ἐπῶν Ὁμηρικῶν καὶ Ἡσιοδείων καὶ Στησιχορείων, Ἐμπεδοκλείων τε καὶ Ὀρφικῶν, ἔτι δὲ πρὸς τούτοις ἐκ τῆς τραγῳδίας καὶ παρὰ Τυρταίου καὶ τῶν ἄλλων ποιητῶν οὐκ ὀλίγα παραθέμενος. . .

**(b)** Cleanthes and Chrysippus

**(i)** In book 2 (scil. of *On the Gods*) he (i.e. Chrysippus) tries, like Cleanthes too, to accommodate to their (i.e. the Stoics') doctrines the poems attributed to Orpheus and Musaeus and those of Homer, Hesiod, Euripides, and other poets.

**(ii)** In book 2 (scil. of *On the Nature of the Gods*) he (i.e. Chrysippus) wants to accommodate the myths of Orpheus, Musaeus, Hesiod and Homer to what he himself said in book 1 about the immortal gods, so that even the most ancient poets, who did not have the slightest inkling of this, would seem to have been Stoics.

**(iii)** Chrysippus, having filled up the whole book (i.e. On the Soul) with verses of Homer and Hesiod and Stesichorus, of Empedocles and Orpheus, and inserting besides these many from tragedy and from Tyrtaeus and the other poets . . .

**(c)** Philo *De aeternitate mundi* 5.17–19 (VI pp. 77.20–78.11 Cohn-Reiter)

πατέρα δὲ τοῦ Πλατωνείου δόγματος ἔνιοι νομίζουσι τὸν ποιητὴν Ἡσίοδον, γενητὸν καὶ ἄφθαρτον οἰόμενοι τὸν κόσμον ὑπ' ἐκείνου λέγεσθαι, γενητὸν μέν, ὅτι φησὶν "ἤτοι μὲν πρώτιστα Χάος γένετ', αὐτὰρ ἔπειτα / Γαῖ' εὐρύστερνος, πάντων ἕδος ἀσφαλὲς αἰεί" (*Theog.* 116–17), ἄφθαρτον δέ, ὅτι διάλυσιν καὶ φθορὰν οὐ μεμήνυκεν αὐτοῦ. Χάος δὲ ὁ μὲν Ἀριστοτέλης τόπον οἴεται εἶναι, ὅτι τὸ δεξόμενον ἀνάγκη προϋποκεῖσθαι σώματι, τῶν δὲ Στωικῶν ἔνιοι τὸ ὕδωρ παρὰ τὴν χύσιν τοὔνομα πεποιῆσθαι νομίζοντες. ὁποτέρως δ' ἂν ἔχοι, τὸ γενητὸν εἶναι τὸν κόσμον ἐναργέστατα παρ' Ἡσιόδῳ μεμήνυται. μακροῖς δὲ χρόνοις πρότερον ὁ τῶν Ἰουδαίων νομοθέτης Μωϋσῆς γενητὸν καὶ ἄφθαρτον ἔφη τὸν κόσμον ἐν ἱεραῖς βίβλοις (Gen. 1. 1–2)…

**T120** Neoplatonici

**(a)** Plotinus περὶ ψυχῆς ἀποριῶν, *Ennead.* 4.3.14.78–80

τούτων δὴ γινομένων φῶτα πολλὰ ὁ κόσμος οὗτος ἔχων καὶ καταυγαζόμενος ψυχαῖς ἐπικοσμεῖται ἐπὶ τοῖς προτέροις ἄλλους κόσμους ἄλλον παρ' ἄλλου κομιζόμενος, παρά τε θεῶν ἐκείνων παρά τε νῶν τῶν ἄλλων ψυχὰς διδόντων· οἷον εἰκὸς καὶ τὸν μῦθον αἰνίττεσθαι, ὡς πλάσαντος τοῦ Προμηθέως τὴν γυναῖκα ἐπεκόσμησαν αὐτὴν καὶ οἱ ἄλλοι θεοί· "γαῖαν

**(c)** Philo, *On the Eternity of the World*

Some think that the poet Hesiod was the father of the Platonic doctrine: they think that the world is said by him to be generated and indestructible, because he says, "In truth, first of all Chasm came to be, and then broad-breasted Earth, the ever immovable seat of all" (*Theogony* 116–17), and indestructible, because he has not asserted its dissolution and destruction. Aristotle thinks that Chasm is place, because before there can be body one must presuppose something that can receive it,[37] and some of the Stoics think it is water, supposing that the name is derived from *chysis* ("flowing").[38] But whichever it is, it is revealed most clearly by Hesiod that the world is generated. But a long time earlier, Moses, the lawgiver of the Jews, said in the holy Bible that the world is generated and indestructible . . .

**T120** Neoplatonists

**(a)** Plotinus, *Difficulties about the Soul*

Because this has happened, this world order, which possesses many lights and is illuminated by the souls, is ordered further (*epikosmeitai*), receiving different world orders beyond the earlier ones, each one from a different source, from the gods of the other world and from the other intellects which give souls. It is likely that this is the sort of thing which is hinted at enigmatically by the myth too, that after Prometheus fabricated the woman all the other gods too adorned her further (*epekosmēsan*), that he

37 Cf. T117a.
38 Cf. Zeno Fr. 103, *SVF* 1.29.6–15.

HESIOD

ὕδει" φύρειν, καὶ ἀνθρώπου ἐνθεῖναι φωνήν, θεαῖς δ'
ὁμοίαν τὸ εἶδος (Op. 61–62), καὶ Ἀφροδίτην τι δοῦναι
καὶ Χάριτας (Op. 65–66, 73–74) καὶ ἄλλον ἄλλο δῶρον
καὶ ὀνομάσαι ἐκ τοῦ δώρου καὶ πάντων τῶν δεδωκότων
(Op. 80–82)· πάντες γὰρ τούτῳ ἔδοσαν τῷ πλάσματι
παρὰ προμηθείας τινὸς γενομένῳ. ὁ δὲ Ἐπιμηθεὺς
ἀποποιούμενος τὸ δῶρον αὐτοῦ (Op. 85–88) τί ἂν
σημαίνοι ἢ τὴν τοῦ ἐν νοητῷ μᾶλλον αἵρεσιν ἀμείνω
εἶναι; δέδεται δὲ καὶ αὐτὸς ὁ ποιήσας (Theog. 521–22),
ὅτι πως ἐφάπτεται τοῦ γενομένου ὑπ' αὐτοῦ, καὶ ὁ
τοιοῦτος δεσμὸς ἔξωθεν· καὶ ἡ λύσις ἡ ὑπὸ Ἡρα-
κλέους (Theog. 526–34), ὅτι δύναμίς ἐστιν αὐτῷ, ὥς τε
καὶ ὡς λελύσθαι. ταῦτα μὲν οὖν ὅπῃ τις δοξάζει, ἀλλ'
ὅτι ἐμφαίνει τὰ τῆς εἰς τὸν κόσμον δόσεως, καὶ προσ-
ᾴδει τοῖς λεγομένοις.


(b) Iulianus Orat. in Hel. Reg. (4) 136a-137c

μὴ γὰρ δή τις ὑπολάβῃ τοῦτον (scil. Ἥλιον), ὃν οἱ
μῦθοι πείθουσι φρίττειν, ἀλλὰ τὸν πρᾶον καὶ μείλι-
χον, ὃς ἀπολύει παντελῶς τῆς γενέσεως τὰς ψυχάς,
οὐχὶ δὲ λυθείσας αὐτὰς σώμασιν ἑτέροις προσηλοῖ
κολάζων καὶ πραττόμενος δίκας, ἀλλὰ πορεύων ἄνω
καὶ ἀνατείνων τὰς ψυχὰς ἐπὶ τὸν νοητὸν κόσμον. ὅτι
δὲ οὐδὲ νεαρὰ παντελῶς ἐστιν ἡ δόξα, προύλαβον δὲ
αὐτὴν οἱ πρεσβύτατοι τῶν ποιητῶν, Ὅμηρός τε καὶ
Ἡσίοδος, εἴτε καὶ νοοῦντες οὕτως εἴτε καὶ ἐπιπνοίᾳ

mixed "earth with water" and put into her the voice of a human, and made her like the goddesses in form (cf. *Works and Days* 61–62), that Aphrodite and the Graces gave something to her (cf. *Works and Days* 65–66, 73–74), and each god gave her a different gift, and she was named from the gift (*dōron*) and from the fact that all (*pantes*) had given one (cf. *Works and Days* 80–82). For all gave to this fabrication which came about from a certain forethought (*promētheia*). When Epimetheus is supposed to refuse his gift (cf. *Works and Days* 85–88) what else could this mean except that the better preference is the one for what is in the intelligible world? And the creator is himself bound (cf. *Theogony* 521–22), because in some way he is in contact with what he has generated, and a bond of this sort is external. And his liberation by Heracles (cf. *Theogony* 526–34) (scil. signifies) that even so he has the power to be liberated. One may think about these matters however one will, but in any case they make clear the gift to the world and they agree with what has been said (scil. by myself).

**(b)** Julian, *Hymn to King Helios*

For let no one think of him (i.e. Helios) as the one at which the myths teach us to shudder, but as someone mild and soothing, who completely frees souls from generation and, once they have been freed, does not nail them to other bodies, punishing them and making them pay a penalty, but instead carries the souls upwards and lifts them up towards the intelligible world. That this opinion is not completely new, but that the most ancient poets, Homer and Hesiod, accepted it—either because they themselves thought this or because they were divinely impelled to-

θεία καθάπερ οἱ μάντεις ἐνθουσιῶντες πρὸς τὴν ἀλή-
θειαν, ἐνθένδ᾽ ἂν γίγνοιτο γνώριμον. ὁ μὲν γενεαλο-
γῶν αὐτὸν Ὑπερίονος ἔφη καὶ Θείας (Theog. 371),
μόνον οὐχὶ διὰ τούτων αἰνιττόμενος τοῦ πάντων ὑπερ-
έχοντος αὐτὸν ἔκγονον γνήσιον φῦναι· ὁ γὰρ Ὑπερί-
ων τίς ἂν ἕτερος εἴη παρὰ τοῦτον; ἡ Θεία δὲ αὐτὴ
τρόπον ἕτερον οὐ τὸ θειότατον τῶν ὄντων λέγεται; μὴ
δὲ συνδυασμὸν μηδὲ γάμους ὑπολαμβάνωμεν, ἄπιστα
καὶ παράδοξα ποιητικῆς Μούσης ἀθύρματα· πατέρα
δὲ αὐτοῦ καὶ γεννήτορα νομίζωμεν τὸν θειότατον καὶ
ὑπέρτατον· τοιοῦτος δέ τις ἂν ἄλλος εἴη τοῦ πάντων
ἐπέκεινα καὶ περὶ ὃν πάντα καὶ οὗ ἕνεκα πάντα ἐστίν;
. . . ἀλλὰ τὰ μὲν τῶν ποιητῶν χαίρειν ἐάσωμεν· ἔχει
γὰρ μετὰ τοῦ θείου πολὺ καὶ τἀνθρώπινον.

(c) Proclus *In Platonis Rem publ. Comment.* I p. 82.9–20
Kroll

τούτοις δὴ οὖν τοῖς τῶν τοιῶνδε θεαμάτων ἐπηβόλοις
λέγοντες, ὡς. . .οἱ δὲ Κρόνιοι δεσμοὶ τὴν ἕνωσιν τῆς
ὅλης δημιουργίας πρὸς τὴν νοερὰν τοῦ Κρόνου καὶ
πατρικὴν ὑπεροχὴν δηλοῦσιν, αἱ δὲ τοῦ Οὐρανοῦ
(Theog. 176–81) τομαὶ τὴν διάκρισιν τῆς Τιτανικῆς
σειρᾶς ἀπὸ τῆς συνεκτικῆς διακοσμήσεως αἰνίσσον-
ται, τάχα ἂν γνώριμα λέγοιμεν καὶ τὸ τῶν μύθων
τραγικὸν καὶ πλασματῶδες εἰς τὴν νοερὰν τῶν θείων
γενῶν ἀναπέμποιμεν θεωρίαν.

wards the truth by godly inspiration like seers—is obvious from the following. For the one (i.e. Hesiod) provided a genealogy for him (i.e. Helios) by saying that he is the son of Hyperion and Theia (cf. *Theogony* 371), hinting thereby that he is by nature the legitimate offspring of him who is superior to all things—and who else could Hyperion be than this?[39] And is not Theia herself, in a different way, called the most divine of beings?[40] Let us not imagine a coupling or marriages, the implausible and unbelievable frivolities of the poetic Muse: instead let us believe that his father and begetter is the most divine and superior being: and who could be like this except him who is beyond all things, him about whom and for the sake of whom all things exist? . . . But let us set aside the utterances of the poets: for, mixed in with what is divine, these contain very much of what is human too.

**(c)** Proclus, *Commentary on Plato's Republic*

If we say then to those who have achieved such visions that . . . and that the binding of Cronus[41] indicates the union of all creation with the intellectual and paternal transcendence of Cronus, that the castration of Sky (cf. *Theogony* 176–81) hints enigmatically at the separation of the Titanic chain from the world ordering that holds things together, then perhaps we would say what they already know and would restore the overly poetic and fictional aspect of the myths to the intellectual doctrine of the divine classes.

[39] Julian etymologizes Hyperion's name as "he who goes above."

[40] Theia's name means "divine."

[41] It is unclear just what passage Proclus has in mind.

# HESIOD

## SCHOLARSHIP AND RHETORIC

**T121** Clem. Alex. *Strom.* 6.2.26

τὰ δὲ Ἡσιόδου μετήλλαξαν εἰς πεζὸν λόγον καὶ ὡς ἴδια ἐξήνεγκαν Εὔμηλός (*FGrHist* 451 Τ 1) τε καὶ Ἀκουσίλαος (*FGrHist* 2 Τ 5) οἱ ἱστοριογράφοι.

**T122** Iosephus *Contra Apionem* 1.16

ὅσα δὲ διορθοῦται τὸν Ἡσίοδον Ἀκουσίλαος (*FGrHist* 2 Τ 6). . .

**T123** Isocrates *Panathen.* 17–19

μικρὸν δὲ πρὸ τῶν Παναθηναίων τῶν μεγάλων ἠχθέσθην δι᾽ αὐτούς. ἀπαντήσαντες γάρ τινές μοι τῶν ἐπιτηδείων ἔλεγον ὡς ἐν τῷ Λυκείῳ συγκαθεζόμενοι τρεῖς ἢ τέτταρες τῶν ἀγελαίων σοφιστῶν καὶ πάντα φασκόντων εἰδέναι καὶ ταχέως πανταχοῦ γιγνομένων διαλέγοιντο περί τε τῶν ἄλλων ποιητῶν καὶ τῆς Ἡσιόδου καὶ τῆς Ὁμήρου ποιήσεως, οὐδὲν μὲν παρ᾽ αὑτῶν λέγοντες, τὰδ᾽ ἐκείνων ῥαψῳδοῦντες καὶ τῶν πρότερον ἄλλοις τισὶν εἰρημένων τὰ χαριέστατα μνημονεύοντες· ἀποδεξαμένων δὲ τῶν περιεστώτων τὴν διατριβὴν αὐτῶν, ἕνα τὸν τολμηρότατον ἐπιχειρῆσαί με διαβάλλειν, λέγονθ᾽ ὡς ἐγὼ πάντων καταφρονῶ τῶν τοιούτων, καὶ τάς τε φιλοσοφίας τὰς τῶν ἄλλων καὶ τὰς παιδείας ἁπάσας ἀναιρῶ, καὶ φημὶ πάντας ληρεῖν

## SCHOLARSHIP AND RHETORIC

### History[42]

**T121** Clement of Alexandria, *Miscellanies*

The historians Eumelus and Acusilaus turned Hesiod's poems into prose and published them under their own names.

**T122** Josephus, *Against Apion*

all the passages in which Acusilaus corrects Hesiod . . .

### Rhetoric

**T123** Isocrates, *Panathenaic Discourse*

They (i.e. my rivals) annoyed me shortly before the Great Panathenaea. For some of my friends met me and told me that three or four of the ordinary sort of sophists—those who claim to know everything and want to be everywhere at once—were sitting together in the Lyceum and were discussing the poets, and especially the poetry of Hesiod and Homer. They were saying nothing of their own about them, but merely performing their poems like rhapsodes and repeating from memory the most entertaining things that others had said about them in earlier times. When the bystanders approved their discussion, one of them, the most daring one, undertook to make accusations against me, saying that I despise all such things and would destroy all the forms of culture and teaching practiced by others, and that I say that everyone talks rubbish except for those

---

[42] Cf. also Strabo, *Geography* 1.2.14, 22, 35.

πλὴν τοὺς μετεσχηκότας τῆς ἐμῆς διατριβῆς· τούτων
δὲ ῥηθέντων ἀηδῶς τινας τῶν παρόντων διατεθῆναι
πρὸς ἡμᾶς.

**T124** Dion. Hal.

**(a)** *De comp. verb.* 23 (II p. 114.1 Usener-Radermacher)

ἐποποιῶν μὲν οὖν ἔμοιγε κάλλιστα τουτονὶ δοκεῖ τὸν
χαρακτῆρα ἐξεργάσασθαι Ἡσίοδος.

**(b)** *De imitat.* 2.2 (II p. 204.14 Usener-Radermacher)

Ἡσίοδος μὲν γὰρ ἐφρόντισεν ἡδονῆς δι᾽ ὀνομάτων
λειότητος καὶ συνθέσεως ἐμμελοῦς.

**T125** Quintil. *Inst. orat.* 10.1.52

raro adsurgit Hesiodus magnaque pars eius in nominibus
est occupata, tamen utiles circa praecepta sententiae,
levitasque verborum et compositionis probabilis, datur-
que ei palma in illo medio genere dicendi.

**T126** Men. Rhet. διαίρεσις τῶν ἐπιδεικτικῶν (III p.
340.24–29 Spengel, p. 20 Russell-Wilson)

ἀρετὴ δ᾽ ἑρμηνείας ἐν τοῖς τοιούτοις καθαρότης καὶ τὸ
ἀπροσκορές· γένοιτο <δ᾽> ἂν ἐν ποιήσει ἐκ συμμετρί-
ας τῶν περιφράσεων . . . παρέσχετο δὲ τὴν μὲν ἐν
ποιήσει ἀρετὴν Ἡσίοδος, καὶ γνοίη τις ἂν μᾶλλον, εἰ
τοῖς Ὀρφέως παραθείη.

who participate in my own instruction. And some of those present were turned against me by these statements.

**T124** Dionysius of Halicarnassus

**(a)** *On the Arrangement of Words*

Of the epic poets, it seems to me that it is Hesiod who has elaborated this style (i.e. the smooth arrangement) most finely.

**(b)** *On Imitation*

Hesiod paid attention to the pleasure deriving from verbal smoothness and harmonious arrangement.

**T125** Quintilian, *Institutions of Oratory*

Hesiod takes flight only rarely, and much of his work is filled with proper names, but his didactic maxims are useful, and the smoothness of his choice and arrangement of words can be recommended: he wins the palm in the middle style.

**T126** Menander Rhetor, *Classification of Epideictic Speeches*

Excellence of style in writings of this sort (i.e. genealogical hymns) consists in purity and in avoiding a feeling of surfeit, and this can be achieved in poetry by means of moderation in periphrases . . . Hesiod demonstrated this excellence in poetry, and one can recognize this better by comparing his poems with Orpheus'.

**T127**  Schol. Hes. *Op*. Prolegomena A.b p. 1.15–2.5 Pertusi

ὁ μὲν οὖν σκοπὸς τοῦ βιβλίου παιδευτικός. . . . διὸ καὶ ἀρχαιότροπός ἐστιν ἡ ἐν αὐτῷ τῆς ποιητικῆς ἰδέα· τῶν γὰρ καλλωπισμῶν καὶ τῶν ἐπιθέτων κόσμων καὶ μεταφορῶν ὡς τὰ πολλὰ καθαρεύει. τὸ γὰρ ἁπλοῦν καὶ τὸ αὐτοφυὲς πρέπει τοῖς ἠθικοῖς λόγοις.

**T128**  Aristoteles

Hesych. in onomatologo s.v. Ἀριστοτέλης (Arist. Fragmenta p. 16.143 Rose)

Ἀπορήματα Ἡσιόδου ἐν ā . . .

**T129**  Heraclides Ponticus

Diog. Laert. 5.87 (Heraclid. Fr. 22 Wehrli)

γραμματικὰ δέ· περὶ τῆς Ὁμήρου καὶ Ἡσιόδου ἡλικίας αʹ βʹ . . .

**T130**  Chamaeleon

Diog. Laert. 5.92 (Chamaeleon Fr. 46 Wehrli, Fr. 47 Giordano)

Χαμαιλέων τε τὰ παρ' ἑαυτοῦ φησι κλέψαντα αὐτὸν (scil. Ἡρακλείδην) τὰ περὶ Ἡσιόδου καὶ Ὁμήρου γράψαι.

**T127**  Scholia on Hesiod's *Works and Days*,
Prolegomena

The purpose of the book is educational. . . . For this reason
the poetic style in it is archaic, for it is for the most part free
of adornments and added ornamentations and metaphors.
For simplicity and naturalness are appropriate for ethical
discourses.

Cf. T53, T60, T95

*Literary Scholarship*

**T128**  Aristotle[43]

Hesychius, *List of Aristotle's Writings*

*Hesiodic Problems*, in 1 book . . .

**T129**  Heraclides Ponticus

Diogenes Laertius, *Lives of Eminent Philosophers*

grammatical works: *On the Age of Homer and Hesiod*,
books 1 and 2 . . .

**T130**  Chamaeleon

Diogenes Laertius, *Lives of Eminent Philosophers*

Chamaeleon says that he (i.e. Heraclides) plagiarized his
own treatise about Hesiod and Homer.

[43] Cf. T2, T37, T102, T117, T119c, and Fr. 303.

**T131**  Hecataeus Abder.

*Suda* ε 359, 2.213.22–23 Adler (73 A 1 DK)

περὶ τῆς ποιήσεως Ὁμήρου καὶ Ἡσιόδου. . .

**T 132**  Megaclides

T 52

**T133**  Antidorus Cum.

Schol. Dion. Thrax 448.6 Hilgard

φασὶ δὲ Ἀντίδωρον τὸν Κυμαῖον πρῶτον ἐπιγεγρα-
φέναι αὑτὸν γραμματικόν, σύγγραμμά τι γράψαντα
περὶ Ὁμήρου καὶ Ἡσιόδου.

**T134**  Zenodotus

Schol. Hes. *Theog.* 5b$^2$ (p. 4.9–10 Di Gregorio)

**T135**  Apollonius Rhodius

Schol. Hes. *Theog.* 26b (p. 7.6–9 Di Gregorio = Apoll.
Rhod. Fr. XIX Michaelis); T52, T80

**T136**  Aristophanes Byz.

Schol. Hes. *Theog.* 68a (p. 15.16–18 Di Gregorio =
Aristoph. Byz. Fr. 405 Slater), 126 (p. 28.3–10 Di Gr. = Fr.
439 Sl.); T52, T69

# TESTIMONIA

**T131**  Hecataeus of Abdera
The *Suda*

*On the Poetry of Homer and Hesiod* . . .


**T132**  Megaclides
T52


**T133**  Antidorus of Cyme
Scholium on Dionysius Thrax

They say that Antidorus of Cyme was the first person to call himself a grammarian; he wrote a treatise about Homer and Hesiod.


**T134**  Zenodotus
Scholium on Hesiod's *Theogony*

**T135**  Apollonius Rhodius
Scholium on Hesiod's *Theogony*; T52, T80


**T136**  Aristophanes of Byzantium
Scholia on Hesiod's *Theogony*; T52, T69

**T137** Aristarchus

Schol. Hes. *Theog.* 76 (p. 17.2–5 Di Gregorio = Arist. Fr. 1 Waeschke), 114–15 (p. 22.1 Di Gr. = Fr. 2 W.), 138 (p. 32.7–12 Di Gr. = Fr. 3 W.), 253b (p. 51.23–52.1 Di Gr. = Fr. 4 W.), 991 (p. 121.7–8 Di Gr.; ἀρχέλοχος mss., corr. Ruhnken, Flach); Schol. Hes. *Op.* 97a (p. 45.11–14 Pertusi = Fr. 6 W.), 207–12 (p. 76.22–24 P. = Fr. 7 W.), 740a (p. 225.15–18 P. = Fr. 9 W.); T49

**T138** Praxiphanes

T49

**T139** Crates Mall.

Schol. Hes. *Theog.* 126 (p. 28.4–5 Di Gregorio = Crat. Fr. 79 Broggiato), 142 (p. 34.6–8 Di Gr. = Fr. 80 Br. = Hesiodus Fr. 57 Most); T50

**T140** Zenodotus Alex.

*Suda* ζ 75, 2. 506.21 Adler

εἰς τὴν Ἡσιόδου Θεογονίαν. . .

**T141** Demetrius Ixion

*Suda* δ 430, 2.41.19 Adler (Dem. Ixion pp. 20–21 Staesche)

εἰς Ὅμηρον ἐξήγησιν, εἰς Ἡσίοδον ὁμοίως. . .

**T137**  Aristarchus

Scholia on Hesiod's *Theogony* and *Works and Days*; T49

**T138**  Praxiphanes

T49

**T139**  Crates of Mallus

Scholia on Hesiod, *Theogony;* T50

**T140**  Zenodotus of Alexandria

The *Suda*

*On Hesiod's Theogony* . . .

**T141**  Demetrius Ixion

The *Suda*

*Exegesis of Homer. Exegesis of Hesiod.* . . .

**T142**  Aristonicus

*Suda* α 3924 (I p. 356.31–33 Adler)

περὶ τῶν σημείων τῶν ἐν τῇ Θεογονίᾳ Ἡσιόδου καὶ τῶν τῆς Ἰλιάδος καὶ Ὀδυσσείας. . .

**T143**  Didymus

Schol. Hes. *Theog.* 126 (p. 28.7–8 Di Gregorio = Did. p. 300 Schmidt); Schol. Hes. *Op.* 304b (p. 102.15–16 Pertusi = p. 300 Schmidt)

**T144**  Seleucus

Schol. Hes. *Theog.* 114–15 (p. 21.13 Di Gregorio = Sel. Fr. 27 Müller), 160 (p. 37.6–8 Di Gr. = Fr. 28 M.), 270 (p. 54.8–9 Di Gr. = Fr. 29 M.), 573 (p. 88.11–12 Di Gr. = Fr. 30 M.); Schol. Hes. *Op.* 96a (p. 44.20–21 Pertusi = Fr. p. 44 M.), 150b (p. 60.16–18 P.), 549a (p. 180.23–24 P. = Fr. p. 44 M.); Schol. Hes. *Scut.* 415 (p. 181 Russo = Fr. 33 M.)

**T145**  Epaphroditus

*Etym. Gudianum* p. 91.18, 177.23 Sturz

ἐν Ὑπομνήματι Ἀσπίδος . . .

**T142** Aristonicus

The *Suda*

*On the Critical Signs in Hesiod's Theogony and Those in the Iliad and Odyssey.* . . .

**T143** Didymus

Scholia on Hesiod's *Theogony* and *Works and Days*

**T144** Seleucus

Scholia on Hesiod's *Theogony*, *Works and Days*, *Shield*

**T145** Epaphroditus

*Etymologicum Gudianum*

in his *Treatise on the Shield* . . .

**T146**  Dionysius Corinth.

*Suda* δ 1177 (II p. 110.11–12 Adler)

ἐποποιὸς. . .καὶ καταλογάδην Ὑπόμνημα εἰς Ἡσίοδον
. . .

**T147**  Plutarchus

Aul. Gell. 20.8.7 = Plut. Fr. 102 Sandbach

quod apud Plutarchum in quarto in Hesiodum commen-
tario legi. . .

Schol. Hes. *Op.* 48 (p. 28.14–16 Pertusi = Plut. Fr. 27
Sandbach), 214–16 (pp. 28.19–79.2 P. = Fr. 32 S.), 220–
21 (p. 81.10–22 P. = Fr. 34 S.), 242–47 (p. 86.18–22 P. =
Fr. 37 S.), 270–73 (pp. 91.22–92.9 P. = Fr. 38 S.), 286
(pp. 96.11–97.2 P. = Fr. 40 S.), 287–90 (p. 97.7–9 P. =
Fr. 41 S.), 317–18 (p. 107.4–6 P. = Fr. 45 S.), 346–48
(pp. 116.25–117.13 P. = Fr. 49 S.), 353–54 (p. 119.1–7 P.
= Fr. 51a S.), 355 (pp. 119.18–120.2 P. = Fr. 52 S.), 356–
60 ‹370–72› (pp. 120.20–121.7 P. = Fr. 55 S.), 375 (p.
125.21–23 P. = Fr. 56 S.), 376[377]-78 (p. 126.4–10 P. =
Fr. 57 S.), 380 (pp. 128.15–23 P. = Fr. 59 S.), 391–93
(pp. 135.23–136.8 P. = Fr. 60 S.), 423–27 (p. 144.2–17 P.
= Fr. 62 S.), 427–30 (p. 148.3–7 P. = Fr. 64 S.), 430–36
(p. 45.1–9 P. = Fr. 65 S.), 504–6 (p. 171.1–10 P. = Fr. 71a
S.), 561–63 (p. 183.1–7 P. = Fr. 77 S.), 578–81 (p. 188.7–
12 P. = Fr. 79 S.), 591–96 (pp. 191.6–192.18 P. = Fr. 81

**T146**  Dionysius of Corinth

The *Suda*

Epic poet . . . and in prose *Treatise on Hesiod* . . .

**T147**  Plutarch

Aulus Gellius, *Attic Nights*

which I have read in Plutarch in book 4 of his commentary
on Hesiod . . .

Scholia on Hesiod's *Works and Days*

S.), 633–40 (pp. 201.22–202.9 P. = Fr. 82 S.), 650–62
(pp. 205.22–206.10 P. = Fr. 84 S.), 733–34 (p. 223.8–18
P. = Fr. 91 S.), 748–49 (p. 228.5–15 P. = Fr. 95 S.), 750–
52 (p. 229.8–14 P. = Fr. 96 S.), 757–59 (p. 231.6–10 P. =
Fr. 98 S.), 780–81 (pp. 242.16–243.8 P. = Fr. 104 S.),
797–99 (p. 248.7–20 P. = Fr. 108 S.)

**T148** Proclus

Suda π 2473 (IV p. 210.9–10 Adler)

Ὑπόμνημα εἰς τὰ Ἡσιόδου Ἔργα καὶ Ἡμέρας . . .

Schol. Hes. *Op. passim*

**T149** Cleomenes

Clem. Alex. *Strom.* 1.61.2

Κλεομένης . . .ἐν τῷ περὶ Ἡσιόδῳ . . .

**T150** Comanus

Schol. Hes. *Op.* 97a (p. 45.8–11 Pertusi = Comanus Fr. 16
Dyck)

**T151** P. Oxy. 4648 recto 14–28

ἠπε[ι-
ρώτης δὲ γεωργ]ὸς ὢν ὁ Ἀσκραῖος καὶ τὰ να[υ-
τικὰ ἀγνοῶν, τὰ δὲ βεβ]αιότατα τῆς γεωργίας, [

**T148** Proclus[44]

The *Suda*

*Treatise on Hesiod's Works and Days* . . .

Scholia on Hesiod's *Works and Days*

**T149** Cleomenes

Clement of Alexandria, *Miscellanies*

Cleomenes . . . in his *On Hesiod* . . .

**T150** Comanus

Scholium on Hesiod's *Works and Days*

**T151** Oxyrhynchus papyrus (third century AD), anonymous prose work on star signs

But the Ascraean, being [a farmer from the mainland and ignorant of sailing] (scil. unlike the educated islander

---

[44] Cf. T120(c).

τὰς ὥρας καταμ]ετρεῖ " Πληιάδων Ἀτλαι|γε-
νέων| [ ....] [τελ]λομενάων" (Op. 383) καὶ ἐπὶ τὸν
    ἄμ[η-
τον τότε ἐξώρ]μησεν, "δυομένων" δὲ ἐπὶ τ[ὸν
ἄροτον, καθάπερ] καὶ ὅτε Ὡρίων ἐστὶν τρυγ[
..........] παρε.[.]. α καὶ ὅλως τινέ[ς
φασιν, ὅταν κ]αί τισι ὁ "ἀκροκν[έ]φαιος" (Op. 567)
    παρ[ῇ.
ὡς δὲ προειρ]ήκαμεν, οὗ δὴ Ἄρατος ζηλ[ω-
τὴς οὐκ ἀγ]εννὴς ἐγένετο, ὡς μηδὲ τὸν [
.......]ον ἐσφάλθαι εἰπόντα (T 73).

## MISCELLANEOUS JUDGMENTS

**T152** Cic. *Cato maior de senectute* 15.54

quid de utilitate loquar stercorandi? Dixi in eo libro quem
de rebus rusticis scripsi; de qua doctus Hesiodus ne ver-
bum quidem fecit, cum de cultura agri scriberet; at Home-
rus, qui multis ut mihi videtur ante saeclis fuit, Laertam
lenientem desiderium quod capiebat e filio, colentem
agrum et eum stercorantem facit.

**T153** Dio Chrys. *Orat.* 2.8

"τὸν δὲ Ἡσίοδον, ὦ Ἀλέξανδρε, ὀλίγου ἄξιον κρίνεις",
ἔφη, "ποιητήν;"

Homer), but knowing the most certain signs of agriculture, measures [the seasons] starting from "when the Atlas-born Pleiades rise" (*Works and Days* 383) and [has set out just at that time] for the harvest, and "when they set" to [the plowing, just as] when Orion is [       ] grape harvest, and some [say] wholly so, [when] it is present to some "just at dusk" (*Works and Days* 567). [As we said earlier,] Aratus was indeed [not] a servile imitator of him, so that [       ] (i.e. Callimachus) was not mistaken when he said, (T73).

## MISCELLANEOUS JUDGMENTS

**T152** Cicero, *Cato. On Old Age*

Why should I (i.e. Cato) speak about the usefulness of manuring? I have spoken about that in the book I wrote on agriculture. On this subject the learned Hesiod did not even say a single word when he wrote about cultivation; but Homer, who lived many generations, as I believe, before (= T6), shows us Laertes trying to alleviate his longing for his son by cultivating his field and spreading manure on it.[45]

**T153** Dio Chrysostom, "On Kingship"[46]

He (i.e. Philip of Macedon) said, "Well, Alexander, as

[45] Cicero seems to be referring to *Odyssey* 24.227; but in fact, there is no explicit reference to manure in this passage.

[46] Cf. also Dio Chrysostom, "Borysthenitic Discourse" 34–35 (= *Orat*. 36.34–35).

"οὐκ ἔγωγε," εἶπεν, "ἀλλὰ τοῦ παντός, οὐ μέντοι βασιλεῦσιν οὐδὲ στρατηγοῖς ἴσως."

" ἀλλὰ τίσι μήν;"

καὶ ὁ Ἀλέξανδρος γελάσας "τοῖς ποιμέσιν," ἔφη, "καὶ τοῖς τέκτοσι καὶ τοῖς γεωργοῖς. τοὺς μὲν γὰρ ποιμένας φησὶ φιλεῖσθαι ὑπὸ τῶν Μουσῶν (sed cf. Th. 26), τοῖς δὲ τέκτοσι μάλα ἐμπείρως παραινεῖ πηλίκον χρὴ τὸν ἄξονα τεμεῖν (cf. Op. 424–5), καὶ τοῖς γεωργοῖς, ὁπηνίκα ἄρξασθαι πίθου (cf. Op. 814–5)."

**T154**  Dio Chrys. *Orat.* 77.1–2

"ἆρα διὰ ταῦτα καὶ τὰ τοιαῦτα ἐνομίσθη σοφὸς ἐν τοῖς Ἕλλησιν Ἡσίοδος καὶ οὐδαμῶς ἀνάξιος ἐκείνης τῆς δόξης, ὡς οὐκ ἀνθρωπίνῃ τέχνῃ τὰ ποιήματα ποιῶν τε καὶ ᾄδων, ἀλλὰ ταῖς Μούσαις ἐντυχὼν καὶ μαθητὴς αὐτῶν ἐκείνων γενόμενος; ὅθεν ἐξ ἀνάγκης ὅ, τι ἐπῆει αὐτῷ πάντα μουσικά τε καὶ σοφὰ ἐφθέγγετο καὶ οὐδὲν μάταιον, ὧν δῆλον ὅτι καὶ τοῦτο τὸ ἔπος ἐστίν."

"τὸ ποῖον;"

"καὶ κεραμεὺς κεραμεῖ κοτέει καὶ τέκτονι τέκτων." (Hes. Op. 25)

"πολλὰ μὲν καὶ ἄλλα φανήσεται τῶν Ἡσιόδου πεποιημένα καλῶς περί τε ἀνθρώπων καὶ θεῶν σχεδόν τι καὶ περὶ μειζόνων πραγμάτων ἢ ὁποῖα τὰ λεχθέντα νῦν· ἀτὰρ οὖν καὶ ταῦτα ἀπεφήνατο μάλ᾽ ἀληθῶς τε καὶ ἐμπείρως τῆς ἀνθρωπίνης φύσεως."

for Hesiod, is he not worth very much as a poet in your judgment?"

"Quite the contrary, but he is perhaps not for kings and generals."

"For whom then?"

Alexander laughed and said, "For shepherds, carpenters, and farmers. For shepherds he says are loved by the Muses (but cf. *Th* 26), carpenters he gives very experienced advice on how big an axle should be cut (cf. *WD* 424–5), and farmers when they should start in on a storage-jar (cf. *WD* 814–5)."

**T154**  Dio Chrysostom, "On Envy"

"Is it not for this reason and like ones that Hesiod was considered wise among the Greeks and not at all unworthy of that reputation of his, namely that it was not by human skill that he composed his poems, but because he had encountered the Muses and become their disciple? So that of necessity whatever occurred to him and he uttered was all 'musical' and wise and nothing in vain. An obvious example of this is this verse."

"Which one?"

"'And potter is angry with potter, and builder with builder.' (*Works and Days* 25)

"It will turn out that many other verses of Hesiod's are quite correct about human beings and gods and also about more important subjects than what has just been men-

# HESIOD

**T155** Plut. *Lac. Apophth*. p. 223a (cfr. Aelian. *Varia hist.* 13.19, p. 430 Wilson)

Κλεομένης ὁ Ἀναξανδρίδεω τὸν μὲν Ὅμηρον Λακε-
δαιμονίων εἶναι ποιητὴν ἔφη, τὸν δὲ Ἡσίοδον τῶν
εἱλώτων· τὸν μὲν γὰρ ὡς χρὴ πολεμεῖν, τὸν δὲ ὡς χρὴ
γεωργεῖν παρηγγελκέναι.

**T156** Ael. Aristid. *Orat*. 26.106 Keil

Ἡσίοδος, εἰ ὁμοίως Ὁμήρῳ τέλειος ἦν τὰ ποιητικὰ
καὶ μαντικός, ὥσπερ ἐκεῖνος . . .

**T157** Gnomologium Vaticanum Graecum 515 Sternbach

ὁ αὐτὸς ἐρωτηθεὶς πότερος κρείσσων, Ὅμηρος ἢ
Ἡσίοδος, εἶπεν· "Ἡσίοδον μὲν αἱ Μοῦσαι, Ὅμηρον
δὲ αἱ Χάριτες ἐτέκνωσαν."

tioned. But this verse too is obviously true and based upon experience of human nature."

**T155**  Plutarch, *Sayings of the Spartans*

Cleomenes, the son of Anaxandrides, said that Homer was the poet of the Spartans and Hesiod that of the helots: for the one gave orders about how to wage war, the other about how to do farming.

**T156**  Aelius Aristides, *Orations*

if Hesiod had been as perfect as Homer was in his poetry and as prophetic as he was . . .

**T157**  Vatican Collection of Greek Sayings

The same man (i.e. Simonides), when asked which was the greater, Homer or Hesiod, said, "Hesiod was born of the Muses, but Homer was born of the Graces."

# TESTIMONIA CONCORDANCE

| Most | Jacoby |
|---|---|
| 22 | - |
| 23 | 22 |
| 24 | 23 |
| 25 | 14 |
| 26 | 25 |
| 27 | 17a) |
| 28 | 17b) |
| 29 | 17c) |
| 30 | 32 |
| 31 | 33 |
| 32 | 34 |
| 33(a),(b) | 35a),b) |
| 34 | 35c) |
| 35 | 29 |
| 36 | - |
| 37 | 31 |
| 38 | 30 |
| 39 | 27 |
| 40 | 28 |
| 41 | 26 |
| 42 | 46 |
| 43 | - |
| 44 | 43 |
| 45 | 44 |
| 46 | - |
| 47 | 45 |
| 48 | - |
| 49 | 47a) |
| 50 | 47b) |
| 51 | - |

| Most | Jacoby |
|------|--------|
| 82 | 58b) |
| 83 | 100a) |
| 84 | 92 |
| 85 | 91 |
| 86 | 93 |
| 87(a) | - |
| 87(b) | 81a) |
| 88 | 82 |
| 89 | - |
| 90(a) | - |
| 90(b) | 84 |
| 91 | - |
| 92 | 85 |
| 93 | 43 |
| 94 | 83 |
| 95 | - |
| 96 | 86 |
| 97 | 69 |
| 98 | 59 |
| 99 | 78 |
| 100 | 72 |
| 101 | 36 |
| 102 | 39 |
| 103 | 40 |
| 104 | 94 |
| 105(a) | - |
| 105(b), (c) | 95 |
| 106 | - |
| 107 | - |
| 108 | 96 |

## TESTIMONIA CONCORDANCE

| Most | Jacoby |
|---|---|
| 109 | 97 |
| 110 | 98 |
| 111 | 99 |
| 112 | 60 |
| 113(a), (b) | 70, 71 |
| 114 | 73 |
| 115 | 62 |
| 116(a), (b) | 77a), b) |
| 116(c) | - |
| 117(a), (b) | - |
| 117(c) | 63a) |
| 118 | - |
| 119(a), (b) | 106 |
| 119(c) | - |
| 120 | - |
| 121 | 74a) |
| 122 | 74b) |
| 123 | 101 |
| 124(a), (b) | 65, 64 |
| 125 | 66 |
| 126 | - |
| 127 | 67 |
| 128 | 102 |
| 129 | 103a) |
| 130 | 103b) |
| 131 | 104a) |
| 132 | 104b) |
| 133 | 105 |
| 134 | 107 |

| Most | Jacoby |
|------|--------|
| 135 | - |
| 136 | 107 |
| 137 | 107 |
| 138 | - |
| 139 | 107 |
| 140 | 108 |
| 141 | 109 |
| 142 | 110 |
| 143 | - |
| 144 | 111 |
| 145 | 112 |
| 146 | 113 |
| 147 | 114 |
| 148 | - |
| 149 | 116 |
| 150 | - |
| 151 | - |
| 152 | - |
| 153 | 90 |
| 154 | 87 |
| 155 | 89 |
| 156 | 88b) |
| 157 | - |

# INDEX

Roman numerals refer to page numbers in the Introduction, Th to line numbers in the *Theogony,* WD to line numbers in the *Works and Days,* T to the Testimonia by number.

# INDEX

Heraclitus, Greek philosopher: T113

Hermes, son of Zeus and Maia: Th444, 938; WD68, 77, 84; Argus' killer: WD68, 77, 84

Hermesianax, Greek poet: T56

Hermophantus, Greek actor: T85

Hermus, river born from Tethys and Ocean: Th343

Herodotus, Greek historian: lxvii; T2, 10, 98

Hesiod, Greek poet: ancient biographical reports: xvi–xvii, lxiv–lxv; T1–35; brother, *see* Perses; date: xxiv–xxv; T3–20; father: xii; T1–2, 25; first-person statements: xii–xii, xvii–xviii; influence and reception: lxiii–lxix; T83–151; initiation by Muses: xii–xiv, lxvi–lxvii; T95; life and times: xi–xxv; name: xiv–xvi; T27–29; oral and written: xix–xxii; self-authorization: xxii–xxiii; and Amphidamas: xxv n.8; T2, 38; and Homer: xviii–xxi, xxiii–xxiv, xxxiii, lxiv–lxv; T1–18, 21, 23, 35, 36, 38, 47, 52, 57, 60, 65, 83–85, 92, 96–100, 110, 114–16, 119b, 120b, 123, 129–31, 133, 141, 151–53, 155–57; vs. Hesiodic: xi

Hesiod's poetry: transmission: lxix–lxxi; *Theogony:* xxvi–xxxvi, T42–47; conclusion, xlvii–il; gods, xxviii–xxxi; other theogonic poetry, xxxiv–xxxvi; structure, xxvi–xxviii; title, xxviii; *Works and Days:* xxxvi–xlvii, T42–51; other protreptic poetry, xlvi–xlvii; structure, xxxvi–xxxvii; title, xxxvii; work and justice, xxxviii–xliv

Hesiodic poetry: *Catalogue of Women:* il–lv, lxv–lxvi, T56–65; date, lv; *Ehoiai,* l; other catalogue poetry, liii; partial recovery, l–lii; relation to Hesiod's poetry, liii–lv; structure, lii–liii; *Shield:* lv–lix, T52–55; date, lviii; relation to *Catalogue of Women,* lviii–lix; relation to Homer, lvi–lviii; structure, lviii; other poems: *Aegimius,* lxi, T79; *Astronomy* or *Astrology,* lxi–lxii, T72–78; *Bird Omens,* lxii, T80; *Descent of Peirithous to Hades,* lx–lxi, T42; *Dirge for Batrachus,* lxiii, T1; *Ehoiai,* see *Catalogue of Women; Great Ehoiai,* lix–lx, T66; *Great Works,* lxi, T66; *The Idaean Dactyls,* lxiii, T1; *Melampodia,* lx, T42; *On Preserved Foods,* lxii, T81; *The Potters,* lxiii, T82; *Precepts of Chiron,* lxii, T69–71; *Wedding of Ceyx,* lx, T67–68

298

# INDEX

# INDEX

Zephyrus, wind, son of Astraeus and Eos: Th379, 870; WD594

Zeus, son of Cronus, king of the Olympian gods: xxix, xxxii–xxxiii, xli–xliii, xlvii–xlviii, liii–lv; Th11, 13, 36, 41, 47, 51, 56, 96, 141, 285, 286, 348, 386, 388, 390, 399, 412, 428, 457, 465, 468, 479, 498, 513, 514, 520, 529, 537, 545, 548, 550, 558, 561, 568, 580, 601, 613, 669, 687, 708, 730, 735, 784, 815, 820, 853, 884, 886, 893, 899, 904, 914, 920, 938, 944, 1002; WD2, 4, 8, 36, 47, 51, 52, 53, 69, 79, 87, 99, 104, 105, 122, 138, 143, 158, 168, 180, 229, 239, 245, 253, 256, 259, 267, 273, 281, 333, 379, 416, 465, 474, 483, 488, 565, 626, 638, 661, 668, 676, 724, 765, 769; T2, 30, 32, 33b, 38, 47, 95, 116c, 119; Cronus'son: Th4, 53, 412, 423, 450, 534, 572, 624, 660, 949; WD18, 69, 71, 138, 158, 168, 239, 242, 247, 259, 276; Olympian: Th390, 529, 884; WD87, 245

Zeus' consort. *See* Hera

Zeus' daughter. *See* Athena; Hebe

Zeus' daughters. *See* Muses; Nymphs

Zeus' son. *See* Apollo; Hephaestus; Heracles

Zeuxippus, owner of a gymnasium at Byzantium: T111

Zeuxo, an Oceanid: Th352